RANCOR &
RECONCILIATION
IN MEDIEVAL
ENGLAND

A VOLUME IN THE SERIES
Conjunctions of Religion and Power in the Medieval Past
Edited by Barbara H. Rosenwein

A full list of titles in the series appears at the end of the book.

RANCOR &
RECONCILIATION
IN MEDIEVAL
ENGLAND

PAUL R. HYAMS

Cornell University Press

Ithaca and London

First published 2003 by Cornell University Press

Printed in the United States of America

Library of Congress Cataloging-in-Publication Data

Hyams, Paul R.
    Rancor and reconciliation in medieval England / Paul R. Hyams.
        p. cm. — (Conjunctions of religion & power in the medieval past)
Includes bibliographical references (p.) and index.
    ISBN 0-8014-3996-5 (cloth : alk. paper)
    1. Law—England—History. 2. Vendetta—England—History to 1500. 3. Reconciliation—History. I. Title.   II. Series.
    KD608.H95 2003
    349.42—dc21

                                        2003007977

Cornell University Press strives to use environmentally responsible suppliers and materials to the fullest extent possible in the publishing of its books. Such materials include vegetable-based, low-VOC inks and acid-free papers that are recycled, totally chlorine-free, or partly composed of nonwood fibers. For further information, visit our website at www.cornellpress.cornell.edu.

Cloth printing 10 9 8 7 6 5 4 3 2 1

The ideal scientist thinks like a poet and works like a book-keeper, and I suppose that, if gifted with a full quiver, he also writes like a journalist.

EDWARD O. WILSON, *Consilience*

CONTENTS

INTRODUCTION

It is possible to state succinctly the premises from which this book was written: I start from an urge to avenge wrong. This seems ubiquitous within Western culture and may indeed even be hardwired into the human psyche. Its signs are certainly visible all over medieval England throughout the three centuries I treat here. It seems to follow that wrong actually is the elemental legal notion of at least England, and perhaps the whole Western world.

This book therefore focuses on *in*justice and wrong rather than on right and justice. To request from people an account of justice today is to risk immersion in a bath of bad philosophy. But when we question ordinary men and women about injustice, many will at once begin to tell stories of real occasions in their own lives when others have wronged them. People feel injustice in a direct and personal manner. When they perceive it directed at themselves, and they cast themselves as victims, they soon begin to ponder whether and how to respond.

Both this storytelling and the calculus of response, as it may be termed, are central to this book. In so many everyday incidents, petty or violent, the way the story is told—by whom, starting and ending at which points—all these matters determine the kind of thrust and impact the tale will have. Different people naturally recount the same events in very different ways. The various narrators necessarily disagree even on the identity of the "real" victim. No good legal historian should assume that the complainant in any legal record necessarily possesses a more plausible claim than does the opponent he accuses of doing him down, nor should he necessarily be considered the *victim* of the wrong. Thus one man's act of legitimate vengeance in redress of shame and wrong may easily appear to another a dastardly and unprovoked crime.

If I talk of a *calculus* of response, I do so without prejudice to the crucial questions of how decisions were actually made. Men and women can react to their perceptions of wrong in a variety of ways. There will be occasion in due course (chapter 2) to question their likely motivations and to consider the balance or tension between ratiocination and emotion. I have found it helpful to envision the decision-making process as occurring in a variety of forms that lie along a continuum. At one end is hot pursuit, the immediate, unthinking return of harm for harm in a bid for vengeance. At the other, a "victim" may feel he must do nothing, perhaps because nothing can be done—the opposition is too strong, the time inopportune, or religious restraints on violence too powerful. The experts have a technical name for this inaction: "lumping it." And even "lumping it" does not exhaust the possibilities. The victim may see no option but flight, in self-protection from his father's or brother's killer, who, perhaps, is ready to return to finish off the remainder of the family. Whether the fugitive's goal is simply to put distance between himself and his enemy by going into exile, or to seek the protection of some great man or spiritually charged sanctuary, the result is similarly off the end of the scale, at a point way beyond mere inaction. These are the extremes of the field I am to survey. In between them, all along the center of the scale lies a plethora of messy, less clear-cut options, some in the courtroom, many outside. These events provide the majority of my material and many bizarre and fiery anecdotes.

THE LITERATURE ON FEUD AND VENGEANCE

Questions of this kind are not unduly prominent in the literature about medieval England. Scholars have tended to content themselves with branding feud and vengeance as archaic and barbaric, before hurrying on to more edifying forms of social and political arrangement. Most English scholars in the times preceding the rise of the European Community have taken pride in England's differentness from its Continental neighbors. They have made much of medieval England's precocious centralization and order. One frequent contrast has been with the contemporary state of affairs in Germany, the former medieval empire. German historians have featured feud much more prominently in their accounts of political development than have the English.[1] This is partly a matter of sources. There are no medieval German plea rolls and writs to lead historians into a concentration on a centrist perspective. But there is equally a shared assumption that centralization is progress and its absence implies political backwardness. England was leading the way. Why spoil the picture by seeking out the ugly creature—feud and violence—that may lurk beneath the fine stone paving of the common law?

1. Since its first appearance in German in 1939, Brunner 1992 has focused attention on feud in Germany in a way never matched in England. Reuter 1991 is a recent and good example of the benefits from such attention.

This kind of approach was greatly assisted by the widespread tendency to view the social order from the top down. The focus has been on the decisions of government much more than on the wishes of the governed. And most accounts of law and order have undoubtedly followed the general trend. Thus law is what jurists write, legislators prescribe, or judges rule. It is not much about what policemen—and their medieval equivalents—actually did or what administrators permitted courts to hear, still less about what ordinary men and women might believe to be their rights and the proper limits to constraints on their freedom of action.[2] Only fairly recently have historians in any number begun to view legal change as also at least partially demand-led and so related to patterns of grievance and the remedies that the aggrieved seek. This book mostly proceeds from that stance. Here I scrutinize the pull of the requirements of litigation and, even more, the impact of those who did not wish to become litigants and so strove to avoid the law and its courts. Given that most grievances never reach a court hearing, the feelings of this last group must surely constitute the matrix within which in general to understand the operations of the law.

The process by which I have come to write this book began with a lecture on feud composed several years ago as a participant in a "circus" of undergraduate lectures on Anglo-Saxon England by various Oxford colleagues. My effort to sketch the place of feud in later Anglo-Saxon England proved enlightening and alluring: to make the whole analysis from the viewpoint of the aggrieved, where I had previously followed the conventional line of starting from legislation and court rules, taught me new things. At first I certainly gave too little weight to royal ideology and aspirations, much less than now appears in this volume. But the way Anglo-Saxon historians seemed to pay lip service to feud without taking it seriously as an integral part of the political culture was disappointing. How, I wondered, could feud, even if an archaism, have exerted so little influence on the society that practiced it with such apparent verve? These were worthwhile questions to ponder. Here was a route toward understanding some of the feelings and resentments of ordinary people, which was always my youthful and unattainable goal. Equally exciting was the fact that feud was then so little studied. Its study was a largely untrodden line through some tracts of a historical terrain otherwise thoroughly muddied by the tramp of many scholarly feet.

The next step was to extend my gaze beyond 1066. Why should the urge to vengeance, delightfully alive before the Norman Conquest, suddenly disappear thereafter, allegedly not to reemerge for several centuries? The con-

2. I tried in Hyams 1996b to investigate what sense ordinary people had of law in the decades around 1300.

sensus of scholars of my generation is to recognize a more nuanced break at the Conquest than had their predecessors. Eleventh-century Normandy now seems in most respects a culture much more closely comparable to its neighbor across the Channel than had once seemed plausible. Could vengeance be an exception?

But feud itself is a very problematic concept, as I show in chapter 1. Even my preliminary study of the phenomenon in Anglo-Saxon England compelled recognition of a further real and context-specific problem. The challenge was to make sense of feud patterns within an understanding that saw late Anglo-Saxon England, like Norman and Angevin England, so largely in terms of precocious state centralization. But early students of feud in third-world cultures then deemed "savage" or "primitive" wrongly viewed feud and law as exclusive alternatives; they understood feud as a feature of, if not fully state-less societies, then at least ones with very weak central governmental institutions. The facts presented the historian with an opportunity to advance the argument rather than merely to receive passively anthropological "truths." One must never underestimate the potential of medieval Christendom to proffer countergifts to the social sciences. Its unique cultural location, en route to the modern West but still very different from it, offers insights into the differences between Western values and those of present-day non-Western cultures that too often serve us as the various "Others" of our world. And the abundant written records of the medieval West, far outmatching those of most other premodern neighbors, enable us to map parts of its belief structure in detail nearly as fine as any but the best modern field study might provide. This heady stuff once led me to an analytical distinction between strong and weak views of feud that I now disown but which helped convince me all the same that there had to be much more to feud than the simple taking of vengeance.[3]

I came to perceive motivation and the way cultures handled it as a missing (or neglected) link in studies of violence and order. By this I mean two separate matters. First, I wanted to understand how involved individuals themselves perceive particular acts of violence and decide what to do about them. I have already hinted at some consequences of this concern. But there is every reason, also, not to be diverted from central attempts to make policy on law and order and efforts to manage societal conflict from the center. In medieval England, as elsewhere, much power lay close to the king and his governmental institutions. This undoubtedly influenced efforts at enforcing old attempts to meet the challenge of violence and social permanence as

3. Hyams 1992, 5-7.

well as any efforts at shaping new solutions. It stood to reason; historians of the English Middle Ages ignore the monarchy at their risk.

Questions about motivation returned me to the concern with wrong from which I began. Through them I hoped to see which conflicts could be compromised and how this was most effectively achieved. This inquiry would situate my work within the recent trend that has finally taken account of the frequency with which medieval contemporaries displayed a preference for concord and satisfaction over punishment and judgment. I hoped further to begin to understand which kinds of troublemaker could be crushed without the sort of disturbing protest that created more trouble than it saved. I might then even spotlight the other kind of troublemaker, possessed of enough power and standing that government must take him into partnership, as it were.

Such is my subject matter here. I have tried to preserve a very broad outlook that draws on the experience and the distinctive materials for three hundred years of history while reserving the right to examine in sometime microscopic resolution the minutiae of legal and institutional specifics. Both range of vision and accuracy of detail are equally crucial; neither can be sacrificed in this kind of study without irreparable loss. Inevitably treatment must be selective. I have looked for compelling exempla to present clear and plausible explanatory hypotheses that will encourage others beside me to test them against more comprehensive data sets. The real goal of this book is thus to persuade future researchers to use some of the same approaches.

SOME APPROACHES TO SOURCES

If I succeed in making my case here, there will be plenty of work for all to do. I certainly cannot claim that all my explanations are beyond criticism or objection. Nor have I assembled, for example, all the instances of raw feud behavior to be found. I can only say that I have interrogated as broad a range of sources as I could and consciously eschewed nothing that came to hand. I have naturally used the legal historian's conventionally recognized materials. Thus the reader will find many familiar texts cited from the Anglo-Saxon leges in chapter 3. I make maximum use of case narratives. For much of the period (pt. 2, chaps. 4–6) these are one-sided accounts, unilateral memoranda usually recording the victor's view of the matter. Such nonprofessional "literary" narratives, almost always external to the legal system, inject dynamics into our understanding in ways that are much needed in legal history. I am fortunate in writing at a time when serviceable hand-lists up to the year 1200 are available as well as (at least for the twelfth century) a fairly comprehensive collection of texts.[4] From the 1190s this mix is enriched with documentation of the new common law itself, a bonus that carries its own problems.[5] I have tried hard to situate these case narratives within a context that includes the most that can be known from outside the courtroom and, where I could, have laid alongside them accounts of comparable disputes that never reached the legal system.

I present my extended readings of many cases in an appendix, in order to keep the argument in my main text uncluttered and to respect my publisher's horror of swollen footnotes. But the case collection reflects a passionate belief that legal historians too often sacrifice the all-important dynamics of litigation and dispute in their concentration on courtroom procedural rules and the history of legal doctrine. In adding my hypothetical reconstructions "in the round," as it were, of these case narratives, I seek to restore to case law a more just balance. This method, I like to think, pays due account to the rules and other essential requirements of the law while adding more of what was really at stake for the parties and their neighbors in the community.

To that end, I obviously have to cast my net far beyond the bounds of law and the various kinds of record it directly generates. Most nonlegal records were produced by churchmen and so document in the first instance the ethos of the Church. Their strength is that, from doctrines of sin and redemption, they make possible a full reconstruction of a Christian view of wrong, though one to which I refer only in passing here. If one seeks to oppose to this, in the way Georges Duby for instance has taught us to do,[6] a secular ethos, two rather different moves are required. One resource is to search entertainment literature, mostly in the vernacular. Old and Middle English and Anglo-Norman have each made their contribution, with occasional further insights from Latin writings. Another, more negative option is to deduce elements of the secular model of wrong by focusing on the practices stigmatized and targeted by the Church's moral teachers in pastoral literature. This second underpins many of the suggestions I make in chapter 2 concerning the role of social emotions. It exemplifies a technique

4. Wormald 1998 and 1992 list but do not edit narratives up to 1066 and 1086. One can locate the best editions of most Old English texts, and many of their shortcomings, from Sawyer 1968. Fleming 1998 lists Domesday suits on a more expansive view of the definition of legal narrative than Wormald takes. Although Van Caenegem 1990–91 unfortunately contents itself for the most part with reprinting existing editions and translations along with their many defects, I nevertheless use its assembly of narratives from the Norman Conquest to the death of Richard I.

5. The problems are discussed in chap. 6. For cases from 1200 on, I use plea rolls preserved in the Public Record Office, London, trying not to privilege too obviously the availability of printed editions.

6. Duby 1983 probably did more to recommend this kind of approach than his earlier work, Duby 1968.

I have found helpful throughout, to tease out multiple meanings from fe-
cund texts. Recent literary theory offers some assistance in this enterprise.
Everyone now accepts the insight that text is liberated as soon as it leaves its
author's hand; previously this understanding was restricted to the more
imaginative historian source critics. The occasions when we find more or
less clear indications that contemporaries regarded some particular understanding of a text as a misreading serve as justification for others less clear. It
certainly ought to have been obvious all along that readers and listeners
bring a good deal with them to their task. Audiences have, for example, always found it hard to receive more than they can fit comfortably into their
existing structures of information and belief. Every lecturer knows that
where his listeners' knowledge is thin, as with beginning students, he faces
an uphill struggle to ensure that a reasonable representation of historian's
truth reaches the lecture notes. We all sometimes hear only what we wish
and so may on occasion draw totally inappropriate conclusions. Medieval
confessors knew this well enough to be wary of educating their flock in sin
through questions designed to promote virtue.[7] Thus texts crafted, for example, to dissuade men and women from any indulgence in vengeance
could sometimes have the opposite effect.[8] The student may make use of
creative misreadings to deduce a positive model from the prohibition of an
opposing authority. This technique has proved fruitful in diverse circumstances. Old English leges and later common-law rules and statutes illuminate for us through a glass darkly the actual state of affairs that provoked
their promulgation. The Church's moral prohibitions reveal something of
the secular models of accepted behavior at whose removal they were aimed.
Received views based on "authorial intention" readings of texts are always a
legitimate target. The treatment of source texts in the rest of this book is
therefore, I hope, straight but never narrow, imaginative yet accurate within
the bounds of the possible.

THE PLAN OF ATTACK

Now that I have explained my general intentions, it may be helpful to set
out my order of attack. In outline, part 1 represents the program I endeavor
to pursue, whereas parts 2 and 3 present its imperfect realization. Part 1 contains two further chapters.

Chapter 1 examines our notions of feud in order to explain as well as de-

7. I cite an explicit statement to this effect by Thomas of Chobham in chap. 2.
8. One nice illustration of this misreading is found in Chaucer's "Tale of Melibee" in his *Canterbury Tales*. Despite the clear message that one should heed an intelligent wife's advice, the host
remarks that he will discipline his own wife when he gets home.

fend my own use of the notion. I seek to persuade myself and others to see feud not as an institution but as a live process with a positive side. I eschew the term *blood feud*, both because of feud's inseparability from peacemaking and because it reaches far beyond any simple equation with the group of blood relatives in the kindred. I suggest that in a world of conscious political choices, blood kinship provides no automatic lock on loyalties, and that prudent political actors, aware of this, seek support proactively and in advance of any trouble. I therefore feel bound to investigate with care the nature and scope of friendship, which competed with enmity, hatred, and feud for control over a single body of neighborly and seignorial acquaintance. One can hardly hope to understand feud and wrong without espousing a convincing position on friendship of all sorts.

I begin chapter 2 by asking how we can best gauge the feelings of past men and women. I want to understand the extent to which their feelings feed into their actions and choices. The fact that questions about the interaction of thought and feeling remain controversial encourages me to secure what help I can from modern studies of emotion. That we can gain salutary information on the rhetoric of emotion in the Middle Ages is of some value. But can we reach beyond this to discern the actual feelings themselves, to evoke and understand their symptomatic physical arousal, their impact on action, and other consequences? I think we can, and so pose further questions on emotions behind the sense of injustice and wrong that fuel so much activity. I try too to sketch the opposing models of rancor and vengeance held by clerics (relatively easy) and laypeople (much harder). I believe that the results demonstrate the existence, as if bursting out of the contested semantic space, of a real-life culture of vengeance within a thought world that affords vengeance a prominent place.

Part 2, offering an alternative narrative of law and society in rough chronological order, opens in chapter 3 with the first extended study of Anglo-Saxon feud for a century. I acknowledge my own skepticism at the recent historiographical trend to maximize the significance of state institutions during the century or so before the Norman Conquest. I do not deny the enlightening discoveries made in the last generation concerning the ideology of a kingship with powerful aspirations toward the extension of central authority and the creation of an administrative apparatus that looked capable of its implementation. Though the achievements are breathtaking, I suspect that scholars have swung the pendulum a mite too far. My skepticism doubts the king's capacity to face down the natural resistance of the noble class on whom all royal power ultimately rests. I approach the subject through critical examination of the Old English *leges*, the law codes that supply evidence for the view today, and which were once a main means to enforce the royal will. More generally, I suspect the king and his advisers had to operate within a feud culture. I strive along this route to locate points of tension between centripetal and centrifugal elements in late Anglo-Saxon law and politics. I end by explaining why these loci may be the most we can achieve, in the absence of evidence that can establish the resulting balance with any precision.

Chapter 4 asks whether the Norman Conquest was for vengeance the caesura it was once thought more generally to be. I have difficulty finding either any great transformation of the existing culture of vengeance that the Normans found in England or any great difference from their own Norman practices. Rather, my inquiries highlight the continuities of the century immediately following the Conquest that conveniently culminates in 1166, the annus mirabilis of Angevin legal creativity. I select two great texts from the early twelfth century for exposure to readings that support this judgment. Orderic Vitalis's great *Ecclesiastical History* and the so-called but unofficial *Leges Henrici Primi*, both much studied, nevertheless each reveal something new for our purposes. I consider at length questions of terminology. An investigation into the post-Conquest penal vocabulary (or lack thereof) demonstrates that the conceptual ambiguity of vengeance and punishment ran deep. Something similar may be said of the general and largely undifferentiated sense of wrong denoted by words like Latin *injuria*. I conclude the chapter by scrutinizing twelfth-century patterns of litigation for signs of the crucial common-law distinction between crime and tort. I find no traces of it into the final third of the century, when the effects of its importation from Roman law finally begin to show. The separate actions of the thirteenth-century common law—the appeal "of felony" and its civil counterpart, the action of trespass—are likewise conspicuously absent from the twelfth-century legal scene. The "undifferentiated" group of procedures to redress wrong continues to reign well into the common-law period of the thirteenth century. The different rules and constraints that governed these procedures, and especially the fact that most or all were seen as remedies for wrong in some general sense, buttress my view that redress of wrong remained a central concern of the age.

Chapter 5 considers the Angevin reshaping of the machinery for the maintenance of law and order, which finally changed this situation. I interrogate the familiar texts of the Assizes of 1166 and 1176 within the context established up to this point. What were Henry II and his advisers really trying to do? And why did they choose these particular methods? These considerations lead me to question some traditional understandings of the grand jury and indictment procedures as they were framed at this time. I am struck by the great investment of effort and resources in these innovations. The king seems to have worked much harder to achieve a more favorable order in his realm than he ever did toward his goals in the reorganization of real property litigation. But did the results justify all the expenditure? When and how did individual complainants begin to benefit by increased opportunity to sue their own cases against those who had injured them? Such questions extend the range of our inquiry from topics that will belong permanently on the criminal side of the formed common law to ones such as the actions of trespass and novel disseizin traditionally classified as civil remedies. This poses a dilemma to be resolved in chapter 6. One essential preliminary concludes the chapter: the attempt to understand the process by which those accused gained, first under the new indictment procedure and later also in appeals of felony, the ability to challenge their accusers' motives. The findings of this inquiry help me to portray the introduction of a public system of law enforcement that was formational of both the nascent common law itself and the more frequently lauded real actions.

The documentation of part 3 is much improved by the internal records of that common law itself. We note the new challenges this poses for historical interpretation. The common law laundered passions from its proceedings in its novel effort to focus procedures more closely on what it deemed to be the central legal issues. The historian needs to reinsert passions and context where he can or receive a distorted picture of the everyday realities behind disputes.

In chapter 6, I first demonstrate the continuation of patterns of feud-like behavior into the brilliant light of the thirteenth-century common law. I then ask how this same light shows the fearful to have managed to protect themselves against violence. Or better yet, how and why some sought a lasting peace with their enemies. I proceed to look further at the mechanics of violent disputes in search of an understanding of support groups and individual accomplices.

The way is now open to return to the "undifferentiated" procedures for wrong, to discern how two distinct common-law actions separated themselves out from it and were progressively positioned on opposite sides of the novel distinction between crime and tort newly borrowed from Roman law. I first posit five diverse premises that had to be in place before the two actions could crystallize from the older procedures. I then explain how the French word *trespas* (and its Latin equivalent *transgressio*) came to denote civil wrongs. Chapter 7 concludes with a detailed examination of the very protracted process by which the two separate actions moved English law toward full acceptance of the all-important distinction between crime and tort, criminal and civil law.

Chapter 8 continues the case for the persistence of some of the old patterns of enmity and vengeance to 1300 and beyond. To show that these patterns remain visible on occasion even within the legal system itself, I search the records of some exceptional procedures that focused on motive. Beyond the courts, I concentrate on the two periods of civil war, because these were exceptional moments when enmities surfaced and were perpetuated in writing. Finally, I end this study with a fresh look at the recent debate on "bastard feudalism." The revisionists' conclusion—that the phenomena signified by this name started much earlier than the school of the late Bruce McFarlane held—appears very pertinent to my overall argument. The revised contention holds, in effect, that men already used lordship in a very instrumental fashion to craft social relations to their will in the thirteenth century and most likely from fairly early in the twelfth century too. They show how relatively little noble practice in the recruitment of support groups for the purposes of confrontation had changed between the Norman Conquest and the death of Edward I. England remained, it seems, some kind of vengeance culture throughout the three centuries of this book and beyond, despite more than one major attempt to transform its ideology of order.

It may be appropriate to add one final word on approach. This is not a book on technical legal history. Some will deny it the right to be called legal history at all. Much of the source material on which it depends is, however, legal, and some of it technical. The same applies to a fair number of the arguments with which I make my case. Legal historians' bad reputation for inaccessibility to the nonspecialist was broken almost uniquely by the divine Maitland, whose writing was completed nearly a full century ago. The exhortations that scholars still receive to write "like Maitland" are, as my own Doktorvater, Derek Hall, told me long ago and with characteristic firmness, not at all helpful. Maitland was (a) a genius, (b) a very poor stylistic model for anyone who wishes his work to be open to critical disagreement, and (c) elegantly adept at covering his periodic philosophical indecision. I should nevertheless like to put it on record that this book is aimed at the broadest and most general audience I can reasonably hope to reach. I have tried to make my points in plain English so that mainstream historians at least, and sane history students at colleges and universities, can follow the argument and disagree with it in fruitful manner. I very much hope that friends and others can hear my voice behind its contentions. I offer it up for criticism and rebuke on that basis.

This has been, literally, a career-busting book. I did much of the basic thinking that underlies it during a year at the Institute for Advanced Study at Princeton, supported there in part by a grant from the United States Institute of Peace. I am grateful to both these bodies and hope they do not feel that the long wait rendered the enterprise uneconomic. At Princeton, I enjoyed the company of a fine group of agreeable neighbors—one of whom, Lee Patterson, told me then that the project was fine but the book would never be written. He was so nearly right! No thanks to my department, I proved his prediction wrong in the end.[9] But I do owe immense debts of gratitude to many Cornell colleagues and other friends, especially to my fellow scholars in our dynamic and stimulating medieval studies program. Many footnotes acknowledge my debts to colleagues; here I mention, for special thanks: Alice Colby-Hall, Tom Hill, Jim John, John Najemy, Danuta Shanzer, Sid Tarrow, and from the wider world, Paul and Vanessa Brand, Charles Donahue Jr., Pat Geary, Henry Mayr-Harting, Barbara Rosenwein (editor par excellence), Patrick Wormald, and Steve White. I am also indebted to John Ackerman, director of Cornell University Press, for his intelligent and sensitive encouragement and consistent interest, and to my other friends at the press for their professionalism and for their help in translating my native English into fair American.

I relish teaching the many Cornell students who have encouraged me to develop and refine the ideas behind this book. Undergraduates present the welcome challenge to impart doctrine that is both as true and as comprehensible as I can make it. Also, I appreciate the intellectual feedback from my Cornell graduate students, particularly Alizah Holstein, Paul Milliman, Amy Phelan, David Rollenhagen, and also Susanna Throop (now at Cambridge). Sadly, Derek Hall and Sir Richard Southern, two of my most influential mentors, have now passed away. I hope they would have liked this book. But James Campbell remains to be honored and thanked for his continuing kindness and stimulation, and also for his many provocations that are influential everywhere and not just in chapter 3.

My wife, Elaine, has suffered this book and its time frame to the point where she has on occasion doubted (sometimes forcefully) its necessity in this form. She has also worked far beyond any call of duty to minimize errors and inconsistencies in the final product. (All remaining imperfections are, of course, my own.) She deserves better, only the very best indeed, but will hopefully be content with this. I could dedicate this book to no other person. I owe to her all the best things in my life, not least my thoughtful, entertaining, and supportive family co-equals, Deborah and David. (Teddy Bears four!)

9. I gratefully acknowledge the assistance and support of senior staff of the Cornell University Library. The libraries at Princeton University and the Institute for Advanced Study, Princeton, also welcomed me as a visiting scholar, as has Dr. Aubertin-Potter (All Soul's, Oxford) over many years.

NOTE ON SOURCES AND CITATIONS

This book draws on source material from many different areas (common law, canon law, Roman law, the Vulgate Latin Bible, and vernacular literatures in English and French) that are usually kept apart. Specialists in each have their own, sometimes mysterious, ways of citing their materials. I have tried to follow these various conventions with reasonable fidelity without concealing from nonspecialists like myself what is going on. The real point is to facilitate the tracing of sources so that readers may check my arguments, and perhaps go on to advance their own different ones, at their convenience. There is also, always, a pressing need to conserve space. These lists should clarify the conventions I have followed.

For the leges and legal treatises of Anglo-Saxon and twelfth-century England, I have followed the practice in Liebermann 1903–16 (i.xi). I do this even though we now know that some of the great man's attributions are incorrect, as one may see from Wormald 1999, which nevertheless persists with the same conventions. They are all we have for now, though my own practice varies on two occasions noted in the list below. All refer to law codes unless otherwise stated.

Abt	Æthelbert
Af	Alfred
Af El	Alfred, author's introduction (Einleitung)
As	Æthelstan
Atr	Æthelred
Cn	Cnut
E Cf	"Leges Edwardi Confessoris"
E Cf retr	"Leges Edwardi Confessoris," second version, for which see O'Brien 1999
E Gu	"Peace of Edward and Guthrum"
Eg	Edgar
Em	Edmund

Episc	"Episcopus," treatise on bishops
Ew	Edward the Elder
Grið	"Grith" (although Liebermann calls it "Sonder-schutz")
Hn	"Leges Henrici Primi," more often cited as *LHP*, from Downer's 1972 edition
Inst Cn	"Instituta Cnuti"
Iudex	"Iudex," treatise on judges
Leges Wmi, Leis Wl	"Leis Willelme" is the French text Liebermann (1903–16) thought original, but I mostly cite the Latin version, "Leges Willelmi."
Norðleod	"Northleoda laga"
Northu	"Northumbrian Priests' Law"
Ps Cn For	Forest law, attributed to Cnut
Sacr Cor	Coronation oath
Swerian	"Swerian: Eidelsformeln"
Wer	"Wergeldzahlung" (Liebermann's coinage)
Wif	"Wifmannes Beweddung"

Books of the Bible are cited after their titles in the Latin Vulgate. Thus Ecclus. is Ecclesiasticus (Ben Sirah), and Ios. is Joshua.

I use a form of standard citation for both the *Corpus Iuris Canonici* (canon law texts including *Decretum*, "Liber Extra," and "Liber Sextus") and the *Corpus Iuris Civilis* (Roman law texts such as the *Digest*). I have kept the references as simple as possible; the abbreviated forms may be found in the list of abbreviations.

It is not just the Bible that the Devil can quote to his own satisfaction. Lawyers use their texts in highly instrumental ways to make cases for themselves and their clients. The range of interpretation must be studied from the professional literature of each group, the two laws and the Bible. I have limited myself here to sampling the most obvious of the glosses produced to help students at the time, through the Glossa Ordinaria or standard commentary used in thirteenth-century schools. I cite this as "gl. ad" followed by the lemma (words being glossed) and the reference. Thus gl. ad Gen. i.1 "In principio," begins the treatment of the Old Testament, and gl. ad *Decretum*, C.1.1.1 "gratia," refers to the first gloss on *Decretum*, part II, Causa 1, question 1, capitulum 1. In his *Decretum*, Gratian included his own editorial comments ("dicta"); I cite these by the capitulum they precede (dac1) or follow (dpc1). Those who need further precision must seek it in the specialist literature, to which Brundage 1995, app. 1, is a good introduction.

I have limited my use of manuscript material in this book to materials in the royal archives, preserved at the Public Record Office, London. I cite rolls and other documents by the class numbers still used there, even though some of these no longer represent our understanding of the sources from which they sprang. These are listed among the abbreviations that follow.

The appendix cites material in the way just outlined. My intention was to give summary references to the documents (often entries on plea rolls) from which I have tried to reconstruct the narrative of each case. In order to help readers follow my trail, I place these references in chronological order and indicate some secondary comment.

ABBREVIATIONS

A-N Dict.   *Anglo-Norman Dictionary.* 1992. Edited by William Rothwell, Louise W. Stone, and T. B. Reid. London: Modern Humanities Research Association.

Anglo-Saxon Chronicle   These annals are cited from Earle and Plummer 1892–99, by the year checked against the translation in *EHD*, vol. 1.

C 144   Inquisitions de odio et athia. Public Record Office, London.

CIM   *Calendar of Inquisitions Miscellaneous (Chancery).* 1916. Vol. 1. London: H. M. Stationery Office.

CIPM   *Calendar of Inquisitions Post Mortem and Other Analogous Documents Preserved in the Public Record Office.* 1904. Vol. 1. London: H. M. Stationery Office.

CP 25   Feet of Fines. Public Record Office, London.

CPR   *Calendar of Patent Rolls.* 1901–. London: H. M. Stationery Office. Cited by calendar years covered.

CRR   *Curia Regis Rolls . . . Preserved in the Public Record Office.* 1922–. 18 vols. to date. London: H. M. Stationery Office.

DB   *Domesday Book.* 1975–92. Edited by John Morris. 38 volumes. Chichester: Phillimore. Cited by county volume and number, and also by foliation of 1783 ed.

DDC   *Dictionnaire de droit canonique.* 1935–65. Edited by R. Naz. Paris: Letouzey et Ané.

Decretum   Gratian. 1879. *Decretum Magistri Gratiani.* Edited by Emil Friedburg. Leipzig: Bernard Tauchnitz. Divided by *distinctio* (Dist.) or *causa* (C.).

Dig.   Justinian. 1967–73. *Digest.* In *Corpus Iuris Civilis.* Edited by P. Krueger and T. Mommsen. 3 vols. Berlin: Weidmann.

EHD   *English Historical Documents.* Vol. 1: *c. 500–1042*
(1979). Edited by D. Whitelock. 2d ed. Vol. 2:
1042–1189 (1953). Edited by D. Douglas and G.
Greenaway. London: Eyre and Spottiswoode.

EYC   *Early Yorkshire Charters.* 1914–65. Edited by W. Farrer and C. T. Clay. 13 vols. Yorkshire Archaeological
Society, Record Series, extra ser. Edinburgh: Ballantyne, Hanson.

Glanvill   *The Treatise on the Laws and Customs of the Realm of
England Commonly Called Glanvill.* 1993. Edited by
G. D. G. Hall. Oxford Medieval Texts. New York:
Oxford University Press. Original edition, Nelsons
and Selden Society Medieval Texts; London: Nelsons, 1965. Cited by book, chapter, and page numbers of edition.

Guisborough   *The Chronicle of Walter of Guisborough.* 1957. Edited
by Harry Rothwell. Camden Society, vol. 89. Lon-
don: Royal Historical Society.

Haveloc   *Le lai d'Haveloc.* 1925. Edited by Alexander Bell. Manchester: Longmans and Manchester University Press.

Inst.   Justinian. 1967–73. *Institutes.* In *Corpus Iuris Civilis.*
Edited by P. Krueger and T. Mommsen. 3 vols.
Berlin: Weidmann.

JUST 1, JUST 3   Justices Itinerant. Assize rolls, and Coroners' rolls.
Public Record Office, London.

KB 26   Coram Rege rolls. Public Record Office, London.

LHP   *Leges Henrici Primi.* 1972. Edited by L. J. Downer.
Oxford: Clarendon Press.

MED   *Middle English Dictionary.* 1952–. Edited by Hans
Kurath, Sherman M. Kuhn, and Robert E. Lewis.
Ann Arbor: University of Michigan Press; London:
G. Cumberledge, Oxford University Press. Also
consulted at http://ets.umdl.umich.edu/m/med/.

MPL   *Patrologia cursus completus.* Series Latina. 1844–64.
Edited by J.-P. Migne. Paris.

Orderic   *The Ecclesiastical History of Orderic Vitalis.* 1969–78.
Edited by Marjorie Chibnall. 6 vols. Oxford: Ox-
ford University Press.

Pipe Roll   Editions of pipe rolls from the Public Record Office, in volumes of the Pipe Roll Society, cited by
the regnal year of the king.

PKJ   *Pleas before the King or His Justices, 1198–1212.* 1948–49, 1966–67. Edited by D. M. Stenton. 4 vols. Selden Society, vols. 67–68, 83–84. London.

RCR   *Rotuli Curiae Regis.* 1835. Edited by Sir Francis Palgrave. 2 vols. London: Eyre and Spottiswoode.

Stricker   *Karl der Grosse, von dem Stricker.* 1857. Edited by Karl Bartsch. Quedlinburg: Basse.

VI   "Liber Sextus." 1879. In *Corpus Iuris Canonici,* edited by Emil Friedburg. Vol. 2. Leipzig: Bernard Tauchnitz.

X   "Liber Extra" of Gregory IX. 1879. In *Corpus Iuris Canonici,* edited by Emil Friedburg. Vol. 2. Leipzig: Bernard Tauchnitz.

CHAPTER ONE
UNDERSTANDING FEUD AND FRIENDSHIP

Vengeance in its more spectacular manifestations always involves killing or threats to kill. Attempts to limit its violent consequences must take this into account. If the biblical license to take an eye for an eye and a tooth for a tooth represents one such attempt,[1] this is because many instinctively seek to avenge a lesser wrong with a greater response. The many early medieval enactments that sanction approved compensation rates for a wide range of physical injuries nicely accord with this biblical ethos, as one might expect from clerical draftsmen. Some codes contain a fairly comprehensive tariff scale for nonlethal wrongs as well. If death is the supreme insult, requiring another death for its requital, lesser wrongs also shame the victims and their friends. There would always be people seeking to gain on the exchange and extort a full life for that eye or tooth.

No book concerned with the redress of wrong in the Middle Ages can escape the duty to consider the "theory" of feud.[2] I present feud here as a kind of ideal type for all potentially violent acts rationalized and designed to redress wrong. Such a view generates questions to pursue through the historical sources for medieval England in parts 2 and 3, to analyze the kinds of redress that men and women seek in different circumstances for the wrongs they see inflicted on themselves. I therefore need to discuss feud's meaning and implications in some detail.

The first part of this chapter turns on the effort to define and understand feud. The rest of the chapter I devote to the topic of friendship. The conjunction is a natural one. We are accustomed to think first of vengeance in terms of a relationship between two individual persons—one wronged, the

---

1. Briefly discussed in chap. 2.
2. To call this "blood feud" begs some questions that most interest me about the restraint and control of blood vengeance. Many scholars' understandings of feud explicitly contrast the taking of actual blood vengeance with the compensation systems designed to prevent this retribution by enabling nonviolent settlement of conflict. I want instead to treat the system of wrong and redress holistically.

other wronging. Classic tales of assassinations in some lonely Balkan pass feed the myth. In reality, others are always involved. The two principals are not isolated individuals. If they were, the avenger might not have acknowledged an obligation to avenge; the dead man was in no position to insist. But beyond this, vengeance in feud cultures is much less a matter to be pursued in isolation from one's friends than was the later duel of honor. The armed assault on an enemy's stronghold is at least as characteristic of feud tales as the solitary ambush. In these house assaults, attackers and defenders each sought security in numbers. In times of known enmities, each side mustered maximum force. These friends were crucial to all hopes of ending feud. Direct peacemaking was often too hazardous. Friends must serve as mediators and help negotiate plausible settlement terms. Then these terms themselves drew others in, as copayers, hostages, guarantors, and the like. I present the taking of vengeance and the making of peace settlements as twin ends of a single system of alternative social control. I argue that the challenge was far too great to be handled by the principals' kinsmen alone. To have a real chance of breaking the cycle of potential strike and counterstrike, others needed to help out. Sensible folk with a horror of endless vendetta had an interest in pacifying the violent if they could, but still needed to be wooed by those nearer the eye of the storm. Because the manner in which contending parties recruited their "support groups" was central to the ethos of feud, I push it center stage as an integral part of the feud model.

PUTTING FEUD IN ITS PLACE

The range of possible responses to wrong in the Middle Ages was obviously much wider than vengeance alone. Feud, however defined, is merely one among many options. To clarify usage, the historian needs to place the term within the whole conspectus of alternate courses of action and the constraints on the choices among them. Scholars have sometimes forgotten that law was one of these choices;[3] consequently, where law ruled, feud must for them inevitably be the enemy of order, surviving only by license or neglect, and until suppressed in the interests of centralized justice. Feud was always extralegal if not anti-legal. Yet feud and law demonstrably coexisted during the period covered in this book. The wronged could only choose direct action, including feud, either by declining law or by acting in the belief that law itself was beyond their reach. This is the first important parameter within which to study the scope of feud.

Beyond it, one can attempt to define the field for the seeking of redress by

---

3. Moore 1978 (103–4) and Black 1989 (75–78) are notable exceptions.

setting out its two extremes as limiting cases. Immediate, hot pursuit of those who harm you is the first limiting case. It proclaims the link between wrong and response. But this swiftness of reaction excludes mature reflection and political calculation. The costs must often have outweighed the attractions of immediate satisfaction. Close to the opposite extreme lies inaction, nonresponse. This strategy of "lumping" may be mandatory for the weak and disempowered. It broadcasts the apparent fact of the injured party's weakness and inability (or unwillingness) to strike back and so invites further oppression. The real extreme case, however, is represented by flight. When someone kills your brother and threatens you, it is unwise to stay around to ask questions. This is the time to leave home, temporarily at least, and perhaps to seek the aid of a more powerful figure by representing the wrong done to you as his also. Initial flight, exile, and appeals to higher powers, both to avenge and to impose or broker peaceful settlements, figure prominently in the stories I tell here.

In between these extremes lie most of the everyday micropolitics in medieval England. The myriad possible shades of response compel prudent decisions from the wronged and may have already been anticipated in the aggressors' calculations. All parties operate under practical constraints. In an ideal world they will ask themselves searching questions, to be answered with the help of friends and counselors. What do they seek from the situation? What is the most they might want, the least they can accept with honor, the best they can reasonably expect? Should they simply flee for protection from further damage and loss? Or can they demand full restitution, to put them and their friends back in the position they enjoyed before the wrongful act and thereby convince their community peers that they have survived attack without loss? Or will nothing less than vengeance suffice, to teach attackers and the rest of the neighbors the lesson that nobody harms *me* with impunity?

These are not free choices. They are subject to material and moral constraints. Confidence in one's physical power and the support of one's friends obviously makes a great difference. In its absence, physical vengeance may not be an option, or must at least be long delayed until a more opportune moment with better odds. In considering such matters, the aggrieved cannot restrict their calculations to their immediate enemies. The view taken by those around them will always matter. The rest of the community has its own choices. It can stand aside to let proper vengeance come, or intervene to prohibit revenge for an act that perhaps seems legitimate in a different context. Execution of a thief caught in the act must not be avenged. Standard models of centralized justice (like the Roman law conceptions taught in the law schools of the twelfth century and later) leave little room for private vengeance; vengeance, if not the Lord's, belonged to the prince, the state. But this too is a relatively extreme position with, as later chapters show, some unexpected limitations. The real crux is the ability of the would-be avenger to convince first himself, then his friends, and finally neutral bystanders that his chosen solution (blood vengeance, or money compensation, or some further possibility) was right and proper. He must argue his case within accepted norms. If he does this in a court, he will plead that his action is justified by the rules in force. In other words, he seeks to make his proof. But the appeal to reason is by no means confined to the courtroom. It is as important that he declare his right and demonstrate the legitimacy and measure of his proposed action when he is about to seek vengeance by direct action. Otherwise he risks shocking his peers by seeming to act *sine causa*;[4] inexplicable violence threatened everyone's safety and well-being. No sensible man wished to mobilize his neighbors into riding against him. A very great deal therefore turned on the way a man told his story, to establish the wrong and his right to avenge it.

Feud was one, often tendentious, way of telling a story. One man's tale of evil crying out for honorable vengeance can easily be met by another's denunciation of irrational, unjustified violence deserving severe punishment. Enemies naturally see the same events in very different terms, but bystanders and the community in general may take third and fourth perspectives that spawn further narratives. All these stories can differ wildly even while sharing the essential facts. Each may be true in its own terms. But some actors will likely stretch the truth, manufacturing facts toward a more winning version of the tale. In later chapters I do my best to disentangle and juxtapose conflicting narratives, and to present when possible my own judgment across the centuries of where the truth lies.[5]

DEFINING FEUD

Scholars have spilt much ink in the quest for an impossibly satisfactory definition of *feud*. Some now suggest that overuse of the term has brought the whole notion to the brink of collapse.[6] One important reason for this conceptual crisis has been the effort to depict both feud and the kinship structures with which it has customarily been linked as institutions. I follow those who see kinship in a more processual light, as a set of shifting choices and

4. Sawyer 1987, 29.
5. Historians do not really need literary theorists to tell them that the contingency of texts precludes the chances of any single complete reconstruction of past events. The chief value of the exercise may be to demonstrate the importance of the various narratives underlying all feud talk.
6. Sawyer 1987, 27–28.

cultural constructions that change through time, and make the case that similar arguments can usefully enhance our understanding of feud itself.[7]

It may be helpful, as a preliminary step, to place the traditional consensus on feud into some notional account of its conceptual development. When Western scholars began serious academic study of the "primitive" world at their borders and its "savage" inhabitants, and sought to describe the workings of their societies, they were faced by a challenging problem. How could these savages have survived and even thrived before the arrival of "civilization" as Europeans knew it? Many found it hard to comprehend what enabled these primitives to avoid descent into chaos when they lacked self-evidently essential institutions like centralized state authority and the rule of law. On-site observers tended to notice aspects of the social arrangements that they found strange, that differed most obviously from the ones they were used to at home. So they singled out unilateral kinship as distinctive of less civilized peoples. The "natives" ostentatiously described their biological relationships in ways so spectacularly different from the structure of European families that investigators were drawn first to list their kinship terms and then to present the results in the alluringly graphic form of kinship charts. These "maps" of native culture proclaimed the solidity of kinship as one institution that could be connected to the others that organized the "primitive" world, and so to form the basis for an overall view. In stateless societies (stateless, that is, by nineteenth-century standards), the apparent absence of identifiable legal systems pushed private self-help into the center of the picture and favored its promotion to institutional status as the "blood feud."

Perceptions of this kind permitted the emergence of many important constructive insights into alien modes of social control.[8] But there were negative consequences too—especially the widely shared assumption that feud and law were mutually exclusive. Few analyses attempted to read the two systems together, to discern the legitimating norms through which feuds were waged and, most important for me in this book, the feud-like impulses that motivated litigants in respectable legal systems.

All this, of course, recalls a historiography fashionable in the past but whose fossilized verities still influence our formulations. European historians of the Early Middle Ages, cognizant of the fact that feud words had originated on their watch, embraced the term and illustrated it with spec-

7. The major influence behind this approach has been Pierre Bourdieu. See esp. Bourdieu 1977, 33 sq., but also, e.g., Comaroff and Roberts 1981. Muir 1993 (esp. xxii–xxiv, 188–89) showed the power of the approach.

8. Arguably the most lasting and important of these is the peace-in-the-feud theory, discussed later in this chapter.

tacular anecdotes of vengeance and countervengeance. Then they graded early medieval political systems by the speed of progression toward the supersession and proscription of feud. Recent literature, influenced by the ethnographers, has softened their negative representation of feud without fully abandoning the attempt to view it in institutional terms. Historians remain disinclined to analyze feud alongside the law courts and within a single system of conflict resolution and social control.

Early medieval Europe indisputably shared common features with the twentieth-century societies so acutely described and explicated by anthropologists. Yet substantial differences are equally obvious. The ostentatious coexistence of feud with lawmaking, law enforcement officials, and courts of all shapes and sizes is among the most notable. Anglo-Saxon England was not the only early medieval kingdom in which fæhðe figured prominently alongside a robust legal system. The examination in chapter 3 of both these, as alternative means within a single political culture by which to seek redress for wrong, is long overdue.

This book, then, treats feud as a process, to be studied alongside a plethora of other options available to the aggrieved for the redress of the wrongs they perceived themselves to have suffered. Although one may present these choices for argument's sake as distinct from each other, the lines between them are patently artificial; one obviously shades into the other. What follows is not intended to argue for a formal definition of feud but to expose the assumptions behind the working understanding of feud-like behavior patterns discovered in the sources for English history in the three centuries between the mid-tenth century and the decades around 1300.[9] From twentieth-century observer accounts and analyses,[10] as much as historians' applications of their ideas to medieval sources,[11] I derive the following premises:

1. Feud starts as an effort to avenge injury, generally violent injury, and often a killing.
2. It represents the injury as the act of an enemy and signals a lasting enmity between the man (or men) who inflicted it and the "victim."

9. Hyams 1992 (6–7) represents an earlier effort at the same goal. I have now abandoned the distinction I drew there between "strong" and "weak" feud, although not the concern with iteration (tit-for-tat actions) that spurred me to produce it.

10. Of a large literature, mostly surveyed in White 1986, I have found Moore 1978 and Boehm 1984 particularly illuminating, and more recently Robarchek and Robarchek 1998 and Gould 2000. Gauvard 1991, chaps. 16–17, is especially helpful because the author uses comparable court-generated source material from late medieval France.

11. Notable among these are Miller 1990 (whose definition is at 180–81), Muir 1993, White 1986 and 1996 (usefully noting the multiple strategies that can be enfolded into the process), and Smail 1996; each refers to previous literature. For Wales, see Davies 1969 and Beverley Smith 1991; for Scotland, Wormald 1980 and Brown 1986. Heyn 1997 is, alas, less comprehensive than one might hope.

3. The wrong that provokes and justifies feud is understood to affect a larger group that included the original victim but was in part known and even recruited in advance of trouble. Its solidarity has been set in doubt and may need reassertion.[12]
4. Given a similar sense of the vicarious liability of the injuring party's associates, they were sometimes targeted for vengeance in the principal's stead.
5. The level of response is constrained by a notion of rough equivalence, requiring the keeping of a "score."[13]
6. Emotions both fuel the response and determine its quantum and nature.
7. The response is ritualized in various ways to proclaim the acts to all as legitimate vengeance.
8. Action from the side of the "victim" nevertheless raises the high probability of further tit-for-tat from their enemies.
9. To dispel this and offer hopes of an end to the violence, something much more than the punishment of individual offenders is necessary, amounting to a veritable peace settlement between the wider groups involved.

The obligation to avenge wrong (no. 1) is understood as something personal, incumbent on the victim or on individuals closely related to him. Because social identities reflect, and are reflected in, group membership, the initial act creates a state of hostility between collectivities as well as individuals (nos. 3 and 4). These support groups, although often described as kindreds, are neither magically available nor necessarily constant in size and power.[14] European societies lacked the unilateral kinship organization that so impressed early anthropologists in Africa and elsewhere. Western bilateral family groups are much less obviously corporate in structure than those behind the classic feud models. Yet these "ego-centered aggregates" mimic the collective behavior of clans and other blood corporations sufficiently closely to justify asking of them similar questions. They call for more, not less, effort in advance of trouble to ensure that the wronged and their enemies receive the desired assistance in time of crisis.[15]

12. White 1996, 120, 125; Gould 2000, 683.
13. Since the word *score*, in the sense of cutting a notch in a piece of wood to record a count, may very well have originated in Old Norse in the context of feud, it is worth noting that cognate forms were slow to reach Old English and do not seem to have acquired their modern meaning of calculation before the fourteenth century; *MED*, s.vv. "scôr(e)" and "scôren."
14. Their conflicts may, indeed, be on a scale that we should more naturally label warfare than feud, as White 1996, 108. See, e.g., the various feuds in *Beowulf* briefly mentioned in chap. 3 below.
15. Here Moore 1978 (108, 113, 115) perhaps exaggerates the "major difference" between corporate kindreds and their more temporary action-set equivalents. But the author's point (125), that

The prudent man has made his basic arrangements well in advance of any emergency. He has fostered the public reputation by which proper behavior in the past earns future aid as needed. He knows that the security of a larger "support group" requires active recruitment by negotiation and the management and constant replenishment of friendship networks in ways that I discuss toward the end of this chapter.[16] He does not use these friends merely to meet fire with fire in violent conflict. They are the ones whose counsel he seeks before he acts or responds to acts by others, for classic feuders look for a clear numerical advantage leading to a clean kill.[17]

Where lives are at stake, emotions are likely to run high (no. 6). This is apparent in the anecdotal sources, both fictional and factual. I begin to plumb the riches of the evidence for the history of emotions in the Middle Ages in chapter 2. To a coward like me, the first and most persistent emotion would certainly be fear. This was sharpest when your side had struck most recently, thus placing you next in the firing line.[18] But it also impeded timely action by men obliged to seek vengeance. The courageous feuder needed to face and overcome his fear. High passions like rage, hatred, or desperation are effective negations. Where they erupt naturally, hot pursuit of the enemy followed at once without powerful restraint. Otherwise a range of responses is possible, all needing validation by the display of appropriate feelings. Some simulated passion to validate the violence they intended and avoid the condemnation of their peers. More often, those genuinely wronged had still to work up the emotional fuel for dauntingly violent action. Some knew from watching how best to psych themselves up for action. Others needed help.

---

perspectives within the kindred differ radically from those taken by outsiders, remains valid and centrally important. Gilds are a serious candidate to fill the corporate role in Anglo-Saxon England (see chap. 3). If we knew more about their operation as controllers of friendship with a special responsibility to deal with deaths, they might be revealed as more central to the process of redress for wrong than can at present be shown.

16. The Old English *leges* indicate that close kin (the group responsible for the *healsfang*) must contribute to payments like *bot*, suggesting that their support was obligatory. II Cn 70.1 (following here the conventional sigla for the *leges* established by Liebermann 1903–16) mentions *neahmagon*, kinsmen beyond the nuclear family who nevertheless have claims to the estate of an intestate. Presumably they were also expected to aid him in his lifetime. The more remote the relationship, the weaker the obligation. One imagines that even they might need some persuasion to put their lives on the line, especially if they were also related to or even just friendly with the other side.

17. There is conflicting evidence. In some cultures, honor requires an individual to seek his vengeance one on one. But the incidents examined in chaps. 3–6 almost always feature a "war band" that is frequently dispatched by the prime mover in his own absence. This pattern bears a ring of reality. It certainly accords with recent theories that only "party-gang" species kill adults of their own kind and that they act only when they are precisely confident of success. Chimpanzees, for example, tend to raid rival communities but only to pick off and kill isolated stragglers, a pattern that has both resemblances and striking contrasts with that of classic feud. See Wrangham and Peterson 1996, 162–67, 221 sq.

18. The recent novel Offutt 1997 depicts this nicely.

When someone was thought to be slow in taking the required steps, relatives and friends goaded him to act as custom demanded. Shakespeare's Mark Anthony, perhaps the quintessential literary case, spurred the citizens of Rome to march against Caesar's assassins by the simple power of the word. Visible demonstrations of young men's duty were as effective as speeches and, because they made better literary copy, better documented. Mothers waved in the face of reluctant sons an ancestral sword or their dead husband's bloody shirt. Old men, relieved by their years from the necessity of bearing arms themselves, feigned shame and took to their beds.[19] In such ways, the young were bullied into the right emotional state to kill and be killed. The payoff came when they had done their duty, in the delicious thrill of the kill and the ensuing applause and admiration from their own.[20]

Against these expectations raised by the vengeance process must be set its potential to generate chaos, a horrific prospect. Here the essential requirement was to mark feud off from other forms of social process. Those involved must, therefore, signal their intentions clearly to bystanders. By following customary rituals (no. 7), they publicized their claim to privileged action,[21] and dissuaded neighbors and superiors from any temptation to ride against them on the ground that their actions constituted the kind of unreasonable violence that all right-thinking folk abhorred and sought to eradicate. Above all, the model to avoid was secret killing, with its aura of cowardice.[22] Hence action needed to be in the open without concealment, explicitly in search of licit redress. These ritualized responses were designed to publicize the all-important message: those who had been wronged by shameful acts deserved in turn to inflict shame against their enemies.

THE CHALLENGE OF CLOSURE

The one major drawback to the process was the great difficulty of bringing it to a satisfactory end. This is a direct consequence of the shame and humiliation whose infliction was the very essence of feud. Survivors had to consider whether and how they could regain honor and standing among their peers.[23] The obvious route was an equivalent violent response, tit for

---

19. William Miller has returned several times to this intriguing matter of goading. See Miller 1983 and 1990, 212–14. Gauvard 1991 (ii.772–74) has data on the critical decision about timing.

20. Wright 1994 (208, 278) and Wrangham and Peterson 1996 (70, 216) both insist on the excitement of animals at the kill.

21. Af 42, 42.1, illustrates this expectation of openness.

22. Halsall 1998a, 15–16. No wonder murder was an especially abhorrent form of homicide. See also Gauvard 1991, ii.758, 761–62, 768.

23. Gould 2000 (699) usefully formulates the point of feud in terms ("to demonstrate solidarity after actions by a rival group had placed that solidarity in doubt") that remove the need for honor in the analysis.

tat. If unrestrained, this response led toward the cycle of recurrent violence that observers have actually found in some societies and some analysts place at the core of their definitions of feud. Horror at the prospect of this vicious circle pressed men toward communal peacemaking.[24] Our understanding of the feuding process would therefore remain woefully incomplete without analyzing the means by which feuding societies strove in an imperfect world to counter this threat. Feud and peacemaking, rancor and reconciliation, wrong and satisfaction—each part of the duality constitutes a necessary side of a single, indivisible coin.

In feud cultures, state coercion alone is unlikely to secure lasting peace among those whose emotions have been aroused by acts of vengeance. The dry, emotion-purged downward-directed penal judgment rhetoric of our contemporary legal paradigms is poorly suited to the task of satisfying sufferers of wrong. (In our own day, victims of violence frequently voice their anger and frustration at procedures empty of personal retribution.) Shame much outweighed guilt to the secular men and women of the Middle Ages; they cared greatly how their lives looked to each other. They expected each other to take very seriously their resentments at perceived wrongs. Even when their emotions did not really run deep, they felt bound to represent them so for public consumption. To stand a decent chance of durability, reconciliation needed to be stage-managed in such a way as to grasp the emotions of both the actual protagonists and the onlookers. Effective publicity to the people who mattered required solemn, easily visible acts that could be read as a public evening of the "score" from some previous imbalance. So "wrongdoers" submitted and were humbled in the sight of all. They made "satisfaction" to the living "victims" or their relicts, whether by payment of compensation in acceptable amounts as honorably assessed or by other acts, such as penitential pilgrimage for a deceased man's soul, valued by the aggrieved.[25] Ideally, peacemakers sought a double goal: normalization, in the sense of ending the immediate conflict, and also restoration or reconstruction of positive relationships between the former enemies, a fresh friendship.[26]

In these twin aspects of reconciliation, women played an important if somewhat passive role. They were transferred from one side to the other as objects of wealth, gifts of the kind that customarily sealed new relationships

---

24. *Mort le roi Artu* 1954, 90, ll. 87–88 (p. 118). See also chap. 5 in this volume.

25. Interestingly, Latin "satisfaction" vocabulary in many narratives about wrongs conveys an obligation of reciprocity without the requirement for mathematical equality or balance implied by other formulations. Compensation was in some societies literally designed to replace the deceased (Moore 1978, 171).

26. The Carolingian anecdote recounted in Bullough 1991 (2) illustrates this double aim.

or reinforced existing ones. Their marriages were intended to produce issue bearing the blood of both former antagonists, hopefully to serve as the thread for peace-weaving in the future. But daughters and sisters were people as well as objects. Just as a woman sometimes goaded her menfolk into vengeance, she could also work in hall and elsewhere to reconcile angry men to her husband's lordship.[27]

To the modern observer, feud constitutes personal relations conceived as international relations. These are conflicts whose resolution demands not the defeat of wrongdoers but a public declaration of peace. This is not the way we normally analyze disturbances of the peace within modern states today. We expect good citizens to condemn crime and applaud its punishment in order to preserve law and order, and to remove, deter, or rehabilitate offenders. We allow citizens no right to choose whether to support the villain or the state. Crime is an offense against the community, a wrong against everyone. An impartial state deals with it most characteristically by the imposition of custodial or afflictive punishment. Throughout the period covered by this book, this characterization of wrongdoing through its public consequences was accompanied in England by more feud-like patterns. When the courts, in implementing this downward justice,[28] order punishment of offenders, they proclaim a radically different view of disputes from one that permitted closure and pacification through treaty between relatively equal parties. Early medieval justice was much more openly political than the new ideals of the twelfth century licensed. High medieval judges were expected to make their judgments of blood and death from a proper zeal for justice in the abstract.[29] We regard the posture of Olympian impartiality they were supposed to strike as fitting within our own ideal of justice but less appropriate to the horse-trading of international relations. Peace negotiations between nations turn on national interest. They occur between entities that have identified each other as enemies. When private enmities were pacified in feuding cultures, the unashamedly partial parties were signaling a similar conception of their essence which we can reasonably label feud.

This peace treaty test delineates not the nature of the disputes themselves but rather the manner in which contemporaries chose to characterize

27. Miller 1983, 175–94; Bullough 1991, 16–17.
28. I use this phrase to denote both the high medieval understanding of crime and the more undifferentiated conception of wrong that preceded it. I do not wish to call the earlier justice "criminal" in order to be able to distinguish attitudes toward wrong in the aftermath of the adoption of the Roman law distinction between crime and tort from practice in the Early Middle Ages. I first argued this in Hyams 1999 and develop my view in chap. 7.
29. I return to this point in chap. 2.

them.[30] In medieval England, there were always alternatives. Kings happily hanged thieves when they could. It seems to us no great stretch to extend this treatment to killers and other peace-breakers who appeared to threaten that descent into chaos feared by all reasonable people. That this switch to public justice was so protracted and gradual implies that the private enterprise alternative, feud, did what was required effectively in its own way. It turns out that one of the things feud could do in the right circumstances was to generate its own peace.

A PEACE IN THE FEUD?

To recognize and establish the theoretical basis for this peace in the feud was one of the great achievements of classic social anthropology.[31] Scholars have sought the answer in some variant of the anthropologists' models. In this view, feud could function as an instrument of routine social control in two ways. Both reflect the high cost and potentially destructive nature of reprisals for wrongful acts. First, a version of the deterrent argument suggests that fear of the violent retaliation threatened by feud serves to deter men from homicides and other violent acts. And second, the expectation of reprisals offers a strong incentive for friends to dissuade each other from committing acts for which they know they may themselves have to pay in money or blood. Feuding groups spread across communities, so men had to face the prospect of being forced to fight kinsmen, colleagues, neighbors, or friends. Blood kin of the disputants might well find themselves confronting their own kinsmen by blood or marriage and so might face excruciating choices. They might even find themselves in principle obligated to fight for both sides at once. Clearly, such "cross-linkage" augmented the pressure for peaceful settlement.[32]

The argument turns on the degree of segmentation in feuding society— that is, how membership of different associations could overlap. Consequently, disputing enemies were likely at some level to belong to the same association, one that stood to lose by their confrontation. The very dynamics of the society, so the argument runs, thus generated both a shared

---

30. Boehm 1984 (205) also describes pacification as "an intrinsic and important part of feuding," which Boehm therefore includes within his definition (151–52 n. 5).

31. Its real progenitor is Edward Evans-Prichard, a giant in his time, in his 1940 book *The Nuer*. But the formulation from which modern discussion starts is that of Max Gluckman, in his essay "The Peace in the Feud," reprinted in Gluckman 1955. I presented my own earlier thoughts on this subject in Hyams 1992 (8–9). I am well aware of the subsequent debate that has refined the notion almost out of existence. I use Gluckman's work here more as license to speculate than as any kind of authoritative model and now realize that I might have got similar encouragement from Brunner 1992 (or its 1965 original).

32. Gauvard 1991 (ii.683, 776) offers a couple of particularly clear cases.

interest in pacification and the means to influence the disputants toward compromise. The notion that the very brutality of "savages" might function as a mechanism for the maintenance of the peace had a nicely paradoxical air about it. In the wrong hands, the theory presented itself as just the kind of assumption of an easy, almost automatic equilibrium ("Look! No hands!") that gave functionalist anthropology a bad name. The underlying logic nevertheless retains a compelling power that still merits consideration.

The theory rests on twin premises. First, the norms must license a victim or his friends to take blood revenge, unless some very weighty factor (such as proposals for an honorable settlement) supervenes. This establishes a high probability that retribution will follow an initial wrong. The threatened violence acts as the sanction to induce the parties to agree on terms, if they can, and to implement the agreement in full afterward. The pressure comes not just from the victim's side that still had a score to settle but from, or on behalf of, the whole community of right-thinking folk who fear an escalation into general violence that will ensnare everyone. The second premise concerns the interest of all associations to protect and promote their own existence and well-being. Intragroup conflict, enmities between members, will harm the entire membership whatever the outcome. The prudent majority thus always possesses an interest to suppress internal violence and bring the contending parties to an agreement honorable enough to have staying power.[33] This is not just a feature of some special kind of segmented society. It is a function of the obvious fact that in any society with more than the most rudimentary political organization, there will be some level at which two enemy individuals or groups belong under the umbrella of a single association—the clan, the tribe, or the kingdom. A few apparent exceptions tend to prove the rule.[34] One can easily see that at least where the shared unit's territorial scale does not overwhelm the technology of power,[35] this collegiality can turn into pressure for compromise. The greater the number of socially influential groups to which an individual belongs, the more likely he is to share valued links with people on opposite sides of any conflict. The "crosscutting" serves to cast some as "hinge persons" with the special opportunity or discomforting obligation to mediate

33. See Boehm 1984 (166) on peace within the tribe.
34. The Waorani of Ecuador with their spectacularly unsegmented society, well described in Robarchek and Robarchek 1998, may be the best case to point. But Turnbull 1973, on the now notorious Ik of northeastern Africa, deserves rereading in this light.
35. The size of the West Saxon kingdom in the later Old English period and the extent of the real power of its kings are matters worth pondering in this connection. I touch on this question in chap. 3, but recognize that sparsity of data ensures that the matter is likely to remain one on which scholars will continue to differ.

between the adversaries. To put the matter starkly, each side may feel that such persons owe them participation in their support group. Thus, should matters come to blows, their position might require a desperately uncomfortable decision to plump for one side and reject ties to the other. Far better, then, to accept the lesser evil and strive to extricate oneself by brokering a reconciliation deal.

Exactly what men and women made of these cross-pulls in any particular situation is, of course, a matter for investigation. Nothing is automatic in the real world. Life is messier and far more contingent than theory, which can merely identify conditions within which self-directed settlements are possible. There will usually be resistance to be overcome, for example, from disputants who fear the long-term consequences of behavior that others might deem cowardly. For peace actually to ensue, enough men must both want a peaceful solution and command the resources and social capital to bring it about. To attain decent odds that the peace will hold, they need to aim at a very public demonstration that the parties are acting honorably toward each other, and that the terms given and received are fair and appropriate. The rituals that implement and demonstrate this settlement are one more distinguishing indication of the distance from the judgments of downward justice. Their ideal result is not merely the end of an enmity but the construction of a fresh or revived, positive amity.

THE "EVOLUTION OF COOPERATION" HYPOTHESIS

This evolution of cooperation has occupied the attention of theorists with very different concerns and methods from those of social anthropologists. Games theorists and evolutionary biologists each reach rather similar conclusions, in apparent ignorance of the anthropological literature,[36] but by routes that offer some further insights. In a classic work (concise, readable, but fiercely contested),[37] Robert Axelrod tried to formalize a general, widely applicable model of cooperation; he sought to demonstrate that (1) this model constituted an "evolutionarily stable strategy" for human beings, which (2) could evolve without the need for direction from above or the existence of any cooperative ethos among its actors—without, indeed, much at all by way of advance planning. Axelrod's methods were remote from those with which we historians feel most comfortable; he honed his theory

---

36. An exception here is Bates 1983, which shows how to reformulate the peace-in-the-feud model in terms of the Prisoner's Dilemma game. But I could not see that this added much to our understanding of the problems.

37. Axelrod 1984. Oye 1986 (7–8) offers a brief sketch of the argument; see also Axelrod and Keohane 1986, 253.

through competitions between game-playing computers. The historical and other confirmatory data seem a later addition more to illustrate the possibilities than to test or prove the hypothesis. Although Axelrod's book may be essentially an exercise in model making, much about his tit-for-tat strategy matches real-life experience and carries the breath of life. The book's argument and subsequent developments convey insights historians might not have discovered unaided.

The problem, as Axelrod saw it, was to explain how humans could ever have reached a situation in which cooperation with others would be the "rational choice" for a well-informed, intelligent individual.[38] The classic answer—that few humans would cooperate until coerced by their superiors—did not seem to him to explain the apparently self-directing communities he observed scattered through nature. The nub of the matter is the establishment of trust. How, without coercion, could rational men come to risk cooperating with their neighbors in a world in which each apparently had so much to gain from betrayal and conquest, and so little to lose?[39]

There is no single strategy for dealing with all situations of enmity. Optimum responses depend on what the enemy is doing and what he intends to do on feedback. So you must take note of the opposition's previous acts and future intentions before coming to your own decision. This calls for intelligence in both senses. You need first to identify and nominate your enemy. As Yitzhak Rabin wisely said in 1993, you make peace with enemies, not friends. But success requires a clear identification of your enemy and a deep understanding of his interests.[40] To put matters at their lowest, "the scope for the exercise of intelligence is considerable."[41]

Axelrod identified a simple, easily comprehensible strategy that would work in certain situations that he claimed to be common, if not all pervasive. These situations must meet three conditions.[42]

1. The parties (not just their principals) must enjoy a "mutuality of interest." This generalizes the segmentation within which anthropologists had observed "peace-in-the-feud" to be possible.
2. The parties must also be aware of the need to continue living alongside those who are currently their enemies. They must therefore rule out the possibility of total elimination of the opposition (mas-

38. Oye 1986, 1–2: "If international relations can approximate both a Hobbesian state of nature and a Lockean civil society, why does cooperation emerge in some cases and not in others?"
39. Frank 1988 offers his own "commitment model" to meet much the same diagnosis with less exclusively rational medicine.
40. Axelrod 1984, 126–32, and chap. 7; Oye 1986, 12–17.
41. Axelrod and Keohane 1986, 231.
42. He and his colleagues describe these in various terms. See Oye 1986, 3–4, 22–23; and Axelrod and Keohane 1986, 253.

sacre or genocide) to remove all fears of further acts of vengeance in the future. "The great enforcer of morality," Axelrod contends, ". . . is the continuing relationship, the belief that one will have to do business again."[43] This "shadow of the future," as he has memorably called it, sobers up the actors to the lasting consequences of their enmities and alerts them to their long-term interests, including the peace option. It enables reciprocity to appear both possible and desirable.

3. The number of players in the game must be low, to keep the odds calculable. It should be a two-player game. For present purposes, the value of this third point is to emphasize the way that people understand feud as a bilateral relationship between rough equals,[44] in which bystanders (including the authorities) operate not as players but, ideally, as if they were officials charged to confine the game to the field of play and the two teams.

Within a situation of this sort, Axelrod says, a party *capable* of retaliation (another crucial premise) can minimize damaging conflict by pursuing the strategy of tit for tat. He should respond exactly in kind, meet strike with counterstrike as swiftly as he can, and continue doing so until the opposition blinks and is ready to propose cooperation, that is, some kind of peace deal. The best option then becomes a favorable hearing of peace overtures in the hope of achieving closure. On the other hand, as long as the opposition continues to attack, he should always counterattack; robust counterstrikes are the only way to inhibit the enemy from exploiting what would otherwise signal weakness. The great risk is an interminable string of defections, endless vendetta. But the opposition should see these dangers too and, realizing that all lose by this route, may choose to try cooperation next time.

A number of factors directly affect the odds on the emergence of cooperation. Interested parties do not have to let things simply run their course. That there are various other ways to lengthen the "shadow of the future"[45] can be seen through the features by which peace settlements explicitly sought to establish positive relationships between former foes.[46] It also clearly helps if there exists from the start "a small initial cluster of potential

43. Axelrod 1984, 60.
44. Axelrod and Keohane 1986 (231) notes the need for equality. The implication, that a feud may migrate upward in society until a victim succeeds in getting his cause taken up by someone of equal status to his enemy, is borne out by actual feud data.
45. Oye 1986, 1, 8; Axelrod and Keohane 1986, 226.
46. Political peace-weaving marriages are the most explicit illustration. Their progeny were close kin to both of the former warring parties. Crosscutting put pressure on these kinsmen on both sides to protect themselves from intolerable conflicts of loyalty.

cooperators" to seed the peace process in other people's minds.[47] In a medieval European context, the obvious cooperator would be the Church, with its message of peace and its success at influencing at least some of the secular nobility and others. Clerical peacemaking is never certain to succeed—it must be done well—but it clearly enters into the equation. Moreover, the anarchy presumed at the starting point may be less than complete, as it certainly was at all times in medieval Europe. In England, kings and their men would ride against troublemakers to coerce them into future cooperation and implement a royal, secular but also Christian view of public peace complementing the ecclesiastical ethos.[48] Even where kings declined to intervene, their supervision of customary processes like feud clarified standards of conduct and set the rules for the game. The West Saxon kings Alfred and Edmund did this and, like some of their successors, arguably went further.[49] King and law each are institutions that can permanently change the payoff structures of feud,[50] even to the point of excluding the game from their society's approved and respectable processes of conflict resolution. The later Anglo-Saxon kings probably tried to achieve this, and their successors from 1166 onward partially succeeded in doing so.[51]

Tracing these institutional interventions proves vital to my subsequent argument. Their power and success go far to explain the statistical balance between full feud as understood here and the more isolated acts of vengeance that lacked iteration. Axelrod calls these latter acts the "single-player game." They are, at least in the thirteenth century, far more common in England than were any sequences of iterated feud, a fact that may be equally true of many other indisputable feud cultures.[52] Furthermore, they are notably more difficult to deal with, for their protagonists are unrestrained by any "shadow of the future."

A moment's reflection on this point carries a profitable general lesson about the system as a whole. If Axelrod's tit-for-tat model is to produce lasting peace, it absolutely demands prudent and intelligent players. What happens when they are lacking? Trouble. A foolhardy player, careless of future consequences, can all too easily convert the potentially stable two-player tit-for-tat game into the explosive single-player version. Such men are dangerous and must be killed, expelled, or otherwise neutralized.[53] The more

---

47. Axelrod and Keohane 1986, 244.
48. The text VI As illustrates this possibility.
49. See chap. 3.
50. Axelrod and Keohane 1986, 238.
51. See chaps. 5 and 6.
52. See Boehm 1984, 109, 198, 217.
53. Axelrod and Keohane 1986, 248; I offer anthropological and historical confirmation later in the chapter.

thoughtful members of feud cultures thus recognized the need to restrain hotheads and move very cautiously in treating disputes that showed any predisposition to escalate.

The tit-for-tat strategy appears more robust than all or most of the alternatives. It has been shown to lead some very different systems into stable state. It has the great virtues of clarity and simplicity. Once all parties perceive it in action, they know where they stand and can adjust their own actions accordingly.[54] Its only precondition is a cluster of believers, an initial pool of the peaceably inclined.[55] The actors do not need to share any moral ethos; they simply have to be able to discern where their interest lies. Even the suboptimal quality of the tit-for-tat solution may be regarded as a strength in the real world. Obviously, each side wants to win, to triumph over enemies and demonstrate its quality to all. But if that is impossible, men of honor win applause by making their concessions honorably and with style. This is the stuff of real-world politics. Resentments may linger and can reemerge later in damaging ways. But to gain time in which to live in peace and die in bed is no small achievement. The venom may even fade to the point where recycled enemies become genuine friends. Peacemaking is an odds game with nothing mechanical about it.

Historians may wish to read Axelrod's argument as the sketch for a recurring pattern of cultural development. Obviously, the tit-for-tat model cannot directly explain feud on the individual level. Its most obvious defect is the impossibility of its crucial requirement of iteration. No dead man can directly counter his own killer; it is too late for that.[56] This forces the argument onto the level of group relations and helps illuminate the rationale behind the support groups on either side of the feud. Precisely because iteration and the "shadow of the future" were so important in the recruitment and maintenance of these networks of amity, the tit-for-tat pattern inevitably figures in every attempt at a definition of feud.[57] To claim the privileged legitimacy of feuding, a would-be attacker must claim to act only because his enemy has defected first and inflicted on him the initial wrong that justified an avenging response. Axelrod shows that swift revenge, in addition to being morally justified within feuding cultures, was also a rational strat-

54. Axelrod 1984, 53.
55. Axelrod and Keohane 1986, 244.
56. Note, however, both the metaphorical attribution of vengeance to the deceased and the way that spiritual acts undertaken by killers as part of their self-humbling within peace settlements were sometimes expressed as intending to replace the murdered in his kin or to relieve his soul.
57. Most scholars would exclude Axelrod's "single-player game" from their definitions.

egy that benefited the actor's interests.[58] To punish defection, thereby discouraging an enemy from believing he could get away with his acts, established your side's credibility.[59] The pattern by which one wrong provoked the next had its hopeful side. Smart actors now viewed peace overtures as rational, perceiving their interest in making a "nice" response. This behavior is close to the predictions of peace-in-the-feud analysis.

All this talk of computers and hyperrational decision-making can easily encourage an overestimate of the run of reasoned calculation over more spontaneous reactions. Emotions like envy,[60] hatred, and anger (one's own as well as the opposition's) have to be part of the calculus. The confrontation and negotiation implied by Axelrod's own schema could produce tense episodes wherein all participants are conscious that they are laying their lives on the line. It is hard to imagine most people treating these circumstances as a mere game. Few normal folk can shrug off all risks to their own skins should their calculations go awry or peace negotiations miscarry. Principals and mediators alike had to summon their courage, stiffen their resolve, and psych themselves up emotionally for the challenge any way they could.[61] I have already indicated some of the ways in which this necessity affects the feud model. The surprisingly adequate documentation for medieval rhetoric about social emotions, coming in chapter 2, encourages the view that feuding was more than just a matter of rational calculation.[62] The lasting value of a "rational choice" perspective here is to document the way that recorded behavior *could* be logically patterned in circumstances in which people genuinely understood their own culture and possessed the self-awareness to recognize the possibilities it offered them.[63]

FRIENDSHIP NETWORKS AND SUPPORT GROUPS

Vengeance may be a dish best consumed cold, as Oscar Wilde once said. It is not for solitary eating. Feud is, in those cultures that practice it, an em-

58. Axelrod 1984, 184–85.

59. Frank 1988 shows in his "commitment model" that there are other ways to convince the enemy to take your overtures seriously; see esp. his chaps. 4 and 10. Cheating (bluff, if you like) and its detection are crucial here; Pinker 1997 (336–37, 412–13) has some thought-provoking material on this topic.

60. Axelrod 1984 (110–13) warns against envy in rational but realistic terms.

61. See Wright 1994, 205, 278–79.

62. This is the argument behind the "commitment model" offered by Robert Frank as an alternative to self-interest models like Axelrod's. He sees this as a step toward a type of "theory of unopportunistic behavior" I might have used here (Frank 1988, 258).

63. Boehm 1984 (xii, 105) claims that his Montenegrin subjects did understand their own feuding behavior. His general stance is more favorable to the "rational choice" viewpoint.

blematic reminder that our individual actions affect everyone who is linked to us at all closely. Harmful acts can have wide repercussions that affect stability of the whole society. The rational man needs friends as much for assistance in committing such acts himself as to guard against the onslaught of his enemies.

Commentators often declare that the collectivities set the scene and occupy center stage at the expense of individual rights. They place at the center of their model the assumption that these groups, usually blood kindreds, "own" the wrongs committed against their members and so control the right or duty of response. Thus we must seek that reciprocal altruism implied by feud models at this group level. The way that individuals are attracted into these groupings and retained thereafter is worth extended study. The obvious principle is that the friend of my friend is my friend too. From that viewpoint one can build in more complex but equally telling extensions, such as the corollary that, as Mao put it, the enemy of my enemy may come to be my friend.[64] The strongest bonds are often those constructed against a common enemy, an Other who compels hard decisions about special loyalties.

Our medieval sources draw us inexorably into the vocabulary of friendship. This is not mere chance. Friendship discourse is central to many feud cultures. At its core is the opposition between friend and foe so fundamental that it is enshrined in many medieval languages. Latin writers opposed without special thought *amicus* to *inimicus*, and desirable, protective *amicitia* to the *inimicitia* they feared. Old English writers contrasted *feond* (enemy, including the enemy of all, the Devil) with *freond*, a nicely rhyming opposition that survived, somewhat softened, into Middle English.[65] One can pursue the opposition into other medieval vernaculars, including the intricate word games of Old French romances on and around *ami* and *anemi*.

Because people defined their friends by opposition to their enemies, we stand to learn about their enmities from an examination of the semantic field of friendship words. There is indeed a strong association between friendship and peace.[66] In the Early Middle Ages, the semantic field occupied by the friendship words themselves referred primarily to immediate kin, followed closely by lords and vassals.[67] From these two directions, peo-

---

64. See Wright 1994, 283–85. Hunt 1989 prints a set of twelve "rules for the maintenance and preservation of friendship" from the later thirteenth century. These draw on a broad "tradition of treatises on conduct and courtesy," to which he gives useful references. Rule 8, "en nul adverseté sun ami guerpir. . . . E tenir foy a tun amy en sa adverseté qe en sa prosperité ové li pussez joir," seems quite to the present point.

65. This is obvious enough from the standard dictionaries, including *MED*, s.vv. "frend" and "fend."

66. Offenstadt 2000, 204–5.

67. Downer, in *LHP* 437–38, marshals texts from the Anglo-Saxon leges to contend that both Latin *amicus* and Old English *freond* "can on occasion mean 'kinsman.'" But his argument is

ple drew their natural friends. All other sources of friends were secondary and resulted from conscious choices.

This fact at once confirms suspicions that revenge is more than the business of an individual.[68] One's kinsmen, lord, and dependants obviously stood to gain or lose status from one's acts. The money required to meet heavy compensation payments came in the first instance from kinsmen, even when the acts that made them liable had occurred without their concurrence or knowledge. Worse still, they could find themselves unwittingly in the line of fire.[69] You and they knew these facts and ought to have heeded one another's interests. A necessary option found in some feuding societies is the right to expel troublemakers from one's kindred or group.[70] There were limits to the obligations of kinship—or to put it another way, friendship carried duties but friends must merit their rights.

The expulsion of those whose friendship was too costly to keep is presumably an atypical, exceptional act. If it demonstrates that friendship was not to be taken for granted, it should also direct attention toward the nurturing and maintenance of friendship as a routine and ever-present concern for the prudent. Members of feuding societies needed to identify their friends in advance, to organize their support networks both for mundane, everyday activities and for that possible future emergency. In the societies for which I have data, prudence appears to have dictated the preparation of alliances extending well beyond the bounds of "blood" kinship.[71] The traditional understanding of feud as kin-based and largely kin-bounded is no longer sufficient. It was more plausible within an older approach that viewed kinship and feud in institutional terms and usually considered political actors to operate within them in ways more reactive than instrumental and proactive. We now rightly approach kinship as a dynamic, cultural con-

---

partly circular in that he assumes that texts concerning feud must refer to kinsmen only. It seems more likely that a number of them (e.g., E Cf retr 36.5; *LHP* 82.26) point less specifically to "the wide circle of kindred" and thus support the speculations in my own text, that feud recruitment was not confined to blood kindred. Bloch 1961 (123–25, 231) is the classic account of "blood friends"; Gauvard 1991 (ii.674 sq.) has critical discussion, suggesting that the support group vocabulary was more developed in later medieval France.

68. See Wright 1994, 339.

69. Miller 1999 (79) notes that in Iceland the range of those deemed responsible for another's act differed according to whether the prosecutors proceeded by feud or through the law. II Em 1.3 is probably enough to show that Englishmen recognized comparable inhibitions on the substitution of close kinsmen and associates for a principal. The risks nevertheless remained real.

70. Moore 1978 (122–26, 171–72) and Boehm 1984 (xii, 75–76, 85–86) illustrate this option, which probably also featured in Anglo-Saxon England (as we shall see in chap. 3). See Offenstadt 2000 (216) for the medieval Netherlands. Hyams 2001 (39–40) uncovers a little more of the early medieval history. Gruter and Masters 1986 and Boehm 1985 introduce a more general literature on the phenomenon of ostracism, which Boehm describes as "acts of distancing when the individual is removed from the group" and as "intended to set an example for the future" (1985, 312–13).

71. Sawyer 1987 (32–33) remarks on the way feuds habitually drew on lordship.

struct, inevitably changing through time, especially in bilateral systems like the European model, where each individual *ego* determined who his close kinsmen were and added to their number through marriage and heir-making. The presence of affines (relatives by marriage) demonstrates the artificiality of the groupings.[72] The fact that people passed their alliances into, and through, their kinship structures demonstrates the prime importance of kinship in such cultures as a great organizing metaphor of social life. It is no wonder that vengeance groups are often described in kinship language as clans, families, and the like. But these are organizing fictions, not sociological definitions. Once we understand kinship as effectively a cultural rather than a biological phenomenon, we must surely go on to ask why reasonably rational and far-seeing members of any feuding society would *not* look beyond their kinsmen for emergency and indeed routine support and friendship.

The bilateral kinship system that distinguishes Europeans from many other parts of the world almost compels people to trace their own kin in radiating circles outward from ego.[73] It is perhaps coincidental that this "expanding circle" is well designed to match the biological realities of genes shared in ever-decreasing proportions as the relationship becomes more remote.[74] Kinship terminology can, we know, wander in directions quite remote from the underlying biology. The "expanding circle" model is best epitomized in the degrees of relationship used by Roman lawyers but eschewed in Germanic Europe, which favored a different, "parentelic" method of calculating kinship.

The background of learned laws seems responsible for the presumably unscientific analog found in early medieval theology. From the days of Origen to the time of Aquinas and beyond, Christian writers talk of an *ordo caritatis*, a taxonomy of love, one might almost say, to encapsulate the moral implications of kinship.[75] They were making a point about the love, *caritas*, due from friends. This friendship diminished in heat as the number of degrees (or joints)[76] separating one from one's relatives increased. Augustine

72. As Gauvard 1991 (ii.637) points out. See gl. ad Gen. xii.8, "fratres enim sumus," for the three ways in which one can become a "brother" in Old Testament texts.

73. One should now read the classic study of Anglo-Saxon kinship of Lancaster 1958 in light of the remarks in Goody 1983, app. 1. Gauvard 1991 (ii. 648–50) documents the "expanding circle."

74. The secondary exposition of the philosopher Singer (1981) makes this point very clearly; the phrase "expanding circle" comes from his title. De Waal 1996 (213) suggests a "floating pyramid" image instead.

75. Herlihy 1991 (7–11) traces the tradition without making anything of the sociobiological parallel. The following paragraph follows his citations.

76. The Germanic parentelic method of tracing kinship sometimes expressed distance from *ego* in terms of a skeleton image, by counting the number of "joints" separating individuals. See on this Radcliffe-Brown and Forde 1950, 15–18.

actually envisioned this in terms of distance from a warming fire. One of the theologians' main concerns was where to draw the line between friends to whom love was due and enemies who had, surprisingly in a Christian context, no such claim. The underlying premise seems to have been akin to the familiar tag: you're either with us or against us. The distinction had to be made. One prevalent view in antiquity branded all strangers as at least potential enemies. Successive authors drew the line in different places according to varying arguments. Origen placed even neighbors in the enemy camp; he thought it necessary only not to *hate* enemies. Peter Lombard seemed to define all those outside the domestic circle as enemies or at least nonfriends. This whole line of thought cries out for careful exposition to show how fathers and schoolmen reconciled its apparent thrust with our expectations of the gentle gospel ethic. Augustine and others pressed believers to love their enemies according to the gospel injunctions. Aquinas concluded one argument in his *Summa Theologica* with the words, "it is therefore more meritorious to love a friend than an enemy."[77]

The immediately apparent, perhaps superficial understanding of the unlearned is more to the present point. It must have seemed to some priests committed to guide their flock from pulpit and confessional sufficient license for the ethics of enmity. Their flocks could be forgiven for reading the overall thrust of the tradition, mistakenly, as lending authority to their secular obligations to identify and pursue enemies. Taken seriously, it challenged the more obvious understandings of the Ten Commandments and the Gospels, as commanding attitudes toward neighbors and enemies that were the very antithesis of this.[78] At the least, by promoting social solidarity as a prime obligation, churchmen were strengthening the extremely secular obligations on which feuding depended.

The tag "amicus amicis, inimicus inimicis" hints at the way people internalized widely shared norms of how to behave toward potential friends and enemies.[79] The mutual friendship oaths sworn by the kings of the East and West Franks in 921–22 allow us a glimpse of the practical implications. "I will be a friend to my friend," the wording went, "and behave just as a friend

---

77. "Ergo diligere amicum est magis meritorium quam diligere inimicum" (Herlihy 1991, 10 n. 62). See also the texts quoted in Mansfield 1995, 36 n. 58.

78. Medieval teachers from Augustine onward believed the Decalogue to have been divided unequally between the two tablets received at Mt. Sinai. English witnesses to this tradition include Powicke and Cheney 1964, ii.902, 1062; I discuss this further in chap. 2. The fact that the fourth through the tenth commandments were all directed at behavior toward one's neighbors ("proximi") seems to me virtually to dictate that the Church generate a social ethic. I shall argue the implications of this elsewhere. Teachings on Jesus' admonition to go beyond the Old Testament view can be approached initially through the Glossa Ordinaria to Mt. v, and so forth.

79. Althoff 1998a, 193.

rightly should to his friend."[80] In the Latin sources of the Early Middle Ages, this kind of friendship language features, as here at the very top of society, mainly to privilege formal associations constructed for political reasons. The rituals and formulae by which this was effected can be traced on the Continent far back into the very early Middle Ages and ultimately to imperial practices in late antiquity.[81] The results resemble political alliances and are often described in identical language. The use by English kings of similar language for roughly similar purposes in charters and other documents issued during the period from the ninth century ends at the Norman Conquest.[82] Kings generally talked the language of friendship when they wished to honor their most important supporters and ministers or the picked men in their garrisons.[83] They secured in their words the real-life practice by which they demonstrated confidence in, and affection for, these friends in very visible ways, such as eating, sleeping, and living alongside them within the same building.[84] The king's interest in friendship was by no means sentimental. He expected active returns from those on whom he conferred his favor. His power rested on the number of friends he could muster in his support. So they were, for example, to help the reeves enforce the laws and lead the rest of the *folc* to the love of God, a task that may have loomed as crucial in a time of invasion.[85] It was his interest that they should stand together as a cohesive group. Wulfstan makes Æthelred, in that air of desperation his laws sometimes carry, order all his friends to love each other honestly, "mid rihtan getriwðan."[86] Perhaps the aim is simply to voice a hope that other kings fostered but never had set into writing. If so, the royal *freondscype* begins to take on the air of a faction of king's friends and retainers with some resemblances to the retinues of much later reigns. To belong to this faction was at least as valuable to its members as to the king. Members gained all-important personal access,[87] which led to other kinds of

80. Martindale 1995, 30–31.
81. Althoff 1990 (31–84) surveys the evidence very thoroughly and is partially translated as Althoff 1998a.
82. Barrow 1999. Post-Conquest kings talked more of their *fideles* than their friends. Although these too were beloved (*dilecti*), the connotations are closer to those of the Carolingian-style fidelity oaths.
83. I wish that the word *fæstingmen* in Sawyer 1968, no. 193 of 841 and the spurious no. 183 (supposedly dated 821 but actually much later), could mean "feasting-men," as suggested in Barrow 1999 (110). This would provide a nice link between political trust and the culture of the royal hall. Unfortunately, however, the root appears to be *fæst* in the sense of fixed, secure, a reference to strongholds (fastnesses). Garrison retainers seems a good guess as to the group intended.
84. Althoff 1998a, 198; Jaeger 1999, chap. 9; Offenstadt 2000, 221–25; see Hyams 1998 (93 sq.) for the intimacies of the royal chamber in a later age.
85. IV Eg 1.5; VI Atr 6.
86. VII Atr 44.1.
87. II Em 4; V Atr 29; VI Atr 36. I have more to say on this below, 93–94, 102.

favor, political influence, and privilege. And having something to give, the king had also something to withhold or withdraw.[88] So Æthelstan's errant reeves were told that future offenses would lose them not merely their property but also "ealra freondscypes." This sounds ominously like a threat to life or limb, and Æthelred reminded his reeves to behave if they wished to retain "Goddes oððe minne freondscype."[89] The thread running through all these legislative admonitions is that friendship must constantly be demonstrated through action. Though one can never rely on the argument from silence in a period so short of evidence, there is a telling absence of references to hereditary friendship, the automatic affection afforded to sons or grandsons of dead friends.

The agenda behind these scattered indications of how Anglo-Saxon kings and their advisers viewed friendship is fiercely political. There is no reason to believe that kings were unique in this. The message—that they expected their would-be friends to live within their friendship or bear the consequences—proclaims an instrumental view of political friendship that was widely understood and shared. The leges enable one to enumerate some obvious, characteristic expectations of friends. Clearly, friends must stick together as a group, stand "swa on anum freondscype swa on anum feondscype" (in friendship as in feud), and treat each other "with true fidelity."[90] On an individual level, they would naturally deposit their valuables with each other.[91] They expected their friends to stand surety for them,[92] advise on and guarantee their marriage agreements,[93] warrant possession of suspect animals or other goods,[94] join in pursuit of enemies and wrongdoers and help negotiate peace settlements afterward,[95] and make good on their share of compensation payments in return for a share of incoming moneys.[96] No wonder, then, that friendship was associated not just with security but with peace, and not merely because of the alliteration with *frið*.[97] The equation of the friendless man with the outlaw is an easy mistake to make.[98] As Wulfstan in sapiential mood proclaimed through Cnut's mouth, the man without friends lacked all the above advan-

---

88. See Leyser 1981 (746–77) on the way the Ottonian kings hired out their manors and horses to the favored few.

89. II As 25.2; VIII Atr 32; VIII Atr 27 declares that a priest forfeited the friendship enjoyed by all men in holy orders if he committed perjury; the principle seems to be that membership of a friendship group demanded proper behavior on pain of expulsion.

90. VI As 7 (London Peace Gild); VIII Atr 44.1.

91. Af, intro. 28 (from Exod. xxii.7 and referring to neighbors as well as friends).

92. II Ew 3; Wif 2.5.

93. Wif 1.1, 7.

94. II Atr 9.2–9.3.

95. VIII Atr 1.1 = I Cn 2.3; Episc 7–8. Abt 65.1; Af 42.1; *LHP* 83.16.

96. II Em 1; V Atr 31.1.

97. VI As 8.2; V Atr 1.2; X Atr 2.1.

98. One manuscript of II Cn 15a makes this slip. See also Ps Cn For 24; II As 25.2.

tages, and judges treated him with special harshness precisely because he could not easily find sureties and oath-helpers.[99] Thus public expulsion from a friendship group was among the harshest of sanctions, which even the king reserved for the most serious offenses such as breach of one's oath and pledge.[100] In a society that proclaimed duties and expectations of this kind, it is hardly fanciful to see men deriving a very significant portion of their social identity from their friendships.

The sparse nonlegislative sources for the functioning of noble society in pre-Conquest England offer little hope of taking these conjectures much further. But they do at least authorize us to think in terms of a more voluntary and instrumental side to political association in general and, more specifically, the kind of support group capable of deployment for the needs of private feud. Even in Anglo-Saxon England, a number of overt voluntary organizations existed to aid the task of securing one's position and providing for future emergencies. The fact that gilds explicitly required their members to settle quarrels with each other peacefully but to stand with their fellows in external disputes makes one wonder about other associations.[101] The publicly organized policing system that assembled private individuals into tithings and suretyship was primarily intended to promote royal justice by ensuring that persons accused of offenses appeared in court to stand to right. But prolonged service within this public system must inevitably have produced less formal consequences. Forcing or cajoling neighbors to put their life and limb at risk by court appearances can have been no simple task and probably involved more physical action than the sources and their modern treatment suggest. The personal relationships that survived this tempering process were just the kind that men in trouble, contemplating violent action of their own or from their enemies, would wish to rely on for their security. Tithingmen especially, with some authority over their tithings, seem well placed to recruit supporters. There could be nothing automatic or forced about this. The recruiter would need to attract his men by whatever means he could muster, from kinship (however remote) as well as from other kinds of more voluntary association—godparenthood,[102] and the ever-elusive fosterage that marked lives from the formative years of a shared youth.[103]

I envision the process of constructing a network of amity to have de-

99. II Cn 35–35.1; cf. VIII Atr 22 = I Cn 5; *LHP* 65.5.
100. II Ew 5.1; cf. VIII Atr 27 = I Cn 5.3; Northu 2.1.
101. Discussed in chap. 3.
102. Lynch 1998; see more generally Gauvard 1991, ii.663–66; and Miller 1983, 160–75. Ine 76 is a key text.
103. See Lynch 1998, 91, 231.

manded care and attention over the many years of a life cycle.[104] The restricted yet fairly free choices feature prominently in the whole business of social relations. For the slow growth of that mutual trust essential to a deep friendship that can accommodate and surmount the stresses of physical danger, repeated contact is needed. Plain geographical contiguity may here be just as effective as intermittent attendance at meetings of gild or tithing, or indeed in a lord's hall. One cannot entirely avoid one's neighbors, and confrontations with them at celebrations and funerals, across one's front gate, or by broken fences fuel a winnowing process through which some become friends and others do not.[105] Kings exploited these existing relationships where they could, for example, to make men stand witness for each other's livestock sales.[106] Choices of loyalty within village and neighborhood made over time prepared for the occasional dramatic incident that forced an actual decision between acquaintances in conflict. One can sometimes show, even for Anglo-Saxon England, how networks created for the purposes of, say, a great landlord brought neighbors from wide areas together in circumstances that facilitated their knowledge and assessment of each other's qualities toward, perhaps, some future emergency.[107] One special selling point of these associations in a segmented society was the way they crossed administrative boundaries of, for example, hundred and shire.[108]

This is the kith (Old English *cyðð*) of the familiar phrase "kith and kin," meaning precisely those whom you know well, in whose company you feel comfortable, your neighbors, or as later generations sometimes called them, *paysans*.[109] Prominent among their number must be many "plain-vanilla" friends of the kind who have largely escaped scholarly notice in the past. They seldom enter our sources unless marked by some special act such as an agreement to share the spoils of war perhaps by becoming blood broth-

104. Gauvard 1991 (ii, chaps. 14–15) has much to tell of the ways in which this was done in France at a slightly later date. It is interesting that her sources have ways of labeling those capable of assembling support groups (ii.636–37, 644–45).

105. Ine 40 and II As 9 give broad hints about the way fencing compelled neighbors (explicitly so named) to build relations with each other. Part 1 of Ellickson 1991 provides eloquent commentary on the implications of this in a modern context. See Gauvard 1991, ii.669–74.

106. VI As 8.7–8; IV Eg, esp. 7–10. Both of these codes again use the *neighbor* word, but Edgar also calls on the village and its *tunesmen*. The twelfth-century *Leges Henrici Primi* frequently refers to *vicini*; LHP 8.5, 26.1, 33.1, 43.9, 57–57.1, 59.2a, 60.2b. Downer finds no obvious sources for LHP 57, "De querela vicinorum," and is inclined to translate *vicinus* as "villager" or "townsman" (LHP 339). But Old French *voisin* and cognates already mean "neighbor" in the twelfth century.

107. Bullough 1991 (19–23) gives one nice illustration from Worcester. See also Rosenwein 1989.

108. Martindale 1995 (30) makes a similar point from Continental evidence.

109. The primary reference of the Old French antecedents of our word *peasant* is to those who live in our area or patch, our fellow countrymen. Contrast Hilton 1975, 3.

ers,[110] or some other formal creation of an *amicitia*.[111] Anglo-Saxons sometimes called these special friends "wine-mægas," possibly with the implication that these were friends as close as kinsmen.[112] We are talking here of relationships that run deep and justify description in the emotional language of love.

Some circumstances foster friendship. Much as with a love affair, the key may lie in the appropriate degree of familiarity, the frequency of meetings, and the contexts in which these occur.[113] Indeed, some occasions—celebrations of births, weddings, funerals, and other rites of passage, and also the public transmission of land as recorded by charter[114]—were especially fruitful opportunities. It is not irrelevant to note how alcohol lubricates intercourse at such events, happy as well as sad.[115] Double-edged occasions ensued, when tongues loosened by beer or mead sometimes said more than they intended or ought, and old resentments resurfaced. The resultant "currents of bitterness and jealousy" encapsulate a polarization process that encouraged both the solidification of new friendships and the emergence of the enmities that made them necessary.[116] Here as elsewhere, amity and enmity proceeded hand in hand. The ultimate bonding experience in medieval cultures came not from feasts and parties but from standing together on the battlefield or at a vengeance killing.

One's presence on such occasions is not enough; how one comports oneself and acts toward fellows who may become friends or enemies also matters. This is true of the most guileless among us, people who passively await the relationships that will befall them. Their fate may be exploitation by more calculating and actively politicizing brethren who set out aggressively to construct their own networks while chipping away at those of their rivals and potential enemies. Theirs is a more conscious strategic response to the trials and tribula-

110. One such agreement is that of Robert d'Oilly and Roger of Ivry before the Norman Conquest, according to a late witness preserved in the Oseney Cartulary, "fratres jurati et per fidem et sacramentum confoederati" (*Victoria* 1907, 383). Domesday Book confirms the plausibility of the story by showing that many of the pair's Oxfordshire properties were linked; see, e.g., *DB*, fols. 155a, 156d. Whether they had consecrated their relationship with blood in some way (see Althoff 1990, 82–84) is not stated, but nasty rituals demonstrably aid bonding (De Waal 1996, 16).

111. Martindale 1995 (21–30) is able to describe in some detail one such special friendship between two tenth-century counts of southwestern France. Although the author does not say so, an unrecorded but formally proclaimed *amicitia* may well lie behind her evidence.

112. Bullough 1991, 16. See the Old English dictionaries for *wine* (not easily distinguished in meaning from *freond*) and its compounds; *winemæga* can also mean simply kinsman.

113. An adage much cited in my parents' generation ran as follows: Let my daughter mix with the rich and marry for love!

114. I argued in Hyams 1991a for reading land charters as records of "occasions" when the parties and their friends assembled to publicize property dispositions in the hope of strengthening their chances of taking lasting effect.

115. Bullough 1991, 6–11 and *passim*.

116. This remark of D. J. Enright's is cited in Bullough 1991, 13–15.

tions of a world full of risks and pitfalls. A considered course of action is virtually required by the many meanings of the Latin word *familia*, a term much used by medieval writers to describe the alternatives to blood kinship.[117]

One can imagine many more ways of freshening and strengthening network bonds than can be documented for the Early Middle Ages. We should not be afraid to inject some cynicism into the argument.[118] The rich tend to have more friends than the poor. Their resources give them many ways to attract retainers, as such artificial friends were more often called in later centuries. A French romance writer said of his villain around 1170 that because of his wealth he had many knights. "Well is him that good man fedes" was the thirteenth-century comment from another Middle English romancer.[119] Money talked, won friends, and so conferred power in the twelfth and thirteenth centuries. It was ever so, certainly throughout the period of this book. Anglo-Saxons referred to their lords as "hlaford," loaf-giver, and patently hoped for rings, weapons, and gold as well, if they were to remain friends. And if not from him, then some more generous lord would do.[120] Wealth, then, was doubtless primary, although some were much better able to use it than others.

Any act that assisted a friend's progress or impeded an adversary's would serve, especially if performed publicly to advertise the ensuing alignments. Among the known devices is the saying of masses "de amico,"[121] one of a number of religious stratagems that spawned their opposites, baleful attempts to use spiritual means to harm enemies.[122] One might also press others to give one's friendship precedence over competing associations in the way we have seen King Æthelred trying to do,[123] or by proscribing opposition groupings as threats to good government and justice.[124] The demanding business of locating oneself within the shifting alliances of local politics demanded constant thought and attention. Because the signals tended to be too inconclusive and ephemeral to furnish lasting reassurance, those whose possessions or status exposed them to the envy of others had to live with tension.

Such postulates make a persuasive prima facie case for dynamic, proactive politicking around the construction of support groups in vengeance cultures.

---

117. Herlihy 1991 assembles a good deal of evidence on this subject.

118. It is already there in the wisdom poems of Shippey 1976.

119. Thomas 1955–64, ll. 5092–93; "Havelok" 1966, l. 1693.

120. Thomas 1955–64 (ll. 2209 sq., 2218, 2248) documents the competition between two royal sons for new knights. The Anglo-Saxon equivalent of this market for retainers may be sought, for example, in evidence for the prospering of some exiles.

121. Bullough 1991, 4–5.

122. I note some of the methods of pursuing enmities with the usually unconscious aid of priests in Hyams 1992, 18–19.

123. VII Atr 44.1.

124. Althoff 1998a, 197–98.

The fact that myriad bonding strategies can be discerned in the sources helps to establish that they were in use. The rich and greedy will lead the way. They cannot risk getting caught outnumbered in situations of physical confrontation.[125] (The term *support group* is perhaps a misnomer; such a group is as important for attack as defense.) Gresham's Law suggests that it only takes cynical politicking by a few to generate universal competition and to compel the more benign and cooperative majority to follow suit in simple self-defense. Soon no one would feel secure enough to rely merely on the "obligatory partisanship" of close kin.[126] Few men can be taken for granted in small communities where everyone knows everyone else; all feel competing pulls. Even kinsmen may need persuasion and material inducements. A fortiori, the uncommitted expected to be wooed, and occasionally they wished to name their own price.

I have felt it worthwhile to discuss friendship at some length and in what may seem an unduly cynical manner. The results liberate us from some limiting assumptions of the older literature. There is no good reason to restrict our search for manifestations of feud to cultures in which individuals passively accepted the dictates of blood kinship in their hour of need. The notion of men whose lives were under serious threat *not* seeking aid wherever it could be found and at whatever price appears profoundly unrealistic. We do not have to replace one false assumption with another, though, and to posit an atomized world of Machiavellian maneuvering. In the rest of this book, I hope to discover what can actually be said about the groupings within which medieval Englishmen ruminated over their resentments and how best to right the wrongs that justified them.

The point is not to replace received views of medieval politics at the national and local levels with some single, all-encompassing, ego-focused, feud-dominated alternative. Nor do I intend to claim a dominant role for feud in the formal sense. The classic models of feud no longer seem convincing; at any rate I do not find them helpful in attempting to understand the medieval European world. Continued recourse to the word *feud* itself is surely justified in view of its etymological origins in the early medieval Germanic languages. I vote for a looser usage than some would prefer for reasons of analytical utility. My notion of *feud* is very close to what others label "customary vengeance."[127] The underlying notion is worth retaining in

---

125. See above for primate analogs. The need for numerical superiority is one criterion by which the prudent calculate the right moment to strike back.

126. The phrase is from Moore 1978.

127. Halsall 1998a (19 sq.) argues very fluently about the conceptualization but does not persuade me of the case for a narrower definition of feud that would exclude many of the very phenomena studied in this book. My own position is much closer to that of White 1996.

order to isolate for study those elements of the medieval political economy not always given their full weight in the literature. This facilitates examination of the human desire to avenge wrongs and the tendency for this desire to provoke further tit-for-tat response. Because my overall goal is to try and understand this emotional dynamic in its societal context, I sometimes include situations in which the full process of wrong and counterwrong, though not apparent, approaches feud-*like* behavior.[128]

I am confident that we should assign to feud and related feud-like behavior their just place in our understanding of medieval society. Redress by feud remained one option among many in medieval England, and perceived grievance always carried much cultural and emotional baggage.[129] The contention that scholars need to be on the watch for manifestations of the feud spirit alongside their more accustomed targets is one that I try to establish in the rest of this book.

128. I note that this usage aligns me with some current scholarship that seeks to supplement the scanty data for the history of lesbianism in the Middle Ages with accounts of situations and behavior deemed "lesbian-like."

129. Once again, analyses of feud models suggest analogy with contemporary international relations. We habitually use the language of friendship in overt observations about loyalty in foreign affairs; the terms of discourse are of friendly parties and nations that merit support, contrasted with unfriendly nations that should forfeit most-favored-nation status, and proscribed groups such as enemy aliens and the like.

CHAPTER TWO
SOCIAL EMOTIONS IN A
CULTURE OF VENGEANCE

Until recently, the subject of emotions in the medieval past has received rather little treatment, despite a surge of interest in the literature of pastoral theology in thirteenth-century England. What I offer here is therefore a personal, preliminary broad-brush sketch, designed mainly to act as further mise-en-scène for the rest of this book. I hope it may also serve to clear minds toward fuller study in the future.

Emotions seem to me an inescapable necessity in the study of wrong. Others have noted that one cannot hope to show how people's acts make psychological sense merely from the rules they purport to follow.[1] The point is especially important in a book based so largely on evidence that comes from law or its applications. The case for trying to inject a tincture of emotional warmth into the analysis—that is, from the somewhat surprising abundance of materials, to document how medieval English people said they felt—can strengthen this book in two different ways. First, it helps to take us beyond the straight rational analysis of their actions. Second, emotion talk about anger, envy/hatred, and some of the other emotional categories of the age leads us directly toward major themes of the book, to confirm the role of vengeance as a moving force in social relations, an integral, possibly central part of the general culture.

I focus here on the role of emotions in public and have titled the chapter "Social Emotions" to indicate that it investigates their contribution to the politics of social life. Readers may object that all emotions are social in an important sense, that to distinguish some only as social is to perpetrate an oxymoron. Admittedly, this is only one of several possible and fruitful approaches to the study of emotions. I am not primarily interested in *affect*, the term by which psychologists refer to generalized feelings that relate to no specific person or thing; happiness is one example. My point is that sev-

---

1. Rosaldo 1984, 140.

eral of the specific emotions on which I focus, and especially some nasty and sinful emotions, involve relations between people and so color the general cultural environment to an unusual degree. I use these to draw attention to the impact of the Church's social gospel of peace and neighborly love, targeted at sinful, secular men and women and propagated through the pulpit, the confessional, and—as is sometimes forgotten—the ecclesiastical court.

HOW MAY WE REACH THE FEELINGS OF OTHERS?

I personally still hanker after the notion that feelings are a universal aspect of human nature. Charles Darwin, for one, saw emotions this way—hardwired, we might say today, into human consciousness, recognized by all humans in themselves and often discernible in others (possibly including other animals) from outward signs.[2] This view, though not in itself altogether mistaken, easily underestimates the important differences made by language and the other riches of human culture. Contexts of human social life differ so much through time and space that the emotional life of different cultures will never *look* the same. Each social context transmits, along with its linguistic expression of feelings, a whole package of preprogrammed patterns of sentiment to the point where it may seem, for all practical analytical purposes, as if we should treat it as a distinct system. In this perspective, medieval Europe is special only in that it lies somewhere along the developmental line toward the emotional world of the modern West, which has informed to date nearly all efforts to understand those of other cultures.

Modern scholarship has generated several interesting and different approaches to the study of emotions.[3] The one I find most promising for present purposes is sociocultural. Its proponents might start from the recognition of how specifically Western most assumptions about emotions are, and how distinctive and unlike those of some other societies these are.[4] Incomplete awareness of this fact has in the past led to the heresy that emotions are "internal, irrational and natural,"[5] with its concomitant adoption of the Western dichotomy between thought and feeling. It has also encouraged the reification of particular emotion words. This is not altogether surprising in view of the salient fact that the Western tradition is marked by series of cardinal sins and virtues, virtues and vices, which seem to have been invented

2. See, e.g., Tavris 1989, 34–36.
3. Abu-Lughod and Lutz 1990 (2–9) briefly outline most of the possibilities.
4. Rosaldo 1984, 146–49.
5. Abu-Lughod and Lutz 1990, 2.

precisely to reify certain emotions and brand them as good or bad.[6] But we ought not to expect a one-to-one match between words and feelings at any stage in history. It is not just that words in different languages denote different combinations of sentiment and arousal. The same emotion words can quite radically change their meaning over time. Old French *doel*, for example, is the linear ancestor of modern French *douleur*, sorrow, grief. But in the *Chanson de Roland* and many other medieval texts, *doel* is as likely to denote anger as sorrow, or rather some subtle mix of each of our modern categories of feeling. This explains the significant finding, for example, that in these same texts, joy is the polar opposite not just of sorrow but also of anger. Apparently, successful vindication of one's honor was expected to generate joy, which might be spread among one's friends. On the other hand, failure brought shame, to which the proper response was either grief (passive) or an active bid for vengeance and a belated but welcome joy to share.[7]

Welcome though such insights are, they address mainly the character of the rhetoric of emotion. One may still doubt how far it is possible to reconstruct with any confidence the actual feelings of the long dead, or even of one's own contemporaries. The mere identification of emotional rhetoric affords us real prizes for understanding the past. I therefore also explore possible indications that might permit us to elucidate actual feelings as experienced by real people, defined by evidence of physical arousal through gestures, facial expression, and posture but, above all, by the actions they elicit. To this end I adopt as my initial base a canny definition not of feelings as such but of *sentiments* as "culturally constructed patterns of feeling and behavior," which people are "constantly negotiating" throughout their life cycle and against the natural world that surrounds them.[8] In this view, emotions are revealed as judgments, "socially contested evaluations of the world."[9] The historian ought to envision, it seems, his medieval actors engaged in a complex dance for position round the deceptively simple reifications that are so much of the surviving evidence, and then he must summon

---

6. Lutz 1988 (8–9) and Tavris 1989 (21) are among those to deplore this practice of reification. My own attempt to explain the idea systems that encourage it (Hyams 1998, 109 sq.) gives references.

7. White 1998, 142–43. Jones 1963 (178–80) gives an interesting, older account and elsewhere provides some other unexpected emotion categorizations. The trespass plaint (on which much more later) provides a connecting link between the two possible responses; the complainant makes it tearfully, to display his shame as grief, but expects with the lord's help toward resolution to achieve satisfaction and vindication.

8. Fajans 1985, 371–72. See Lutz 1988, 149: "emotion concepts . . . can be seen . . . as having been constructed in the same environmental crucible as the language of such things as ritual, land tenure or ethnicity."

9. Abu-Lughod and Lutz 1990, 11.

up from his imagination the body language that accompanied them and did much of their political work.[10] Men and women used emotion concepts dynamically, to lead to action by themselves and to block or change the actions of others. They summoned up emotion words as part of their "negotiation over the meaning of events, over rights, over morality."[11]

The best illustration of this concept may be the notion of fear, simply because it is so frequently used to justify acts, including violent acts like killings, that would otherwise be deemed illicit, sometimes indeed to transform them into moral imperatives.[12] The relevance of fear to vengeance is obvious enough. Although such uses of fear words only partially cover the semantic space of the notion,[13] they can help to explain even very complicated conflict situations. In some of the worst of these, we find each side claiming to fear the other and presenting this fear as proof of their oppression, and thus, a license to act freely, beyond the normal rules, against their enemies. We hear similar arguments almost every day from widely separated parts of the world, now Ireland or the Middle East, now the Balkans, even the Department of Homeland Security. They must also have figured in some feuds, though they are not particularly evident in either chronicle and charter feud narratives or the heroic fictionalized accounts of vernacular entertainment literature.

That medieval historians have so few firsthand accounts of motives and feelings of actual feud participants is unfortunate, for the talk that might be glimpsed thereby is intrinsic to the feelings we seek to recover. Talk constitutes the nonvisual evidence for emotions by being an integral part of the process. "Feelings," one observer has remarked, "are . . . social practices organized by stories that we both enact and tell," whereas another notes that "talk about emotions provides [people] with a way of making sense of other people's motivations as well their own."[14] The historian can only remind himself of these keys he cannot possess and seize upon the extant scraps of talk texts to reconstruct wherever possible the conventions that may have ruled. But talk, and the rhetorical talk about talk, serves contemporary purposes that far outweigh their evidentiary value later. Emotion discourse proceeds from within the emotional process and is therefore formational, not

10. We have an occasional contemporary hint, as in the remark of Thomas of Chobham cited at n. 71.

11. Lutz 1988, 5; see Rosaldo 1984, 141.

12. Lutz 1988, 183–84 (and see 207); Abu-Lughod and Lutz 1990, 14; De Waal 1996, 69. Also Tavris 1989, 96–97, on the "excuse epidemic."

13. I have in mind here, for example, both the almost autonomic "fight or flight" reaction of the biologists and the claims of Rosaldo 1984 (14) about the possibility of managing fear.

14. Rosaldo 1984, 143; Myers 1979, 344.

merely descriptive.[15] Each time emotion thoughts are voiced, the speaker and his audience rehearse and adjust the concepts they connote to the current and pressing needs of their lives. The words of the historian's sources are at best experience frozen into textual form, a transformation often impossible to reverse.

Yet the real-life storytelling to which we owe distantly our own accounts of feud and other conflict is one of the most effective ways to keep emotions alive and hot, or reheat them when tepid or cold.[16] Even the most constructivist account of emotions should remark on the physical arousal produced by passionate emotions, which is visible to onlookers with sometimes spectacular results.[17] Our own capacity to measure the physical effect of words and feelings in the laboratory or the doctor's office should dispel any suspicion that because we are dealing here primarily with words, emotions are in any sense trivial.

Although this account of emotions has obvious implications for how a vengeance culture might function, it says little explicitly. For this, I perform a half-turn now to a philosopher, clearly much influenced by the same ideas, who adds his own insights under the decidedly nontrivial head of justice. Robert Solomon argues for an emotional basis to justice, one that stems largely from the "nasty" passions, as he calls them. Echoing Nietzsche's disturbing remark that morality is the vengeance of the weak, he speaks of a justice that transcends the old dichotomy between reason and thought. "What we call reason," he says, "is often a matter of emotion versus emotion."[18] Lurking behind is "a cauldron of sometimes competing passions, all of which have as their basis an almost visceral sense of what the world should be like." Each emotion carries within itself a "quantum of reason" and must argue its case, as it were, on the bearer's behalf, to persuade others to accept his or her viewpoint and case.[19] Justice is revealed as a set of judgments made in advance but still needing to be argued out.[20] Children must learn the criteria from their own experience or from that of others passed on.

Within this process, the nastier passions figure strongly.[21] We start from

15. The fashionable notion of discourse, in some definition such as Foucault's, as cited in Abu-Lughod and Lutz 1990 (9; "practices that systematically form the object of which they speak"), is very helpful here.

16. Tavris 1989 (139, 300) notes that the process of talking anger out, too easily recommended by some moderns, can equally fan the flames. This was, of course, the whole point of early modern "revenge narratives" (as in Muir 1993, xxv–xxvi) and of the various forms of goading.

17. Tavris 1989, 88–90, 117–18; she also notes that different emotions produce an identical arousal. In Hyams 1998 (113), I retell a fine anecdote from Wolfram von Eschenbach's *Parzifal* that illustrates how hard it can be to conceal strong emotion.

18. Solomon 1990, 223.

19. Ibid., 44, 47, 201.

20. Ibid., 155–56, 212, 219–21, 249.

21. Ibid., 26, 34, 43, 243, 245.

"indignation and outrage at injustice" as "a dynamic engagement in . . . a world . . . we resent and act to change."[22] Resentment itself results from a "very special kind of evaluative perception" of "what is right and proper." It constitutes a "claim—even a theory—about injustice in the world."[23] Passions often dismissed as negative really argue *for* a positive view of how the world ought to be.

This is the context for hopes of vengeance. Those who seek it always have some reason, or we should not call it vengeance.[24] We seek it "because we care about someone or something" and because we know we are expected as loyal members of particular groups to live up to ideals of honor, shame, and so forth.[25] Our quest is fierce because it proceeds from a personal involvement and is fueled by an extreme animus hard to satisfy within a modern legal system.[26] One senses so constantly a goal of balance, or fit, or leveling the score, as to make one suspect that such a goal is hardwired.[27] This, then, is the emotional context within which to analyze the urge to vengeance and its manifestations in the thought and action of our period. Vengeance is neither mechanical in a knee-jerk fashion nor wholly negative in aim or motivation; rather, it proceeds from a clear and/or passionate sense of wrong and seeks to restore not merely the status quo ante but the way things *ought* to have been. In other words, inherent in vengeance is its own view of justice, which sometimes coincides with that of official law, or at other times presents an alternative that challenges the "official" view.

SOME USES OF EMOTION LANGUAGE IN POLITICAL DISCOURSE

Before I argue that this view of emotions illuminates both official understandings of them as well as unofficial, counterviews, it seems logical to demonstrate first the prevalence of emotion language. In fact such language very often arises where I, for one, did not expect to find it—for example, in chronicles and constitutional documents. The writers who used this vocabulary of emotions in some very dry contexts were drawing on a well-known and very old literary heritage.

J. E. A. Jolliffe gave us the most familiar example forty years ago in a book long admired but seldom emulated.[28] His demonstration that the Angevin

22. Ibid., 43, 243.
23. Ibid., 247, 268.
24. Ibid., 275. This insistence on the rationality of vengeance recalls the views in Black 1989, mentioned in chap. 1.
25. Solomon 1990, 225–30, 289–96.
26. Ibid., 256–57, 261–62.
27. Solomon 1990 (113–15, 268, 276, 282) talks of this being "instinctual" and remarks that contending parties may calculate balances very differently or even use different arithmetic.
28. Jolliffe 1955.

kings used their "ira et malevolentia" (anger and ill will) as a political tool provoked little further study of the political use of emotional displays.[29] Jolliffe did, however, convey a dual message to thoughtful readers. The passages he adduced strongly suggested that kings, like other alpha males, needed and responded to the massaging of their egos along lines that mimicked emotional personal relations. The corollary was a cost to the petitioner or miscreant, first in the form of humiliating status concessions but later often entailing money. It seems likely that most of what our sources describe was enacted for show and public consumption. Displays of royal anger, terrifying though they might prove to those at the receiving end, were usually under tight political control.[30]

I have noticed another conventional cluster of emotion words prominently used in administrative and legal discourse. These phrases target the effect of social relations at the level of everyday royal administration of finance and law. The royal investigation of 1170 known as the Inquest of Sheriffs was designed as an inquiry into administrative abuses that arose (significantly) shortly after the 1166 innovations in public prosecution of crime (examined in chap. 5). Royal instructions laid down a procedure to be followed in each shire. All witnesses were as usual to swear to tell the truth and conceal nothing. The investigating justices were then warned to be on the watch for reasons why witnesses might be less than fully frank, "for love of anyone or from hatred, or for payment or reward [vel precio vel praemio], or out of fear, from any promise or for any other reason."[31] This list translates into a series of questions to which written answers were required, a powerful indication of serious intent. Had anyone been unjustly accused under the assize (of Clarendon), the justices were to ask, for example, "for reward or on account of some promise or out of love," and if so, who received the money?[32] This curious mix of emotional and financial motives recurs in routine administrative records and documents to the end of the period.[33] It remained an utterly

29. See, however, Leyser 1987.
30. The most recent authoritative treatment of *ira regis* is Althoff 1998b; his views may be compared with my own (Hyams 1998) expressed in the same volume.
31. Prologue to "Inquest of Sheriffs," in Stubbs 1913, 176. The briefer second-person version (for the justices themselves?) published in Morey and Brooke 1967 (523–24), contains fewer emotion words, although its clause v (= clause 6, for which see the following note) does mention the reward motive.
32. "Inquest," clause 6, in Stubbs 1913, 177; see clauses 8 (on foresters) and 11 (on sheriffs pardoning "for reward or from love").
33. The 1194 articles of the eyre (Stubbs 1913, 254) required an oath that juries conceal the purloinment of no royal property "from hatred or from grace or favor toward anyone." See also other relevant texts printed by chance in Stubbs 1913 (359, 458), concerning tax assessment (1237) and distraint of knighthood (1284).

conventional grouping, an open-ended rather than fully comprehensive list,[34] which never quite settled down into common form and was paraded for special effect at times when reform was in the air.[35] It proclaimed that identity of royal interests with the public good, which legitimated Angevin untrammeled power, "vis et voluntas" (force and will), through the Carolingian language of "publica potestas" (public authority). The language was a convenient tool whenever royal ministers wished to convey to royal subjects the canons for probity of the public acts upon which public justice depended. It was easier to represent these guidelines in terms of what people should *not* do rather than to fix one definition of proper public conduct. Several items on the list already had a long history in English royal rhetoric. Eleventh-century Old English legal texts speak in very similar terms when listing the factors that invalidated the actions of bent judges and untrustworthy accusers.[36]

Any reasonably attentive reader will be struck by this consistency of content in lists that are not verbal repetitions of each other but can be expressed in various terms and different languages.[37] The explanation seems to be an origin in Roman law that was perhaps transmitted into the Early Middle Ages primarily through the ever-influential encyclopaedist Isidore of Seville. Isidore had listed in his *Sententiae* four ways by which "human judgment" was perverted. First, fear of another's power makes us afraid to tell the truth. Second, we are corrupted with rewards through our desire or hope of gain. Third, hatred induces us to exert ourselves against some enemy. And finally, love may make us put ourselves out on behalf of a friend or kinsman ("propinquo").[38] When, about the mid-twelfth century, Gratian inserted this text into his *Decretum*, he introduced it in open-ended, now-familiar language. He deplored the perversion of judgment "from hatred or friendship or for a gift or out of fear or by any other means whatever [vel quolibet modo]" and added yet another patristic condemnation of judg-

34. The prologue to the "Inquest of Sheriffs" had ended "et ulla re." The texts cited in the previous note similarly allow for cases not in the list.

35. See Treharne and Sanders 1973 (90, 102, 120, 134, 272) from the period of "reform and rebellion" after 1258.

36. See the treatises "Judex," 3, 7, 14 (angry judges, etc.), and "Swerian," 4 (Liebermann 1903–16, i.474–76, 396–99), as well as the laws concerning "sins of the tongue," mentioned in chap. 5. Much of this material continued to be read into the twelfth century, as translations and adaptations attest.

37. Contrast similar sentiments expressed in quite different terms in Charlemagne's "Capitulare Missorum Generale" of 802, clauses 1, 4, 9, 25, etc. (Schneider 1968, 28–30, 33); see "Capitulare Missorum" of 805, clause 19 (Schneider 1968, 43). Some other texts, such as the "Admonitio Generalis" of 789, clause 63, and the "Admonitio" of 825, clause 8 (Schneider 1968, 14, 49), use more comparable language.

38. *Decretum*, C. 11.3.79. Liebermann identified Isidore's *Sententiae* as the main source for the treatise "Judex" cited previously.

ments perverted "from kinship, friendship, hostile hatred or enmities [vel hostili odio vel inimicitiis]."[39]

Schools-trained advisers of the Angevin kings knowingly drew on ancient and learned traditions here.[40] Their formulas inject a whole cluster of "nasty" social emotions into the public forum, purportedly to establish and publicize canons for proper public behavior, but equally to justify their master's initiatives in the extension of government and law. That they were able to do so successfully nicely documents the suggestions already rehearsed about the judgmental and evaluative functions that emotion words can perform. Our list is patently deployed for purposes of accusation and condemnation, which its targets will likely have contested where they could. Its range, passing easily from words of palpable emotion down to ones that imply very rational but destructively improper action, accords well with the predictions of theory drawn from very different observations.

A final point about this list concerns the word by which contemporaries indicated that an offense of this kind had been committed against justice through conduct corrupted by one or more of these improper motivations. This word *malitia* is often found in the dictionaries as a virtual synonym of *malum*, meaning evil in some form. It was as often used to talk about evil acts between fellow humans as for sins against God, although all acts that harmed one's neighbor naturally also constituted sins against God.[41] Usage for offenses against the proper enforcement of public justice seems primarily directional between humans,[42] and to concern motives that invalidate otherwise licit acts. In its adverbial form *maliciose*, the notion serves again to aggravate the seriousness of actions that might not otherwise come within the aegis of public justice as felony or (eventually) trespass. I consider this directional usage within the sphere of public affairs to be the semantic springboard that set *malitia* off on its journey from denoting evil in a general way to being a specific label for aggravating directional evil, in the sense made famous by the phrase "malice aforethought."[43] When priests in the

39. *Decretum*, C. 11.3.78 dpc and C. 11.3.79 (misattributed to Augustine, actually from Jerome).

40. Bartholomew, bishop of Exeter, under Henry II, 1161–84, adopted our Isidore text into his Penitential (clause 93, in Morey 1937, 258), presumably by way of Gratian. See also in the 1220s, Bracton 1968–80, fols. 143–143b (ii.404–5).

41. Chobham 1968, 24–25, 232. See Mansfield 1995, 41 sq. This certainly seems the thrust of Ecclus. xxv.26 (and see xxv.17): "Brevis omnis malitia super malitiam mulieris," which comes in the middle of a savage antiwoman diatribe, but the glosses divert the attack to idolaters and heretics, again human.

42. Chobham 1968 (418) proscribes even anger against animals as *malitia*, also a directional usage. Giraldus 1861–91 (ii.360) tellingly warns that *malicia* stems not from the times or the land but from human beings. Brand 2001 (274) translates a 1290 judicial offense as "wrongdoing."

43. I hope to return to this topic. In the meantime, Green 1985 (54–56) shows what there is to explain about "malice aforethought," and Kaye 1967 (376–77) reads the phrase as indicating prior hostility. Early examples like *Guisborough* (342) and *Rotuli Parliamentorum* 1783 (i.160a; a 1304 pe-

diocese of Coventry addressed their flock at Sunday mass, they were supposed to enjoin them to flee the seven sins as they would the very Serpent itself. After *malicia* kills souls, they were reminded, these then become the Devil's food evermore, without hope of redemption, for the Devil likes rotting flesh.[44] Through the wishful episcopal thinking here—such well-informed sermons were rare—one can sense a shared view of social sin. The impact of this cluster of offenses against the standards required in public life was thus strengthened by its ability to tap a powerful vein of the Church's moral discourse against evil without sacrificing any independence of secular justice. This may be as important for our argument as the more obvious fact that malice and its constituent parts supplement our evidence for enmity and hatred as routine problems of everyday public life, especially in the vicinity of the law courts.

TWO MODELS OF SOCIAL EMOTION:
SOME THIRTEENTH-CENTURY INDICATIONS

It is easy enough to show that questions about the best permissible responses to wrong would find, during the Middle Ages, different answers from clerical and lay respondents. Both framed the questions their own way. Laymen talked of avenging acts done by an enemy whom, they were happy to admit, they hated for his past actions and now for himself. Clerics spoke more about sin, love of one's neighbor, and the overriding need for peace within the love of God. I focus here on the more abundant evidence from the later end of the period that makes possible the juxtaposition of these two approaches to wrong, thereby to demonstrate some interrelations between them. But I realize that here I can merely open the area for further discussion and use my tentative results to set up inquiries into English developments in law and social relations. Nor should we exaggerate the gulf between Church and laity. There were "striking similarities between the feuding culture of Benedictine monks and that of the noble kin groups from which the monks were recruited."[45] Yet the carefully worked out ecclesiastical position on vengeance, violence, and the factors that led toward them and away from some earthly simulacrum of heavenly peace palpably opposes

---

tition against interference with indictments) support his view. *Très ancien coutumier* LXX (Tardif 1881, 65), includes among the Norman duke's pleas of the sword, justice "de assultu excogitato de veteri odio," which seems to have everything bar the actual word (ca. 1204).

44. Treatise on the seven *criminalia* appended to Coventry 1224–37, in Powicke and Cheney 1964, 214.

45. White 1998, 149–50, and more generally Little 1993.

many significant aspects of secular ways, and thus challenges laymen to generate their own.

The Church's model is much the easier to establish and document. Given the rarity of direct anecdotal evidence, the historian must mostly deduce the secular countermodel from the behavior patterns the Church targeted. In materials created for preachers and confessors or to guide the business of the church courts, the prominence of "nasty" passions is to be expected. Churchmen needed first to identify and oppose sin before they could attempt to lead their flock toward positive virtue and salvation.

I therefore start with pastoral works produced by English churchmen in the thirteenth century and some of the writings of the Western Church—the Glossa Ordinaria (Ordinary Gloss or standard commentary) to the Bible is the outstanding example—which were their sources and inspiration. From the various sinful social emotions, I single out anger and hatred for examination. Although pride, often termed the mother of all sins,[46] is certainly just as pertinent to the themes of this book, I set it aside here and leave it for other occasions and probably other hands.[47]

Medieval Christians started from a biblical sense of justice. Even churchmen had to take note of the Old Testament version, which corresponds in a number of ways to Robert Solomon's view of justice already outlined.[48] It was, as he says, "decidedly personal" and almost always involved revenge, whether by God, His chosen people, or individuals.[49] The problems that this inevitably raised for priests and confessors schooled in the gospel of love are epitomized in the famous injunction to take "an eye for an eye, a tooth for a tooth."[50] The standard Gloss, which rarely attacks the social consequences of Bible texts directly, nevertheless evinces a degree of discomfort in this instance. The injunction was aimed mostly at the original wrongdoer, it suggested, and the remarks about teeth really meant to indicate words anyway.[51] But Jesus' teaching of love even for enemies is in inescapable conflict with the message of the *lex talionis* that justified and restricted vengeance can be licit. More powerful arguments than these are

46. E.g., Chobham 1968, 538–39.

47. In an ideal world, I should certainly have wished to analyze Pride and examine its opposition, long habitual among modern scholars, to Shame. But this has been complicated by the interesting, if perhaps ultimately unconvincing, critical denial of this opposition in Stewart 1994. It deserves a book of its own.

48. He makes this explicit in Solomon 1990, 9–10, 272.

49. The "divine feud" waged by God or one of his saints is one manifestation of Old Testament influence here.

50. This appears three times in the Old Testament: Exod. xxi.23–25; Lev. xxiv.17–20; Deut. xix.21. The theme is then taken up quite explicitly in one gospel only, Mt. v.38. Luc. vi.28–30 also offers the other cheek, but without any express reference back to the Old Testament *lex talionis*.

51. Lev. xxiv.17, gl. *qui percusserit*; Lev. xxiv.21, Deut. xix.21, gl. *dentem pro dente*.

required. The Gloss follows Augustine to turn the emphasis away from vengeance itself, which may properly be adjudged by the law courts, to the motivation behind it; "the lust for vengeance is vicious." This confirms the standard Christian message that removes the right to act from the individuals involved and confers it as a duty on properly authorized judges and courts. To take vengeance is to return evil for evil, whereas a just judge, motivated by the love of justice, imitates God in returning good (meaning justice) for the original evil. The result may feel similar for the wrongdoer, but there is all the difference in the world between justice and vengeance.[52] Even so, seeking justice through process of law is no more than a first step available to the uncultivated *rudes* unable to reach beyond it to the fuller justice of the Gospels, whose goal is salvation and which dictate nonresistance to evil. All Christians, laymen included, should not only not retaliate against their enemies; they should bear their injuries patiently as Christ and the saints had before them.[53]

This counsel of perfection permits *vindicta* to be administered to wrongdoers for their correction by someone without anger in authority. Behind lies an evolutionary scheme by which vengeance should proceed from its ancient Old Testament state of being a largely private matter toward a more perfect justice left to God, for He alone may take vengeance, either directly or through judges possessing ordinary jurisdiction. The two main Latin words denoting vengeance, *ultio* and *vindex*, and their derivatives probably came to connote punishment in this way. Hence the claim that God has a monopoly on vengeance, made in very familiar statements from both Testaments to the effect that "Mine is the vengeance, and I shall take it."[54] Being much clearer than the eye-for-an-eye texts, they gave the commentators much less trouble.

Although all three texts make the same point in terms all but identical, the Gloss chooses to regard the Deuteronomy formulation as superseded.[55] The version in Paul's epistle to the Romans bears in consequence the main burden of comment. Paul does not argue against vengeance in principle: "He [Paul] does not order that they be unwilling to be avenged by God, but that the saints do not indeed make their claim in order to slake their hatred,

---

52. Mt. v.38, gl. *audistis quia dictum*. See later in this chapter for Thomas of Chobham's very conventional feelings about litigation for wrong.

53. Mt. v.38, gl. *non resistere malo*: "Iusticia legis rudes instruit in initio iusticie, id est non plus quam est illatum reddere. Iusticia evangelii que ducit homines ad regnum est non resistere malum." Ibid., gl. *prebe ei ad alteram*: "Non tantum non repercutias, sed si vult alteram [?] se rite patienter feras hoc de iniuria corporis."

54. Deut. xxxii.35: "Mea est ultio, et ego retribuam in tempore"; Heb. x.30: "mihi vindicta, et ego retribuam"; Rom. xii.19: "Mihi vindicta: ego retribuam, dicit Dominus." See Solomon 1990 (273) on the New Testament requirement of restraint.

55. Deut. xxxii.35, gl. *mea est ultio*: "Paulus de hoc loco supersit."

but the just man is delighted when he sees vengeance. He orders, moreover, that instead of avenging themselves, they give carte blanche to God." Vengeance (if one may so translate the ambiguous *vindicate, vindictam*) should be sought for positive reasons rather than from hatred that kills the soul, and its execution should be left to God. The Gloss foresees the obvious objection: "If therefore the good man wants God to punish his enemy, surely this is to return evil for evil [as is specifically forbidden in Rom. xii.17]? In this way, he neither loves nor blesses his enemy. But," he answers, "the good man takes his enemy rather to be corrected than punished, even when the punishment comes from God, so that he may delight in the penalty not because he hates him but because he loves God for His justice. Even if it does rain on the just and the unjust alike [Mt. v.45], yet in this world He seizes the rough and condemns the stubborn in the end."[56]

The Glossa Ordinaria, compiled in its lasting form mostly at Laon in the first half of the twelfth century, largely consists of extracts from the Fathers of the early Church. Its purpose was much more to transmit to medieval clerical readers of the Bible an introductory guide, as it were, to patristic understandings of the *sacra pagina*. In this way, the Fathers set for the Middle Ages many of the doctrinal parameters for exegesis and teaching. Readers in the schools and elsewhere, with access to glossed Bibles, imbibed their views at source whenever they read their Bible. Because these were at least the teachers of teachers, theirs must have been in large part the lines of argument on, for example, the social sins that reached most ordinary priests, and through them such laity as listened. A common topic was the social sins, including the very notion that relations with one's neighbor were central to the virtuous life as seen in the Decalogue. One of the most central items in the Old Testament, the Decalogue is possibly the shortest, most trenchant and memorable text any major religion can boast of. In its manuscript form, it may not have struck the Fathers as so clear and simple as does our own neatly printed text, helpfully divided into chapter, verse, and, ultimately, rubrics too. It comes, after all, in two versions, differing in small but possibly significant details, and although each claims to contain ten commandments, neither explains clearly what these were or where one ended and the

---

56. Rom. xii.19, gl. *date locum ire*: "Non precipit ut vindicari nolint [!] a Deo, set quod clamant sancti, non quidem propter exsaturandum odium, sed laetabitur iustus cum viderit vindictam. Precipit autem ut, non ipsi se vindicantes, dent locum ire Dei, qui dicit. . . . Si ergo vult bonus ut Deus inimicum puniat, nonne est hoc reddere malum pro malo? Vel ita non diligit nec benefacit inimico. Set bonus magis capit corrigi inimicum quam puniri, etiam cum Deus punit ut delectatur de pena, quia non odit eum, sed de Dei iusticia quam Deum diligit, quia et Deus (quem in hoc sequitur) si pluit super iustos et iniustos tamen et in hoc seculo asperis corripit et pertinaces in fine damnat."

next began.[57] Augustine (who else!) had puzzled over its numbering and internal organization, and engineered a solution that found its way into the Ordinary Gloss. The commandments were to be divided into the first three pertaining to man's relationship with God (and so naturally associated with the Trinity) and the remaining seven on man's relations with his "proximus," his neighbor.[58] This arrangement became standard with the dissemination of the Ordinary Gloss (if it had not been so earlier). The consequences were of the highest importance to Church doctrine and pastoral theology. The Decalogue figured on those exiguous lists of basic documents of the faith that all priests were supposed to possess.[59] Some at least must have read and meditated upon them. More strikingly, the image of the two tablets of the Law, among the most familiar of medieval biblical graphics, made visually obvious the conventional division, which singled out the last seven commandments as the rules for dealing with one's neighbor.[60] In this way, even the dullest country priest gained some sense of the importance of teaching peace and love between neighbors. Few priests can have remained unaware that they were expected to teach their flock fraternal love and neighborliness.

The greatest of thirteenth-century pastoral bishops, Robert Grosseteste, pressed home the message in a short work indisputably aimed at the grass roots. His *De Decem Mandatis* seeks to promote social peace through the dissemination of *caritas*, love. "Ama ordinate!" the prologue proclaims, meaning something like "Love everyone, okay?"—an apt injunction for an evangelical crusade.[61] The starting point was the division of the commandments into three and seven. The goal of all adjudication should, he held, be "peace among men," and perfect justice (meaning divine, not human, justice) ought to require no sanctions.[62] Everyone (every man, at least) was a neighbor in

57. There is a vast literature on the Decalogue, although remarkably little modern study of its transmission and influence in the Middle Ages. Jews and Christians diverge over its organization. There are at least five different modes of numbering the commandments, and the division into verses dates only from the thirteenth century.

58. Augustine 1958, no. lxxi, 1–2, pp. 102–3, went into gl. ad Exod. xx.1, where it is followed by a corroborative passage attributed to Isidore, which I have yet to trace but which must again have helped spread the Augustinian solution. I owe much to the kindness of Gary Macy, himself a temporary neighbor (at the Institute for Advanced Studies, Princeton), when I first noticed and started to grapple with this topic. In addition to Exod. xx.1–17, the Decalogue is also rehearsed in Deut. v.6–21.

59. I say something about the expectations in thirteenth-century England later in this chapter; see Goering 1992, 84, 89, 90, 92–93. But those statutes and teachings were totally conventional and uncontroversial. Mansfield 1995 (65 n. 18) cites the references for actual parish inventories extant from the period.

60. Vecchio 1989; McGee 1976, ix–x and chap. 3.

61. Grosseteste 1987, 4–5 (prologue), 91.

62. Ibid., 80, 81.

this definition, infidels and enemies not excluded.[63] All must be loved, for all come from the same root, according to the Decalogue, whose special authority derived not from human investigation but divine wisdom. It goes without saying that none should be harmed. The fifth commandment ("Thou shalt not kill") receives some prominence.[64] When Grosseteste adopts the biblical line that the manner of a killing may aggravate its seriousness and thereby affect the quantum of punishment, he cites as example hatred killings. He also totally rejects any notion of licit vengeance, on the ground that evil should be requited with good, not more evil.[65]

Significantly, this presentation by the Decalogue—to compel pastors to teach good social relations toward neighbors—broadcast the duties of neighbor to neighbor as a token of the general obligation to eschew sin and love God with all one's heart. In turn, this message influenced what laymen and their courts considered wrongs, and what they thought were proper courses of action. The very simplicity of the message proclaimed by the Decalogue's division into three and seven requires emphasis; medieval culture was not normally characterized by sound bites and slogans of the kind that mold us today. In consequence, teachings that could be expressed in forms of words easily comprehensible by ordinary priests and their charges may have benefited disproportionately.[66]

A further illustration of this point is the enumeration of short, easily memorized lists of cardinal sins and virtues. The existence of these lists, and the kinds of number games that Christian writers played with them, is well known.[67] The varying schemas of seven (occasionally eight) mortal sins have an obvious relevance to our theme and merged with the sense of duty toward neighbors just discussed. Augustine, unlike Gregory the Great, had privileged for special attention those particularly offending against neighbors, as the shrewd thirteenth-century administrator and pastoral writer, Thomas of Chobham, was aware.[68] In his *Summa Confessorum* (completed shortly after 1215) and other works, he instructed his priestly readers in the reasons for the three/seven division of the Decalogue and even generalized the lessons. They should, for example, understand the fifth commandment

---

63. Compare this with the *ordo caritatis* discussed in chap. 1.

64. Interestingly, his most extended treatment is of the fourth commandment ("Honor thy father and mother").

65. Grosseteste 1987, 62, 63.

66. I have in mind here distant analogies with legal maxims, as suggested in the appendix to Hyams 1999, and of course proverbial sayings.

67. I give references to some of the literature in Hyams 1998, 109–10.

68. Baldwin 1970 (i.34–36) is a convenient introduction to Thomas (*obit* ca. 1233–36), successively Paris theologian, sub-dean and official at Salisbury, and a prolific writer.

to apply not just to killings but to all cases of wrong ("iniuria") against a neighbor.[69] He underscored the importance of such matters in his advice on the confessor's duties. Priests must instruct penitents not just about the love of God, but also how, and in what order, to love their neighbors. To this end, they were to instruct them on the seven criminal sins. Many, he warns, do not know what these are. They should therefore be made to learn by heart the types of sin and so to internalize the minimum canons of virtuous behavior.[70] The sad fact is that parishioners hesitate to confess spiritual sins of their own accord; they are especially loath to admit to anger and *invidia*, not always seeing these as sinful. Indeed, the priest must be careful lest in prompting them to confess he unwittingly passes on to them sinful ideas they had not considered. Yet men show emotions like hatred and anger on their faces, and if the signs are that obvious to us mere mortals, they must be equally obvious to the Devil, who will encourage them to act out their thoughts.[71]

This sense that spiritual sins carried imminent danger of action against neighbors and the community fueled much of the massive pastoral effort that the canons of the Fourth Lateran Council of 1215 sparked among English bishops and their followers. It produced a fine corpus of episcopal statutes to promulgate the decisions of councils and canonists at the diocesan grass roots and a further plethora of pastoral treatises.[72] Their writers were especially concerned to ensure that village priests were equipped to combat sin among their parishioners. Both the Decalogue and the schema of cardinal or mortal sins figured among this minimum textual equipment, from which, one could hope, priests would serve the confessional and preach sermons as often as four times a year.[73] Thus armed, confessors at least might interrogate would-be penitents in the kind of reasonably organized fashion most likely to draw from them information about their sins.[74] Knowledge of the Decalogue will have compelled some to ask trenchant questions about individuals whom parishioners might have wronged, and

69. Chobham 1968, 28–31; note that he regarded all sins against neighbors as equally against God (24–25, 232).

70. Ibid., 43–44, 326–27.

71. Ibid., 327–28, 418, 474.

72. Goering 1992, chaps. 2–3, seems to me the best recent synthesis of this material. I learned much long ago also from Gibbs and Lang 1934.

73. Powicke and Cheney 1964, 268, 304, 345, 403, 423, 516, 609–10, 721, 900–905, 1017–18, 1025, 1062 sq. Grosseteste, who placed his canon on the subject right at the head of his Lincoln statutes (1239?), established an influential pattern here for the rest of Middle Ages.

74. This is clearly the intention of Thomas of Chobham and his slightly earlier contemporary, Robert of Flamborough (Flamborough 1971, 62, 179 [secs. 9, 197]). See also Powicke and Cheney 1964, 172 (Worcester II, 1229, clause 8).

the best will also have held out to their charges the seven principal virtues "through which man is ordained to himself and his neighbor" as an important step along the route to Heaven, which simpler souls might easily miss.[75]

IRA AND INVIDIA — ANGER AND ENVY-HATRED

Inevitably, sins received most attention, with particular interest in the threat of action that caused actual harm to neighbors. Pastoral writings aimed at local secular priests are much less focused than monastic texts on internal sins of thought, especially in regard to anger and envy-hatred (*invidia*). Archbishop Pecham's 1281 Provincial Council at Lambeth, placing "anger or hatred" ("ira vel odium") third on the list of capital sins, defined it as "a passion for vengeance and harm to another." If retained in one's heart, anger led to hatred and thence to persecutions by word and deed and possibly on to killings.[76] Although anger might be merely venial, Bishop Alexander of Coventry and Lichfield instructed his priests early in the thirteenth century, the sun never sets on persistent wrath, identified by a "boiling lust for revenge," which ages into clear hatred and may be regarded as homicide even when it does not actually lead to a death. The simple oppression of a neighbor, even a challenge to his property rights, could easily provoke him to curses and hatred in response, and thereby kill his soul as well as one's own, in effect, by provoking feud.[77] Thomas of Chobham had earlier explained that "hatred is deep-rooted anger [inveterata] together with . . . an urgent will to harm another or the desire that he be harmed by a third party."[78] A few years later, Walter Cantilupe, bishop of Worcester warned his priests that anger made a man as if mad and very fierce "so that he will avenge himself and harm his neighbor"—by various means, from blasphemy all the way to a swift strike that might even lead to the neighbor's death.[79]

Churchmen clearly saw in anger a clear and present danger not merely to sinners' souls but equally to the bodies of their neighbors. Anger was much more than a sin of the mind; it led to hatred, and the hatred to violent action. Even if the action was not motivated, that is, conceptualized, in terms

75. Powicke and Cheney 1964, 904–5 (Lambeth 1281, clause 9).
76. Powicke and Cheney 1964, 904: "appetitus vindicte et nocumenti alieni." This echoes Aquinas's definition of anger (Gauvard 1991, ii.765).
77. Powicke and Cheney 1964, 216–7 (1224–37). The sun conceit, referring to Christ, comes from Eph. iv.26.
78. Chobham 1968, 420.
79. Powicke and Cheney 1964, 1067. This treatise is there attributed to Peter Quinel, bishop of Exeter, who published it in his diocese in 1287. It started life, however, as a *summula* on confession composed by Walter Cantilupe, at about the same time as his statutes, ca. 1240, according to Goering and Taylor 1992.

of vengeance—and churchmen might want to play down that possibility—vengeance from the "victim" was a very likely response. The supremely damaging potential of anger and hatred is certainly worth remembering as we turn to examine the nature of thirteenth-century moral teachings on these two sins.

Behind the Church's characterization of anger lay a hydraulic model, widely distributed across cultures, of actors frustrated because their desires were blocked.[80] This was not, of course, the whole story: the phenomenon of righteous or justified anger was another dynamic force often used as a device to deploy social condemnation against an enemy or adversary. The mere knowledge that such a resource exists helps to keep social relations honest and to evoke and publicize behavioral standards for the community to teach its children.[81] The medieval Church recognized the positive potential of good anger and tried to control it. The anger of God, especially in the Old Testament, raised the possibility that humans too could exercise good anger. To distinguish this sentiment from the sin of anger, one focused on the consequences for both the angry person and those toward whom it was directed and who had perhaps provoked it. Thomas of Chobham, however, was ambivalent on the subject. Zealous anger ("ira per zelum") was, if not a vice, at least a punishment. It sprang from a mental disturbance ("perturbatio . . . ex motu rationis") that could blind one to reason. It was, therefore, normally to be resisted, licit though it may be against vices and those who committed them. Christ never got angry, he said on one occasion. Yet elsewhere he instances His anger when expelling the moneychangers from the Temple. Laymen certainly on occasion invoked Christ's anger against their enemies.[82]

Thomas regards anger as almost always a very serious sin, one quite "abominable to God," especially, he emphasizes, when it pushes men to harm each other. A capital "crime," anger concealed God's will contrary to the third petition of the Lord's Prayer, "Thy will be done." Thomas deplores the fact that so many contemporaries took it so lightly.[83] Anger was the only sin that absolutely disqualified one from service at the altar. An

---

80. Lutz 1988, 177–79. Solomon 1990 (256–57, 282) points out that Aristotle also associated anger with the urge to get even or take revenge. Ailred of Rielvaux illustrates this stance all too well in his Life of Edward the Confessor, MPL 195, col. 783: "Expavit domina et incaluit cor ejus et in meditatione ejus ignis exaestuans erupit in vocem increpationis et indignationis, et quasi diabolico praeventam spiritu blasphemam dirissimis sermonibus verberaret."

81. Lutz 1988, 154, 161, 169. This has some relevance to the peace-in-the-feud model discussed in chap. 1. Pinker 1997 (404) points out that anger protects those left vulnerable by their niceness.

82. Chobham 1968, 414. See "Havelok" 1966 (ll. 542–45), where the hero calls on Christ to give him vengeance.

83. Chobham 1968, 38, 416–18, 518. Thomas regarded a pastor's sentence as unjust if launched "propter iracundiam vel invidiam" (ibid., 201).

angry person's alms were unacceptable to God. Anyone who became aware of a live anger while on his way to receive the Eucharist should go at once to reconcile himself with its object, or at the very least determine to do so as soon as possible.[84]

The focus of attention is naturally on the soul of the angry person. But it is also obvious that the probability of evil action ahead was only slightly less prominent in the moralist's mind. Thomas knew that "percussio" (blows) often followed from anger. This was permissible only if administered as a punishment or correction ("ad penam vel ad emendationem"), or occasionally in order to extract the truth from some wretch who was concealing it, a remarkable concession to the use of torture and, to my knowledge, unique in England at this early date.[85] Genuinely sinful anger ("ira per vitium") was pardonable only if it ended without action; the intention to harm someone was of its very essence. It could work through shaming words, or by damaging body and possessions. The evil consequence was to inject fraternal anger and hatred that might lure men to curse each other in situations where fraternal love should rule.[86] Anger became a mortal sin as soon as it began to provoke "contumeliam vel iniuriam," which places shaming alongside physical harm. Shaming humans was always punishable.[87]

Invidia was up there next to anger in the list of capital sins. The most obvious translation is "envy," because the Middle English and Old French words behind modern *envy/envie* are indisputably descended from the Latin. In practice, however, it slides so easily toward hatred as to persuade one that here too is a medieval emotion whose semantic space does not quite coincide with the modern Western schema. It is the converse of the affective sympathy men have for their kinsmen and loved ones.[88] Those who commit it envy and hate God as much as themselves and their victims. All good comes from God. As some slightly later episcopal statutes warn, nothing is so terrible as self-hatred. Invidia is like a bone disease, eating into the marrow, especially deplorable in clerics who were themselves supposed to be the

84. Mt. v.23–24 was a passage much cited on the heinousness of *fraternum odium*. Lauren Jared first alerted me to the importance of this text in medieval pastoral thought in a paper presented to the International Congress of Medieval Studies at Kalamazoo in 1990, titled "Horizontal and Vertical Communities in the *Summae* of Peter the Chanter and Thomas of Chobham." Its earlier monastic usage had established the connection with the Eucharist.

85. I briefly survey the slow advance of torture justifications on the Continent in the thirteenth century in Hyams 1999, 81–83. The received view is that they had little effect in England.

86. Chobham 1968, 327, 415, 417–18. On cursing, Little 1993 is the authority.

87. Chobham 1968 (415–16) analyzes various possible manifestations of anger in a manner followed and much extended by later scholastics. Hyams 1998 (111–12) gives some nearly contemporary examples from Peraldus and others.

88. See Frank 1988, 15; De Waal 1996, 85–86; Pinker 1997, 390–91, 400.

bones that bore Christ's weight.[89] It was so lugubrious a sin that it seemed to fail Augustine's test that all sins aimed at delight, unless perhaps the sinner delighted to see evil happening to someone else.[90]

Invidia ought to be excluded by the Lord's Prayer. The pious person who says "Thy kingdom come" and means it cannot himself be envious of anyone.[91] He can, however, slip into invidia by feeling hurt when good things happen to a neighbor. An *invidus* can be so jealous of his neighbor's good fortune that he schemes to do him evil. But he may also often defame his victim "by malicious words or lies" that impede his business or lose him the favor of his lord.[92] If a priest finds his penitent has lied, he should ask searching questions about any damage caused. The liar might, for instance, have caused someone to incur the hatred of a former friend or someone from whom he had hopes of good things. If so, it is up to the liar first to restore his victim to the good man's graces and then to make up his losses. The very least he can do is to own up and seek pardon.[93] Invidia poses the confessor some testing problems. Penance is harder to award than it is for some other sins; "a man often harms his neighbor in many different ways through invidia [also pride], by detracting from him, by taking away his good reputation, by losing him material goods." The goal should be exact restitution, to counter the damage actually done, by repaying the victim, say, the same number of prayers removed from him by hatred.[94]

"Fraternal hatred," a most unnatural state, is high on the list of matters that any confessor needed to raise with would-be penitents. For Thomas of Chobham, it constituted the second of three essential preliminary questions.[95] It aggravated other sins, which then required higher than average penances.[96] Some people were especially vulnerable to it. Champions, men who hired themselves out to fight judicial duels, were, to Thomas's way of thinking, in such a perpetual state of fraternal hatred that they must be totally barred from the confessional. To have a chance of gaining eternal life, a person needs to love his neighbor as himself, but "no-one can

89. Powicke and Cheney 1964, 216, 307 (Coventry, 1224–37: "gutta inossata"; Worcester, 1240: "ossium . . . putredo").
90. Chobham 1968, 535.
91. Ibid., 38.
92. Ibid., 327.
93. Ibid., 547.
94. Ibid., 235, 419–20, 534. This is a striking illustration of the all-pervasive notion of keeping score in order to restore a balance. Though central to peacemaking in feuds, its strong presence here suggests a climate of clerical opinion that would have favored the rise of trespass at much this time.
95. Ibid., 242.
96. Ibid., 571.

love him whom he wishes to kill."[97] Even innocent, nonprofessional duelers are in a very awkward position morally. It is probably all right to defend a duel demanded by the other party.[98] But such a dueler should first lay aside all rancor and then will himself to work for even this neighbor's salvation.[99]

If this is Thomas's view on the likely chances of salvation for those compelled to fight to the death by court process in an established and largely approved legal system, one can understand how strongly he abhorred feuding vengeance.[100] He was horrified when someone went to church and asked God in the Lord's Prayer to "forgive us our debts" yet could not forgive the offenses of his own enemy. This is like asking for your own death, he says, which is why many teachers advise their listeners never to speak the words "dimitte nobis." We must all "lay aside rancor and all hatred" against those who wrong us. Laymen may, it is true, nevertheless seek satisfaction by suing for material loss caused and wrong done to them, although granting pardon was better for the victim and his soul.[101] These were counsels for an imperfect world.

Hatred seemed a serious matter largely, although not entirely, because of the possible consequences. Because clerics always feared that these would include killings, the subject arises in the context of the fifth commandment, "Thou shalt not kill." Bishop Walter Cantilupe warned his flock that they could commit this breach in many indirect ways. Hatred unto death wills another to die and was thus—even without further action—homicide, "because he who hates his brother is a homicide."[102] In a somewhat similar vein, Archbishop Pecham interpreted the same commandment as including all kinds of consent to killing and, implicitly, "every unjust act harming another," since one should love one's neighbor as oneself.[103] Husbands tended to hate their wives, for a whole variety of reasons, which, according to Thomas of Chobham, helped to explain why they also killed wives more often (even?) than sons killed fathers.[104] The Church had always treated this sort of fratricidal or parricidal killings with special seriousness.[105]

97. Ibid., 293.
98. Ibid., 427–28.
99. Ibid., 244.
100. Yet he took the conventional view and did not think to question capital punishment (ibid., 128–29, 304–5, 422–26).
101. Ibid., 319–20.
102. Powicke and Cheney 1964 (p. 1064) again under the name of Peter Quinel, bishop of Exeter, who republished the text in 1287.
103. Ibid., 902–3 (Lambeth, 1281, chap. 9: "omnis iniusta persone lesio").
104. Chobham 1968, 458. For data on this, see Given 1977, 56–58.
105. See chap. 3.

This discussion of clerical attitudes toward the select sins of anger and envy-hatred identifies vengeance as a significant aspect of the world in which our writers operated. Thomas of Chobham's advice to his priestly clients does much to confirm this prominence. His Christian dislike of vengeance extended to a deep suspicion of all litigation. A good Christian should show to all, including an enemy, the *obsequia humanitatis*, greet him as a friend in the street, and offer him the kiss of peace at Mass. The *perfecti* (monks, friars, and perhaps secular clergy too), held to a higher standard, should never sue on their own behalf in secular courts, although—naturally—they might do so on behalf of their house or saint. As the canons put it, "no cleric may avenge his own wrong, but should seek justice for himself from his own [ecclesiastical] judge."[106] The most they were permitted was to report on their enemy to an ecclesiastical judge.[107] They must renounce rancor and follow to the letter the Gospel injunction to love their enemies.[108]

Imperfect persons—that is, laymen and laywomen—were not expected to meet this counsel of perfection by reflecting gospel values of love, in their daily lives. Nor were they required to surrender their claims for debt and other wrongs.[109] But the Christian ideal was ever present, and anyone with a grievance against another could, says Thomas, easily choose some good man to mediate and make peace for him outside the courts.[110] Presumably, if one were sued, it was permissible to defend oneself. But even here nothing was simple. Thomas warned of the extreme care needed in homicide cases over the plea of self-defense. The natural right to defend oneself is one thing; taking revenge is quite another.[111] Self-defense was a permissible plea only when escape was impossible. When a person could have escaped but chose not to, there was always suspicion of at least an element of concealed vengeance, that "per iram ad vindictam," anger had roused the accused to vengeance and that, thus inflamed, he had inflicted harm "ex vindicta," for vengeance. Violent reactions in the heat of the moment, "flagrante maleficio," while the evil still burned, were legitimate. But delay suggested pre-

106. *Decretum* 23.4.27, cited in Chobham 1968, 306. I cite some modern Christian doubts about litigation in Hyams 1996b, 90–91.
107. The probable reference here is to *denunciatio evangelica*, on which see Lefebvre in *DDC* v.557–69. Mansfield 1995 (53–54, 119) illustrates this procedure without using the name.
108. Chobham 1968, 245, 320, referring to Mt. v.44. I assume that the ban on clerical litigation extends only to secular courts, although Thomas does not expressly say so.
109. Ibid., 244, 320. Thomas surely has trespass in mind here.
110. Ibid., 204. See Chaucer, the general prologue to *Canterbury Tales*, ll. 258 sq.
111. Ibid., 70, 439–40. This discussion can usefully be compared with the common-law materials on hot response (and malice aforethought) collected in Green 1985, 54–56.

meditation and the presence of hatred, as did a disproportionate response such as the use of a sword against an attacker's stick.[112]

All these points were very well known. The priest should consider the details of an incident very carefully in their light, to exclude any possibility that he was really dealing with vengeance. The well-known Roman law tag, "vim vi repellere," justifying the repulsion of force with force, held only when stringent legal requirements were met.[113] But the Church's expectations were higher still, for vengeance must be left to God.[114] Thomas permitted vindication only for wrongs done to the public interest; private wrongs were excluded, and so were all suits by clerics. Laymen could act within the king's peace against breaches of that peace (a telling reference), although it was best if they too forbore.[115]

The guiding premise behind all Thomas's discussions is the sad recognition that laypeople do seek to avenge their wrongs by inflicting physical harm on the alleged perpetrators, even killing where they could. This experienced pastor's understanding of the true nature of "fraternal hatred" thus confirms a major theme of this book, which raises terrifying challenges for priests. Thomas states the problem directly in another work aimed at his fellow preachers. "Again, it is very difficult to preach to those wrongly harmed ["per iniuriam"] that they should not seek vengeance. For *they* believe it to be just that each man avenge his own wrong; even though the Lord says to the Romans [Rom. xii.19]: 'mihi uindictam et ego retribuam'— vengeance is mine and I am the one to pay back."[116]

Readers of Thomas's *Summa Confessorum* received an astonishing elaboration of the problem in an exposition of the seal of the confessional. What should a confessor do, he asks, if his supposed penitent admits that he is out to kill (or to burn down the house of) some great man who has killed or disinherited his father? The confessor can neither ignore the matter nor tell those who most need to know about it. This has all the signs of a case that experienced confessors might actually expect to meet. Perhaps Thomas had once himself been in a similar situation. In his perplexity, he turned to hints dropped by Augustine. The confessor should go to the penitent's father, some other close relative, or his best friend ("amicus familiarissimus") and

112. Ibid., 439–40. The time factor, weighing hot response against a delayed and more considered reply, might be critical in feud cases.

113. This was one of the best-documented maxims in England. Add to the brief reference in Hyams 1999, 89 n. 92: Darlington 1928, 169.

114. As discussed earlier in this chapter.

115. Chobham 1968, 440–41. The advice to lay people was "ut non suam uoluntatem . . . iniuriam in damnandis malefactoribus attenderent, sed solummodo pacem regis observare curarent, et iniuriam pacis vindicarent." Thomas once again shows obliquely his familiarity with the common-law remedies of his day, appeals, and trespass suits.

116. Chobham 1988, 271 (emphasis mine).

emit some oblique hint to restrain him or accept responsibility as his accomplice.[117] Should this approach fail, a second possibility is to warn the man against acting in the presence of priests or other good men. The snag here was that one must first be certain that none of the witnesses would inform on the man and make him subject to a possible death penalty. The third suggestion is my personal favorite. The confessor is to approach the threatened man and question him as to whether he might by chance have offended anyone recently by, for example, killing or disinheriting that person's father! If so, the best course would be to make peace swiftly (here offering his services as mediator), or else . . . it will go badly with you.

Thomas patently found secular acts of vengeance all too normal in his own day. His dicta are compatible with the presence of the extended tit-for-tat strings of such acts that we term feud. He felt no need to discuss these directly, since confessors deal with one soul at a time. The Latin term he might have used for them is *inimicitia*, among whose possible meanings some incautious lexicographers include "feud."[118] In fact the word, although its primary meaning is obviously "enmity," is hardly specific enough to indicate a continuing situation meeting the kind of preconditions indicated in chapter 1 as essential to full feud. For a century or more after the Norman Conquest, no single English word may have existed to denote feud the way Old English *fæhðe* once had.[119] *Inimicitia* needed to be qualified by some intensifier to denote feud; the enmity had to be capital or mortal. This apparent borrowing from Roman law terminology entered the various vernaculars to denote a state of heightened and lasting enmity.[120] Originally, the phrase denoted a state of social relations that invalidated certain otherwise proper acts of litigants, their procurators, and the judges in the courts. It was in this sense very much akin to the similar invalidating factors, emotional and fiduciary, already discussed. One important difference was its reception into custom and formal law on some parts of the Continent. The parties to a declared *inimicitia capitalis* in these areas might licitly take their vengeance, providing they followed the customary rules. Behind lay a claim of a now familiar kind that the killer was entitled to privilege as acting under

117. Chobham 1968, 257–58. A half-serious threat of murder is made in the confessional during a 1990s movie, *The Runaway Bride*. But Thomas's details—a house assault after the killing of the lord's (?) father—sound like classic feud.

118. E.g., Niermeyer 1997, 538, s.vv. "inimicitia," "inimicus."

119. *MED*, s.v. "féd(e)." Dobson 1956 confirms the post-medieval origins of modern English "feud."

120. *Dig.* 3.3.8.3, 4.8.15, 17.1.23; and cf. 5.1.15.1. Robert Bartlett set me on this path with a conference paper from 1990, "Mortal Enmities: The Legal Aspect of Hostility in the Middle Ages," later published as Bartlett 1998. *Très ancien coutumier* XCI (Tardif 1881, 101), notes as one justification for the refusal of assent by a lord to a tenant's land grant the existence of "mortales inimicitias inter illum et genus eum ex una parte et dominum et suos ex altera"; this looks like full feud.

some emotional (if not moral) imperative to avenge wrongs against himself or his friends and so had been unable to restrain himself.[121]

Neither formal English law nor any post-Conquest custom of which I am aware ever went this far. This defense is precisely what Thomas of Chobham was at such pains to exclude in the passages just discussed. Self-defense at common law was always much more heavily circumscribed. Mortal enmities were never privileged by medieval English law. They were always extralegal. But English writers and their audiences nevertheless shared the special awe with which their Continental neighbors regarded instances of mortal or capital enmity. The same was true of English courtrooms. In 1198 four knights of the shire, after a formal visit to Geoffrey Picot at home to ascertain if he were really sick in bed and so check his formal excuse for nonappearance (his essoin), reported in court that he was not. Geoffrey then did come to court, to plead that the justices disregard the knights' word, because they were all, he said, his mortal enemies.[122]

Epithets like capital, mortal, or public are likewise frequently found in political discourse, used to intensify enmities and place their proponents in the firing line. Kings and political leaders used the notion to warn those who flouted their wills on especially serious issues that they were exposing themselves to summary treatment. The message was clear and simple—if you are not with me, I shall regard you as against me and treat you as an enemy whom I can and should kill. The disturbances in Henry III's reign following the collapse of the reforming coup of 1258 provide a number of pointed instances in very public documents.[123] A nice illustration of less formal but still sharp usage comes from a fine story whose alleged dénouement found it a place among the miracles of Saint Wulfstan of Worcester. A young man, Thomas of Elderfield, had an illicit affair with his lord's wife. After the husband's death, Thomas repented of his sin, refused his mistress's matrimonial advances, and endeavored to disentangle himself from the liaison. This daughter of Eve conceived for Thomas "mortal enmities," but she bided her time until a second marriage provided her with a likely instrument for her vengeance in the shape of a husband. Thomas's

---

121. This claim may or may not be true. White 1998 (145, 146, 150) notes various possibilities ranging from a political pose, a mere cover for violence, to a rebuttable contention of "hot anger." Gauvard 1991 (ii.757, 775–76) notes the use of the phrase in house assaults, for example, but seems to indicate that it constituted at best a ground on which to seek pardon.

122. *RCR* i.308, 321–22. Geoffrey was his mother's attorney in an appeal that spun off from a protracted land suit in the Cambridge shire court. Lady Stenton comments (*PKJ* i.25), without catching all the points at which the suit surfaces on the rolls. *Très ancien coutumier* XCI (Tardif 1881, 101), suggests that Norman law took a similar peripheral view of mortal enmity.

123. See chap. 8.

death was the couple's evident object, and their efforts came very close to success.[124]

The notion of mortal enmities was pervasive in medieval society. A learned legal concept had been drawn into the general culture. All kinds of writers used it for a myriad of situations involving strong feelings of hostility, when somebody hated badly enough to kill. The rationale was usually vengeance of some kind, although the previous wrong might be fairly remote. Enmity lay in the eye of the beholder and might originate in an emotion such as shame that the enemy neither shared nor recognized as his responsibility. The notion's ubiquity in a vast array of entertainment vernacular literature in Old French as well as Middle English must surely indicate a strong popular inclination even in England to view sympathetically killings made under its influence.[125]

A SECULAR MODEL OF VENGEANCE: SOME POSITIVE EVIDENCE FROM LITERATURE

The most feasible path to the documentation of a fragmentary secular model of vengeance must lie largely (but not exclusively) through "entertainment" literature of this kind. Stephen White used Latin chronicles as well as chansons de geste and early romances in his study of "political anger" in France during the eleventh and twelfth centuries. His conclusions establish preliminary hypotheses for the whole francophone area of western Europe, which undoubtedly included England after 1066. He found emotional language common but restricted to a "tiny repertoire of emotional shifts."[126] Emotions were far more prominent than in, for example, Icelandic sagas. The degree of cultural significance ascribed to this fact depends on the historian's view on the juxtaposition of other works that make less recourse to emotion language. Still, White shows that his literary texts do indeed reflect the conventions of appropriate use in certain areas of everyday life. They establish, for example, the typical situations in which men and women imputed anger to their fellows and where its display was to be expected. For example, anger was deemed appropriate to high-status

---

124. Hyams 1986 tells the story; the precise reference to "mortales . . . inimicitias" is Darlington 1928, 169, ll. 14–15. Also Bracton 1968–80, fols. 79, 81b (ii.231, 237) (from William of Drogheda); and *Britton* 1983, III.iv.33 (ii.46).

125. See Tobler and Lommatsch 1925–95, iii.306, vi.308–9. Random examples include Benoît de Sainte-Maure 1998 (1160–70), ll. 587, 5600, 13762, 16074, 16311, 17657, 17816, 17912 (the last three of which are nicely secondary). See the end of the next section.

126. White 1998, 134–35.

males, where a man (or for that matter, some supernatural being) was out to take vengeance in response to some past (political) act.[127]

To elucidate these findings, White draws on theoretical sources similar to those canvassed at the beginning of this chapter. Anger and similar emotions effect "a quasi-judicial appraisal of the act," which opponents may contest.[128] The angered person is pressing a trespassory type of claim that some act "against" him was wrongful and harmed his honor. His anger therefore carried a normative dimension. The location of all this rich information within narrative sequences suggests that we place them within "a relatively stable, enduring discourse of disputing, feuding, and political competition."[129] They therefore speak for a succession of emotion scripts requiring the individual to display different emotions for different purposes.[130]

White's important schema tells us much about the public emotional display of a variety of sentiments (not just anger) in the political dramas of medieval France and its neighbors. He does not claim to be writing about actual feelings at all, though he is obviously aware of their existence in the societies he studies as in our own. We must therefore ask whether his material can tell us anything about those feelings of men and women who walked the real world and sometimes were (but at other times, were not) physically aroused by their passions. My hunch is that in the end it does. Behind good forgeries must always lie genuine coin of the realm. White focuses on some quite individual situations. Lordly anger and political emotions were patently not forces beyond the actor's control. They were sometimes demonstrably simulated for effect and on other occasions provoked by goading.[131] The whole point of a plea to your lord (of the type I term proto-trespass) was often to shame him into anger so that he would take up your cause, perhaps make feud on your behalf, or at least award you redress.[132]

But even the greatest of kings got genuinely angry on occasion, and some of them gained a reputation for their temper tantrums. Henry II was notorious for his.[133] It is impossible to set aside all descriptions of anger in the chronicles and elsewhere as mere political display. The existence in the ver-

---

127. Ibid., 137, 138–40. The absence of similar references to the anger of high-status females suggests to me that some interesting gendering was occurring.

128. Ibid., 140–41.

129. Ibid., 142.

130. Ibid., 142–45, sketches the way some of these scripts might proceed.

131. Ibid., 145, 148–49.

132. Ibid., 146–47, citing both Hyams 1992, 12, and an amusing illustration from the *Renart* cycle. The discussion in chaps. 5 and 6 of proto-trespass and its thirteenth-century development into the common-law action is pertinent here. This literary evidence reveals the common-law "tickets," by which litigants sought to obtain for their pleas a hearing in a royal court, as fossilized relics of ancient goading.

133. Hyams 1998, 102–3.

nacular literature of a "common motif" of appeasement suggests of itself that men and women at times felt the need to cool their companions' ire by appealing to their sense of honor, doubtless in ways conventionally expected to prove effective. Strong emotions must sometimes have run out of control, even occasionally perhaps those begun as political display.[134]

Genuinely experienced feelings lie behind at least some of these secular behavior patterns. White himself believes that some of his literary evidence confirms the reality of the emotions that underlay the taking of vengeance within "a 'technology of power' that cannot be neatly classified as either overt or symbolic violence."[135] Many of the stories written to move contemporary audiences still seem positively glowing with heated emotions from the feuding culture to which White ascribes them. The most obvious illustrations come from such twelfth-century masterpieces as *La chanson de Roland* or *Raoul de Cambrai*, but works like these that may have originated at the beginning of the twelfth century or even earlier continued to be copied, and sometimes reworked, throughout our period and long after. Some scholars have proclaimed, it is true, that the genre shift in French literature from epic to romance marked also a shift in Western sensibility generally.[136] Prolonged study might conceivably be able to show that attitudes toward vengeance and feud changed as this older view implies it should. If so, the transformation must have been remarkably subtle, for it has so far escaped this historian's eye in his quite extensive reading of Old French literature. Many themes once deemed characteristically epic pass across the break with scarcely a shudder. Among these, beyond question, was vengeance. Many romances contain vengeance episodes, with a plethora of mortal enemies to be killed off by characters possessing an apparent knowledge of the rules of the game. Historians who doubt that romances can focus as much on the psychology and pursuit of vengeance as on love need only read some of the crusading romances and Arthurian ones like the "Prose Lancelot" and *Perlesvaus*. The case is almost at its strongest with the unfortunately named "insular romances" from thirteenth- and fourteenth-century England, which retain rather more of epic themes and rather less of romance sensitivity than their French counterparts.[137]

---

134. White 1998 (145) explicitly distances the French noble anger he is discussing from the battle rage of early medieval warriors. On the possibility that a political act can eventually take over the actor himself, I recall the classic biography of Hitler by Alan Bullock. The best way to deceive others is to start by deceiving yourself (Frank 1988, 131–33).

135. White 1998, 141 (citing inter alia *Roman de Thèbes* 1995, ll. 7453–62), 151.

136. But see now Kay 1995.

137. Crane 1986 is an excellent, often insightful survey of entertainment literature produced in England in the twelfth and thirteenth centuries and beyond. The author introduced me to several of the works I considered for the next section. She clearly, however, does not expect her title (*Insular Romance*) to raise expectations that she will cover any of the literatures produced outside

Vernacular authors of the twelfth and thirteenth centuries certainly obey fairly clear conventions in their use of emotion language, yet appear to address something more than surface display. They frequently seem to try to convey feelings that their audiences have, or could have, experienced themselves, and some works show how these might motivate people within a culture of vengeance. In certain works, the theme is nearly as pervasive as the more celebrated love aspects of romance.

To document these points from material directly relevant to the English experience, I sample some lesser-known works that were produced and consumed within the polity subject to English kings and their law during the twelfth and thirteenth centuries. So as not to labor the relatively obvious, I do not here focus on the common theme of honor and the avoidance of shame.[138] Instead I focus on the same emotions of anger, hatred, and fear that are, demonstrably, equally essential to patterns of vengeance for wrong.

For this brief pilot study, I use two sets of twin romances, versions of the same tale composed in England—one in French from around 1200 and then again in Middle English half a century later. Thomas's *Romance of Horn* dates from about 1170, while its Middle English counterpart, "King Horn," might be as early as ca. 1225. The Anglo-Norman "Lai d'Haveloc" may be dated between 1209 and 1220, and was first Englished as "Havelok the Dane" sometime during the second half of the thirteenth century. Thomas's French romance is both longer and much better stocked with emotion words than is "King Horn," but the opposite is true of the other doublet, albeit in a less spectacular way. The "Lai d'Haveloc" is quite brief; "Havelok the Dane," more expansive. In the absence of specialist studies comparing emotion discourse in the two languages, it is not obvious which was the more predisposed to emotion concerns. The use of works composed in the two separate languages over such a period may serve as a reasonably fair test of the ideas they carry about emotions, a control to ensure that we are not dealing just with the semantic idiosyncrasies of one language or literature. This approach may perhaps suffice to provoke more extensive historical study.

Audiences evidently expected that feelings would make themselves apparent to the onlooker's eye. When Rigmel in the *Romance of Horn* found that she had attracted the wrong suitor to her chamber, she colored from anger and irritation, "de ire e de maltalent ad la color muée."[139] Rigmel was indeed

---

England in the rest of the islands. In my view there is also precious little romance (and much knockabout "geste" action) in some of the works she treats, but that may be a matter of taste.

138. *Pace* Stewart 1994, this opposition (of honor and shame) seems to be alive and central to at least the cultural patterns of the medieval West. See Gauvard 1991, chap. 16, for a recent discussion.

139. Thomas 1955–64, ll. 872–73; cf. l. 1869: "od chiere mut marrie."

apparently easy to read; our author's description of her moments of joy establishes her as the lady "of the laughing face."[140]

I think I often see emotion words used in a genuine attempt to convey feelings that the characters would naturally experience in the situations they met. Fear is one illustration. It seems reasonable enough to fear threats to life or the arrival of unknown fighting men, also nightmares and the shining of bright lights from the mouth of a sleeping companion.[141] Kings and great men ruled in part by dint of the fear they inspired.[142] I confess to finding few illustrations of the artificial display of fear, by word or action, to excuse violent action in the name of vengeance.

Much is also made of grief and sorrow. Medieval romances engendered as many tears as do modern ones. Men as well as women mourned the deaths of loved ones with tears, and political failure could turn their joy to grief.[143] Rymenhild's love for Horn brought her pain and sorrow and seemed to her likely never to end unless she took some positive steps. These seem genuine enough feelings. But their visible manifestations had their effect on those who witnessed them. Horn proved as affected by Rymenhild's tears as any modern lover would be, innocent though she may have been of any will to manipulate him.[144] The fact that emotions in one person had predictable consequences on others made aware of them raises the possibility of instrumental use of emotion display; however, none of these four authors treated emotion as artifice.

Displays of anger, for example, were frequent and important to the plots, as the variety of words (especially in French) used to describe them shows. But even these are mostly presented as actual, not feigned, arousal. It is not too surprising that our hero found his blood boiling (more precisely, his heart gave off sparks!) when someone killed a beloved ally. But a competitive prince too easily beaten at the shot putt also became very angry "in his heart" ("en sun quoer").[145] Arousal by anger can cause a man to lose control, to become literally beside himself.[146] Equally, it can move him to action, often violent, although this may take time and effort. After a pagan adversary reveals that, long before, he had killed Horn's father, Horn's first reac-

140. Ibid., ll. 3960, 5109, 5135; cf. l. 5136.
141. E.g., ibid., ll. 20, 158–59; *Haveloc*, ll. 401 sq., 459, 837; "Havelok" 1966, ll. 477 sq., 1164 sq., 1258.
142. Thomas 1955–64, ll. 1760 sq.; "Havelok" 1966, ll. 277–79, 2568–69.
143. "King Horn" 1966, ll. 897–98. Thomas 1955–64, ll. 3532–33, 5170–71; cf. ll. 3563–70.
144. "King Horn" 1966, ll. 265–67, 429–34, 677–80, 1092; see ll. 988, 1056, 1417–18, for Rymenhild weeping with no lover to comfort her.
145. Thomas 1955–64, ll. 2624, 3000–3001: "li quor li estencele." See *Jordan Fantosme* 1981, l. 243: "Irrur ad en sun cuer, li sanc li estencele."
146. Thomas 1955–64, ll. 4017–18. The representation of anger as a temporary madness is very common in Old French literature.

tion was to gaze at his beloved Rigmel's ring. Only then did anger fill his heart and make it swell with "rancorous pride." After that boast, no peace was possible between them.[147] The anger not only impelled vengeful action but was also its necessary cause.[148]

Envy provided another motivating factor. In the *Romance of Horn*, the Old French *envie* carries little of the hatred, which we have seen to characterize its Latin equivalent, *invidia*.[149] Nevertheless, the emotion appears both long-lasting and deep, as is shown by a proverb twice quoted in the text: "Envy will never die."[150] It may even be characterized as "mortal envy."[151]

My evidence here is obviously restricted. It serves to encourage me to pursue the matter more fully through Anglo-Norman and Middle English literature on another occasion. There is ample warrant for placing all these works within a vengeance culture. The theme is very prominent, one might virtually say central, in our two fullest works, the *Romance of Horn* and "Havelok the Dane." The latter closes with a kind of plot summary that concludes: "And hou he were wreken [avenged] well / Have ich said you everich del." We are left with the assurance that we have had all the details of a worthy vengeance, that the characters feel this as a deeply ingrained principle of life and action. They are not surprised by it; they expect one violent act to be requited by another. Everybody recognizes, for example, the dangers of leaving alive after a killing those who will in time feel impelled to avenge it. So the dead men's sons should be killed, though the story line requires that this does not actually happen.[152] Vengeance was an absolute compulsion, what I most want in the world, Horn said.[153] It was not a matter that could lightly be abandoned. Havelok would not give up his quest for vengeance for anything, "ne for love ne for sinne," "for lef ne loth."[154] He pursued it hard, because its achievement brought joy. "For shall I nevere more be blithe / Ne hoseled been ne of priest shriven," said Havelok, until revenge had been taken against his enemies. His happiness hung on his taking his vengeance before he would once more receive the Eucharist or go to confession.[155]

Instead, men mostly sought to act swiftly and take their vengeance while they could. As the French author said approvingly of Horn, "Where he intended evil, he avenged himself very soon, and where he intended good, he

147. Ibid., ll. 3168–71. See "King Horn" 1966, ll. 875–79; *Jordan Fantosme* 1981, ll. 1807–10.
148. Thomas 1955–64, ll. 4009, 4782, 4798, and *passim*.
149. Ibid., ll. 1772, 1935, 4852, and *passim*.
150. Ibid., ll. 1875, 2580: "Ja ne murra envie."
151. "King Horn" 1966, l. 691; *Jordan Fantosme* 1981, l. 13.
152. Thomas 1955–64, ll. 42–47; "King Horn" 1966, ll. 111–14. See Thomas 1955–64, ll. 2907a–2910a; "Havelok" 1966, ll. 325–27, 509–12.
153. Thomas 1955–64, ll. 3892–93.
154. "Havelok" 1966, ll. 2375, 2379, 2775.
155. Ibid., ll. 2033, 2597.

did it without show."[156] "If it were done when 'tis done, then 'twere well it were done quickly," was how Macbeth would later make a similar point. This kind of action by a ruler sends a message that wrong will swiftly meet its proper response but that otherwise men can expect restraint.[157] It respects the recommendations of Axelrod's games theory; the opposition knows what to expect. Some situations call for even greater dispatch for rather different reasons. Those faced with imminent death, pagans as well as Christians, feel a compulsion to take their revenge in advance, as it were, for fear of shaming their descendants.[158] In the *Romance of Horn*, the dying Egfer claims to feel in some sense healed ("gari") and able to die peacefully and without pain once he knows that his killers have themselves been slain.[159] To gain this compulsory vengeance, driven men have no compunction in calling on God or even invoking the supposedly peace-loving Christ.[160]

Yet settlements were not out of the question. Had the pagan Rodmund not resorted to treachery, Horn would have offered him his life in return for baptism and exile overseas.[161] Offers were made but agreement not reached, so demanding in this literary world were the calls to vengeance.[162]

What restrained a person's legitimate hopes of joy at an enemy's discomfiture was the general feeling that the proper goal was a restored balance of some kind. Men therefore hesitated to rub their enemies' noses in their defeat, as we might say. A relatively trivial example makes the point. The disguised Horn eventually left the chessboard at which he had been constantly winning. It would have amounted to presumption ("surquiderie") to stay longer, once he had avenged his lord's defeats at the hands of his own sister.[163] There was such a thing as an "evil vengeance act." One such occurred when men, angry at their failure to capture a castle, stripped the bark off the fruit trees outside the wall—an act so described perhaps because of the de-

156. Thomas 1955–64, ll. 1765–67: "E la u veut le mal, mut tost s'en est vengé; / E la u veut le bien, mut est de humilté"; cf. ll. 3724–25.

157. There are other possible patterns, too. When a man is expected to take counsel and bide his time, precipitate action provokes criticism.

158. The *Romance of Horn* is quite explicit on shame as the spur to vengeance. Thomas 1955–64, ll. 881–86, 2603–6, 2642–49.

159. Ibid., ll. 3493–96; cf. 3444–47, 4748–49.

160. Ibid., ll. 1136–39, 1319–21, 1470, 1549–50, 2898–2904 (almost a crusading tone); cf. ll. 3334–35 (St. John), 3371–74 (pagans call on Belial). In "Havelok" 1966 (ll. 542–46, 1362–65, 2402–3), it is Christ whom Havelok invokes. But the vengeful Christ is a common-enough image; the *Bible Moralisée* (1995, Ivc and 54) illustrates Gen. ii.2 with Christ trampling his enemies into Hell.

161. Thomas 1955–64, ll. 4823–31; cf. ll. 4517–23; "Havelok" 1966, ll. 2717–19.

162. *Havelok* (ll. 270–74) hints that one party might need to force the other to reconcile.

163. Thomas 1955–64, ll. 2769–73; cf. ll. 2740–44 for the circumstances of the games, and ll. 3885, 4080–81, 4832–34, for the imagery of debt, reward, and repayment that underlies the treatment of vengeance here.

structive nature of the gesture.[164] Another criterion for the legitimacy of vengeance goes unmentioned in our four romances and much other literature. It is the likely need for the would-be avenger to proclaim his intention, or in some other way to mark himself out as different from any casual or motiveless purveyors of violence.[165] Our texts indicate that the state of enmities, including who was whose enemy, was quite well known in contemporary society. The *Romance of Horn* frequently refers to these known enemies by an interesting term, *faidis* or *faidé*.[166] This may, as some suggest, imply an oath of enmity; it undoubtedly implies the existence of a recognized state of enmity, as denoted by the Germanic word *faide*, the probable direct ancestor of modern English *feud*. Another name for foes was, naturally enough, *mortel enemi*,[167] associated with a mortal enmity between the protagonists.[168] Either form of locution serves to make the necessary point—that our authors and their audiences shared a culture in which feuding and its concomitant emotions featured prominently.

CONCLUSION

The historian can, and should, mine the topic of medieval emotions and describe their impact on actual politics. I have shown how medieval emotion talk corroborates the importance of vengeance in the English political culture of the time. En route, the character of this talk begins to locate for the medieval West a place on the road toward the emotional discourse current in our own world. The Middle Ages remain some way down that road. Their emotion categories, and uses thereof, do not always coincide with ours. England derives from its mindset and its people's own emotional resources an alternative understanding of justice that was always present, lurking beside the more respectable models of law schools and theologians. This vernacular or secular model served as a check on the formal model, and in doing so it depended largely on nasty passions à la Robert Solomon, with vengeance in some form as its preferred sanction.

People made instrumental use of this emotional discourse to seek their political ends. They did this at all levels of the system, from high politics to family squabbles. The result was a line of political rhetoric, which historians

164. *Jordan Fantosme* 1981, l. 1679.
165. I argue for viewing the *exfestucatio* and/or the allegedly "feudal" defiance as just such a ritual act, in Hyams 2002.
166. Thomas 1955–64, ll. 249, 269–70, 3072, 3178, 5015. See the editor's note on the lexicography (ibid., ii:129).
167. Ibid., l. 3519; the usage of *Jordan Fantosme* 1981 (ll. 432, 1177, 1584) in each case personalizes political enmity.
168. Thomas 1955–64, l. 887: "haunge mortel." See the equivalent verbal phrases in *Haveloc*, l. 556; *Jordan Fantosme* 1981, ll. 131, 668.

must take seriously and on its own terms, without necessarily believing as fact all they find there. Our preliminary samples demonstrate how emotion was used both to justify high-handed royal actions and to establish moral standards of conduct in public life and the law; therefore, one can seldom be confident that behind displays of *ira regis* lay genuine royal arousal and heated feelings of actual anger.

Emotion was nevertheless a force to reckon with at more mundane levels of everyday life. The very efforts of thinking churchmen to promote an enforceable Christian social doctrine governing relations between neighbors prove this point. Fortunately, we can study this social theology in remarkable and illuminating detail. The model of social relations which pastors felt bound to dispel from their lay flocks is much less easy to describe with equal specificity. Historians must struggle to reconstruct the system from the shards of behavior targeted by the moralists and the distortions and romanticizations of entertainment literature. When we ferret out the "Do's" and "Don'ts" featuring in such sources, we find them to be quite different from the Church's own precepts. In a large number of different ways, they emerge as at least congruous with, even conducive to, a vengeance culture.

The system both belongs to Western Christendom as a whole and is specific to England and the diversely discerned actions of the English. There is much more evidence to be examined than could be considered here. The single notion of the "two conceptions of the neighbor in the Middle Ages" deserves its own treatment at book length. Much remains to be written about the history of emotions.

One final, important point: I find it impressive that the rhetorical clusters I have been examining here travel so well through society. I can see no good reason to believe that their acceptability was limited to the nobility or the social levels inhabited by authors of entertainment literature. They fulfill the criteria suggested by Georges Duby for cultural diffusion in that they apparently pass through English society in both vertical directions.[169] They deserve very close study as we further develop our analytical tools for understanding medieval secular culture. Notions of malice and mortal enmity, for example, originated in the higher levels of learned culture and yet were translated into truly demotic and vernacular guises. Similarly, the dynamic idea of anger, so important to the themes of this book for its propensity to lead from personal arousal into actual hatred and violent action, permeated medieval society. I should like to think that contrary emotional currents bubbled and flowed upward from some "popular" consciousness too. It would be very odd if thirteenth-century England and its Continental neigh-

169. I have Duby 1968 in mind here.

bors were really the almost passive beneficiaries of emotion language and concepts from learning and schools so recently revived. One is almost driven to assume some emotional counterflow. The difficulties of proving some such hypothesis from a largely oral culture are quite another matter. My very preliminary investigations have patently only scratched at the surface of high medieval problems that require careful attention to the preceding period.

PART II

Undifferentiated Wrong and Its Redress

CHAPTER THREE
REDRESS FOR WRONG IN THE GOVERNANCE OF LATE ANGLO-SAXON ENGLAND

Every student of the Anglo-Saxons accepts the existence of feud as a feature of society before the Norman Conquest. Yet there has been no serious study for over a century of intense scrutiny and debate on just about every aspect of English culture in the period.[1] Scholars have marginalized the subject; although a set topic, feud is seldom permitted to affect the main currents of Anglo-Saxon history. Anglo-Saxon England, possessing the state-like characteristics now identified by scholars, emerges in modern accounts as a society very different from the ones in which scholars have usually located, described, and analyzed feuds. Much recent scholarship has depicted England during the century and a half separating Alfred from the Norman Conquest as a highly centralized society, one more closely subject to royal leadership than most of its neighbors. Such centralization was rarely attained in the later medieval period, with the possible exception of the often-lauded "Angevin kingship" itself.[2]

In attempting to juxtapose the evidence for feud with the case for "the Late Old English State," I have come to suspect that feud was quite central to Anglo-Saxon political culture. The major questions on the maintenance of order—where to strike the balance between an individual's direct action and that of the king? Or between private initiative and public authority?— remain unanswered, amid sources that are patently incapable of sustaining any quantitative judgments. I unapologetically adopt the premise that in arguments *a silentio*, all assumptions about the existence of a particular practice or pattern are equally weak.

It is easy enough to establish the overall significance of feud within Eng-

---

1. Laughlin 1876. Hyams 2001 was an earlier version of this chapter.
2. The best guide remains Campbell 1982.

lish culture during the hundred and fifty years before the Norman Conquest. However, the royal *leges* are the key to the history of feud as a process,[3] for this quintessential testimony to the king's central authority is congruous with the existence of a feud mentality. That is, this feud culture was a prime target for much legislative activity. To explain how private efforts to manage and resolve conflict could have worked in this kingdom, I take as my cue a modified version of the anthropologists' theory of "peace within the feud," even though royal authority is far more prominent than in the almost stateless societies that first generated this approach. The progressive strengthening of royal aspirations is easily visible in the extant law codes. I summarize and dissent from the views of scholars for whom this constitutes a central theme of political development in the last century of Anglo-Saxon England, leading to the formation of an "Old English state." To explain how their "maximalist" findings might be reconciled with the view argued here, I discuss at some length the ordinary pattern of litigation in the public courts. The picture of a largely litigant-driven schema that emerges resembles that familiar from Angevin England. The primary matrix for the legal pursuit of grudges and grievances could be characterized as an individual "undifferentiated action for wrong" much like that which I depict in chapter 4 as splitting in the late twelfth century into the common law's appeal "of felony" and civil action of trespass. In this view, Anglo-Saxon England in its last period was a feud culture with public courts and an active monarchy.

This hypothesis differs markedly from much recent scholarship, most notably that of respected period authorities like James Campbell and Patrick Wormald, who have argued persuasively for the centrality of royal leadership in late Anglo-Saxon England. When I term the general position these scholars share "maximalist,"[4] I intend neither to disparage nor to mock genuine achievements that have greatly advanced our understanding of the period. I simply mean that they tend to make more of the sparse and difficult evidence for kingship and royal government than I myself feel able to do. My own preference leans toward skeptical caution. These maximalists do not, for my taste, adequately juxtapose undoubted royal aspirations and robust attempts to actualize them with the resistance of individuals equally

---

3. I say *leges* because these were neither official statutory codes nor mere private law books. On all such matters the authority to check is now Wormald 1999.

4. The fact that James Campbell titled his Campbell 1995a "The Late Anglo-Saxon State: A Maximum View" strongly suggests that he for one would wear the label with pride. It is in fact one not infrequently used elsewhere to clarify scholarly issues (e.g., Sims-Williams 1998, 25; Carpenter 2000, 47).

keen to defend and perhaps further their own opposed interests.[5] They seem to subscribe to a harder-edged vision of state formation than many of the specialists on the subject in later periods would accept.[6] I see no reason to expect any tenth-century polity to resemble a state from the nineteenth century. I also find little contemporary evidence of the sharp division between royal government (that is, the state) and society, which the maximalist views would seem to require. Instead, I see assertive royal aspirations compelled to co-exist with something much less than an actual royal monopoly of the means of violence. To establish this does not refute maximalist contentions about governmental practices in tenth- and eleventh-century England. It does, however, suggest that late Anglo-Saxon government be situated in a context with some rather different implications, and cautions us against speeding to a final verdict concerning the actual level of royal power from the existing data.

Royal authority is clearly central to Anglo-Saxon England. The king's role in all noble affairs over a wide area of the country is paramount in the sources. Politically active contemporaries could never afford to neglect the king in their calculations. The impressive line of vernacular royal leges proves that Anglo-Saxon personal vengeance operated in a context that ostentatiously included public, royal courts willing to exert pressure against private acts they deemed illegitimate. It also reveals the literate Anglo-Saxon's complex cultural legacy from a Christian and Roman past, substantially mediated through Frankish sensibilities. Even postulating the most minimal, restricted, and clerically concentrated "craft literacy,"[7] Anglo-Saxon historians cannot employ the "tabula rasa" assumptions that underpin some writings about feud in African oral cultures.

FEUD IN OLD ENGLISH LITERATURE

Old English literature establishes the cultural centrality of feud. First of all, the language includes the word *fæhðe*, cognate to German *Fehde*, which most scholars seem happy to translate as "feud."[8] We should of course be chary of assuming an institution because of the existence of a term. Still the Anglo-

5. Both scholars are naturally well aware of the problem of distinguishing aspirations from achievements; Wormald 1999, 300, 430–31, 449, 477, 482, and esp. 308, promises proof of the "actual efficacy of tenth-century government" in his next volume.

6. In thinking about matters of state definition, I have found helpful the critical survey of major theorists in Axtmann 1993.

7. Wormald 1977b; Clanchy 1993, chap. 1.

8. Bessinger 1978, and Bosworth and Toller 1973 (s.v. "fæhð," "fæhðe") collect texts and establish the general point. I discussed the equation with *feud* in chap. 1.

Saxon doubtless thought he understood the reference. The prima facie importance of feud fairly leaps out from *Beowulf*, the sole surviving long poem from the era. It contains references to more than a dozen feuds.[9] The one that Hrothgar and the Geats experienced against Grendel and his mother is a mainspring of the poem's whole action and tension. Beowulf is the outsider who volunteers to join in someone else's feud against the advice of his own friends, in part to establish himself and his reputation.[10] References to other feuds abound.[11] The poet's condemnation of extraordinary fratricidal killings serves to distinguish them from, and to highlight, the routine nature of legitimate feud.[12] Such unnatural intragroup offenses, which make the achievement of a decent settlement impossible, set a context for other feuds. The dying Beowulf congratulates himself on never having been drawn into such traffic.[13] Many of the poet's listeners will have suspected their neighbors to be less prudent. They recognized the negotiation of an honorable settlement as an intrinsic part of the game. The payment of monetary compensation and the offer of a woman in marriage as "peace-weaver" were always worth careful consideration.[14]

Beowulf must have been popular, if ever, during the last century of Anglo-Saxon England. Its poet draws much of his work's passion from the emotional discourse of vengeance and enmity. He uses vengeance language even for confrontations between whole peoples where we would prefer the language of warfare.[15] Feud seems close to the center of his thought world. That much the same can be said of a substantial number of other poems in the Old English corpus is weighty testimony to the centrality of feud in Old English culture as a whole.[16]

9. (1) God v. Cain for killing of Abel, ll. 106–14; (2) Grendel (and his mother) v. Hrothgar, ll. 151–58 and *passim*; (3) Beowulf v. enemies of Geats, ll. 422–24; (4) Ecgtheow v. Wylfings, ll. 459–72; (5) Unferth v. his brother, ll. 587–89; (6) Sigemund f. Waels v. various enemies, ll. 877–79; (7) Finn and his Frisians v. Hengest and his Danes, Finn episode and Finnsburgh fragment; (8) Geats v. Frisians, ll. 1206–9 etc.; (9) Heathobards v. Danes, episode of Freawaru; (10) Dragon v. Hrothgar and Geats, ll. 2280 sq.; (11) Onela v. Ohthere, his brother, for the Swedish throne, ll. 2379–2400; (12) Haethcyn v. Herebeald, ll. 2435 sq.; and (13) Swedes v. Geats, ll. 2946–98, 3000–3003. I have used throughout the edition of *Beowulf* edited by F. Klaeber (1950).

10. Ll. 1187–90, 1997–98.

11. Nos. 3–5, 7, 11, and 13 are digressions, but the references in nos. 1, 6, 7, 9, and 12 concern characters in the main plot.

12. See Beowulf's gibe at Unferth (no. 5) as well as nos. 11 and 12. My colleague Tom Hill helped me to understand the importance of the fact that Beowulf and Unferth do *not* come to blows.

13. Ll. 2737–43.

14. See for money *Beowulf*, no. 4, and ll. 2093–94, 2435 sq.; for marriage alliances, no. 9 and ll. 1942–44. Sklute 1990 demonstrates the obscurity of the notion of peace-weaving, but see also for some possible implications of the whole image Leach 1961, 131–32.

15. *Beowulf*, nos. 3, 8, 9, 13 and perhaps 7.

16. This subject deserves separate treatment. Among poems to be so considered would be "The Wanderer," "The Seafarer," the "Sword" riddle, "The Wife's Lament," "The Husband's

If the Anglo-Saxon read and heard such sentiments in his hall and cloister, this would indicate that he lived in the kind of society that might funnel an urge to redress wrong into feud. Narrative testimonies to this are understandably few. All come from the highest social strata, of kings and great nobles. Perhaps most convincing is the famous saga of the West Saxons, Cynewulf and Cyneheard preserved in the *Anglo-Saxon Chronicle* annal for 755, which depicts a string of patent feud killings.[17]

Cynewulf had deposed a remote kinsman, Sigeberht, who was soon killed dishonorably when a swineherd avenged the earlier killing of his own lord. Cynewulf then ruled Wessex with apparent success for thirty years, until in an attempt to exile Sigeberht's brother, Cyneheard, he incautiously let his enemy catch him virtually unguarded in a love nest. He was killed. His few followers on the spot refused Cyneheard's offer of "money and life," choosing death with their lord, which duly followed. The next day a much larger group of the dead king's men caught up with Cyneheard and besieged him in the same spot. They were so avid for their vengeance that they too refused all offers, and withstood even the reminder that the besieged included their own kinsmen. After reasserting loyalty to their dead lord, they pressed on with their attack until all but one inside were dead.

For the present purpose, the crux of this dynastic struggle lies in the two peace offers refused by Cyneheard before the final bloody dénouement. The second, desperate effort was sweetened by an appeal to links of kinship. The attackers' famous response, that "no kinsman is as dear to us as our lord," has sometimes been read as an indication that lordship was by this time superseding the pull of kin loyalty.[18] It really demonstrates that no loyalty was seen as absolute, not even lordship. The protagonists had little option but to negotiate and argue out their attachments and support. The offers demonstrate that some kind of peace could well have emerged from this feud. But that would have weakened the story, which might then never have reached us.

One other feud story from an only slightly lower social level usefully spans the period between Æthelred's reign and across the Norman Con-

---

Message," and the masterly final section of "The Battle of Maldon." Most of these can be given a preliminary scan in the English translation of Bradley 1982. Much prose, including Wulfstan's "Sermo Lupi" (ll. 62–64, 141) (Whitelock 1963), is also pertinent.

17. I follow here White 1989. He retells the tale itself at 1–4.

18. Another comparably famous remark is that of the southern German princes in 1082 in justification of their refusal to fight for Henry IV against the Saxons: "they would on no account fight against innocent men, Christians and their own kin" (cited in Leyser 1979, 46).

quest.[19] Æthelred was apparently seeking to strengthen his party in the north. Earl Uhtred, his man there, repudiated one wife in order to marry into a rich York family. Part of the deal was, apparently, to dispose of one Thurbrand Hold, a Danish enemy of his new father-in-law. Although the "contract" failed, Uhtred stayed faithful to Æthelred even after Cnut's invasion and eventual seizure of power. Thurbrand made him pay for this constancy by slaughtering him and all forty of his war band in an ambush, allegedly with Cnut's knowledge and assent. After a surprisingly brief interlude, Uhtred's family nevertheless regained the earldom and his son, Earl Ealdred, duly killed Thurbrand. Later Ealdred made overtures to his victim's son, Carl, and negotiated a full peace settlement involving ritual brotherhood and a joint pilgrimage to Rome. The pilgrimage was delayed. Carl hosted Ealdred at a banquet in his own hall and then had him too killed. The earldom now passed from Uhtred's kin until William I appointed Waltheof (II) in 1072. The new earl caught Carl's sons feasting at hall in their turn and killed all but one, plus all the grandsons. Our sources end at this point.

Our main authority for the tale was a Durham monk writing close to 1100. At that time, the site of Earl Ealdred's murder in 1038 was still marked by a stone cross. In seeking to promote Saint Cuthbert's recovery of his lost lands, the monk also preserved for us characteristic allusions to other associated feuds. He gives every impression of a man fully familiar with a secular literature of feud. His monastic eye and property-directed perspective cannot hide the underlying saga-like cultural context. In northern England, Danes and Englishmen lived and caroused hard together, then sometimes went on to hate and fight just as hard. And when their descendants once again met to feast and drink in someone's hall, and the songs and stories began, there was ever the possibility that a stray boast or goading remark would rekindle long quiescent passions.[20] Audiences would have supplied context from stories they had heard elsewhere. Details like the account of the unsuccessful effort at a peace settlement in Cnut's time would have authenticated the reality of feud. They may, too, have remembered some prehistory of the enmities now lost to us.

Some have dismissed this tale as atypical because of its location in the law-

19. EARL UHTRED'S FEUD. (Case names given in small capital letters indicate that their stories are told in the appendix.)

20. It is striking that two of the killings in Uhtred's feud took off from hall hospitality. If saga-like stories of ancient resentments sometimes figured as after-dinner entertainment, as one must assume, then we must also expect that equally saga-like gestures sometimes led to fresh violence. Feud-like assaults around 1200 commonly seem to have deliberately targeted families at dinner-time; one good example is CUSIN (MONACHUS) V. FITZJOHN.

less north, beyond the normal range of West Saxon royal justice.[21] But our Durham monk did not write in a vacuum; indeed, he enjoyed ostentatious intertextuality with monastic brothers from Worcester and elsewhere in the core realm. The events he recounts *are* exceptional in that they involve the greatest families in the area. Few aspired to earldoms, and fewer still were courted by kings. But those who did are hardly likely to have been deterred by everyday policing arrangements not backed by immediate royal power. We cannot therefore deny the possibility that the story was routine at least on this social level.

The special case of competition for kingdoms supports such speculations. Until the ninth century, no clear mechanism existed to govern royal succession. Commentators talk less of custom than power. Northumbria, for example, had eight kings from three different families between 759 and 796, well within the lifespan of a single king blessed with better fortune and skill. Between 685 and 802 no king of Wessex was succeeded by his close kin.[22] Behind these crude statistics—pretty much all we can learn—may once have lain tales of enmity and feud that could have been comparable to the Cynewulf saga.

These two tales of Cynewulf and his rival and of Earl Uhtred's Northumbrian feud come three centuries apart and from different ends of England. Some scholars read the gap in date and location as further reason to downplay the significance of feud. Given the dearth of narrative sources, however, it seems as reasonable to take the little we know about kings as some indication of what we cannot know about the rest of warrior culture.[23] Feud culture was something that pre-Alfredian kings shared with their nobility. Exiles, for example, were common both in the extended royal kin-groups and generally among the nobility. Often the threat of feud vengeance was the explanation.[24] Kings and their would-be supplanters shared the noble feuding culture of their day.[25]

21. Kapelle 1979 (23) defends northern manners. Wormald 1997 (560) dismisses this feud as atypical.

22. For the data, see Campbell 1982, 56, 114 sq., 138; and Rollason 1983, esp. 4, 5–9, 20, touched on below. Cf. the comments of Gillingham 1994, 38–39.

23. Campbell 1995b (34) pertinently observes that "in the tenth century, . . . the royal family was very much part of an expanded noble cousinhood."

24. I know of no general study of exile, the theme of the Old English poem "The Husband's Message." The eleventh-century German poem *The Ruodlieb* (1985) offers an apposite Continental analogue; see, e.g., Campbell 1995b, 32.

25. See *Bede's* 1969, iv.21 (400), for Theodore's mediation between the Mercians and Northumbrians, ca. 679; *Anglo-Saxon Chronicle* s.a. (687, 694), cited from Earle and Plummer 1892–99, for the somewhat similar negotiation of a vast sum in compensation for the Kentish burning of a royal West Saxon invader; and Haddan and Stubbs 1869–78 (iii.274–75) for the bishop of London's appeal to Canterbury over unsuccessful peace settlement activities ca. 705.

Another indication of a pervasive feud mentality in the upper reaches of Anglo-Saxon politics is the approving repetition much later of feud stories from the days before Alfred. One finds in England, mostly between the seventh and ninth centuries, "a tradition of the veneration of murdered royal saints . . . unparalleled elsewhere." Behind these stories lie the politics of succession and dynastic conflict fought out in feud-like manner but on a battlefield of holiness and spiritual power. The creation of such a cult was "a means of expressing and focussing opposition" to the killers. The claim was that God, not fallible man, led the feud band. With His aid, the dead man's line would return and their enemies—the unrepentant ones, at least—would receive their just desserts. Such logic led leaders of successful coups to represent their monastic foundations as attempted expiations of their actions. On at least one such occasion, our sources talk of *wergild* (blood money). Was this enough to end the enmity? Political maneuverings on this theme are well illustrated in the competition for control of the bones and story of Edward the Martyr in the decades around 1000.[26]

THE ANGLO-SAXON LAWS AND FEUD

To test the surmise that feud was a prominent part of the shared culture of kings and their nobles, careful examination of the corpus of highly stylized Old English law codes is indispensable. Scholars have now learned to understand these as kingship treatises not actually used in litigation and thus of most significance as indicators of an ideology of royal governance.[27] More recently still, their testimony has been adduced in favor of "maximalist" views of Anglo-Saxon kingship. The legal texts are badly in need of the kind of critical examination that was once called deconstruction, in order to transcend traditional concerns with authorial intention and examine the range of possible readings to which the leges and the manuscripts that contained them are susceptible. We need to know how they could have been read and used.

The targets against which these texts were aimed may be quite as important to social historians as the hopes of compilers and their employers. High aspirations were not always matched by actual achievement. I offer here a tentatively minimalist reading in the hope that a more balanced picture will

26. Rollason 1983 assembles the evidence in a most suggestive manner. For the *wergild* image, see Cockayne 1864–66, iii.426. On the considerable modern discussion of the cult of Edward the Martyr, see, e.g., Keynes 1980, 163 sq.

27. Patrick Wormald has most fruitfully followed the lead given here by J. M. Wallace-Hadrill. See briefly Wallace-Hadrill 1971 (148–49), then Wormald 1977a, Wormald's other papers noted below, and of course Wormald 1999; also Kennedy 1995, 174–78.

emerge. The evidence will never be adequate to compute the actual level of royal power.

The Old English word *bot* and its verb *betan* carry a primary sense of remedy, amendment, or cure and denote in most contexts the process of compounding or compensating for a committed wrong. *Bot* refers to the payment in discharge of the debt created by a wrong.[28] The wrongs covered in the leges include many to be classified as crimes in the thirteenth century. Pre-Alfredian leges stipulate the level of *bot* appropriate to different acts and identify the groups by whom or at whom they were committed. So pervasive a feature of the early law codes must have been a major concern and motive of their composers, and may still have attracted later copyists and readers. These compensation regulations were plainly available for use by anyone who viewed vengeance as a natural and licit first response to perceived wrongs.

Such readers would need to know the tariffs for appropriate compensation (*wer* and *bot*) and where they fitted into these classifications. To share a blood price with one's peers was to be assured of an equivalent level of honor and respect. It declared in advance the measure of loss friends suffered through your death. Only repayment of this amount in appropriate style could restore them to honor according to the worldly ranking enjoyed by all.[29] Compensation must accord with status. This was one's defense against the calumny that the passing of money constituted the dishonorable sale of a dead kinsman for the highest price, a replication of the treachery of Judas. The system required no writing and could comfortably accommodate normal change. Christianity brought with it both writing and a new need to adjust customary blood prices. The normal processes of intertextuality ensured that, once set down on parchment, new regulations elaborated on the old. It was necessary to assign places within the hierarchy of status to priests and monks, to protect them from violence. This may be why the early leges were written down. Whatever kind of "Roman" model the composers of the earliest leges may have had in mind,[30] the regulation of feud settlements appears central to extant codes, with the implication that "early English justice was essentially that of the blood-feud."[31] The important developments

---

28. Hall 1960, s.vv. "betan," "bot." See Liebermann 1903–16, ii.336.

29. II Cn 42, 49, are quite explicit on injuries to churchmen. (I follow here for the most part the sigla established in Liebermann 1903–16 for the law texts he edited. The Note on Sources and Citations in the introduction gives further detail.) Recent challenges to simple deductions about social status made from the laws do not affect their contemporary use as indications of honor gradations.

30. Cf. *Bede's* 1969, ii.5 (150), on which see Wallace-Hadrill 1988, 60–61; and Wormald 1999, 29–30.

31. Wormald, in Campbell 1982, 98–99.

under Alfred's tenth-century West Saxon successors make best sense within this context.

Despite the powerful case for the tenth century as an era of forceful advances in royal power, gradualist readings of the tenth-century codes retain some attractions. Consider first Alfred's pathbreaking code, which contains some of the fundamental maximalist texts on royal lordship, starting with what some claim as England's first treason law.[32] Yet most of its clauses treat matters of compensation in the traditional way found in earlier codes, such as Ine's, which Alfred copied along with his own. More than fifty of the seventy-seven chapters into which Alfred's own code is conventionally divided detail the *bot* due for various kinds of injury.[33] Two chapters deal explicitly with feud,[34] depicted as a licit procedure so long as certain basic rules were followed. Before any formal resort to violence, the aggrieved must first seek their ealdorman's aid, and only if that proved vain, proceed to the king. The point seems almost certainly to strengthen a vernacular customary requirement that feuders should inform the neighbors publicly of their grievance or cause of action before moving.[35] The would-be avenger must give fair warning of his intentions, in the manner most feud cultures require, and thereby permit a cooling-off period for possible peace overtures. The king, whatever his preferences, felt able to assert no more than a right to police the accustomed system. The two enactments (assuming they really were new) look like an attempt to regulate more effectively a policing system still essentially dependent on private enterprise. Understandably in a turbulent invasion period, royal law privileged lordship over the claims of kinship. As leader of national defense, Alfred had to stress the very special nature of his office and blood. He could hardly claim kinship with everyone. So he made his appeal through paramount lordship.

During the century and a half that separates Alfred from the Norman Conquest, royal action against "crime" (in the sense of serious breaches of acceptable behavior) visibly intensified right across the board. The *leges* evince a new level of royal interest in violence and disorder committed outside the royal circle. From almost their first mention of forfeiture, a novelty

---

32. Af 1.1 is general in language and not obviously restricted in scope to royal lordship. I am not quite convinced that Alfred intended anything more than a general requirement that men should be loyal to their lords and carry out their commitments as made. The whole code is characterized by a persistent emphasis on the duties of men to their lords, a theme of special value to a king, who had many men but acknowledged no superior. I come back to this law later in the chapter.

33. Af 10–39, 44–77.

34. Af 5, 42. In the often-neglected "introduction," Af El 13, 42, draws from Exodus texts that hint of a typology of homicide that distinguishes between excusable and culpable killings and counsels generous treatment of at least one's enemy's livestock.

35. See *LHP* 83.6–6a and my speculations on the supposedly "feudal" defiance (Hyams 2002).

that seems to have come swiftly in the years around 900, charter title narratives confirm that the king was confiscating book land (land held by charter) from offenders.[36] Other physical and financial sanctions progressively sharpened. By the eleventh century, the king and his draftsmen could demand against various kinds of putatively serious offenders communal action leading to afflictive punishment, including death. These texts say less about compensation payments to the victim and/or his kin and much more of what was due to God and the king. They raise fines due the king to the level of systematic savagery. The tenth century was thus one of those periods when optimists believed they could win their "war" against crime by tougher punishments combined with moral exhortation.

Æthelstan (924–39) merits a special place in the story. He was the first to make explicit provision for the exclusion of convicts from Christian burial.[37] Apparently the combination of moral pressure and brutality in earlier codes had proved predictably ineffective. His codes manifest a heightened degree of horror at wrongdoing, perhaps reflecting a new equation of all serious offenses with a kind of infidelity, as if wrongdoers were thereby deemed to be as heathen as the Danes. Another of Æthelstan's innovations demands the removal of any especially powerful wrongdoers from their kindred and region.[38] The king was encouraging men to get rid of awkward and uncontrollable kinsmen whose offenses cost them dear in compensation, but to do this for the public good as well as their own and so to counter the deplorable trend toward the flouting of oaths and pledges to the king and his *witan*. This public pressure on kindreds to act against their antisocial members was the obverse of an ancient coin whose reverse included the often-repeated prohibition of feuds or lawsuits against men who had legitimately executed convicted offenders.[39] It is among Æthelstan's laws that we find the ordinances of the "Iudicia Civitatis Londonie," briefly mentioned below, which probably represent the royal regulatory takeover of a private frith-gild.[40]

36. Wormald 1988, 278–79; 1999, 149, 160, 306–7.

37. II As 26.

38. III As 6; cf. IV As 3–3.2, VI As 8.2, and II Em 1.1.3 (discussed later in this chapter). III As 6 is a strong candidate for listing among cases where the king takes on and adapts to his own ends an existing, perhaps more casually enforced customary norm. I give parallels from other societies on the next page.

39. II As 11 (compensation for dead thieves), 20.7 (vengeance against one convicted of *oferhyrnesse*, contempt of the moot summons). Cf. III Atr 7, which (although to the same effect as II As 11) has significantly different procedural details, and E Cf 36–36.5. Ine 21.1 and *Beowulf*, ll. 2435–43 (accidental killing by Hrethel's son), confirm that the anguished dilemma was far from new. Hurnard 1969 (88–92) shows that thirteenth-century men still sought vengeance or compensation for the "justifiable homicide" of legitimate executions. I discuss this issue further in chap. 8.

40. VI As. Patrick Wormald pointed out to me the intriguing fact that the 30d. fine for noncooperation here (clause 2) and in Edgar's Hundred Ordinance (I Eg) coincides with the property qualification for gild membership; cf. Wormald 1999, 369.

One senses here a Milsomian policy of royal enforcement in the public interest of private custom as it *ought* to work.[41]

From the reign of Æthelstan's successor, Edmund (939–46), comes the central text in the whole argument, the code hailed by scholars as a pioneering effort to minimize bloodshed and the spread of feud. *II Edmund* was apparently spurred by Archbishop Oda's recent call for "peace and unanimity," something with which feud killings were patently incompatible.[42] Although Continental leges offer few close parallels,[43] we should not rush to exaggerate its innovations. Given the selectivity and chance that has formed our corpus of leges, we must allow for the possibility that the king and his clerical advisers were defining more precisely what men had previously taken for granted.

The king declared that, having had some success with theft, he now wished to move against other "illegal deeds of violence" (1.1).[44] Interspersed with regulations on killings and feud are peremptory royal rulings on *fihtwite* and *manbot* (2), on abuse of sanctuary (3), and on the very royal pleas (seemingly designed to view feud situations as offenses against the king) of *mundbryce* and *hamsocn* (6). The apt climax is an apparently ringing prohibition of feud (7): "The authorities must put a stop to vendettas."[45] En route (1.1.3) the king had considered the consequences of the decision by a killer's kin to abandon him. Edmund certainly appears intent on moving aggressively against interpersonal violence and inexorably drawn to proceed against feud as a major source of disorder.

Let us look more closely at the details. The abandonment of a kinsman under pursuit, one whose violence had grown too costly to the kindred, was probably established practice, albeit open to criticism. Similar practices can be documented from other feuding societies;[46] they are effectively a required premise of the peace-in-the-feud model. Edmund's law simply lent public approbation to this rational strategy. Its novelty lay in the offer of royal aid to the kindred; he would have his men ride along with them if the situation turned ugly.

To maintain peace, one must be ready to ride to war. Edmund was out to

41. Kennedy 1995 (181–82) ends on a rather Milsomian note of kings telling courts to do the right thing.

42. Whitelock, Brett, and Brooke 1981, 73, for chap. 8, cited in Wormald 1997, 555.

43. Wallace-Hadrill 1971 (107–8) singles out Charlemagne's *Admonitio Generalis* of 789 as "the earliest piece of legislation against feud."

44. Doubtless this meant property disputes and inheritance, as in the better-documented days of the thirteenth century; chap. 6 treats the matter.

45. The translation is that of Robertson 1925, 8–11.

46. The data adduced in Moore 1978 (122–26) and by other anthropologists (see chap. 1) make II Em 1.1 look rather less "drastic" than does Wormald 1997 (555–56, 558). We have just seen Edmund's successor, Æthelstan, acting in similar fashion; for III As 6, see earlier in this chapter.

encourage peaceful solutions (2–4). He wanted the killer's party to settle with their enemies, always a tricky procedure.[47] The perpetrators should do penance before they sought the king's pardon and protection. They must, that is, first satisfy God and the victim's kin, whose claims apparently took precedence. The setting of penance and appeasement of the opposition were each necessary conditions for future peace,[48] which neither guaranteed.

We should study *II Edmund* alongside the contemporaneous treatise Wer, as tenth- and eleventh-century readers did.[49] This juxtaposition shows that the king intended no outright prohibition of feud.[50] The conflated texts stipulate a deliberate, precise procedure to restore peace and ensure a full series of necessary payments to different people—to the king, and to the victim's kin and lord. There must be no mistake or the consequences could be catastrophic.

We can distinguish three main normative stages. First, representatives from each kin hammered out an agreement, to enable the restoration of royal peace (*mund*). This they sealed with a suggestive ritual involving the laying of hands on weapons. The king sought both to maximize the chances of ending the violence and to secure his own cut in the shape of *mundbryce*, his fine for the breach of his peace. He could, if he chose, summon all "lawful" men to ride with him against peace-breakers. But his clear preference was for the warring parties to make their own peace. Without some such preliminary agreement, direct interference was in any event much riskier for all concerned. Next followed a series of public payments. Custom (*riht*) set the initial schedule. Further installments of the *wergild* were negotiated under supervision within the year.[51] Wer 6.1 presents the third and final stage as an extra, for use where the killer aspired to regain "fulle freondrædne" (the mutuality of full friendship) by proceeding "mid lufe." This entailed a full public reconciliation of the kind known from other times and places.[52]

Edmund's draftsmen probably envisioned the full schema of Wer. If so,

47. Mediators help a bit. See later text in this chapter for the apparent introduction of a mediator to the Quadripartitus translation of Wer 6 on restoration of the parties to royal *mund*.

48. Our extant penitentials may distort the realities, but Frantzen 1983 argues persuasively that we may take their general message seriously. Whitelock, Brett, and Brooke 1981, nos. 42–43, gives sample letters for penitents from ca. 1000 that support this view; all deal with homicides for which feud would not normally be a licit option.

49. Wormald 1994 (124–25) virtually proved that readers received Wer and similar unofficial treatises alongside I–III Em. He further suggests that the final part of II Em, with the details of settlement procedure, may have been added to the genuine code from Wer, itself written to fill gaps in the code (Wormald 1999, 310–11, 374–78).

50. Wer 6.

51. Wer 6: "witan graedan"; cf. Quadripartitus: "sapientes instituent."

52. The Quadripartitus translation has "liceat per amorem procedere, si perfectam velit amicorum consocietatem habere."

the first sentence of *II Edmund*, clause 7, "Witan scylon fæhðe sectan," is open to retranslation as something like "wise men [or elders = mediators or arbitrators] should [work to] reconcile feuds."[53] The possibility of approved arbitration between warring parties makes good sense of the law's concern for negotiation. The aim was to conclude *fæhðe* speedily, and without further bloodshed if possible. Care was required or violence might erupt again. The careful stipulation of procedural machinery was designed to avoid such ructions.

ROYAL JUSTICE IN THE LATER LAWS

Other readings of *II Edmund* assume the dominance of royal law which they purport to prove. Later legislation charts the actual emergence of this dominance. Codes subsequent to *II Edmund* increasingly single out habitual evildoers—the men of ill repute—for special, harsher treatment.[54] Edgar expressed his royal will that men bring their disputes into the public courts under the ordinary *folcriht*; he emphasized too the common duty to ride together in pursuit of cattle rustlers and strengthened older requirements that accusers should act from proper motives.[55] This last enactment is nearly contemporary with the new coronation oath binding the mature king to forbid iniquities and do justice with equity and mercy, thereby securing the peace for all Christians.[56] Kings must offer royal justice to those who applied in a proper manner. But this does not mean that Edgar and his advisers intended any serious claim to monopoly jurisdiction over even the most serious disputes.

Not until the reign of Æthelred (978–1016) do the leges assert the existence of bootless offenses, wrongs so serious that redress may no longer be taken by private agreement with the wronged. Æthelred probably began the

53. Quadripartitus translates: "Sapientium est sedare factionem." Liebermann 1903–16 (iii.128) recognized the possibility that "witan" here might mean arbitrators but preferred a more official rendering: "Notable sollen Fehde beilegen" (i.189). Arbitrators may have some kind of official standing; see Robertson 1925 (297) for comment on this and Old Norse *saetta*, with which she associates this unique Old English *sectan*. My colleague Tom Hill advises me that *sectan* should probably not be considered an Old English word at all, unless it is an error for *settan*, meaning settle or something similar. It might even be a loan-word from Latin (*sectare*), with a cutting image and perhaps carrying the implication of a suppression (a cutting down) from above. He also stressed the law's sapiential tone, with its implication that the reconciliation of feuding parties was the kind of thing that *witan* were expected to do when acting properly.

54. Laws lay on the *tyhtbysig* a heavier burden of exculpatory proof; e.g., see Hyams 1980, 107. This concept of public reputation within public justice must surely have influenced twelfth-century arrangements.

55. I Eg 7; cf. III Eg 1.1. For pursuit of rustlers, cf. I Eg (Hundred Ordinance) 2–3.1, 7, with II Ed 4–5.1.

56. Stubbs 1913, 69.

accumulation of these bootless offenses under Wulfstan's tutelage. He first made breach of his own special peace bootless and then added homicides aggravated because committed in churches. Wulfstan has him place the compensation procedure under episcopal supervision, drawing the clergy more into secular law enforcement and placing God and the king ahead of the victim's kin.[57] All men, not just the victim's friends, shared a duty to pursue wrongdoers and peace-breakers, because everyone suffered the consequences of their evils.[58] Cnut's code both extended the list of bootless offenses and strengthened the emphasis on royal punitive action. He did explicitly declare a royal monopoly claim to certain offenses.[59]

It is important to understand just how radical that claim was. Genuine bootlessness means in principle that the injured parties—the family, lord and men of the victim—might receive no compensation and have no claim of their own against the offenders and their party. Many of these offenses patently relate to feud circumstances.[60] Later lawmakers sweetened this bitter pill by permitting private civil suits for damages alongside public, criminal prosecutions. Even Henry I, in asserting around 1130 his royal right to pardon killers (homicide always being the strongest case of wrong), expressly reserved the kin's right to pursue their own claim for compensation.[61] The declaration of even a few offenses as bootless marks an astounding degree of royal self-confidence, which must have caused serious reverberations among the nobility on whom royal authority rested. The mildly minimalist position I strike here already claims a great deal for the West Saxon kings. In its light, I doubt the need for more extreme readings of the leges.

Written laws, of course, often report legal change after the event. It is therefore possible that these laws postdate developments from Alfred's reign or those of his immediate successors. My inclination, however, is to read the story essentially as suggested by the texts themselves. The first phase established the royal contention that serious offenses could no longer be aban-

57. III Atr 1; VI Atr 51; VIII Atr 1.1 = I Cn 2.3.
58. IV As 6.3; I Eg 2; this hue and cry is discussed later in this chapter.
59. II Cn 64. There is still no general agreement on the principles by which the lists in II Cn 12–15 were drawn up; Hurnard 1949 is the classic account.
60. I have in mind here griðbreche, forsteall (often meaning "ambush on the roads"), and hamsocn (including the classic house assault, as documented in chap. 6) first grouped in IV Atr 4.2.1. Although the standard accounts of these offenses in Hurnard 1949 (307–10) and Harmer 1952 (79–81) are silent on the possibility of a feud context, the hints are there in the sources, as Cooper (forthcoming) ingeniously argues. Af 42, although it does not use the term, and II Em 6 treat hamsocn in the midst of reviewing feud regulation. VI As 1.5 pairs the attempts to rescue a thief captured on stræt with those to take vengeance for one executed. LHP 80.2, 4, 11–11a, assumes that both it and forsteall are likely to be aimed at an existing enemy. Even Liebermann 1903–16 (iii.128 n. 2) notes that hamsocn usually comes after a killing.
61. On this, see chap. 4.

doned to private treatment governed only by feud custom. The royal claim, that some demanded punitive sanctions under the king's own aegis, followed logically.[62]

The purpose behind the formulation and written presentation of these laws in the king's name was to improve that doing of good justice to which he had pledged himself at his coronation. It would be surprising if the compilers did *not* argue for an extension of their master's authority and control. The historian must therefore apply to the Old English leges the same critical skepticism extended to other prescriptive texts such as the Carolingian capitularies.[63] They are certainly not simple descriptions of the state of the realm the king sought to rule. One promising route is to consider the likely target situations against which the leges were framed.

Simon Keynes has subjected laws of the late tenth and eleventh centuries to acute and learned examination in very much this spirit. He noted that "the tenth-century kings experienced considerable difficulties in maintaining the rule of law and order" in a kingdom where men sometimes refused the direct commands of the king. Despite the legislative lament of *II Edmund* and similar laws at the "manifold deeds of violence" facing the realm,[64] both legislators and their audience accepted the legitimate claims of lord and kin to authority over their own groups. Each had a proper role to play in the accepted system of law and order. The laws confirm the position of lordship as the major restraining authority other than the king. Every man was expected to have or get a lord.[65] The laws, when read together, buttress rather than attack the legitimate domination of lords; the exceptions are overmighty subjects and kin groups.[66]

The leges, on which any answer must rest, are quintessentially contingent texts that defy a single, definitive reading. The very few eleventh-century Englishmen capable of reading are unlikely to have consulted any individual code on its own. Their manuscripts generally contained laws from various kingdoms, interspersed with certain legal treatises and other less obviously authoritative matter.[67] How did such readers deal with the material? The

62. Wormald 1997 presents the stages of central royal control in a nicely nuanced manner differing in some respects from the schema argued here.
63. Fichtenau 1957 taught this lesson to a whole generation of Anglophone historians.
64. Keynes 1990, 69. I was much encouraged by Prof. Keynes's kindness in letting me see this paper before its publication.
65. The plight of the lordless man is well documented. Hyams 1980 (235–36) shows the lord's responsibility for his men's offenses and some of the countervailing implications of the texts on which it rests.
66. Keynes 1990, 70–71, 78–80.
67. Wormald 1994 (122, 124–25) and 1999 (374–78, 383–84) show, for example, that I–III Em usually appear with Swerian, Wif, and very significantly, Wer. Wormald has also observed (1997, 558) that II Em is a notable absentee from the otherwise comprehensive legislative sources of I and II Cn.

fact that they seem never to have cited law books in any actual case ought to counter any assumption that the leges tell us all we need to know about actual legal process.[68] When we ask how contemporaries read the leges, our best clues come from post-Conquest compilations and translations.[69] These depict a literary reader, distanced from the constraints of actual legal argument, consulting his texts in bookish fashion, to extract from them whatever he wished to find.[70] He might draw conclusions directly contrary to the spirit of the original draftsman or compiler. He might even derive from these quintessential royal efforts to set central standards of order through Carolingian-style downward-justice arguments to justify the taking of traditional private vengeance. Resistance readings remained an option in the twelfth century;[71] they must have seemed attractive to earlier readers too. The authors of royal leges in the tenth and eleventh centuries were all members of a monastic reform party committed to a controversial royal view of peace and justice. Their views dominate virtually all surviving written sources. Their political victory was inevitably less complete. Adversaries remained to read the leges after their own fashion. We cannot exclude the likelihood that defenders of *secularium prioratus* (meaning the secular domination of church property) also argued on occasion for licit feud and vengeance-taking.

WAS THERE A PEACE IN THE ANGLO-SAXON FEUD?

Yet Old English society never did quite dissolve into chaos. How did it survive if the aspirations of the laws fell so far short of full attainment? Scholars have sought the answer in some variant of the anthropologists' peace-in-the-feud model. In this light, some depict feud as an instrument of positive social control. Fear of the violent retaliation feud requires could serve to deter men from homicides and other violent acts, or at least give them pause for thought. The high cost of reprisal provided an incentive for friends to dissuade the most violent men from acts for which they know they, too, will in the end have to pay. Feuding groups spread across communities, so men had to face the prospect of being forced to fight kinsmen, colleagues, neigh-

68. Wormald 1977b, 112–13. Much must have gone unrecorded in writing. Kennedy 1995 (140–41) and Fleming 1995 (103–5, 106, 118) have both stressed the importance of "combined courts" in the late Old English period and on to the Domesday Inquest and beyond, yet the laws carry no hint of them.

69. See, in addition to the previous note, Wormald 1995, 243–66.

70. Brooke 1931 long ago revealed in detail the highly selective manner in which Archbishop Lanfranc abstracted his canonical collection from his pseudo-Isidorian sources.

71. The compiler of the *Leges Henrici Primi* arguably did something of this kind in providing ample material from which a resistant twelfth-century reader might, if he chose, justify feud along Anglo-Saxon lines, as I show in chap. 4.

bors, or friends. Blood kin of the disputants might well find themselves confronting their own kinsmen by blood or marriage, and so might face excruciatingly difficult choices. They could find themselves obligated to fight for both sides at once. Clearly, such "cross-linkage" augmented the pressure for peaceful settlement.

Anglo-Saxon England was beyond question a highly segmented society in much the sense originally envisioned by the anthropologists. The basic bonds to lords and kin were supplemented by various artificial and voluntary groupings, such as tithings and gilds. In such a society, leaders had a clear interest in managing and restraining enmities and violence among their own followers. Anglo-Saxon kings, lords, and others seemed to have understood that vengeance within the lordship was damaging both to their following and their own control over it. One good indication is the special horror with which killings within the family and lordship were regarded.[72] No prudent lord wanted to see his own following riven by feud. Even in tenth- and eleventh-century England, one may guess, lords acted as both peacemaker of first resort and the main source of redress for grievances held by one follower against another. This is a pattern whose significance I examine further later in the chapter.

Men were still killed in nasty ways. Peacekeeping was imperfect and incomplete. The peace-in-the-feud model guarantees no easy equilibrium. Its value lies in suggesting lines along which contemporaries *may* have thought and acted to preserve their world from the threat of a relapse into chaos. One key premise is that such actions needed to be consistent with the honor of those concerned.

For individual actors, the constant nagging question was how best to meet their social obligations and political challenges so as to conserve honor. Here the leges are again helpful. The social groupings into which their compilers divided society for the purposes of wergild payments (for example, two, six, or twelve hundred–shillings groups), also afforded men a literal sense of their own worth, an apparently objective measure of what they might with honor accept for the killing of a close kinsman. We should probably not take the sums as fixing an automatic price. Instead, they set an acceptable range within which to seek or resist acknowledgment of the special strengths of the deceased, perhaps his reputation, his warrior skills, and wisdom as a counselor. To compare this system of valuation to horse-trading or dealing in used cars misses the overt concentration of all parties on honor

---

72. Wallace-Hadrill 1962, chap. 6, distinguishes nicely between intrakin and interkin feuding. The penitentials are significantly more merciful to vengeance killings for close kin than to parricide or fratricide; e.g., Frantzen 1983, 7–8, 67, 75–76.

and face. All the same, the wergilds of the leges must have operated in real life as rough indices of social worth.

The evocative accounts of the murder of two Kentish princes of the seventh century, Æthelred and Æthelbert, by Thunor on behalf of his master, King Egbert, give some idea of how the compensation process might work.[73] King Egbert, assisted by various miraculous signs, soon realized that he had angered God beyond any safe measure. He therefore assembled his witan and thegns to advise him how best to deal with the situation. On their advice the king recalled Mildrith, the dead princes' sister, from Mercia. She was to choose an appropriate form of compensation. Mildrith in her turn consulted her own close kin and other friends. Then she made her choice through a process of prayer and consultation with the family's most powerful and influential friend, God, who could be relied on to enforce the settlement. Mildrith ultimately demanded land on which to build a monastery, the bounds of the island territory to be perambulated by Mildrith's pet magic hind, presumably under God's supervision.[74] Our texts expressly call the island, Minster-in-Thanet, a wergild (or *precium* in the Latin versions). Royal leges do not normally specify precise tariffs for the blood of kings and princes. One should not dismiss the generality of the patterns of negotiation disclosed by this unique case. The negotiating atmosphere depicted here illustrates how the tariffs and related regulations of the law codes could work in real-life situations.

Endowment of a monastery required a massive investment of wealth. The compensations specified by the laws for more conventional cases were also very substantial. The size of the payment impressed the seriousness of the wrong on kinsmen and others sucked in from both sides to heal the enmity. It gave expectant recipients an immediate interest in preserving the settlement; they stood to gain most once the promised payments were finally made. As kinsmen, obligated to assist in the payments or entitled to stand among the receivers, they expected to be in the front line during the hot phase of hostilities before a settlement emerged.

Such support groups are also pursuit groups. Prudent men created, nurtured, and refreshed their support networks well in advance of actual trouble. When the crisis did arrive, mustering one's friends was still a very polit-

73. The basic facts of this story were already circulating by the early eighth century and were still being retailed long after. Rollason 1983 (5, 13) assembles the materials. For a more exhaustive examination of the Mildrith cult and its development, see Rollason 1982. I focus on the texts in Cockayne 1864–66 (iii.426–28) and Symeon of Durham 1882–85 (ii.3 sq).

74. Quantum of compensation is an obvious sticking point. Rollason 1982 (49–51) considers the possibility that the island's eighty sulungs of land can be interpreted as two princely forty-hide wergilds. The killer protested the amount, and the earth duly opened up to swallow him; the spot was thereafter known by his name, Thunor's Low.

ical action, turning in principle on reciprocity, yet drawing most frequently on the firm bonds of blood or lordship. The commonsense suspicion that feuds are as likely to involve lords as kinsmen is confirmed for Anglo-Saxon England by the existence of *manbot*, compensation to a lord for the loss of his dependant.[75] No good man, certainly no prudent man, would turn a deaf ear to his lord's appeal that he ride beside him on feud business, or even do the work under his orders but in his absence.[76] But common sense goes further. Why should a killer (to take the simpler case), under threat of revenge death, confine struggle for survival to summoning kinsmen, whose obligations were in any case relatively clear? The smart operator surely worked in good times to accumulate from others with whom he had no blood ties new debts against some future pressing need. One common method was the marriage alliance, which created quasi-kin links of affinity. Icelanders went much further, and there is reason to think Englishmen did too. There were many honorable ways to secure support, acquire and reinforce friendship. Men and women understood kinship in cultural ways even when they talked blood and biology. Enemies are frequently recycled friends, as the rhyming opposition of Old English *feond* and *freond* should suggest. But strangers too can become enemies without previous close relations. Why should anyone limit his friends to those linked to him by existing formal relationships? In reality, desperate men seek aid wherever they can. They doubtless start with those under some kind of obligation to help them: first kin, then established lords and any mutual-aid organizations (gilds) to which they belonged.

The regulations of the Cambridge thegns' gild, written down at the end of the tenth century, nicely depict socially responsible arrangements for the member thegns' deaths.[77] Gild brothers swore on the relics a qualified oath of mutual loyalty, promising "to aid him who has most right." Each in turn could expect instant assistance in his hour of need; all he needed to do was to inform the reeve of his closest gild-neighbor and the chain message should do the rest: "And if anyone kill a guild brother, nothing other than eight pounds is to be accepted as compensation. If the slayer scorn to pay the compensation, all the guildship is to avenge the brother and all bear the feud. If then one avenges him, all are to bear the feud alike." Any brother who slays "as an avenger by necessity and to remedy the insult to him" can be confident that the rest will contribute to any wergild payment he incurs.

75. II Em 3, 7.3, Wer 6, VIII Atr 3, and I Cn 2.5 all call for the enforcement of *manbot* alongside other payments. Ine 70 may suggest that Alfred too was sympathetic.

76. Killing at the lord's behest may be one of the situations that lies behind the phrase "dæd-bana oððe rædbana" in VIII Atr 23; I Cn 5.2b; *LHP* 85.3. Compare the thirteenth-century evidence adduced in chap. 8.

77. Thorpe 1865, 610–13; translated by D. Whitelock, in *EHD* I, no. 136.

Not so, however, should anyone kill "through his own folly." Such a man is alone responsible to the victim's kin and must then repurchase his gild membership with the same eight pounds that is due for a gild brother's death. In other words, he is also liable for his gild-*wer*. Men must not eat or drink with the slayer of a gild brother, unless compelled to do so by the presence of the king or a bishop, a powerful hint at the peacemaking potential of these great men.[78] Other regulations cover verbal insults, the drawing of weapons, and the nonlethal wounds they cause. But the real focus of the text is on death. Men patently joined this gild to offer each other honorable Christian burial after a good death or to avenge a bad one, always with due care for the salvation of their souls. Nowhere is there any suggestion that vengeance and salvation might be inconsistent with each other. And there is just enough outside evidence from Æthelstan's London peace association (VI As) to suggest that the Cambridge thegns were not unique and that some, perhaps dozens, of other noble groups in late Anglo-Saxon England were committed to similar standards of behavior.[79]

Aid is not always forthcoming and seldom free. Beyond one's immediate coterie of obligation, the asking price inevitably rises. For this reason, soliciting aid from outsiders in the Early Middle Ages sometimes led to the creation of new lordship.[80] The prudent man tried to provide for his future needs without incurring debts on a scale that led to bankruptcy or permanent and dishonorable dependant status. To succeed, a man had to have a good previous record, to stand well in his community, and to have successfully maintained and extended a network of his own friends by putting himself to bother at their request. Prudent men accumulated credit in good days for conversion to harder currency in evil times. Affines, spiritual kinsmen (through the baptismal font, "gossips"), blood and foster brothers, mere neighbors, and plain vanilla "friends" might each prove forthcoming, even,

78. I speculated about ecclesiastical peacemaking in Hyams 1992 (17–20). Despite the dearth of direct evidence, I still suspect its importance. Churchmen were promising candidates to perform the mediations implied by laws like those discussed earlier, especially when the taking of sanctuary intervened. Wulfstan, keen as ever to save souls where he could, urged bishops to work for reconciliation and peace when secular judges with whom they sat in court were likely to be amenable to such overtures; Episc 3–4 (Liebermann 1903–16, i.477). See also n. 25 in this chapter, and Scholz 1966, 140–41. There is some suggestive evidence from later periods too. For secular (including royal) peacemaking, see later text in this chapter.

79. See VI As 7: "We have declared," spoke Æthelstan in his peace ordinance aimed at London, "whoever it be whose hands avenge wrongs done to us all [a key phrase], we shall all stand together, both in friendship [freondscype] and in enmity [feondscype]—whichever may result. And he who is before others in killing the thief shall be the better off for his action and initiative by twelve pence taken from our common property." This translation is slightly amended from Attenborough 1922, 163.

80. Helmstan's case looks to be an illustration. See Keynes 1992. This is directly relevant to the "drift to subordination" that Stenton once thought to discern as a dominant trend of the late Old English period.

or especially, while they were serving as public officials. Exactly who would volunteer on demand is another question. Some were good only for lip service; others helped face off the opposition in court, and a few, possibly a very few, honored their promises to the death on the battlefield.

The leges bolster clues culled from the narrative materials. The repeated emphasis on oath-helping bespeaks a reliance on public reputation that would compel men to cultivate friendship networks seriously. From the tenth century, the king required men to be in tithing, a territorial institution designed in part to turn to royal advantage the fact that men depended on the esteem and support of the neighbors and peers alongside whom they lived, fought, and performed their public duties.[81]

In speculating about support groups and peacemaking, I expect a substantial degree of personal choice and initiative. The blithe assumption that in time of trouble one's family and friends would automatically risk their lives on one's behalf was a risky strategy. Men and women probably saw in their future needs a weighty argument for deference to the lord from whom their best and perhaps only chance of useful aid would come. But the more politically astute among them will surely have fostered in their everyday relations in a troubled world whatever claims friendship and other relationships might afford over all potential allies.

FINDING PEACE: SANCTUARY, THE HUE, AND THE KING

After a killing, there was much to do in very little time. One cannot overnight muster friends to one's defense, stay summary execution, and negotiate a peace settlement. But the penalty for delay was swift death. The fugitive offender's immediate challenge was thus to survive until the would-be avengers cooled off and peace overtures became possible. He desperately needed a breathing space. So even the bravest might seek the temporary protection of some benevolent power, appeal directly to some "big man" such as the king perhaps, or accept exile in some distant court. Christ himself seemed to some the biggest "big man" of all, and a model of peace-giving for kings and others to follow.[82]

The attractions of flight into the protection of a powerful man demand careful examination. We may imagine the fugitive prostrating himself at the great man's feet or adopting some other patently submissive posture. He

---

81. Morris 1910, chap. 5, still remains the standard account.

82. Grið 31.1. Wormald 1999 (394–95) situates the treatise *Grið* (Liebermann 1903–16, i.470–73) within the developing thought of the later part of Wulfstan's career, toward 1014. The Old Norse source of the word *grið* makes it worth considering the speculations of Yver 1928 (319–20, 333–45) as to a complex origin that included possible Scandinavian influence.

had to make visible to all about them that he was, as the Normans would say later, putting himself at the great man's mercy.[83] Anyone who failed to demonstrate clearly that he was indeed a *friðbena*, a suppliant for protection, risked instant death. So the show of submission was an essential and ostentatious sprat to catch a much-needed mackerel. The fugitive was in desperate need of at least temporary security from the great man, as a means to two further ends. First and intensely practical, one avoided immediate death at the hands of a "victim's" friends. Second, one won a breathing space within which one's own friends could negotiate, offer terms, and strive to make peace with the opposition. The leges, in allowing that others than the king might offer this kind of temporary stay of violence, were recognizing some of the realities of a feuding culture. Bishops, ealdormen, and other secular powers might all serve their turn on occasion.[84] That said, the king was always much the most desirable target. He alone could remit bootless offenses and grant peace to men who had committed outlawry offenses.[85] Royal counselors must have told him on occasion that peacemaking could enhance power and prestige.[86]

All relevant texts imply political "business" in the king's immediate physical presence, a drama of tense rhetoric and horse-dealing between declared enemies. The king had his opportunity to display his talents as peacemaker. It is a fair bet that participants understood themselves as pleading for aid and protection. In other words, they are part of the case for what I shall call proto-trespass. If all went well, the proceedings culminated in some ostentatious piece of ritual reconciliation; if not, then perhaps in a shameful hanging. The fugitive sometimes found himself awaiting judgment in jail for a spell.[87] But this was less a custodial punishment, something that was highly rare at this date, than protective custody.[88] These decisions cannot have been instantaneous. They must on occasion have seriously distracted kings and their companions from routine and other pressing business pertaining to battlefield, hunt, or bower. They doubtless disliked being bothered by

83. Grið 9 ("on cynges dome" whether he should live or not), 15. The later amercement is discussed in chap. 4.
84. Grið 4–5. I read II Cn 12, 15, as likely to imply that recipients of royal grants of *mundbryce* or *griðbryce* were entitled to offer the same kind of protection as the king. Indeed, II Cn 13, 15a, specify that such rights did not extend to those who had committed offenses deserving of outlawry; only the king could pardon *them*. If this is right, the context is feud rather than "crime."
85. Grið 9, 15; see II Cn 13, 15a, as in the previous note.
86. It seems probable that the king and his men sought control over peacemaking in the way implied by the later common-law rule against unlicensed settlements out of court. Ine 52 had assumed the illegality of illicit compacts ("Be ðyrnum geþincðe"); VI As 11 condemns the reeve who allows them, and V As 3.1 implies something similar. Although all these texts were available to the author of *LHP* 59.27–28 in the Quadripartitus translation, he shows no sign of using them.
87. II Cn 35; cf. *LHP* 65.5.
88. Grið 16 sets out the unpalatable alternatives.

any but the most significant of fugitives. Such considerations explain why laws that strove to limit "over-hasty resort to the king" were both needed and frequently reissued.[89]

Of even greater importance is our effort to elicit the obscure prehistory of another bedrock concept of the common-law world, the king's peace itself. What the king conferred on the fugitive who managed to reach his presence was his *grið*, with the kinds of consequences just mentioned. Some of his subordinate officials could perhaps make the grant on his behalf.[90] Possibly private individuals too, those to whom the king "desired to show special honor," might by virtue of a grant of *griðbryce* enjoy a similar power.[91] One wonders if flights in quest of protection against imminent violence were not a relatively common feature of everyday life.

The king's *grið* itself came in two main manifestations. There was first the king's routine peace, breach of which carried a relatively moderate fine. The king seems indeed to grant this *griðbryce* more or less at his will; we find it included in lists of other routine privileges like sake and soke. This is perhaps all that royal officeholders and most private grantees could mete out. But the king could also act personally to shelter a threatened person or monastery with his more solemn and portentous personal peace. He did this in person by his own hand (*handgrið*) or (possibly with slightly less stringent consequences) by his writ and seal. It was presumably for this special, solemn peace that personal access to the king was crucial. Did the king ever allow private individuals to adjudicate allegations of the breach of this special *handgrið*? This question may be as pertinent to old controversies concerning the existence of private jurisdiction before the Conquest as more obviously franchisal formulas like sake and soke. Anglo-Norman evidence suggests that specially favored individuals may indeed have enjoyed this level of autonomy on occasion.[92]

Inevitably, my remarks here about the protection afforded to fugitives by the king and other "big men" have been speculative. The nature of our evidence and its survival leave no alternative. The leges do nevertheless license a reasonably firm sense of a plausible connection between royal grants of peace and private feuding practice. It seems we should regard grants of spe-

89. This is the phrase used by Wormald 1997 (573) apropos of the laws from III Eg 2 to II Cn 17 and across the Conquest that struggle to enforce the rule that men should always start their suits in the local public court of the hundred.

90. III Atr 1. 1–2. Since this Wantage Code appears directed at the Danelaw, this possibility (like that of presentment by the twelve elder thegns in clause 3) may not have existed in English areas; cf. Wormald 1999, 326–27, 371–72.

91. The conventional view of II Cn 12–15 is that grants like *griðbryce* convey in the first instance merely the right to receive fines for their breach.

92. O'Brien 1999, 73–74. The classic account of "Anglo-Norman Franchises" remains that of Hurnard 1949.

cial peace to individuals as ad hoc, made to meet specific situations of enmity, and not necessarily intended to be permanent or of extended duration.[93] But terrestrial protectors were not the only option in the tenth and eleventh centuries. Often the closest and always the best-documented protectors were dead saints in the ecclesiastical sanctuaries dotted all over medieval England. A small number of especially holy ancient sites offered deep protection on Old Testament authority,[94] and thousands of churches and chapels extended a more routine protection to fugitives of all kinds. Everybody knew somewhere within reach that offered refuge in need.

Historians have not satisfactorily integrated the colorful evidence for the major sanctuaries with the history of law enforcement and feud. Many studies have followed the hallowed and risky retrospective method of *Domesday Book and Beyond*, reading back from the better-documented and sometimes weird manifestations of sanctuary rights in the later Middle Ages toward misty origins. When one assumes the perspective of centralized law and an established distinction between crime and tort, sanctuary inevitably seems anomalous, a quixotic, irrational gift to protect the criminal from the state and due retribution. The villain apparently needs merely to set his foot in privileged territory. Sanctuary is reduced to a children's game.

Tenth-century leges do indeed suggest a royal takeover of sanctuary rights, in a direction that tries to integrate them into a central royal policy for the repression of serious disorder. The association of Æthelstan's name with several sites indicates royal interest. The equation of fines for breach of sanctuary with those for breaking the king's special peace[95] suggests that contemporary royal grants of peace to churches may represent the confirmation of sanctuary rights.[96]

The most important consequence of this regulatory takeover appears to have been a general scheme that lasted through the Conquest and into the twelfth century.[97] The fugitive's best option was to reach the peace stool placed at the sanctuary's very center. This most sacred and highly protected

93. Obviously monasteries are a special case. Their needs for protection were constant. The formulas of monastic grants of peace and protection are thus likely to imply permanence. I suspect, however, that kings once made unrecorded, in many cases unwritten, grants of peace to laymen in their dozens or even hundreds.

94. The main Bible references are Num. xxxv.9–29; Deut. iv.41–42 and xix.2–13. They distinguish between accidental, unknowing acts, which merited protection within cities of refuge, and willed acts motivated by enmity, which did not. See further Exod. xxi.12–14; Ios. xx.2–6. Offenstadt 2000 (206–14) usefully collects Continental data.

95. Hall 1989, 428–29. Campbell 1995b (39) makes a relevant point about the network of local shrines. Note also Af El 13, which makes a *friðstowe* of the biblical altar of Exod. xxi.14 and denies sanctuary there to culpable homicides.

96. This may be the implication of II Eg 3.

97. Cox 1911 presents much of the evidence in picturesque fashion. Hall 1989 (426 sq.) argues for the notion of "a general Anglo-Saxon scheme."

sanctuary—"swa deope friðsocne," as the laws called it—carried the highest fines and most solemn anathemas, to ensure absolute security in almost any circumstance.[98] Surrounding this were concentric bands of territory, each one a little less holy and thus less stringently protected than the last, until they opened out into the general *banleuca* of the church. Late Old English law already required supervision to prevent the fugitive's escape and, more to the present point, to ensure that he met his obligations.[99]

The intriguing questions are two: who were the fugitives, and what were they fleeing? Neither royal justice nor feud can supply the whole answer for the later Old English period. Few of the texts specify exactly what justifies their saints' intervention. They tend to refer in general terms to fugitives "for whatever reason."[100] This phrase must cover refugees from war and natural disasters, runaway slaves or serfs, as well as fugitives from justice and vengeance. The compassion of God and His saints was all encompassing. Even so, the primary situation envisioned must surely be feud, as Alfred's reference to a feuder ("fahmon") fleeing on foot or horseback makes explicit. A twelfth-century text hints that many sanctuary customers were fleeing from men who felt themselves wronged to an extent that justified blood vengeance unless proper compensation was forthcoming.[101] Even when the fugitive was fleeing from trial and punishment, by far the most likely assailants were those who felt themselves directly injured by his acts, kinsmen and friends of the victim, in hot pursuit of their personal vengeance.

Sanctuary arrangements show strong parallels to other regulations in the leges concerning feud and the prosecution of theft.[102] The basic purpose in each case is to construct an appropriate truce that allows time for negotiations toward some more lasting peace. In this light, sanctuary is a special case of the house protection allowed by the laws in cases of straight feud, a supplementary church-protection as it were.[103] The alleged wrongdoer sometimes claimed to have acted accidentally, without any intention to do

98. VIII Atr 1. It is probably to breaches here that Whitelock 1963, ll. 39–40, refers.

99. Hall 1989, 431–32. For those incapable of buying off the claims against them, one possible option was enserfment to the saint in whose power they found themselves, to become his *grithmen*. Riggs 1963, 14–16; Hall 1989, 433. Scholars have yet to make the obvious comparison with *sanctuarii* and *tributarii* on the Continent. I wonder if the eventual fate of Thomas of Elderfield that I described in Hyams 1986 owes anything to this conceptualization.

100. Af 2: "for hwelcere scylde"; cf. Symeon of Durham 1882–85, i.203 ("Historia Sancti Cuthberti," chap. 13); Leis Wl 1; Cox 1911, 130–34 (twelfth-century Beverley); Searle 1980, 68–70; Hart and Lyons 1884–93, i.57.

101. Af 5. Where E Cf 5.2a originally gave a strong hint in the same direction, its later recension, E Cf retr, uses "wrong" language in keeping with its late-twelfth-century date and specifies the entitled recipient as "cui damnum intulit." Hunnisett 1961 (37, 45, 75) cites some thirteenth-century evidence of flight for fear of reprisals and also of forcible rescue and extraction.

102. Riggs 1963 established the basic point here, with arguments that I largely follow.

103. Riggs 1963, 4, 34.

harm. So he sought sanctuary before his wrong became public knowledge in order that he might make amends and head off any chance of vengeance or feud.[104] This met the Church's interest; it loaned the holy powers of its saints, to lighten the fugitive's fear of human retribution, without deleting his moral responsibility for sinful deeds; he must still relieve his soul with penitential acts. Churchmen habitually returned runaway serfs to their masters against the masters' promise to concede them their lives.[105] The Church had no wish to protect troublemakers to sin again and lose their souls.

The rules for the compensation and/or punishment of theft provide a broader context for sanctuary arrangements. Local people were bound by a very ancient obligation to pursue and arrest a hand-having thief. This did not end at the church door. They now had to stand guard and prevent his escape.[106] The overall concern was to prevent an escalation of violence and thus to ensure that the licit execution of a thief did not lead to further trouble later.[107] In the course of the tenth century, flight itself became a capital offense, so that the king effectively assumed the obligation of feud against outlaws on behalf of all.[108] In this and other bootless cases, sanctuary would provide limited comfort to fugitives,[109] except perhaps for the exceptional few with powerful friends able to move the king to mercy.[110]

Most who reached sanctuary did so under close pursuit. The duty to raise the hue and cry was already a feature of Anglo-Saxon law. This obligation— that anyone who witnessed a crime must publicize the fact by blowing his horn and shouting, so that all within earshot should join in the pursuit of the wrongdoer—is, like sanctuary, generally understood within a context of public criminal justice. But the scattered and fragmentary references in the leges strongly suggest a popular origin in neighborly and communal aid to private vengeance, whose royal takeover may long have remained incomplete. There was much less of the later emphasis on defaults and more on execution as licit vengeance.

104. Ibid., 36–37, explicates Af 5.4 in this way.
105. Ibid., 21–22.
106. Laws from Ine 5 onward define these duties. See Riggs 1963, 10–13, 19.
107. As noted earlier in the chapter, executions easily provoked the thief's friends to seek vengeance for his death.
108. Riggs 1963, 41 sq., cites II As 1.2, VI As 12.1, and VIII Atr 2.1.
109. In this it resembles the later institution of the approver, a convicted felon whose life was spared on condition that he accused and convicted his former associates by duel. Although they might live for a while at the king's expense, almost all approvers were eventually hanged. This is thought to have been a twelfth-century innovation (Röhrkasten 1990).
110. VIII Atr 3 and I Cn 2.5 provide for the payment of *wer* to the king as a kind of ransom in addition to the traditional *wite* and the *bot* due to lord and kin. There may be some connection between this limited facility and the later option of ritual abjurations of the realm. Cf. Hunnisett 1961 (chap. 3) on thirteenth-century procedure with Riggs 1963 (47–48, 61).

The treatment in the leges represents the kings' efforts to use and control this organic, natural popular response to disorder to the common profit and their own,[111] much as they took over and regulated sanctuary at about the same time. The origins of these two public procedures apparently lay in private and popular responses to violent wrong. Their royal takeover helped both to extend the kings' own peace and also to integrate them into it. But in thus asserting their control over the responses of their free men to wrong and disorder, the West Saxon kings were also tacitly approving and reshaping legitimate vengeance.

HOW DID FEUD COEXIST WITH LATE OLD ENGLISH KINGSHIP?

The West Saxon kings of England in the last century or so before 1066 project a profile of power undeniably different than those of the Continental confrères to whom they sometimes married their daughters and sisters. The age that saw the disintegration of Charlemagne's empire and the emergence of Europe was not a great one for royal authority. England was long an exception to the trend, sometimes spectacularly so. English kings appear to have exercised an unusually close control of crime and disorder.[112] According to Patrick Wormald, a distinctive system originated around 900 in the watershed reign of King Alfred "the Great."[113]

Wormald contends that the West Saxon monarchy enjoyed a substantially higher degree of central control over law and order than its Continental contemporaries and, very possibly too, its Anglo-Norman successors. He adduces in support a wide and ingenious set of illustrations, starting with the provisions of the leges themselves, documents designed precisely to demonstrate this royal authority. He demonstrates the extraordinarily high proportion of extant case narratives that directly or indirectly concern nonpo-

111. The plethora of local regulations as to how to shout the hue suggested to Pollock and Maitland 1898 (ii.578–79) its voluntary and popular origins. II Cn 29–29.1 seems to be the first clear reference to a public duty enforced by the fine for *oferhyrnesse*. Before this, matters are less clear. VI As 3 is perhaps an ad hoc decision for special circumstances, but VI As 4, 8.3–4, show that London gildsmen were under obligation to pursue fugitives. It is not clear whether III Em 2 is mandatory, and E Gu 6.6 = II Cn 48.2 ("mid hearme"), which some twelfth-century readers ("cum clamore") equated with the hue, is for a special case. See, for brief discussion, Liebermann 1903–16, ii.465–66.

112. James Campbell does not mince words in Campbell 1995a. He sees no paradox in the currency of the "idea that there was something especially free about England" within a "state . . . in which . . . crime [was] severely punished" (49). Campbell 1995b builds on this structure with further, telling examples.

113. The following summary of one possible maximalist position was initially constructed before the appearance of Wormald 1999. The exact nuances of Wormald's position will only become clear with the publication of his second volume. Campbell's version differs from his most importantly in its greater stress on the state system's very ancient roots rather than on Alfredian innovation (Campbell 1995a, 43–45).

litical "crime."[114] He documents the impact of increased recourse to capital punishment in the appearance of recognizable "execution cemeteries" from about 900 onward, just about the same time the king began to take forfeitures for an ever-increasing range of serious offenses.[115] Lesser sanctions sharpened alongside, until pecuniary fines could destroy a convicted man's social standing. Much as in ninth-century Francia, where many of the ideas originated, this wide authority over "crime" was founded on the obligation of all free men from the age of twelve upward to swear an oath of fidelity.[116] This committed them to keep the peace, to turn suspects over to the public courts for justice, or to ride them down for the king. The oath sought a positive commitment of the king's men in his cooperative enterprise. It also converted their offenses and defaults into perjury, an offense against God that drew spiritual penalties as well as secular punishment. Further positive reinforcement was achieved through police regulations by which each man of repute was to find himself a surety (*borh*), to guarantee his good behavior and/or court appearances, and to join the police associations of tithing and hundred. Wormald has marshaled the evidence in unprecedented force. Cnut's second law code argues strongly for the existence of a conscious system of royal law enforcement in the years before 1066, the solid substance behind Norman references to the good old "Laga Eadwardi."

But Wormald further argues that the system's origin in essentials dates back at least to Æthelstan's time and perhaps even to that of Alfred himself.[117] He associates the changes in peace maintenance with a new and much strengthened ideology of royal justice. Churchmen taught the king that he had to punish breaches of faith or risk God's anger. Reformers like Archbishop Wulfstan pleaded in their writings for royal leadership of a

114. Wormald 1988 (280) estimates that four out of five law suits concerned "crime." In Wormald 1992 (62) he notes from Domesday Book thirty-seven forfeitures "for what passed as crime" alongside only twenty-nine other cases from the twenty years separating the Domesday Inquest from the Conquest. These calculations are made from his own deliberately strict criteria of inclusion, explained in Wormald 1988 (250–55) and 1992 (62 sq.). Anyone who opted for "looser" criteria, my own preference, would slightly lower the percentage but not materially change the picture. I avoid "crime" words myself, for reasons I explain in chap. 5.

115. Wormald 1988 (278–79) summarizes the evidence for what he calls in Wormald 1999 (306–7) "a new approach to crime." It is striking that these forfeitures went in the first instance to the king. This was not the later solution, which accorded forfeitures in due course to the lords from whom the offender had previously held his lands. Even if kings swiftly regranted all such lands, as often appears, in the manner of the later German custom of *Leihezwang*, the arrangements attest to substantial royal authority and control. Reynolds 1999 (105–10) usefully surveys the evidence for execution cemeteries.

116. Text in Stubbs 1913, 73, and echoed in III Em 1. The term *fealty* carries too much late medieval baggage for my taste; I might prefer *loyalty*, as does Wormald 1999, but follow the usage of Susan Reynolds.

117. The attempted royal takeover of sanctuary (discussed earlier) may be added to the evidence.

Christian people. Their new ideology not only permitted but positively commanded royal intervention. The result was an ideal of royal responsibility for a public justice considerably more assertive than that found anywhere else in eleventh-century Europe. In the circumstances, it is easy to understand the effective absence from England of the Continental peace movement, which substituted partial episcopal protection of selected classes of the population for potentially full royal authority over all.[118]

Taken together, these data argue compellingly for a high degree of royal authority and control in the maintenance of law and order by the king qua king. We have seen already a shift in the character of the existing law books from the tenth century on. The lynchpin for the whole structure of public justice under the king was the oath of fidelity, whose first appearance, right at the beginning of Alfred's law code, marks a huge leap forward in the claims of royal justice. "First," the king is made to say, "we direct what is most necessary, that each man keep his oath and pledge [að 7 wed]."[119] Wormald cites Carolingian parallels from the previous century and deploys English evidence to suggest that *this* oath was specifically royal and state-like.[120] The "að 7 wed" tag reappears in a variety of tenth- and eleventh-century contexts. At least from Wulfstan's time it integrates the secular legal obligations of the laws into a broader Christian schema of salvation. Wormald's contention, that because the texts are all so similar they must from the start have conveyed the same message, nicely supports his perception of Alfred's reign as the moment of change. But I am not yet myself quite persuaded to abandon the view that the original intent was to promote fidelity in the general sense and only later sharpened by reforming clerics like Wulfstan to single out loyalty to the king.

During the century and a half that separates Alfred from the Norman Conquest, royal action against offenses marked out as especially serious visibly intensifies right across the board. Fiscal and corporal sanctions strengthened. Theft (especially cattle theft, rustling) became a dominant concern of the leges, which say less about compensation payments to victims and more about what was due to God and the king. By the eleventh century, the king and his draftsmen were loudly calling for communal action against thieves and some other types of offender, with afflictive punishment, including death, awaiting those caught.

This is a masterly piece of imaginative scholarly reconstruction. Yet the

118. Cowdrey 1970 remains a useful summary conveniently constructed from an English viewpoint. See, further, Head and Landes 1992.

119. Af 1.1. The translation is Whitelock's from *EHD* I.

120. Wormald 1999 (283) signals an argument reserved for chap. 9 of his vol. 2. Campbell 1982 (162) and Keynes and Lapidge 1983 (306) already convey the documentary bones of the case.

sparseness of the documentary foundations on which all tenth- and eleventh-century arguments rest precludes finality. Our current picture of England, allegedly the most powerfully organized "state" of its time nevertheless falling victim to two foreign invasions in the course of the eleventh century, remains a paradox awaiting elucidation. As Wormald concedes, better narratives, if we possessed them, would certainly reveal more of the power struggles (and feuds) that must certainly lie behind the leges. The key interpretative issue is, then, to find convincing justification for the leap from the prescriptions of a Wulfstan for Christian kingship to the will of the king himself, and from legislative aspirations to the achievements of power. My reluctance to accept the whole maximalist hypothesis rests in part on the absence of a royal technology of power to facilitate the implementation of the king's orders far from his physical presence. Enforcement of the royal will remained problematic much later.[121] Granted that the population and bounds of the West Saxon monarchy were much smaller than in Tudor times, our confidence that royal commands first reached their targets, then convinced them to obey, requires a certain suspension of disbelief. One would expect some resistance from an Old English nobility whose calculations of self-preservation and interest cannot always have coincided with the wishes of royal advisers.

OLD ENGLISH LITIGATION IN A FEUD CULTURE

I shall try to explain and seek to justify my skepticism through a couple of thought experiments that start from the options of an "average" disputing thegn in some shire far from the royal court. Even the local courts were public and royal in a much more obvious sense than any contemporary equivalent across the Channel. What then was this average thegn's normal response to a court summons? Did he always feel that he must jump to obey?[122] Only rarely can the king have been aware of local court cases. Our thegn might calculate the odds of the king getting round to mounting an expedition against him if he refused or simply ignored the order. At moments of palpable national crisis, or if the king were close at hand or particularly

---

121. Elton 1972.

122. Leyser 1981 considers this point for tenth-century Germany but goes on to argue a somewhat maximalist case. Old English knows a *fyrdwite* (for default of military obligation) but no *motwite* for court default. Scholars say little of the circumstances in which *fyrd* default brought about property forfeiture or worse. See Hollister 1962, 22–23, 29, 66 sq., 96; John 1966, 139–40; Abels 1988, 19, 114, 124–27. The literature on contumacy and contempt of royal commands in general is still thinner. Keynes 1980 (136–37) cites from Ælfric 1967–68 (ii.659) a most suggestive *exemplum* concerning a thegn's refusal of a royal *gewrit*. There are whole groups of texts in the leges on *oferhyrnes* and on the king's grants of hand-given peace, but no obvious Old English sources for the much clearer *LHP* 10.1, 13.1, 79.2.

dear to him, he might perhaps obey. But it is not obvious that the average thegn would defer to a single expression of royal will about run-of-the-mill events on *his* patch.[123]

Now consider such a thegn with a grievance of his own. In what circumstances will he sue in the hundred court prior to a time-consuming appeal to the distant king?[124] Most medieval noblemen in trouble or faced by an enemy thought first of self-help. It is hard to believe that the English thegn was any different. At best he sought out some accessible counterpower to make the best bargain he could for protection from justice.[125] Consider in this context the declaration made by early eleventh-century judges of the Hampshire county court about the undesirability of pressing suits to their logical conclusion in the proof-oath: "better set the oath aside . . . because thereafter would be no friendship."[126] Even here in the immediate circle of the king himself, local political circumstances were normative, concord (that is, a deal or consent settlement) preferable to judgment.[127] And if judgment in a conventional lawsuit was so dangerous to future expectations of peace at the micropolitical level, how much more disturbing might the actual execution of a well-connected thegn prove?

One may therefore doubt how frequently the swingeing provisions of the leges could have been enforced against the powerful. And if indeed most cases of full afflictive punishment concerned small fry, real nobles may, like their twelfth-century successors, have suffered at most outlawry and temporary exile, except for political offenses. Our exiguous evidence of justice in practice at least shows that a convict's friends would try to buy him off the death sentence when they could.[128] We cannot know how often they succeeded, but our cases document an attitude that influence was always worth trying because everything was potentially negotiable. Then again, anyone who knew the king personally and managed to reach him presented him with awkward political choices simply by throwing himself onto the royal mercy. This is the implication of enactments that seek to screen just this access.[129] All medieval law experienced difficulty in dealing with the great. The main political constant was the shadow of the future, the awareness of

---

123. Keynes 1990 (78–80) gives details of two cases of thegnly resistance to royal commands, which he does not see as "instances of problems peculiar to Æthelred's reign."

124. He should. See n. 89 above.

125. II As 3 tried to deal with the "dominus qui rectum difforciabit et malum hominem suum manutenebit."

126. Robertson 1956, no. 66, p. 136, with a slightly different translation.

127. See Keynes 1992, 96: "[Helmstan] emerges as a king's thegn who twice committed theft, but who with a little help from his friends managed to survive and even to redeem himself from . . . outlawry."

128. Wormald 1988, nos. 154, 171, 173. Cf. Kennedy 1995, 152.

129. II Em 4; V Atr 29; VI Atr 36.

king and nobility that each needed the other and would have to accept each other's company for the foreseeable future. It seems unlikely that the quantum of actual royal coercive power over the politically significant minority was adequate to sustain a wholeheartedly maximalist regime.

Even if it were, the designation of Alfred as originator of the system looks questionable. His greatness largely resided in the political skill and hard effort with which he gained and kept the loyalty of the thegns on whom he relied for the defense and extension of his kingdom.[130] In desperate times, kings needed as many carrots as sticks for their nobles. If English politics looked especially bloody to eleventh-century Norman observers, that blood may have been spilt at least as often in private feud as at royal command.[131] In this perspective, the political actors' justifiable fear of bloody retribution from above looks almost as much an extension of private competition as an index of a special royal coercive authority. In this view, the king, for all his occasional sacral aura, must sometimes have figured in the competitive game of factions and support groups as just one more especially powerful player, another "big man" as the anthropologists say.

The quite substantial Old English evidence for individual prosecutions of wrong, "appeals" in the Continental and post-Conquest sense, tends to support such a position.[132] Appeals, in everything except their (French) name and their characteristic dénouement of trial by battle, undoubtedly figured prominently in pre-Conquest law. We have no way to know what proportion of the "wrong" market they covered. But the higher that proportion was, the more confidently we may guess that thegns and others viewed the public courts and their justice instrumentally as an extension of a feud-based system of private redress for personal wrongs. The clearest case may also have been the most common. The victim of theft had the right to set off in hot pursuit of his thieves, summoning neighbors and bystanders to help. Capture red-handed permitted immediate execution.[133] Knowing this, escaping thieves did not stay around to discuss the matter and sometimes mustered their own support groups. Violence and pitched battles might ensue, from which feud and further potential violence could follow.[134]

130. See, for illustration, Nelson 1986.

131. The contrast between old-style English politics in the eleventh century ("a much rougher game than contemporary Norman politics") and the gradual chivalrization of Normandy is the main theme of Gillingham 1994. He takes as a given the persistence of open feud before the Conquest while conceding that there may have been an earlier move toward a more humane politics now reversed.

132. What follows is very much indebted to Kaye 1968 and to drafts of material that will reappear, perhaps much changed, in the second volume of Wormald 1999.

133. For this summary procedure involving no trial, see Goebel 1937, 347 sq., 357, 360, 367.

134. A relatively clear example is Wormald 1988, no. 54, recorded on a royal diploma of 992/95.

Even in the courts, individual initiative ruled. By far the most common pattern must have been for an individual to bring a plaint into court—that is, to tell his tale (Old English *talu*), support it by his oath, and thereby to put his own body (and those of supporting co-swearers) at risk, as security for the truth of his assertions.[135] This was not apparently done directly by an engagement to fight a proof duel in the way already familiar abroad and from Norman England later. Trial by battle seems, somewhat surprisingly, unknown to Old English law. Precisely how the complainant was at risk remains somewhat obscure, but life, limb, and unpleasant ordeals like the triple iron come to mind. The stakes rose for both parties as penalties for serious offenses increased in the course of the tenth century.

Almost all our texts confirm that individual accusation was the expected normal case. These include the special rules of the leges for suits against monks and other clerics,[136] and the reading of Old English law at the beginning of the twelfth century by the author of the *Leges Henrici Primi*.[137] This individual suit (or appeal), like the often-repeated requirement to begin all suits in the hundred court, was at the lowest a required preliminary on whose failure the king, now informed on the matter, might take decisive "public" measures.[138]

Scholars seem not to have noticed the best evidence for the ubiquity of this general pattern. It is late but convincing. It consists of a series of mysterious references in charters and elsewhere to someone called a *sacrabar*. Until 1969, an erroneous but authoritative theory held that this represented a Scandinavian "public prosecutor" operating in the Danelaw to screen court accusations.[139] The putative prosecutor has now been exposed as a fiction. The scattered references come from all over England and, when combined with other evidence of custom in the repression of violence and disor-

---

135. The unofficial treatise "Swerian" (Liebermann 1903–16, i.396–99) 2, 4, 6–7, together with II Cn 22.1a–2 and its many precursors, specifies the oath forms. Some of these forms committed irate complainants full of patent enmity to swear that they were not motivated by either hatred or friendship; the formula, "hete 7 hole," is a characteristic piece of Wulfstan's alliterative phrasing. All this raises some paradoxical questions and suggests one possible origin of the common-law writ *de odio et athia*, to be discussed in chap. 5.

136. IV Atr 23–25, I Cn 5.2b–c, and II Cn 39 are texts that strongly suggest that feud by and for the kin of priests and monks (and a fortiori laymen) was not unusual.

137. *LHP* 64 makes the basic case; see chap. 4 of this volume. Kaye 1966 (xxvii) takes it for granted that the individual appeal minus trial by battle already existed before 1066.

138. See II Cn 30 for the situation in which three men *ætgædere* accuse a *tyhtbysig*, someone of established evil reputation. Were these perhaps three separate accusations (in the manner that can be found in the later common law) rather than a communal prosecution supported by three co-complainants? It is routine in the thirteenth century for royal justices to order a jury to inquire for the king into allegations brought to the court's attention by a failed appeal.

139. Stenton 1964 (55–56, 124–37) expounds the fictional "pre-feudal . . . public prosecutor" of the local courts of eastern England first posited by her husband in 1927 from Steenstrup's 1882 suggestion. Kaye 1968 exploded the notion. Kennedy 1995 (159 n. 112) cites recent comment.

der, nicely document the general requirements for the prosecution of manifest theft and other wrongs.

The Old English word *sacrabar* perhaps meant case-bearer, that is, the man who brought and took responsibility for the accusation. The important underlying principle—that in all normal circumstances nobody be put to his defense except by an individual accuser or complainant subject to the same risks—was rehearsed as late as clause 38 of Magna Carta.[140] To put the accused to his proof, or in the case of manifest theft, to justify his execution (usually by beheading on the spot where he was captured), an individual complainant had to be present to proclaim his right and make his suit. Several points are important here. The principle was not restricted to manifest theft in the thirteenth century. It seems a general feature of all private suits (suits between party and party as we might say) that put a man to defense of life and limb, and was intended to protect men against the chance that their enemies might use public process to murder them under color of right. The eleventh-century safeguard was to compel the presence of an accuser to put his own life and limb literally behind his accusation in order to coerce a full defense by oath, ordeal, or other means. Without this, in a principle progressively abridged by royal legislation on men of ill repute,[141] the defendant might conclude the matter with a simple oath of denial, the blank denial of a later age. In the very different thirteenth century, when the courts were struggling to divide wrongs between crime and tort, either individual suit or presentment by court or jury established a case requiring answer, but the need to protect men from malicious prosecution by their enemies remained. Understandably the laws were compelled to consider the possibility that one side or other would wish to continue their enmity after an alleged execution by further litigation or by plain violence. What appears dimly through thirteenth-century texts must once, mutatis mutandis, have been eleventh-century practice. Theft was perhaps regarded at this stage as one kind of wrong within the same all-embracing conceptual bag as others.[142] This bag included, we should note, the "theft" of landed property.[143]

140. I sketched these distant origins of the U.S. Constitution's Sixth Amendment confrontation clause in Hyams 1999.

141. See n. 54.

142. It is not inconceivable that thefts might have been regarded as party-and-party matters (i.e., tort) on some occasions but at other times as matters of public moment, hence "crimes." Such dual perspective options were a feature of the common law from the thirteenth century onward.

143. This is Wormald's discovery. He noticed that Old English *reaflac*, generally translated as theft in some aggravated sense such as rapine or rapacity, could denote land seizures (Wormald 1997, 576–77, 588). Writers had in mind the serious kind of misbehavior that a king swore to prevent at his coronation and from which a judge must keep his ministers (Iudex 10, Sacr Cor 1.2, in Liebermann 1903–16, i.216, 475). Most instances of the word are general and unspecific, much like the kind of serious offenses in Continental lists of vicarial jurisdiction. See VIII Atr 4 = I Cn 3; II

The most common context for these *sacrabar* references was the pursuit and prosecution of manifest theft, two procedures with a more than etymological association in the eleventh century. The leges undeniably licensed, even required, the owner of rustled cattle to pursue his thieves if he could, with the help of his friends and neighbors. If they caught the malefactors red-handed, immediate private-enterprise retribution would follow, evidently on their say-so since there was no requirement for public trial. That they sometimes stretched the meaning of "hand-having" is all too likely. Kin of alleged thieves undoubtedly viewed some of these executions in quite different terms, as a shameful killing to be avenged. Their attempts to appeal at law or take revenge outside it are attested to by the laws.[144] Homicide was probably treated similarly. In the unusual case of "open *morð*," Cnut's laws require that the killer be handed over to the victim's kin, presumably for them to execute. Beyond supervising the ordeal, the king claims little part in the process.[145]

These few texts hint at a world of activity that supplements but does not necessarily contradict any maximalist interpretation. Men relied in the first instance on their own strength and the power of their connections to seek redress of wrongs. When they eschewed direct self-help as in open feud, they still followed much the same logic and patterns. They entered the courts in search of the same vengeance or honorable settlement that they and their ancestors had expected to achieve through the prosecution of feud. Prudent kings may well have encouraged important men to act in this manner. Self-serving kings cultivated support groups of their own friends much as other noblemen did,[146] but sought to restrain lesser men from their enmities, to bring them into "their" courts, where they could act as royal judge and pacifier. Litigation is politics by other means.

But kings were peacemakers as well as warlords and emblems of down-

---

Cn 47 (where it is associated with *wiflac* = Latin *raptus*), 63, and more generally Liebermann 1903–16, ii.181. Robertson 1956, no. 24, a manuscript anathema, nicely illustrates the level of disapproval. But *LHP* 57.7a, 7c, patently includes land seizures, as does Robertson 1956, nos. 59 (p. 122, l. 24), 63 (p. 130, l. 6; and cf. p. 128, l. 16), while Robertson 1956, no. 66 (p. 136, l. 28), is only slightly less clear. ÆTHELWOLD V. LEOFSIGE seems to illustrate the offense. I consider the implications of this conceptualization for the theory of a "criminal" origin to the assize of novel disseizin in chap. 5.

144. See n. 39.

145. For the owner's satisfying privilege of acting as sacrabar-executioner, see Pollock and Maitland 1898, ii.160, 496. The precise date at which *morð* took this meaning of secret killing is problematic; see further Kaye 1967, 366–67; O'Brien 1999, 79. Note that when "open *morð*" (which I take to mean secret killing come to light) was proved, the convict was handed over to the victim's kin, presumably for execution, with the king's role being less than the bishop's; see II Cn 56, and also for ordeals, II Cn 53, 53.1.

146. The esteemed lawgiver, Cnut, certainly acted thus in EARL UHTRED'S FEUD. See chap. 1.

ward justice. Some rulers, committed by their coronation oaths to stand up for peace and against *reaflac*-like iniquities, took their duties as seriously as they could, given the harsh, often violent micropolitics of the court in which a king was also a player. The king was as well equipped to pursue his goals by brokering deals as by other routes. Men would remind him of this when he forgot. He ought normally to possess more prestige and clout than any rival. All the factors that support the king as adjudicator also assist his peacemaking. Analogues from better-documented periods later indicate that this peacemaking could have been a significant feature of politics and law in the late Old English state.[147]

Let us speculate further along feud-inspired lines. All lords, kings included, who fail to keep the peace and protect their own inevitably lose authority and standing. Each therefore has an obvious and strong interest to quell damaging conflict within his own following, among his own supporters. Each must decide whether to join forces with one party to bring the other to heel, or try (more attractively) to knock heads together and broker acceptable face-saving settlements that conserve both men's service. Blessed are the peacemakers, for they shall save face. Thus, in some respects, royal interests differed little from those of other lords in their realm, outside the context of the distinctive promises they made at their coronation.

To illuminate the likely importance of this widely occurring pattern, let me again posit our average reasonable thegn nursing one more grievance against a rival too powerful for private action.[148] He needs a comparable *potens* on his side. His best option may be to call upon a lord for the aid to which their mutual hold-oath already committed each of them in principle. But to persuade a great man to hate as his man hates, as the oath of fidelity put it, will be difficult when the object of hatred is another follower; no lord can easily take over the feud for one of his men against another. A more promising line tries to evoke that love of what he loves and spur one's lord to assume the responsibility for the restoration of concord or love among all his men. With decisions to make, the prudent lord will wish to consult other interested parties, peers of the disputants and others. The complainant and his friends make their plaint, then his adversary counters, each in as persuasive an epic style as he can muster. The lord and the rest of his men then try to make a peace on the basis of their own view of distributive justice, giving to each what they are felt to deserve in order to restore balance within the lordship. The process, politics as much as rhetoric, may be harsh and crude.

147. As discussed earlier and in chap. 6.
148. See Leis Wl 26; Pollock and Maitland 1898, i.464.

Ritual humiliation may be demanded to compensate for past misdeeds and much wealth change hands. Yet the underlying structure of the proceedings is quite familiar to legal historians. An aggrieved man makes a plaint to his lord that he has been wronged, petitioning for a grant of redress. Edward the Confessor even granted written privileges to monasteries, prohibiting anyone to do them wrong, an act without meaning unless he was prepared in principle to do them justice against those who did not heed his warning.[149] This looks for all the world like the warm body later mummified in common-law jury trials as the action of trespass for damages.

It begins to look as if the late Old English state contained almost all the elements of the later Angevin system for the maintenance of order, absent only that crucial distinction between crime and tort that has always seemed intrinsic to the common-law solution. These individual "appeals" to king or lord sprang from a sense of wrong pursued in a form that varied according to circumstances. In every case, complainants increased their chances of a strong, positive response by showing that what was involved fitted a known character of serious offense, the kind for which kings, reeves, and judges hanged and beheaded lesser men. Were these not crimes in the later sense? It is hard to ascertain how contemporaries thought about the matter. Churchmen certainly possessed biblical models of crime, but most people probably used the more undifferentiated conceptualization of wrongs still visible in the twelfth century.

The argument here challenges us to reread the corpus of Old English legal narratives,[150] restore some of the silences of the leges, and also something of the lost dynamics of Old English society. Anglo-Saxon royal commitment in principle to ostentatious justice is not in question. Kings were responsible for many land forfeitures and a host of shamed execution corpses. Even if few really great men were punished for nonpolitical offenses, as I suspect, this pitch for control of downward justice remains impressive. Few Continental kings claimed as much. Old English downward

149. Harmer 1952, nos. 12, 114, 116. Twelfth-century writs to a similar end used the Latin word *iniuria* where the Old English draftsmen referred to *unriht* or *unlagu*, but the aim is patently the same. These Old English terms (and *bearm*) were available for use by the common law at the time when the French *trespas* became the preferred term of art.

150. Wormald 1997 (562–63, 572) accepts that "lawsuits are not peaceful antithesis to feud, but an alternative . . . way of pursuing similar objectives . . . concerned with upholding a party's sense of its place in society, its honour," but finds "few instances of . . . informal or ad hoc adjudication." The highly exclusive criteria he adopted in his studies of these narratives are unfortunate. So much depends on the way the story is recounted. Often a major value of these "unilateral memoranda" is that they present the point of view of one gloating or resentful party. Our reading needs to allow for both the very different opposition views and the crucial choices of when to start and stop the "story."

justice already comprised in the eleventh century many features that went to shape notions of crime in our Anglo-American common law.

But effective kings can possess high claims and real powers over the life and death of those they can reach, without their regime approximating an autocracy or a totalitarian state. The task of government at a distance was infinitely harder in eleventh-century Europe when the technology of domination was so much weaker than today. We are thus left with an impossible task: to strike a balance between private and royal initiative in the prosecution of wrong, from utterly inadequate data.

My main contention in this chapter has been that all this undeniably royal authority operated within a culture permeated and informed by a resistant notion of direct personal action against perceived wrong. A treaty with the Danes from the 990s simply assumes that there will be enmities within both camps; each agreed not to harbor the other's enemies.[151] In the century before 1066, resentful men avenged themselves with blood when they could. They might with difficulty be persuaded to accept the honorable alternative of a peace negotiated with due concern for their acknowledged social status and standing in the community. One could work to pacify even the hottest feud in this way. Yet litigants entered public courts almost as deeply imprinted with thoughts of feud and vengeance as did the men and women of Icelandic sagas. Rancor at wrongs, real and imagined, colored their understanding of their law codes; no modern prejudice for the "rule of law" existed to stop that. To twelfth-century legal writers as to me, their individual lawsuits looked like the Norman "appeal." They pressed them when they thought they could achieve their ends by open, public demonstration of the wrong they had suffered. When they doubted their chances of courtroom success, they did not seek their day there, for participation from childhood (the age of twelve) in the functioning of the public legal system had taught all men that failure could be taken literally out of their hide. Self-help through direct action then became an option. If this seemed beyond their resources, they might seek aid from a lord (old or new), either to avenge their wrong against an outsider or to broker an honorable settlement with some peer. Nobody doubted the vast differences within this range of apparent options. Sensible men pondered the options with their friends at length before reaching for their spears. I doubt that Englishmen or their womenfolk compartmentalized these options. But they were not content to leave

---

151. II Atr 6.2, and cf. 6–6.1. This clause's discussion of breach of the treaty's peace (*friðbræc*) distinguishes carefully between the special political enmity that the treaty was designed to resolve and the routine domestic enmities that required vengeance or their own peace settlements.

the violence option to the forces of evil. The fact that many actions thought respectable, legitimate, and rational in the eleventh century were ruled by the later common law (again literally) out of court must not be allowed to distort our understanding of the treatment of wrong in late Anglo-Saxon England.

CHAPTER FOUR
VENGEANCE AND PEACEMAKING
IN THE CENTURY AFTER THE
NORMAN CONQUEST

M ost modern studies of the hundred years after 1066 ignore the existence of feud. The historiographical focus has remained largely on constitutional and cultural progress toward that precocious centralization of government of which English historians once boasted but now lament. There is still something to be said for this more conventional approach. To frame Anglo-Norman England against a succeeding "Angevin leap forward" remains valid; however, the period stands to gain from examination through the eyes of victims and purported victims, claimants and litigants. That process may well modify our valuation of the Angevin law reforms themselves, mute the applause, and deepen our understanding of how and why the changes were possible. Beginning with this chapter, my treatment of data is more selective because of the ever-expanding volume of evidence. I assume the conventionally recognized case for progressive centralization without attempting to restate it.

The real challenge is to establish that the urge to vengeance should figure prominently in the story. I can then demonstrate how this urge affected the general culture and helped to shape both English law and the various arrangements for peacekeeping. Therefore I begin with an assessment of the relevant ways in which the Norman Conquest did or did not change English approaches to the treatment of wrong. I single out two special witnesses, the historian Orderic Vitalis and the author of the so-called *Leges Henrici Primi*, for closer interrogation about their views in the first decades of the twelfth century. I then proceed to demonstrate a virtually ubiquitous belief in vengeance among laymen and laywomen and a range of ecclesiastical responses to this. Lest the beliefs seem confined to theory, I set out a series of vengeance anecdotes from real life, showing (1) that some of the direct action approximated to feud, and (2) that this understanding nicely illuminates several familiar phenomena of twelfth-century public life. The chapter ends with an exposition of the notion of "undifferentiated wrong," which, I argue, remained central to dispute resolution and most law in the age preceding the common law.

Among recent attempts to reestablish the Conquest as a cultural caesura, the series of remarkable, probing articles by John Gillingham is particularly pertinent to the present purpose.[1] For him, 1066 marks a genuine sea change in sensibility. William's Frenchmen brought with them chivalry, "a secular code of values . . . in which a key element was the attempt to limit the brutality of conflict."[2] They were more humane and civilized than the somewhat backward English.[3] One central test of this new humanity examines the way these peoples treated their enemies. Specifically, the question is: Did Frenchmen continue to kill enemies whom they had at their mercy in the way that had been traditional almost everywhere one looks in early medieval Europe? The answer, it turns out, is that it depended on who these enemies were. It would be foolish perhaps to expect Normans, heirs in their conquests to the terrifying Vikings of yore, to outlaw all killings other than those committed in hot blood. Instead they narrowed the field for approved killing to spare the people most like themselves, to retain their captives' costly war equipment but ransom their lives for what they could get. This approach made sound economic as well as political sense with equals who could be restrained from future aggression by depleting their resources so severely that they could not easily afford to take up arms again for a while. It also earned them applause from admiring ladies and the clerics in charge of their souls. But all this was for equals only. It heralded the advent of a new chivalry of knightly peers from France and the Francophone-dominated European continent (joined in a noble fraternity with a long future extending perhaps into the distant Europe of 1914, as depicted in Jean Renoir's *Règle de jeu*).

Excluded from this exploitative compassion was a vast newly defined "Other" of men who could not expect to merit equal treatment. This category included unbelievers, slaves, and the Celtic peoples of the countries bordering conquered England.[4] William of Malmesbury and Orderic Vitalis were the first major English writers to observe and register these subtle

1. The important pieces are Gillingham 1992a, 1992b, and 1994. Each of these builds on but also realigns his earlier work. I hope for a full synthesis in due course.
2. Gillingham 1994, 32.
3. Needless to say, Wormald 1997 (560–61) disagrees. Searle 1988, esp. chaps. 14–15, sees the eleventh-century Norman nobility as very much into feuding loosely defined.
4. Gillingham 1992a; 1994, 43–44.

ideological changes, and can be seen gradually formalizing their observations into something like a new understanding of barbarian.[5] This new barbarian "Other" could claim no right to mercy; the constituent members lacked the required common humanity.

This important categorization became associated with other better-known developments such as the twelfth-century rise of humanism and the emergence of a courtly ethos. Gillingham makes many sophisticated suggestions to explain the links. Most germane to the present point is the way in which this distinction between a civilized "us" and the barbarian "them" cleared space for the equally new code of chivalry and its associated ethic of restraint. In Gillingham's view, this is largely incompatible with a feud mentality: "Societies in which secular nobles regard the blood feud as acceptable were, in my view, unchivalrous."[6] Gillingham deals mainly with political evidence on great men and great events. Nevertheless, because he has no reason to draw sharp lines between royal wars and private enmities, his arguments carry far-reaching implications for the contentions of this book. Indeed, his conclusions might seem to exclude feud behavior and thought from twelfth-century England. Certainly I shall bear his ideas in mind throughout this chapter.

PENAL TERMINOLOGY

A good place to begin the analysis is with the mare's nest of Anglo-French penal vocabulary after 1066, precariously balanced among three relevant languages—Latin, French, and English. In an interesting study that deserves better recognition, J. P. Collas observes that there was at the time of the Norman Conquest something of a "penal void" in the French language.[7] On neither side of the Channel were there good French terms with which to describe the imposition of penalties. The Latin transitive verb *mulctare*, for example, with the sense of a financial penalty, had by this time been lost and never succeeded in entering the medieval Romance languages. Francophone Englishmen did eventually develop a way to express what we call "fines" through the transitive verb *amercier* with its corresponding noun *amercement*. The notion that an offender might place his life and limbs at

5. See Wormald 1997 (554) for some ninth-century sources not explicitly mentioned by Gillingham.
6. Gillingham 1994, 33. But Gillingham 1992b, 78, cites advice to the young Parzifal that explicitly licenses vengeance for a "mortal wrong," which clearly means feud. Difficulties with the cited translation do not affect the main point, that vengeance killing is licit for a very chivalrous knight. Some of the many indications in thirteenth-century literature that *inimicitia mortalis* and vengeance were very much part of the culture of chivalry were canvassed in chap. 2.
7. Collas 1964, xv, xvi.

the mercy of a king and then have to wait to learn on what terms he might be permitted to save them seems especially appropriate to a conquest situation. William should have possessed on such occasions all the cards for exacting heavy penalties or imposing peace on disputing parties, as he preferred.[8] The temptation to associate the vocabulary with the first generation of Norman occupation must, however, be resisted. First, such situations of abasement were not unknown in Anglo-Saxon times.[9] Second, the end result was ordinarily a modest money payment or fine. Collas argues on linguistic grounds for a development too protracted and complex for the Old English *wite* to have played any great part in the story. He cannot see the emergence of amercement in its common-law usage until the later twelfth century.[10] This sets the changes down very close to the Angevin innovations in law enforcement that I discuss in chapter 5.

More narrowly historical arguments suggest an explanation for Collas's linguistic findings. Consider the mystifying evidence for William I's abolition of capital punishment, a spectacularly unlikely achievement for the conqueror of an occupied and resisting nation.[11] Gillingham shows that neither Norman law nor twelfth-century English practice appears to favor the application of the death penalty to nobles.[12] He does not consider in any detail the post-Conquest tradition for William's merciful substitution of mere mutilation.[13] The legislative authority for this view is not only of uncertain date, provenance, and authority but also strongly reflects Old English enactments pressing the need for royal mercy, more especially the need to permit offenders to repent before death.[14] One possible explanation is, in fact, the reflection of the violence of the Conquest itself. Nostalgic retrospection to the good old days showed that kings and their advisers were more aware of their obligation to respect bodies redeemed at such cost, as their laws expressly said, by Christ's Atonement.

Historians, I think, should not overemphasize the occasions when chroniclers laud William for choosing to allow his rebels to keep their skins intact. That those convicted of serious offenses might on occasion bargain successfully for their lives marks no great change from the pre-Conquest realities.

---

8. I discuss royal peacemaking further later in this chapter and in chap. 6.

9. Wormald 1997 (561–62) makes this point. Althoff 1997 describes in the contemporary German *deditio* what is evidently the source of our behavior pattern.

10. Collas 1964, xxv–xxxi. Hurnard 1969 (12–13) took a somewhat different view.

11. Pollock and Maitland 1898, i.88–89; cf. Wormald in Hudson 1996b, 14.

12. Gillingham 1992b, 82.

13. "Hic Intimatur," clause 10 (Liebermann 1903–16, i.488), on which see Wormald 1999, 402–5.

14. V Atr 3; VI Atr 10; II Cn 2.1, 30.5. The Anglo-Norman compiler seems to have combined the two provisions of Cnut. See also from the twelfth-century II Inst Cn 20.2.1, which adds the intriguing words "ne culpe inulte remaneant"; and Leges Wmi 40.

There is certainly no sound evidence for routine commutation of death to any standard payment resembling the thirteenth-century amercements at this stage. That institutionalization of *misericordia* makes better sense where Collas's arguments place it, in the later twelfth century as routine royal justice began to reach men far below noble rank.

Gillingham's vision of a softening of shared mores obviously carries important implications for the evolution of afflictive punishment over the longer term.[15] It is not clear that the break comes at the Conquest. We therefore need to examine further the extent to which 1066 did indeed mark a cultural caesura in the respects most relevant here.

CULTURAL CONTINUITY ACROSS THE NORMAN CONQUEST

Prima facie, it seems unlikely that the advent of the Normans would change the ethos of vengeance and punishment in any very abrupt manner. Eleventh-century Normandy was culturally similar to its neighbor across the Channel. Frenchmen too sought their vengeance for the wrongs they suffered, and conceptualized their rights in much the same feud-like way we found to be normal to the Old English situation. It would be surprising if the Normans contradicted the ethos of the French literature they read or heard on both sides of the Channel. Moreover, conquests encourage the victors to compete for the spoils and demand care to guard against attempts at vengeance from losers.[16] The Conquest certainly offered William and his sons the opportunity to realize more of the aspirations toward central justice voiced in the leges than Old English kings had perhaps managed for themselves. This must surely have been one of the attractions that drew them across the Channel. How much success the Normans had is another matter. Whereas some scholars would locate here the amalgamation of the Old English practices of surety and tithing into the medieval system of frankpledge, others believe that this step had already been taken before 1066.[17] They see the *murdrum* fine as an existing procedure to protect aliens from murder by native Englishmen that William extended for the benefit of his Frenchmen.[18] Although these puzzles are not soluble with

15. The contention of Gillingham 1992a (400–401), that the twelfth-century contrast between England and its neighbors deemed "barbarian" stemmed from a socioeconomic gap, seems debatable. Because England already enjoyed a similar advantage before 1066, while Normandy did not, the determinants appear more likely to have been cultural than economic.

16. Liebermann already noticed that feud remained a factor of which twelfth-century legislators had to take account. Liebermann 1903–16, ii.266, 320.

17. Hudson 1996a (61–66) follows Wormald in assigning an Old English origin to Frankpledge.

18. Most recently O'Brien 1999 (77–80) argues persuasively for a pre-Conquest origin to the *murdrum* fine, as does Cooper, forthcoming (on slightly different grounds).

full certainty, I suspect that the conquering Normans inherited a system ripe for exploitation from the top.

But all the evidence suggests that when their own individual interests were at stake, they approached the law courts in quite as instrumental a frame of mind as did their English predecessors. The law's potential for such use is amply illustrated by analysis of the feud materials in the *Leges Henrici Primi* (discussed later in the chapter), by case narratives from narrative sources such as the *Liber Eliensis*, and by incidents such as that which drew forth the Nunnaminster curse,[19] a textbook demonstration of how frustrated litigation can pave the way for recourse to extracurial sources of vengeance. In this context, private individuals continued to use the old ordeals in the Norman period.[20] And kings too often saw justice as a means to take their vengeance against wrongdoers,[21] justice exercised by virtue of the *ira regis* they were still expected to feel toward the enemies of the realm and themselves.[22] There is ample warrant here for the pursuit in Anglo-Norman culture of a higher degree of interest in vengeance for wrongs than a casual reader of Gillingham's work might expect. But the greater volume of available evidence enables a more nuanced approach. To this end, I initiate my inquiry with the assistance of two important contemporary witnesses, the author of the *Leges Henrici Primi* and the monastic chronicler Orderic Vitalis.

TWO SPECIAL WITNESSES

Orderic composed his major historical work, the *Ecclesiastical History*,[23] at various stages over the first third of the twelfth century. A Benedictine monk, he was obsessed with the goal of heavenly peace and wrote increasingly about a real world failing dismally to reflect this. He found the theme unavoidable, even in a work that had begun as an account of his own monastery. Human disorder affected ecclesiastical life at every point. His interest thus transcended the merely negative aspects of secular life. He probably started writing about laypeople to record their difficult

19. Hyams 1992 (4–5) quotes the curse and briefly elucidates the probable sequence of events over the decade leading up to 1086.
20. E.g., *Orderic* iii.160.
21. Eadmer 1884 (102) is a classic account of royal instrumental use of the ordeals and judicial process, if one accepts the story as told.
22. I argue in Hyams 1998 for the persistence of these licit displays of royal anger later than does Althoff 1998b in the same volume.
23. I concentrate here on the *Ecclesiastical History*, whose editor presents her own view of her author very succinctly in Chibnall 1984. Other helpful surveys can be found in Gransden 1974 (151–65) and more briefly by Lucien Musset in *Dictionnaire des lettres françaises* 1992 (1087–88). One could now extend the analysis with the aid of Van Houts 1992–95.

struggle to defend their turf on this earth without utterly destroying their chances of salvation into the world to come. But the narratives enthralled him and drew from him more positive sympathies. He was keen to depict the emotional forces working on men and women he knew personally, and whom he admired or disliked according to their treatment of his house or duchy. Beyond this, he was naturally affected by the sensibilities of his own day. The martial achievements of the First Crusade, for example, patently moved this cloistered monk too. He reveled in the anecdotes and legends soon to produce the first surviving written medieval romances. His focus is increasingly often on the duchy and its leaders, more especially on the struggles of William I's sons for domination over their father's heritage on both sides of the Channel. Orderic's accounts of these intrafamily combats highlight his longing for firm secular leadership and order in his own Christian commonwealth. He generally applauds instances of royal justice, including its periodic penal severity; correspondingly, he deplores the ducal weakness of Robert Curthose. He never appears to have felt any qualms over capital punishment. These firm conventional preferences for central justice corroborate the importance of his favorable spin on that avenging of wrongs that is my main interest here. This shines out from his work almost as if against his will and greatly enhances his value as a witness.

My second special witness is thought to have been a bishop writing in the second decade of the twelfth century and thus conceivably within Orderic's circle of acquaintance. We know much less about him, and little beyond what his legal treatise the *Leges Henrici Primi* tells us. Despite its title, the work carries no official authority, and historians have tended to use it as a convenient Latin entrée into Old English law, without going too deeply into its status.[24] Its close association with the large-scale translation of Anglo-Saxon law codes that provided its major vernacular sources should not be allowed to obscure its originality.

The hints of connections to the contemporary schools are one good index of this. The author often makes a real attempt to organize his material around Boolean distinctions of the "if . . . or . . . else" type. Although his efforts are, after the fashion of very early scholasticism, not always successful, his text merits comparison with *Glanvill* at the end of the century, once one sorts out the textual shuffling that sometimes obscures his plan.[25] His systematizing instinct—once insufficiently appreciated—is revealed clearly in

24. Wormald 1999 (411–14, 465–71, 473–74) is the major exception.
25. *LHP* 49.1 should, for example, be read within a group of clauses that goes back at least to clause 45 or further but has probably got out of order. Downer, in *LHP* 338, makes a good case for reading *LHP* 23.5–24.4 in a similar way.

his taxonomy of theft.[26] Such tasks were, at the beginning of the twelfth century, harder than they seem in hindsight. The intelligence and independence of our author's attempted classifications make him a good witness to the ways in which other intelligent people could, if they chose, read their leges in the twelfth century.

In the intellectual milieu of the early-twelfth-century "legal" writings available to an English bishop, his approach is truly original. The works we label "pseudo-Isidorian" deeply influenced Gratian and his canonistic predecessors. Although recent scholarship has advanced our knowledge of these older canonical collections, their influence on the later English scene has yet to be determined.[27] Our author clearly derives from pseudo-Isidore many of Western law's future principles on procedural protections in court.[28] But the many passages for which scholars have found no ancient sources, and the Old English enactments that the author demonstrably knew but ignored, are just as intriguing. Such conscious omissions enable us to tease out the author's canons of legal acceptability, his intent in writing, and some part of his vision of the world.[29] His worldview included an awareness that the urge to avenge wrongs was very widespread and often licit. Just how central that recognition was to his overall purpose requires further investigation.

The prefatory quotation of Henry I's coronation charter of 1100 removes any doubts that the author's ideal is one of central royal justice. The goal is peace,[30] for the protection of *pauperes* otherwise defenseless against evildoers unrestrained, malicious officials, and corrupt judges.[31] Frequently, the means is an emphasis on concord alongside judgment.[32] "True peace" is never an inappropriate goal, even at times when litigation is prohibited.[33] Yet once proceedings have begun before public justice, there is to be no

26. *LHP* 59.21–22.

27. Fuhrmann 1973 (i.229–32, ii.419–23) is the main witness. But see also Philpott 1993 and 1994.

28. *LHP* 48–49 can serve as illustration, but borrowings in this area are all over the book. I attempt a general account of the massively important medieval transformation of procedural protections in Hyams 1999.

29. The superb manuscript researches that lie behind Wormald 1994 and 1995 prove that the different leges circulated in blocks or clusters. When someone knows one part of the block, the chances are very high that he must know the other texts in it. This immensely strengthens the case that an omission might be a conscious choice.

30. *LHP* 3.1, 7.3a. I adduce some of the evidence for this important royal function of peace-making below.

31. *LHP* 7.2.

32. *LHP* 49.5a may get the sentiment "pactum enim legem vicit et amor iudicium" (alluded to also at 7.3a) from the genuine Isidore, who also perhaps inspired *Glanvill* x.14 (129). Cf. further *LHP* 54.2–3, 5; 57.1a. Hyams 1991a surveys forces bearing on peaceful agreements in the twelfth century.

33. But *LHP* 62.1–1a is rather less direct than its source, I Cn 17.2, and the divergence is especially marked in Latin translations that talk of *ira* or *inimicitia* for Old English *sacu*.

reconciliation without a license for which one party or the other must pay.[34] The absolute need to restrain lawlessness is restated in the strongest terms. "Justice and worldly coercion" are essential to divine laws as well as secular, "so that"—in true Weberian style—"the more serious offenses must be punished by the justice or mercy of the prince alone."[35] Every effort must be made to ensure that royal commands are obeyed.[36] Bootless offenses are a public concern.[37] Occasional Carolingian echoes that associate the repression of wrong with the sworn obligation of loyalty to the king, and recommend the adjournment of the hand-having thief's execution until royal officials are able to be present, confirm the underlying royal initiative.[38]

THE UBIQUITOUS BELIEF IN VENGEANCE

One might conclude from a first reading of the *Leges Henrici Primi* that private feelings about vengeance played little role in Anglo-Norman political culture. This would be a mistake. The conquering French were, as their descendants' entertainment literature shows, quite as likely to burn for revenge as were their English victims, and the spirit of the times was not such as to dissuade them. To illustrate this point, I offer evidence of attitudes toward the crusade and toward the Jews, and on the monks' own feelings with regard to their property.

We should do well to regard the crusade as the locus classicus for any demonstration of the positive values that could be set upon vengeance and enmity. "The crusade was at one level a war of vengeance," concedes a scholar known for his sympathy toward crusading ideals.[39] Many participants of the First Crusade in 1095 saw their enterprise in just such terms. The Turks had injured and dishonored Christ. His faithful followers should now avenge these injuries against His enemies, who thereby become theirs, too. The exact conditions of this holy feud differed; some felt they were

34. *LHP* 59.27. For Normandy, cf. *Très ancien coutumier* LV.1 (Tardif 1881, 44).

35. *LHP* 11.16–16a. Is there any comparably trenchant declaration of a royal monopoly of punishment from before 1066? See also *LHP* 1, 52, 53.2, 63.4.

36. See especially the references to *ouerseunessa* scattered throughout the text. *LHP* 53.1–1b shows the consequences of ignoring this, although it may soften the impact of its source (II As 20) and include private court-holders within its scope. Cf. also *LHP* 35–36 and note that this kind of text insisting on obedience is, as always, double-edged in its implications.

37. *LHP* 11.1a, 12.1a.

38. E.g., *LHP* 26.3, 30.1, but 55.3, 3b, appears to understand *fides* as applying to any lord and not just the king.

39. Riley-Smith 1984, 68–70; also Forey 1985, 185; and Tyerman 1988, 11–12, 34, 192. *Lancelot du lac* 1991–93 (ii.340) shows very clearly from ca. 1225 how this feud view of crusading could encourage the taking of vengeance against those who were deemed to have behaved as badly as a Saracen.

fighting on behalf of God Himself or because of the injury to Christ's person, others for the Eastern Christians. Not all chroniclers made the point as explicit as did Baudri of Dol when he told his readers, "If an outsider were to strike any of you down, would you not avenge your blood-relative? How much more ought you to avenge God, your father, your brother, whom you see reproached, banished from his estates, whom you hear calling . . . for aid?"[40] Orderic was certainly not averse to such reasoning. The vile Allah-lovers in the East deserved to have vengeance wreaked upon them. The crusade was a call to exercise "divine vengeance" by making war on God's enemies. Anyone who resisted truth and justice is to be called "God's . . . enemy," and good crusaders hated them all equally—Jews and heretics as well as Saracens.[41]

This last point is confirmed in the work of a brother Benedictine, Thomas of Monmouth, who began writing his life of Saint William of Norwich in about 1149–50, although he did not complete it until 1172–73.[42] He repeatedly presents the Jews of Norwich in such terms as "always enemies of the Christian name and religion." That there should be no doubt what this meant, he declared at one point that the hierarchy of saints in Heaven and the numerous army of martyrs stood ready to fight "tyrants and enemies of the Christian name in defense of the faith of Christ."[43] Those who aided the Jews felt God's anger and died before their time.[44] So natural did the need to avenge wrongs seem to Thomas that he was prepared to understand the Jews' own actions in similar terms. He retails the convert Theobald's myth of the annual sacrifice required by the Jews to explain their motive: "so that they might thus avenge their wrongs on Him for the sake of whose death they were excluded from their fatherland and exiled like *servi* into alien lands."[45]

Monks, although professed men of peace, may be eager customers for vengeance whenever their property comes under threat, for two reasons. First, the religious are especially vulnerable to invasion and coercion. They cannot in any normal circumstance fight fire with fire. So they are to be found first in line for royal justice but otherwise particularly dependent on supernatural sanctions.[46] Perhaps none of this should matter, since monks in

40. The translation is from Riley-Smith 1984. Fulcher of Chartres has the pope enunciate very similar sentiments in his speech at Clermont (Riley-Smith 1981, 41–42). On conceptualizations of God's feud, see further White 1996 (110, 126–29).
41. *Orderic* v.4, 16, 44, 320, 348; and cf. vi.124.
42. Jessopp and James 1896, on which see Langmuir 1984.
43. Jessopp and James 1896, 42, 43 sq., 63, 71.
44. Ibid., 111–12, 165–66. In favor of the first victim, the royal sheriff, there was little to be said, but Thomas had in many ways admired Prior Elias.
45. Ibid., 93.
46. Hudson 1994, esp. chap. 8.

their renunciation of the world vow also to abandon personal property. But their houses require endowments and hold these in the name of the saints to whom they dedicated their churches. It is the *saints* who resent their losses and may be ready to avenge them. Thus men sworn to peace and poverty pursue property and honor for their saints, not for themselves, and the results can be regarded as holy feuds.

In the 1070s, for example, it seemed to the monks of Bury that Bishop Herfast of Thetford thought he could ride roughshod over their charters under the impression that he could always buy his way out and divert Saint Edmund's vengeance.[47] Then one day while the malicious bishop was riding in the forest, a branch caught his eye and left him helpless, in pain, and facing at least partial blindness. The Bury monks at once recognized this as their saint's revenge, and one of them cheekily advised the bishop to seek the saint's aid, adding a strong hint that he would raise his chances of recovery if he also ended the litigation. The bishop came to Bury and was received with the solemnities due his episcopal status. The abbot then invited the royal justices who happened to be in Bury holding pleas to attend a special assembly in the vestry. Bishop Herfast there admitted that "he had sinned in word and will against God and Saint Edmund" and repudiated the counselors on whose advice he had committed the guilty acts. After this public confession, he proceeded in floods of tears to the high altar and deposited there his episcopal staff, in pledge both of his promise to restore the crosier at issue and also his hope for forgiveness from God and the martyr. He then performed the penitential ritual to gain pardon for sin. He prostrated himself beneath the altar and sang the seven penitential psalms while the abbot and brothers gave him formal absolution. It worked: he recovered his sight, although with a warning dimness in one eye. This omen was, alas, needed, for Bishop Herfast did not keep his word. When he tried to reopen proceedings, he was struck dumb at the hearing in the king's presence, which had the extra merit of ensuring the widest possible audience for the saint's vengeance and to warn all what to expect if they too wronged Saint Edmund.[48]

When the ethos of vengeance can be so easily documented in the world of monks, the quintessential men of peace, it follows almost beyond question that the secular evidence is even clearer and more abundant. Much of this has already been laid out in an earlier chapter. The urge to take vengeance reeks from every corner of twelfth-century French literature, romances as well as epic chansons de geste, and that literature seems as strongly repre-

47. Van Caenegem 1990–91, no. 9.
48. Ibid., nos. 217, 223, also illustrate the force of saintly vengeance within a litigation context. In each case, the fact of vengeance was perceived in retrospect, as may also have been true of the Bury case, whose details were recorded by a Bury monk, Herman.

sented on the English side of the Channel as beyond it.[49] The so-called epics of protest laud the recourse to private vengeance whenever royal justice failed to meet expectations, admittedly much more a French than an English theme at the time.[50] When English versions of these works and original English romances begin to appear, from the late twelfth century, attitudes toward vengeance are as prominent as in their French forbears.

It is always dangerous to deduce patterns of actual behavior directly from entertainment literature, but enough noble anecdotes exist to make one confident of a reasonable match between ideal and reality. I draw on many of these later in this volume, but a few samples can make the preliminary point. People usually knew when someone harbored a grudge or enmity against them or any mutual acquaintance. A knight in the 1070s told his lawyer of a previous occasion when he had needed a *saintly* defender against the Abbot of St. Augustine's, Canterbury, who had endeavored to disinherit him out of hatred. Robert de Mowbray expelled the monks of Durham from lands of theirs before 1121 "on account of a hatred he had against Bishop William."[51] Men hesitated to provoke such strong resentments for fear of physical revenge. Orderic explained Rufus's self-restraint after the revolt of 1095–96, for example, in this way. The king rewarded his friends but only fined most rebels, in the knowledge that their noble kinsmen could all too easily take vengeance in Normandy. Yet kings were in a stronger position than most to face down reactions of this kind. Orderic deduced from the "swelling fury of the Normans," which followed Rufus's death, that the "rigor of princely justice" had previously restrained much of the anger and malevolence he saw now being released in acts of violent revenge for past wrongs.[52] It was correspondingly important to publicize the end of an enmity so that all could draw the proper conclusions and repair the torn fabric of peaceful social life. The stage management of public reconciliations was not therefore confined to the most dramatic and violent of feud situations but rather was a common need frequently felt after more mundane disputes over property and the like.[53]

ECCLESIASTICAL RESPONSES TO AN ETHOS OF VENGEANCE

Another way to approach the secular ethos is to consider the good Christian critiques it inevitably provoked from churchmen. There were three obvious

49. Short 1992 virtually set the onus on the French to deny that their written literature was born in England.
50. Calin 1962.
51. Van Caenegem 1990–91, nos. 16, 223; cf. also no. 235 (1124).
52. *Orderic* iv.285, v.300.
53. Van Caenegem 1990–91, nos. 319, 343.

responses. First in logic comes outright condemnation, along lines already fully apparent in the New Testament. We have already seen that this could not be the whole or sole ecclesiastical reaction. Churchmen needed and believed in the licitness of divine feud—vengeance by, for, and on behalf of God and His saints. This was the second type of response. And there was also a middle way: to shelter those at the receiving end of attempts at vengeance, to try to restrain their pursuers, and to encourage the parties to come together and make peace. In this third response, churches offered sanctuary and sought to reconcile and make peace. The challenge that feud posed to churchmen's thinking is thus more nuanced and complex than one might expect. A pair of atypical case studies illustrates the way that ordinary religious too must at times have felt themselves to be between the proverbial rock and hard place.

Bishop Wulfstan of Worcester, the Old English prelate to survive longest and most successfully into the Anglo-Norman world, illustrates the different pulls unusually clearly. He preached peace in so exemplary a fashion as to attract that arch-proponent of religious peace, William of Malmesbury, to compile a life. Yet he was also a profound believer in the rightness of God's vengeance. Although we have unusually full information on his dilemmas, the doctrine with which he tackled them appears to be perfectly orthodox and fully representative of the best religious practice of his day.

His biographer describes peacemaking activities against violent feud through colorful anecdotes I have recounted and analyzed elsewhere.[54] The good bishop labored to persuade feuding brothers to reconcile with an (in his view) accidental killer. Nevertheless, in the last resort, he was prepared to threaten anathema (in effect, divine feud action) on the ground that their refusal to make peace placed them squarely in the camp of the Enemy of all, the Devil. His biographer, Coleman, had his own experience of peacemaking when deputizing for his bishop. The message of the *vita* seems clear and uncomplicated: good Christians should oppose all vengeance (along with its violent consequences) in order to raise their chances of achieving any semblance of heavenly peace in this world.

But this is too simple. When Wulfstan and others worked to counter feud by summoning up God's divine power against recalcitrant disputants, they were themselves buying into a version of the ethos of vengeance. Wulfstan's point is that to take personal vengeance against the ways of God is to become God's enemy and thus subject to the possibility of His divine feud.

54. *Vita Wulfstani* ii.15–16 (Darlington 1928, 38–40), on which see Hyams 1992, 2–4. Mason 1990 (269–75, 286–94) explains the relationship between Coleman's lost Old English *vita* and the extant Latin adaptation by William of Malmesbury.

The proper corollary is to declare with the Bible that "vengeance is the Lord's," and to leave it to His suprahuman judgment whether and how to take it. A resentful victim might hope that the Lord would choose him as an instrument of this divine vengeance. He had certainly better not oppose the divine will, whatever it might be.

Another anecdote that reinforces the point concerns the most powerful figure of the region around Worcester during the middle period of Wulfstan's episcopate.[55] Æthelwig, abbot of Evesham, was for a time after the Conquest the most important royal representative in the southwest Midlands. He naturally used some of this authority in his own interest. For example, he coerced some of Worcester's richer tenants into his lordship by a mixture of trickery, force, and persuasion—"Unde non minima altercatio." The monks of Worcester, disgusted at his pretense of protection against the threat of a Danish invasion, could do little beyond recounting their rights for the record. Even Wulfstan, a man often totally uninterested in secular business, had to respond to this contempt of his saint. Predictably, however, his efforts to deploy his fatherly authority as Æthelwig's bishop and confessor, or even to sue him, proved fruitless in the face of such well-organized secular power.

So it was that Æthelwig died without having done satisfaction for his wrong to Worcester and hence remained technically the monks' enemy. As one monk noted, he had neither paid the bishop nor been absolved by him.[56] Yet the saintly Wulfstan was so moved by the news of his death that he at once began to pray for Æthelwig's soul in good New Testament fashion. The result was that he was stricken with the same illness that had killed Æthelwig. Soon, despite the best efforts of his human doctors, he looked at death's door. Gradually Wulfstan came to recognize through prayer and vision that he had to cease praying for his enemy. At once and without human aid, he recovered his health. Hemming noted the appropriate lesson: when God opposes prayer for pillagers, He is showing us how serious a condemnation they deserve for invading monastic property. The historian can infer from this a monastic view that it was sinful to oppose divine vengeance on those who harmed God and His saints.

Christians had to avoid not vengeance per se but rather its appropriation into human hands.[57] Peacemaking ought, therefore, to have preoccupied

---

55. *Hemingi* 1723, i.270–73. Comment on the anecdote in Mason 1990, 122, 125–27; for Hemming, see further *Hemingi* 1723, i.294–95 and index, s.v. "Hemming." Also Smalley 1987, 47–48.

56. *Hemingi* 1723, i.272.

57. There are doubtless many other hints of the Byzantine subtlety with which the pious sometimes contemplated human anticipation of divine vengeance. Richard Abels brought to my attention Bede, "Aliquot Quaestiones Liber," on Rom. xii.19 and Deut. xxxii.35 in MPL 93, col. 457C. The exemplary story in Ailred of Rielvaux's life of Edward the Confessor, i.35 (MPL 195,

clerics; indeed, Wulfstan and his Worcester followers remain the best exemplars in the generations after the Conquest. Whereas the patterns and dynamics of feud anecdotes suggest generalized clerical peacemaking, the relative dearth of direct evidence must indicate a greater role for royal justice than that found abroad. It would still be a mistake to abandon the search. Among the more obvious candidates for peacemaking à la Wulfstan are Anselm of Canterbury, Ailred of Rielvaux, and Hugh of Lincoln,[58] all strong proponents of an ethic of friendship and peace among monks compelled to play a role in the secular world.[59] Others will perhaps emerge alongside them once we look for them.

Orderic Vitalis was not that kind of worldly monk. He showed little inclination to leave the cloister at St. Evroul, where he spent virtually all of his life; he did not venture into the nasty, violent world outside to play any active role, even as peacemaker. Nevertheless, as his *History* shows, he was well furnished with both connections and information about events far from St. Evroul, and he was very concerned at their consequences for good and evil. The attitudes of this careful observer of the outside world toward feud and the pursuit of vengeance are as little susceptible to simple classification as Wulfstan's.

Certainly, Orderic did not always disapprove in any simplistic way the seeking and taking of secular vengeance. In the course of the *History* he recounts very many anecdotes on the subject, mostly without a hint of criticism. For example, when King William imprisoned Earl Morcar in 1071 "absent any obvious offense," Orderic approvingly relates the decision of Morcar's brother, Edwin, to avenge this wrong with Norman blood; but he also condemns the young man's betrayal and says that the French too mourned his death.[60] Here and in other places, he recognizes and apparently sanctions secular feelings concerning the licitness of vengeance and, implicitly, of feud too.[61] He constructs his moral analyses with laudable prescholastic casuistry, on premises that include his full awareness that God and the saints also on occasion wreaked vengeance on their enemies. His book XI records many unpleasant deeds of violence and treachery. At its

cols. 783–84), is especially impressive for its wedding of proper divine vengeance for wrongs done to his saints, with Ailred's own peacemaking activities noted just below.

58. See, for Ailred, Daniel 1950, 46, 57–58; and on his general attitude, MPL 195, cols. 750–51; for Hugh, see Douie and Farmer 1961–62, i. 123–24; ii. 31–32, 71, 102–3; cf i. xxxvi and ii. 218.

59. I hope to present evidence on each of these on another occasion. We would surely know of other acts of peacemaking by Ailred, for instance, had his letter collection survived.

60. *Orderic* ii.256–58.

61. The best illustration is perhaps BRIONNE V. GIROIE. But there are many others, e.g., *Orderic* iii.308; iv.64, 156–60, 256–58; v.56–58, 84; vi.332–34, 514, 520–22.

start, he placed a poem saying among other things that lawbreakers deserved the penalties of celestial anger.[62] The caveat that humans ought to bear in mind was that no vengeance was possible for them without God's will.[63] He inferred the hallowed scriptural principle that vengeance was best left to God. But this did not imply that one had to remain passive and silent. Orderic thought it perfectly proper to inform God of the facts and seek his aid, in trespassory terms very similar to those in which other men complained to their earthly lord. So when a jackdaw stole eggs through an open window, a monk could address God directly: "O Lord, avenge us on the enemy who takes away what Thy compassion gives us." The bird duly died.[64] As this mundane example shows, vengeance was, for some monks, as much a part of the texture of daily life as for their lay cousins.[65] The proper framing of their complaints of wrong was necessary to move divine as much as worldly protectors. The ideal result might be that the protector did it all, and kept their pure hands clean of blood. Certainly that was what the monks preferred. But laymen at least might have to assist God in the prosecution of His and their enmities, and they might be quite happy to oblige. I mentioned earlier the locus classicus of the Crusades. Indeed the monastic logic of Orderic and his fellows about licit divine vengeance, and especially perhaps crusading, might encourage laymen to take vengeance into their own hands on the ground that they were simply carrying out God's work—a venial sin, if one at all.

Naturally, this is only part of the story. As a patently pious monk, Orderic was constantly reminded of higher Christian standards than secular vengeance—the duty to show mercy and pursue peace in New Testament fashion. His own monastery's patron Saint Evroul had in his own lifetime, he thought, lived up to that ideal, having never avenged any of the evils done to him. When informed of losses, he just shrugged his shoulders and recited the long-suffering Job's words, "The Lord giveth, the Lord taketh away; blessed be the name of the Lord." He was moreover an excellent peacemaker admirably equipped with honeyed words to resolve discord.[66] To Or-

62. *Orderic* vi.8. Rufus's death was God's vengeance for his tyrannies (v.284–90). There are other instances of clear divine vengeance as well (vi.166, 490–92).

63. The Byzantine emperor had to learn this lesson (*Orderic* iv.12).

64. *Orderic* iii.278: "Domine, vindica nos in adversario, qui aufert quod nobis donat tua miseratio." Cf. also ii.230–32 and iii.326, where his own house was the loser.

65. A more serious and disturbing case is *Orderic* v.284–90: a Gloucester monk, after a vision of Rufus's tyranny, begged Christ to avenge him justly and with clemency as "the avenger [*vindex*] and judge of all." He was told to be patient, since vengeance would indeed come in time. Rufus met the abbot's warning about the vision with belly laughs and went on to his death in the New Forest.

66. *Orderic* iii.296. The broken quotation is from Job i.21.

deric this was more than an ancient exemplum for inspiration alone, as he showed in an anecdote from William I's Maine expedition of 1083–84. A beardless youth hidden behind the walls of a besieged town shot Richer de l'Aigle just below his eye. The great man's friends were furious and at once rushed off to avenge their noble companion by killing the youth. With his dying breaths, Richer called them off, "for the love of God" as he said, adding: "I have to die this way for my sins [peccatis exigentibus]." His friends released the youth and turned instead to hear their lord's dying confession.[67]

Orderic is thus in some ways an even more interesting case than Wulfstan. No sensitive reader of his *History* can doubt either his full-hearted acceptance of his monastic vocation or the sincerity of his final plea for prayers. Yet he remains one of our very best sources for the continuing recourse to feud-like behavior along with its concomitant sentiments on licit and deserved vengeance so prevalent in his day. He was perhaps fueled by drives similar to those that impelled younger contemporaries to revive the quest for the literal sense of the Bible. Only by close observation of the way things actually were might one hope to uncover the signs of truths deeper and ultimately far more important than the events themselves. His readers may have gleaned all kinds of thoughts about the politics and material relations of this world. By the end of his task, if not long before, Orderic's gaze was fixed on the stern face of the great Judge awaiting them all and the inexorable vengeance that should be His alone to wreak on the impenitent or to withhold from those who repented.

A SOCIETY FOCUSED ON WRONG AND ITS REDRESS:
A VENGEANCE CULTURE

Orderic's powers of observation and record are as much to the point as his conclusions. They reveal to us a society he patently thought to be riddled with ideas of vengeance and actual tit-for-tat action that could sometimes escalate to veritable feud killings. No reader can miss his sense of men nursing their grievances over long periods and awaiting the day when, hopefully, they would find the right moment for action and vengeance. After 1066, the English prayed for the "ultionis tempus."[68] In 1075, the northern earls persuaded Waltheof to join their revolt; they argued that the day of vengeance had arrived for his recent injuries and for all of them to recover their lost

67. *Orderic* iv.48–50. Another merciful victim appears just below.
68. *Orderic* ii.184.

honors. Poor Waltheof was only temporarily restrained by his oaths to the king and the knowledge that "no good song was ever sung of a traitor." So off he rode, to his doom.[69]

Orderic unblushingly recounts many rattling good yarns of blood and vengeance in his *History*. Although some are tales of long ago,[70] many come from his own day. One receives from him no sense of a world in transition, in which older notions of vengeance for wrongs suffered were passing out of fashion.[71] To the contrary, the reader of his *History* can easily imagine his age as drenched in notions of feud and vengeance restrained as much by religious and other drives for peace as by royal justice. Orderic constantly employs feud language in the general accounts of the history of Normandy and the careers of its kings and dukes. The protracted rivalry with Anjou over control of Maine offers several different illustrations. In 1069, resistance to Norman rule erupted into a rising in which the citizens of Le Mans "took such vengeance on the Normans" as to throw the whole area into disorder. William angrily responded with immediate preparations to resist invasion and take a "deserved armed vengeance" of his own.[72] Orderic tellingly depicts each side as having its own version of the story told to justify classic feud-like consequences in its own favor. Maine remained a bone of contention. A generation later at the time of the First Crusade, Rufus refused to let Count Helias fulfill his vow to take the cross unless he surrendered the county to him. Helias bravely responded that he remained committed to fighting in the Lord's name "against Christ's enemies" but would now face battle nearer home, because anyone who resists truth and justice thereby proved himself "God's enemy."[73]

Distinctions between the discourses of personal enmities and international relations were far less clear in the twelfth century, even to an Orderic. In 1119 at the Battle of Brémule, the English knight William Crispin caught up with the fleeing French king, Louis VI, whom for some reason he held in special hatred and now tried to hack to pieces with his sword. Louis's mail hauberk saved his life, but then the king had to fling himself over the body

---

69. *Orderic* ii.314. There is no sign of condemnation in Orderic's account. Gillingham 1994 and Wormald 1997 are the most recent writers to comment on the unusual nature of his execution at a time when capital punishment seems otherwise on the retreat.

70. *Orderic* ii.24, iii.308; BRIONNE V. GIROIE.

71. E.g., *Orderic* iv.200 (brother takes over inheritance along with associated feud), 200–202 (lord feeling responsible for killing makes peace with victims by marrying daughter to deceased's nephew), 214–16 (three-year period when Evreux and Conches families took no prisoners), 288 ("ancient enmity" erupts into violence).

72. *Orderic* iii.206. Cf. Le Patourel 1976, 85–86.

73. *Orderic* v.320; cf. v.258.

of his assailant to protect him from swift vengeance by his own friends.[74] All concerned patently took such matters very personally.

Something similar must often have held for revolts. Here Orderic is probably a faithful witness. In the twelfth century, men still justified or condemned those rising up against their lords in terms of their good faith, past service, and honorable treatment. One cogent example is the revolt of Duke William's uncle, William of Arches, in 1054.[75] Orderic describes Duke William as "animosus" when he suppressed the rising and killed, among others, Ingram, count of Ponthieu. One consequence was the invasion of the furious French king, leading to his decisive defeat at the Battle of Mortemer. Among the French partisans on that occasion was Guy, the new count of Ponthieu, "who had come to avenge the death of his brother." After a while, Orderic tells us, to the joy of the ordinary people there emerged "negotiators of a lawful peace," who shuttled between the warring lords to negotiate the return of captives and the making of treaties. One can read this either as the settlement of a feud or as the textbook end to a public war.

Orderic's willingness to narrate political events in the language of private wrong seems to me a point of real importance. I want to underscore it more closely from his treatment of William Rufus, a reign perhaps a little less heavily trodden by commentators.[76] In 1088, Rufus had to face a rising by his own uncle, Odo of Bayeux.[77] His council warned him of the danger and urged him to take action as king against "disturbers of the peace." Rufus was anxious to do just that. Angered by the rebels' inadequate initial peace offer, he threatened to hang them all. This horrified his own supporters, who all had kinsmen and friends among the opposition. They urged clemency.[78] But Rufus argued for the rigor of the law, on the ground that sparing the wicked stole peace and quiet from the innocent. The debate waxed warm and learned around various passages of the book of Samuel, until the doves convinced the king, at least for a time, that he should control his rancor and benignly permit the rebels to reenter his service so that he might once again

74. *Orderic* vi.238. Orderic did not himself approve of this rash attempt to strike down the Lord's anointed.

75. *Orderic* i.159; cf. the fuller and somewhat different account of the affair in iv.86–88.

76. One could make as strong a case also for Henry I. See *Orderic* iv.156–60 ("miserorum strenuus vindex" against Robert de Bellême), iv.256–58 (vengeance against his brothers for disherison), and vi.12–18 (attempts to reconcile with brother Robert after the 1101 invasion). For comments on Stephen, see *Orderic* vi.520–22 (hanging rebels as "ultionem sceleris" in preference to taking gold is both good for the king's reputation and pleasing to peace lovers); and on Louis VI of France, see vi.422.

77. *Orderic* iv.124–34.

78. They added to their biblical authorities for clemency a contemporary poem lauding the noble lion whose anger spared the prostrate. This unlikely model must refer to some bestiary text such as White 1954 (9). I discuss royal anger and clemency in Hyams 1998.

enjoy their *amicitia*. Although he spared their lives, the king was still angry. The rebels did not regain their property and had to troop out of the besieged town through the ranks of their jeering enemies, a patent if customary humiliation that Bishop Odo struggled in vain to escape. Rufus then bided his time, awaiting his opportunity for revenge while selectively converting some of Odo's supporters into fawning followers of his own through selective offers of pardon and benevolent treatment.[79]

Rufus's circumspection is again evident after another rebellion a few years later in 1095. He was careful both to reward those who had stood by him and to restrict the punishment of the guilty to fines. He acted so, says Orderic, out of respect for their kinsmen, who might wish to avenge themselves in Normandy. The king had no option but to take account of their strong feelings.[80] The king had in fact much incentive to be circumspect, once William of Eu and others had been mutilated for their parts in the revolt.

Orderic thought Rufus all too similar to the more violent of his nobles. Plainly, he suffered from an anger problem and was quite sensitive to mockery. At a siege toward the end of his life, the defenders killed the knight standing right next to him with a lucky stone and then compounded the insult by loudly mocking the king. Rufus, already frustrated by his inability to bring matters to successful closure, was so unbalanced ("contristatus") by the incident that his advisers advised him to withdraw and, significantly, "punish his enemies with some other kind of vengeance."[81]

This well-known element in Rufus's character was, intriguingly, a factor in the decision of his uncle, Odo of Bayeux, to take the cross and go on crusade. He reckoned that Rufus's "rancor" against him from past quarrels precluded all his hopes for a peace deal. Rather than submit as a defeated enemy, he preferred to go on pilgrimage. The king was magnanimous (perhaps meaning proud), Orderic tells us, but so angry by nature and so tenacious of memory "that he did not easily forget a wrong done him without avenging it."[82]

---

79. Barlow 1983 (89–90, 267–68) puts these incidents into context. *Orderic* iv.285 notes that after another rebellion a few years later in 1095, the king took good care to reward his own friends and also not to drive the ex-rebels' Norman kinsmen into a further round of vengeance by exaggerated punishment.

80. *Orderic* iv.285. Barlow 1983 (354–59) gives a good account of the actual sequence of events. This incident is worth bearing in mind when one considers the contention of Yver 1928 that the Norman dukes had outlawed feud in their domains. There was no Norman equivalent to the Old English laws that banned vengeance for lawful executions.

81. *Orderic* v.258–60. Barlow 1983 (99–100) explicates the choleric humor of this short, red-headed man in contemporary terms.

82. *Orderic* v.208–10; he recalls earlier illustrations of the theme, as from iv.230–34.

Now that I have sketched the intellectual milieu, let us look at a few anecdotes of feud from real life. Several of these cases treat revenge killings and
their prevention or limitation by the peacemaking process.

The murder of William Maltravers, although not technically a feud act
because it lacked the tit-for-tat element, is good evidence nevertheless for
the continuing feud ethos in twelfth-century England.[83] The killers believed they had suffered more than enough to justify his death. Maltravers
was a royal *fonctionnaire* to whom Henry I granted the Lacy honor of Pontefract sometime between 1115 and 1118 on characteristically harsh terms.
Doomed from the outset to be the outsider imposed on an unwilling honor,
he was virtually compelled to oppress Lacy folk in order to satisfy the demands on himself. Loyal Lacy vassals gave him a cool reception but could
do little while his royal master ruled. As soon as Henry was dead, however,
a Lacy knight called Pain swiftly disposed of the now unprotected Maltravers. Later litigation named at least one alleged accomplice and hinted at Ilbert de Lacy's complicity. One imagines that the Lacy coterie applauded the
news of Maltravers's death as a proper act. Certainly when Stephen pardoned Ilbert and the rest in 1141, he included no condition that they should
make peace with the dead man's kin in the manner supposedly required
since the 1130s.[84] The affair proclaims a local solidarity at once seignorial
and kin-based.

In the Durham feud of a generation earlier that resulted in the violent
death of Bishop Walcher, the solidarities seem more obviously constructed.[85] The deeper causes of conflict here go back to the Conquest and
the form taken by the Norman takeover of the north. For nearly a decade,
Walcher had been both bishop and earl. He ruled largely through foreigners whose arrogance of conquest alienated many of the local people. Two of
his trusted servants were, however, English, and their rivalry struck the
spark that set the conflagration. Although Leobwin was a native Northumbrian, Ligulf was a relative newcomer who had fled the south country before the advancing Normans and was favored by our monastic reporters for
his devotion to Saint Cuthbert. The *invidia* between this pair reached the

---

83. Van Caenegem 1990–91, no. 306, is the highly laconic record; see also *EYC* iii.1440, 1455,
and Howlett 1884–89, iii.140. Comment in Wightman 1966, 66–74, 243–44; and Green 1986,
260–61.

84. I consider further the significance of this case in the broader history of royal pardons later
in the chapter.

85. BISHOP WALCHER'S MURDER 1080.

point of violent shaming public words in the bishop's presence. A humiliated Leobwin hired a hit man from the bishop's close kin, and the deed was done by storming Ligulf's house at night in a style that was classic feud in all but the total absence of advance warning. Very few indeed escaped from the household to bear witness or seek revenge.

Once the news emerged, the bishop, who does not appear to have been privy to the plot, recognized that he was now nevertheless very much in the firing line. He struggled both to broadcast his own innocence to the countryside and to buy time in order to reconstruct an *amicitia* with some chance of outlasting the heat of the moment. After arranging a preliminary truce, he attended in person the peace negotiations at a rural church. Perhaps inevitably, relations broke down in the face of Leobwin's recalcitrance. Besieged in the church, the bishop had to follow his knights out to the enemies waiting to kill them. And so too, most unwillingly, did Leobwin, the source of all the trouble, when the firing of the church left him short of other options. Although the repercussions did not end there, our sources do.

This story's main events parallel familiar Old English lines. One killing will certainly engender another unless the right steps are taken. That Bishop Walcher knew what to do, despite his distant upbringing and the disregard for local sensitivities displayed by much of his following, establishes the important point that the rules were well known. Walcher might still have saved his episcopal skin, especially since everyone knew that violence to an earl would inevitably provoke a royal punitive expedition. He died because of Leobwin's cowardice and his own tactical error of an unwisely close supervision of the negotiations for his own safety.

These and similar anecdotes establish clearly enough that at least some inhabitants of Anglo-Norman England still internalized feud norms and could deploy them as needed.[86] The fullest accounts concern areas remote from the power centers round Westminster and Winchester. Certainly feud may have lingered in marginal areas like Northumbria and Cornwall, but it was also a significant part of the fabric of social life or culture in the heartland of England. Behind the line of argument that feud can only have existed where royal authority was relatively weak, however, is a misperception that feud is incompatible with central state institutions, most especially a central system for the administration of justice. I have refuted this erroneous idea on general grounds earlier in this book. Here it is important to

---

86. I detail Bishop Wulfstan's treatment of one palpable case of feud, over what was claimed to be an accidental killing, in Hyams 1992 (2–4). The incident is probably post-Conquest (before 1095). I also discuss there (1–2) a nice case of cursing nuns for which one can establish a context in pre-Domesday land litigation. Another highly suggestive case from about 1100 with much later repercussions is FRAWIN OF CORNWALL V. THE SONS OF TOKI.

recognize that even if all the stories did originate in peripheral areas of the realm (which is not in fact the case), men told and listened to them much more widely.[87] It would be odd if men who heard and apparently enjoyed fictional feuds totally closed their ears to real life analogs—possible but odd. I prefer to assume that their tastes comprehended occasional dramas of vengeance and high passions as those of their cultural descendants still do today.

The continuing evidence for the vitality of sanctuary is another straw in the same wind to indicate a widespread recognition that vengeance killing remained a real and frightening possibility. In such dangerous situations from which flight into temporary protection was sometimes the only sensible option, the fugitive's first decision remained much as in the eleventh century—whether to seek out an earthly or a celestial protector. Let us consider first earthly powers. Men still opted to place their security in the hands of some private lord, although the details are not easily extricated from narratives, which sometimes present the protecting lord rather than his fugitive man as author of the dispute. The king's role is better evidenced. For example, access to the king's person undoubtedly offered a desperate man, in the twelfth century as at almost any time during the Middle Ages, the chance of absolute if temporary security. Political imperatives compelled kings to do all they could to keep their personal peace inviolate. Moreover, they continued in this period to extend this peace to favored beneficiaries, private individuals and religious communities alike, and as they chose. The translations and adaptations of Old English law on the king's peace by twelfth-century legal writers put this beyond doubt. Their treatment integrated the old rules with what looks like living law.[88]

Cases from the thirteenth-century plea rolls convince me that the immediate value of a royal peace grant was to afford the recipient assistance in defending himself against his enemies. In other words, I deduce that the king's peace may still have operated in a feud culture for much of the time. But it is the swelling number of recipients of such grants that historians have noticed, rightly, as an important signpost to a major route toward the "king's peace" of the common law. This peace still came in two forms.[89] The less solemn *grithbryce* covering emendable offenses figured prominently in a

87. An excellent case to point is the Worcester sources both for Bishop Wulfstan's peacemaking referred to in the last note and for BISHOP WALCHER'S MURDER.

88. See O'Brien 1999 (74) for the "fuzzy but quite simple" picture presented by *LHP*. E Cf 26–28 strongly hints that abuses of the royal peace by some recipients was one reason why kings turned to place their trust into the frankpledge system. Cf. also the echoes of *grið* in Inst Cn III, 56–57.

89. E Cf 12 and 27 in fact portray the royal peace as "multiplex," differing in where and when granted. But this does not seem particularly pertinent to the present purpose.

very wide range of privileges granted to religious houses and others.[90] But numerous references to royal grants of a special peace by hand or seal (writ) in Domesday Book and elsewhere demonstrate the continuation of the claim that kings alone could remit offenses otherwise bootless and unemendable.[91]

I am attracted by the belief that this special peace was granted on a scale substantial enough to provide the main route to overall royal jurisdiction over crime and disorder—the key perhaps to the emergence of the common law. But proof is hard to find. One argument runs roughly as follows.[92] Henry I expressed his will to punish all violent acts against property as breaches of this special peace when he ordered in his coronation charter that "amodo" his "firma pax" should be observed throughout his kingdom. I can, however, see no compelling reason to read this as a general—certainly not a permanent general—grant of special peace. Henry and his successors continued to grant their peace through a variety of formulas (including some expressed as firm peace) to religious houses and others, which shows that men still felt it worthwhile to purchase a privilege they knew to be not automatically available to all. The adjective *firma* surely expresses the firmness of the royal will,[93] and is no index of royal confidence that his order will be obeyed.[94] Henry had sworn at his coronation "to prevent rapacities and all iniquities by all at any level of society." His subsequent charter proclaimed that there was now, once again, a king in England, that he was that king—determined to re-impose law and order and keep the peace as a king should.[95] Men who heard his oath or read his charter might be impressed by his words. But they would not, if sensible, believe that he could by words alone expel violence from England once and for all. That is why prudent men continued to buy from him and his successors special grants, in writing and so with lasting consequences. These converted violent acts against the grantees and *their* property into breaches of the king's

90. Hurnard 1949, esp. 303–5; cf. O'Brien 1999, 74. Yet "The Owl and the Nightingale," ll. 1730–35 (Wells 1907, 140), appears to take "griþ-breche" seriously enough in the early thirteenth century.

91. *DB* i.172a, 252a, 262c, 280c, 298d, 336c (shire customs of Worcs., Salop., Ches., Derby, Notts., Yorks., Lincs., but declared to have been universal before 1066; *DB* i.252a).

92. Garnett 1986, 114–15, followed by O'Brien 1999, 74.

93. Cf. the Quadripartitus translation of III Atr 1 on a bootless peace in the Danelaw, "þæt his grið stande swa forð" as "ut pax eius firma sit."

94. Garnett (1986) wants us to read clause 12 of the coronation charter in conjunction with the provision of clause 14 that apparently requires heavy emendation (financial penalty to the king) for property thefts committed since Rufus's death unless restored. But this second clause at least looks like a temporary decision to meet the exceptional circumstances of a royal interregnum, a time when later men would say there was no king's peace because there was no king. Garnett's rendering of the word *amodo* as "henceforth" similarly does not strike me as forced; the point could simply be to emphasize that the previous laxness was over.

95. Stubbs 1913, 116, 119.

special peace, thus aggravating the consequences and raising the price. Perhaps this would work to dissuade potential aggressors and so gain for purchasers a better peace than others enjoyed. We must, I think, assume—from the surviving written grants of peace and more complete evidence of surrounding periods—the existence of other oral, ad hoc grants of special peace. These grants, so useful to fugitives and their friends, attracted anyone who, with reason to fear an imminent attack, had sufficient resources to procure royal favor.

The commonsense notion that, in troubled times, sensible people sought out powerful protection was clearly familiar in the twelfth century. Men and women comfortably transferred its implications to God and his holy friends and sought sanctuary in their hour of need. Much of our knowledge of the pattern of ancient sanctuaries in northern England comes from a confirmation to the archbishopric of York of rights of sanctuary attributed to Henry I. The fact that this charter may be a twelfth-century forgery if anything strengthens the overall case.[96] Many of the royal sanctuary grants mentioned in chapter 3 were confirmed in the old terms during the course of the twelfth century. The peace stools at York, Hexham, Beverley, Ripon, and Durham were still surrounded by a penalty for the sacrilege of their breach. Those who reached them still enjoyed a grace period of thirty days, which they could now use under the visible protection of one church ("cum signo ecclesie") to reach the safety of another as well as to seek through mediators to make some accommodation with those hunting them down.[97] Publicizing the fact of one's saintly protection in some highly visual way must have been crucial to advertise it from a distance to those who might shoot first and ask questions later. Something like the prominent crosses that abjuring fugitives were required to carry on their route to the sea would have filled the bill nicely.

To handle hostile questioners, testimonial letters like those still extant from the Confessor's shrine at Westminster may have been both a lifesaver and a literal godsend.[98] These once again seem to envision trouble coming from victims and their friends, and carry almost no reference to royal jus-

96. Van Caenegem 1990–91, no. 172, conveniently reprints the text of an inquest of 1106. Hall 1989 (426, 428) judges the royal confirmation dubious but concedes that Stephen later accepted it as authentic when copying its terms in a grant to Beverley.

97. Van Caenegem 1990–91, no. 17A, is the main text. The signum of a church must have been something rather bigger and more easily visible than a pilgrim's badge, to warn potential attackers that you were not available for killing. The mediators' prime task was "pacificare hominem cum illis cum quibus male egerit," but they might also help gang members looking for the chance to turn over a new leaf ("si vero aliquis inter malos existens consorta illorum mutare voluerit" [ibid., p. 141]).

98. *Monasticon* 1817–30 (i.310, nos. lxi–lxiv) prints a selection. No. lxii demands for the fugitive not just the liberty of his body but also "pacem regis."

tice. Perhaps there was some connection between the nascent cult of Edward the Confessor and the unofficial legal collection "Leges Edwardi Confessoris" (written well on into the twelfth century), which still viewed sanctuary as a respectable part of the law of the land and required by the tendency of victims to hunt down those who had injured them. This text holds in quite general terms that once an offender reaches sanctuary, no pursuer may arrest him in any way except through the good offices of the bishop. The best hint as to the likely identity of these pursuers comes from a clause that enjoins restitution "to him from whom he has stolen" or, as a later recension puts it, "to the one to whom he has caused loss" ("cui damnum intulit"). That a victim's enmity could still place an offender at risk after he had sought refuge and formally abjured the realm appears from scattered later cases of attacks on the road to the ports.[99] Even in this context, our text's only explicit reference to royal justice comes in a further clause dealing with a fugitive's illicit return from his exile, an act naturally regarded as a royal offense; such a man was not to be received "without the consent of (a) royal justice."[100]

We have seen how closely the pattern of action around sanctuary was integrated into the overall scheme of law enforcement before 1066. Something similar remained the case into the twelfth century, as is evidenced by a new procedure for royal pardon in homicide cases that was apparently introduced by Henry I in the last few years of his reign. Sanctuary arrangements, still probably "the most important single means of securing mitigation of the prescribed penalties" of the leges,[101] were a significant determinant of the procedure's shape. A previously undocumented pattern of pardons emerged "in or shortly before 1130."[102] It expressly reserved for the victim's friends the right to proceed against even a pardoned offender and put him to the defense of his life and limb "legali lege." Their power to compel their enemy to undergo mutilation or worse by royal justice di-

---

99. Hunnisett 1961, 48–50. Mason 1988 (nos. 238–40, 279, 349) demonstrates that monks of Westminster continued to assume well into the thirteenth century that sanctuary breaches come from *adversarii*.

100. E Cf 5–5.3. E Cf 6 assigns breach of church-peace in general to episcopal jurisdiction. Leges Wmi 1 suggests a broader link between general peace confirmations and the narrower rights of peace in sanctuary.

101. Hurnard 1969, 3.

102. Ibid., 15–19; O'Brien 1999, 82–83. The evidence for innovation at this particular time is simply the sole extant pipe roll from Henry I's reign (referring to 1129–30) and the slightly later E Cf 18. Pipe rolls would only record pardons for which payment was not made on the spot. The actual introduction could have been earlier by several years or even more. Cf. also Inst Cn's suggestive translation of I Cn 2.5 (Liebermann 1903–16, i.283). For the royal monopoly of pardon in outlawry offenses, see *DB* i.262c, 280c, 298d, 336c.

verted thoughts of private vengeance into more acceptable channels, while preserving their chances of monetary compensation.[103] The early popularity of this kind of pardon is impossible to document. Henry's precedent may not have been followed under Stephen, although it probably survived in Normandy,[104] and it was taken up again later by Henry II at the start of his reign.[105]

Let us try to summarize the evidence for actual feud. The position is not altogether dissimilar from the pre-Conquest situation discussed in chapter 3. We possess anecdotes and enough other evidence to argue that full feud action persisted as a possible option for some and to suggest that it was not so rare that prudent men could afford to omit it from their calculations. This is not to say that it was a normal occurrence. Once men have ridden off in hot blood to seek vengeance, matters have gone to extremes. These are the exceptional cases. But they buttress a more far-reaching contention that the everyday world of twelfth-century England was one in which men were on the alert for wrongs done them and ready to seek their redress as and where they best could.

A LEGAL WRITER PROMOTES ROYAL LAW BUT ACCEPTS THE EXISTENCE OF PRIVATE VENGEANCE

Laymen, lords, or their counselors could reach for assistance to an unlikely source, a royalist legal treatise, the *Leges Henrici Primi*, written in a society in which royal authority proclaimed itself the guardian of order and the prime dispenser of earthly justice. It is striking to find that the author, despite a persistent effort to put royal justice first, nevertheless felt that feud persisted and still required regulation by the law and some extended and not unsympathetic treatment from him. His frequent recourse to Old English

103. The king's aspiration "to facilitate the introduction of yet sterner measures" had perhaps been meeting with "a good deal of obstruction from his subjects" (Hurnard 1969, 10, 20).

104. *Très ancien coutumier* XXXVI.1–2, LXXXVIII.3–4 (Tardif 1881, 30, 99), is quite forthright about the need for a killer to make peace with the deceased's *amici*; otherwise he faced an appeal (if not actual feud) to force him into exile.

105. Hurnard 1969 (15, 18) believes that the new form was quite popular from the start but concedes the lack of evidence for its continuation in the next reign. The facts of the Maltravers case (as discussed earlier in the chapter) suggest that no such pardon was used on that occasion. *EYC* i.466 (1157–63, but very probably 1158) strongly suggests that Henry II took the form up (again?) almost as soon as the usurper Stephen was dead. The casual reference of *Glanvill* vii.17 (91) to "aliena jura" shows that the king continued to respect kinsmen's right to appeal even after royal pardon. Wormald 1997 (562) sees this combination of royal power with kin rights as an intermediate stage in his schematic development already reached by Edgar and surpassed in the eleventh century.

materials obscures a sincere effort to portray the conditions of his own day. He is an especially good witness to the situation, "both complex and ill-defined" of law enforcement in his day, about the middle of Henry I's reign.[106]

Feud discourse creeps into what might otherwise have been perfectly normal statements about legal procedure. Discussing the equation of the oaths of six *villani* with that of a single thegn, he says of the latter, "and if he [a thegn] be killed, he may be fully avenged [vindicaretur] on six *villani*" or compensation paid as for the same six *villani*.[107] The context for this kind of statement is the persistence of the Old English system of compensation for wrong, evident from other sets of twelfth-century leges.[108] Overall there is ample indication that the author of the *Leges* targeted prominently in his teaching those who took vengeance into their own hands.

In this he resembled his Anglo-Saxon predecessors. His overt line is very consistent with someone purporting to write in twelfth-century Latin a law code for Henry along Old English lines. He appears to favor on grounds of public policy a line of increased royal leadership in the tough repression of disorder tempered by more royal mercy.[109] He envisions the king as the dominant regulator of feud arrangements and recommends that he seek an equitable balance by leaning toward peaceful settlement of complaints that might otherwise lead to feud violence. In so doing, he includes several procedural rules made in the tenth century to regulate settlements and reduce the dangers of open feud.[110] To restrict the circle within which men were entitled to seek vengeance or compensation, he cites with approval the principle that "he who has sinned should make atonement," indicating that a lord who followed it might expect to have peace from all.[111] He further evidences a preference for peace over conflict in a straight citation of the biblical Golden Rule to encourage judicial compassion.[112] A little later, and with-

---

106. The assessment is that of Hurnard 1969 (6–7).

107. *LHP* 64.2b. One might choose to translate *vindicaretur* as "punished," but Downer, whose translation I slightly amend, is with me on this point and comments more broadly on the author's language (*LHP*, p. 416–17). Cf. also *LHP* 90.7–7a on the absurdity of claiming vengeance for a killing caused by someone falling out of a tree.

108. Hudson 1996a (80–82) takes a different view. E Cf 12.6 and 18 show that not even penalties for breach of the king's peace or receipt of a royal pardon for homicide exempted wrongdoers from making their peace with the victim's kin and cites an Old English proverb: "Bugge spere of side oðe bere." See also Leges Wmi (7, 18–19) and the ca. 1130 reform of royal homicide pardons discussed earlier.

109. *LHP* 10.1, 11.16a, on which see the comments in Hurnard 1969, 13–14.

110. *LHP* 59.4–4a, 12–12a. In addition to II Em 7–7.1, as noted by the editor, it is possible that the author had also used the treatise Wer.

111. *LHP* 41.13, 15.

112. *LHP* 28.6: "what you do not wish to be done to you, you should not do to another."

out any obvious written source, he says that settlements ought to be of a type acceptable for oneself and that an aggrieved complainant ought indeed to swear an oath that he would accept similar terms from his opponent after a similar offense.[113] One is reminded of the rather less restrained Icelandic procedure for self-judgment. In framing such settlements, the parties made a distinction, already familiar from Anglo-Saxon feud enactments, between compensation paid to make up losses suffered (we might say damages) and payments intended to regain the *amicitia* of the victim's party. The ideal recipient would return the whole payment, to make it clear to all that the aggrieved retain no sense of insult and shame. The offender might in his turn offer his body to the victim and his friends for possible revenge, to show that he to whom justice is still in some sense due is a man to be feared and one whose *amor* is far better worth having than his *odium*. Finally, the injured party should accept part or all of the proffered payment as appropriate, presumably as a signal of good will and to proclaim the symbolic redress.[114] We see something very much like this in practice at almost exactly the time our author was writing.[115] He felt strongly that people should not enrich themselves from judgments, possibly also that neither party could be totally innocent.[116]

His treatment of lords and their role in dispute settlement among their men preserves a comparable balance between royal and private initiative. A lord is expected to produce any man in his household or (perhaps) service to answer any charges made against him in local courts.[117] Having done so, his own responsibility ceased. This is notable enough, given the very strong sense of the bond between lord and man that suffuses the text and the fact that even in the thirteenth century, a lord was placed under serious suspicion of complicity when a killer left from or returned to his house.[118] In principle, no vassal should oppose his lord in court and still less on the battlefield; he must suffer his lord's offenses without response for a time. Even to shame the lord was an offense so serious as to trump the usual requirement of an

113. *LHP* 36.1d–2b. This discussion, although situated in a context of which I can make no good sense, shows some understanding of the psychology of settlements.
114. *LHP* 36.2–2b is not easy to translate with confidence. I have made the best I could of it. Feeling against unfair enrichment from litigation can be documented from our own day.
115. Van Caenegem 1990–91, no. 185 (1109–10). A hundred court ordered a habitual and nocturnal turf thief to pay the monks of Abingdon silver pennies to the huge value of five mancuses. The abbot of his clemency refused to accept more than a single penny from each mancus and ordered the five pennies received to be conserved in the archives "pro memoria hujus emendationis."
116. Cf. *LHP* 39.1, 49.7, 84.1–2, and the comment by Downer, in *LHP*, p. 349.
117. *LHP* 46.6–15.
118. See the discussion in chap. 6.

eyewitness accuser.[119] On the other hand, any lord who without excuse deserted his man "in his mortal need" thereby lost his claims to lordship.[120]

No reasonably careful reader of the treatise as a whole could fail to recognize that the author favored peaceful solutions to all problems and expected royal justice to provide the lead in this direction. The theme of a quest for firm peace suffuses his work. Among the indications is the advice not to hit out, if caught up in a sudden quarrel.[121] Our author, well aware that "it takes two to tango," knows that the putatively innocent party often deserves a share of the blame and that the macho sin of pride is likely to lead to the unnecessary loss of lives.[122]

Few people actually read legal treatises through from start to finish. Often, instead, readers are searching either for problems or for solutions they have defined in advance. Will this treatise or code enable *me* to justify this course of action or that procedure, a reader often asks. Patently, our author himself has been selecting, rearranging, and interpreting his sources, sometimes even cherry-picking. It is a just judgment, especially appropriate to postmodernist authors, that as they select from others, so they will in their turn be skimmed, read selectively, and often, in their turn, gutted so that their data may be distorted and diverted to support others' purposes.

One should imagine a twelfth-century reader inclined to seek vengeance to its bloody climax or—perhaps more likely—to use this threat to secure not just pecuniary compensation but restoration of face by the humiliation of a former enemy. Self-help remained among the resources of even the most law-abiding citizens at this time, doubtless expressed in vernacular terms that owed as much to saga and chanson de geste as to any legal lexicography. One can scent these things even behind our author's text. He knows, for example, to expect trouble at "potationes," drinking sessions at market or in the gildhall, and suggests that potential troublemakers (those with known enmities, for example) be invited to leave early.[123] These considerations naturally raise the question: What kind of answers might such a man find in the *Leges Henrici Primi*? Ex hypothesi, he would naturally expect

---

119. *LHP* 32.2, 43.9, 44.2. It was still accepted a century after this that a lord did not have to accept an enemy into his homage (e.g., on acquisition of land within his lordship), and the common law too was much embarrassed at the possibility of a duel between lord and man.

120. *LHP* 43.8.

121. *LHP* 83.7.

122. Cf. *LHP* 84.1–4, discussed earlier.

123. *LHP* 81–81.1a; cf. 87.10–10a, laying down that all the participants at small parties (less than seven persons present) that ended badly should share the burden of paying the wergild. The violent renewal of old enmities under the influence of alcohol is a persistent theme, mentioned in chap. 3.

to observe certain rules about feuding, including a list of the situations in which vengeance was illegitimate.[124]

He would be heartened to find that when certain conditions were met, killers had to be handed over to the kin of their victims. Where a Welsh *servus* cannot or will not meet his obligation to pay his English victim's *wer*, for example, his lord must hand him over unless the lord is willing to make the payment himself.[125] It is obvious from some passages that the word *wer* still carries the old connotation of a life for a life. Murder is the limiting case. Kinsmen are supposed to surrender an avowed murderer to his victim's kindred "so that he may experience the mercy of those to whom he displayed none." This must mean that they can licitly kill him.[126] If they do, he will be—as a passage with no Old English source dryly notes—released from his obligation to contribute to the *murdrum* fine.[127] Residual doubts are dispelled by a provision for aggravated unemendable killings by sorcery or poison, which similarly state the point to be "so that he [the culprit] may experience the mercy and judgment of those whom he himself did not spare."[128] If this happened at all frequently,[129] it helps to make sense of the fact that even in the thirteenth century the victim's kinsmen and friends apparently executed in person some judgments of mutilation and death.[130] Our bellicose reader will surely have understood that his ultimate right to blood vengeance remained the final sanction behind peacemaking and compensation.

Vengeance killings are sometimes equated with ones carried out in self-defense or under duress, hence legitimate and not subject to penalty by royal wite.[131] In other words, they were not merely excusable (requiring royal pardon) but justifiable, and so ineligible for further punishment or vengeance.[132] Certain other cases of legitimate vengeance are almost as clear, most notably when a husband finds another man with his wife behind closed doors or beneath her blanket.[133]

On such occasions, the right of vengeance descended in the first instance

---

124. This is how he would read *LHP* (11.11b, 64.5, 66.1, 68.9, 74.1, 75.3, 75.5a, 88.8) on such matters as killing within the kindred and executions.

125. *LHP* 70.3, 5–5a, whose source (Ine 74) is explicit about the alternative.

126. *LHP* 92.15. *LHP* 71.1a and 92.19 (both taken from II Cn 56) confirm that murderers at least may be surrendered to the opposition. Cf. *LHP* 92.3b, 15a.

127. *LHP* 92.3b.

128. *LHP* 71.1a, 1c; these are cases elsewhere called murder.

129. *LHP* 92.15, 19, points to the clear cases of conviction and confession.

130. Hyams 1986, and see also in chap. 6.

131. *LHP* 83.6a, 88.19. The meaning of duress in 88.19 is established in 87.6–6a; it sounds very reminiscent of the cases of forced executions in the thirteenth century (Hurnard 1969, 88–92).

132. The terminology is that of Hurnard 1969, chap. 1.

133. *LHP* 82.8.

according to the rules of inheritance. A man's children and close blood-kin stood first in the line of fire, even when the killer was a woman whose husband and in-laws might, the author observes, be innocent of complicity.[134] Because this was sometimes an unwanted duty much more than any kind of right, it had to be possible to renounce troublesome kinsmen, and the treatise recognizes just such a right.[135] After blood kinship, the other bond that required and justified sharing someone's duty of vengeance was lordship. When your lord was under attack, coming to his defense was usually legitimate and involved no liability to wite. Similarly, a lord could always come to the aid of his man.[136] But the prudent man would certainly wish to recruit support beyond immediate kin, and outsiders spoiling for a fight sometimes volunteered their services. References to the important process of mustering a support group seem somewhat tangential. One law distinguishes between men you have invited to join and those who came along without being asked. A principal is responsible only for the death of his invitee, not for volunteers.[137]

This reminder that supporters were also risking their lives raises once more the question of the relationship between actual tit-for-tat vengeance and the payment of compensation in substitution for blood. It seems clear that our author considered the two equivalent, at least within his own preference for peaceful solutions. When the protagonists are equal in status and wergild, "unus pro alio jaceat" (one should lie slain for the other), he tells us in explicating the compensation system.[138] Elsewhere he habitually equates the payment with the life it protects.[139]

Our author patently seeks to direct the system toward the restoration of a balance by peaceful means where possible. From his perspective, it was clear that at the end of the day neither party should gain or lose.[140] The best illustration smells strongly of the schoolroom. A hypothetical poses the following question: What is to be done when one man falls out of the air (from a tree or other structure) on top of another and kills him? To insist on vengeance or even compensation in such a case is a demonstration of severe mental obstinacy in opposition to all common sense. If the victim's kinsman

---

134. *LHP* 70.12.

135. *LHP* 88.12b, from II Em 1.1.

136. *LHP* 82.3–4, 90.19. It is slightly less clear that the same rules applied to the defense of kinsmen (82.7), but see also the next note.

137. *LHP* 88.9–9a. In the thirteenth century, the common law routinely referred to such support groups (often but not always seignorial) as a *forcia* (see chap. 6). But friends and *placitatores* could be just as helpful to face off one's enemies in the courtroom (*LHP* 49.2a; Brand 1990, 211; Wormald 1997, 566).

138. *LHP* 70.8–9.

139. *LHP* 68.1 (from the Old English treatise Wer), 88.11b–c.

140. This may be the message behind the somewhat obscure *LHP* 70.9, 88.11.

insists, the most he is to be allowed is that he may, if he must, climb the same tree and hurl himself in similar fashion onto the (inadvertent) killer.[141]

It is most unlikely that enraged kinsmen in hot pursuit of redress for a slain brother shared this austere juristic preference for fair play and perfect equilibrium. That is no doubt why our author devotes some considerable space to the creation of conditions favoring peacemaking. He does not content himself with a simple rehearsal of the tenth-century rules.[142] He adds some helpful advice on how to get a good result. The kindred should negotiate as a unit. They should take care to make their payments in due time,[143] and in general to act "per justitiam," which I take to mean "according to the rules" but which may also imply recourse to the local royal justice.[144] The prince and his ministers are encouraged to mediate—an undernoticed provision that points to an important but neglected aspect of kingship.[145] Henry I needed little urging to act the peacemaker when it suited him. In the 1120s, for example, he sent William Peverel to end a serious dispute between Robert de Ferrers and Burton Abbey over some disputed woods. Word having apparently reached the king informally, he decided to lend a helping hand. William went beyond mere damage limitation to attempt the creation of a new and positive *amicitia*. He flourished the royal order at the parties to bring them to terms in the Ferrers Castle at Tutbury. Robert, "moved by the fear of God and compelled by the king's command," swiftly proclaimed himself the abbey's special friend, bound to maintain and defend the monks. The monks then formally recorded the agreement.[146] Henry intervened in similar fashion and sometimes in person on other occasions, as earlier kings had and successors were to do.[147] Our evidence is very much the product of chance in charter drafting and survival. The very direct documentation from John's reign of feud settlements made from the top, which is set out in chapter 6, comes from sources unavailable in the twelfth century, a suggestive fact from which we ought to assume some, possibly very many lost instances from earlier kings.

---

141. *LHP* 90.7–7a. Although the editor has located no source for this, it claims to be derived from "antiquis institutionibus," that is, to constitute a legal chestnut. The fact that the natural death of an arrested murderer does not cheat his victim's kin of their rights, while his execution by his enemies does, is another pointer to the juristic preference for equilibrium (*LHP* 92.3–3b).

142. *LHP* 76 follows Wer quite closely.

143. *LHP* 59.4; contrast *LHP* 4a.

144. *LHP* 88.17, 20a. Is the local justice expected to mediate?

145. *LHP* 83.2; the limitation to peacetime clearly demonstrates that the enmities envisioned here are feuds.

146. Van Caenegem 1990–91, no. 252 (1121–27).

147. Cf. ibid. 138, 263, 283 (1093–94, 1121–29, 1133–35) for other Anglo-Norman instances of royal peacemaking. Mayr-Harting 1965 (41–42), Kemp 1968 (106–8), and Richardson and Sayles 1963 (256) document the continuing interest of Henry II in making peace among the clerics themselves.

Would-be peacemakers with less than royal clout needed to build trust by confirming the opposition's honor and permitting the saving of face. Such is the impression of the procedure conveyed by another account without obvious debts to Old English precedent, that underscores the need to look honorable not just to one's enemies but to the inevitable bystanders too. Negotiations should at least be free, leaving the other side the option to reject what it cannot accept.[148] The trick, as always, is to give the opposition room to accept the fact of their loss and the possibility of assuaging grief with an honorable payment instead of blood. Naturally this takes time. Our author, understanding this well, updates the old rules concerning a cooling-off period to include possible recourse to royal justice. Indeed, he warns that should the victim's kin prove unwilling to use their peaceful options, "the king may do his justice."[149] To put it at its lowest, once the enemy has offered to stand to right or pay proper compensation, vengeance is always unlawful.[150]

There is a nice double lesson to be taken from this examination of the *Leges Henrici Primi* so far. A reader driven by thoughts of vengeance and feud could certainly find justification and inspiration in this text. But to do so he would have to read very much against the grain. The author's clear intention is to promote royal leadership in the maintenance of the peace so essential to his episcopal and other ecclesiastical colleagues. His basic view is very much comparable to those of other contemporaries relatively lightly touched by the Gregorian winds of change. One may well ask whether the author's peace aims resemble more those of his Old English sources or his common-law successors. The answer is clear on this occasion. He still conceptualizes his law in the old manner, with hardly a hint of the distinction between crime and tort that is so central to European law from the thirteenth century onward. Although we know him to have been fairly familiar with canonical materials that might have led him toward this ultimately Roman distinction, there is little sign that he felt the need to move beyond an analysis of undifferentiated rights and wrongs.[151]

Crime language, and its corollaries, figures in the book but ranks low among the various efforts at categorization of cause and lawsuit. On one occasion, the author divides wrongs into emendable, unemendable, and those belonging to the *ius regium*; on another he distinguishes in terms of proce-

148. *LHP* 36.1d–2b, 70.11 (on lesser offenses). Cf. *LHP* 88.16.
149. *LHP* 82–82.1, 88.11 (from II Em), 88.20a, 89.12–12c, 92.15a. Much of this goes back to Alfred's code. Cf. also *LHP* 83–83.1b on chance meetings with an enemy.
150. *LHP* 70.10a, 83.3; and cf. *LHP* 86. The implication is that in other circumstances vengeance may be licit.
151. The next few paragraphs supplement Hyams 2000.

dure between private prosecutions and manifest offenses.[152] When he uses crime words, the opposition with tort (or civil causes) is absent; they are merely especially serious wrongs singled out for their evil effects.[153] The antithesis to crime and the *causa capitalis* with which he frequently links it is the *causa communis*. This term covers lesser offenses distinguished by appropriately lighter penalties.[154] Despite odd hints of an equation with emendable offenses, which might suggest tort, our author focuses on the seriousness of the act and its penalty.[155] He apparently shares with his secular contemporaries the feeling that behind most legal action there lies a notion of wrong that he was not inclined to analyze in any precise manner.[156] He understands in this way even those unemendable offenses that put one in the king's mercy. In the list is contempt of the king's writs "and anything that does shameful wrong to the king's person or mandates." The shame language used here, so reminiscent of later usage in trespass cases, can be read as confirmation that we should understand the wronged king as "one party to conflict."[157] It is also a strong hint of the ubiquity of that "single undifferentiated *action* for all serious private secular wrongs" to which some have pointed in the world before the common law.[158] Let us now turn to document this very important phenomenon.

UNDIFFERENTIATED WRONG: AN ELEMENTAL CONCEPT BEFORE THE COMMON LAW

The clearest statement comes from the Norman *Summa de legibus* written ca. 1236. Its author says: "*Iniuria* is the action for unwarranted harm caused to anyone, from which every dispute arises as streams flowing from a single source."[159] By this date two different procedures by which a wronged man

152. *LHP* 9.1, 1a, 6, 12; 57.7.

153. *LHP* 47 rubric, 61.18, 85.2a.

154. Downer, in *LHP*, 428.

155. *LHP* 61.14. Downer's suggestion, in *LHP*, 429, that they require different methods of proof, seems doubtful; cf. *LHP* 49.6.

156. *LHP* 9.4 (*iniuria*); 51.1 (*culpa*).

157. *LHP* 13.1: "et quicquid ad propriam personam suam uel mandatorum suorum contumeliatur iniuriam." Downer translated this syntactically awkward phrase: "and anything which slanders injuriously his own person or his commands." The phrase at the end is from Wormald 1997 (579).

158. The phrase and the insight are from Richardson and Sayles 1941 (cxxxiii). Much of what follows springs from the pioneering study of Richardson and Sayles 1941 (cviii–cxxxiv, headed "The action of trespass"), and Harding 1981 (xxxii–lviii, "The origins of trespass, tort and misdemeanour"), arguing along very much the same lines.

159. *Summa de legibus* L.1 (Tardif 1896, 134). Cf. *Summa de legibus* L.4 (Tardif 1896, 135): There were four kinds of *iniuria*, two against the person and two more against property. "And from these four streams all other disputes arise. So it appears that these four proceed from *injuria*; it is the mother of all disputes." This great treatise, written at almost exactly the same moment as the sec-

could initiate suits for redress in public courts were widely known in both Normandy and England. These are in outline already familiar from the last chapter. But it was only in the course of the late twelfth and thirteenth centuries and with the birth of the common law that the two procedures developed into discrete legal "actions." Those scholars who have argued for this way of seeing the antecedents of the criminal appeal of felony and the civil action of trespass have described them as growing out of a single undifferentiated action existing before the split. To put the matter in these terms smacks of hindsight. It is easy to exaggerate the degree of formality in the twelfth century before there was a controlling jurisdiction to impose similar procedures on all. There can have been no single action in any way analogous to the later common-law "forms of action."

"Appeal" here is the Old French *appel*, that dramatic challenge by which a man threw down his gauntlet to commit himself to proof, a genuine commitment of life and members by calling out his enemy to fight within the four benches of the court. This colorful act and the rules that governed it grace a whole range of literary works from the age of epic on into that of romance. The accompanying rhetoric, so redolent of enmity and resentment, nevertheless gave no sign that the procedure was limited to cases of felony, as in the later practice of English royal courts.[160] Proof after 1066 was by a duel in which both parties put their life and members to the test. All concerned knew that the loser faced physical penalties—mutilation or death.[161] This raised the stakes. Not every complainant was willing to place his own skin so obviously on the line. The more prudent or timid could put their complaints to the justice of a higher power in similar terms but directed to the different end of redress rather than outright revenge. And this decision path led in the direction of common-law trespass.

In the age before the common law, a man who felt himself seriously aggrieved (yet not so scared as to "lump" it or flee)[162] thus had some options to consider with the counsel of his friends. These can be represented schematically as follows.

1. He could seek vengeance by direct action, self-help on his private initiative. At its most basic, this is *feud*.

---

ond "recension" of "Bracton," should be read alongside that book as a distant witness to their common origin in twelfth-century Anglo-Norman legal tradition.

160. Even in thirteenth-century England, appeals without words of felony continued in the shire court (Harding 1981, liv).

161. Or his principal faced the penalty, if a champion had fought the actual duel, as was common in the twelfth century.

162. A really scared man (e.g., a feud killer) might seek sanctuary or protection from the king's hand. I examine the history of such grants of special protection in chap. 6.

2. He could bring an individual accusation of wrongful behavior against his adversary and back it up with his own body in the offer of battle. This is the *appeal*, a stylized and tamed alternative to actual feud.
3. Or he could complain to a "big man" with the power to do something about it, usually in medieval England the king or some very great lord. He would petition for redress—compensation not just for the injury (e.g., restitution of property) but for his shame and loss of honor too.[163] I have called this *proto-trespass*.

The most likely consequence of each of these strategies was some kind of settlement, although a driven or resentful "victim" might always press matters on to a conclusion in any of them. The pros and cons were well known and figured in all prudent calculations. This process of strategic decision-making reveals the fundamental unity behind what otherwise appear (especially with common-law hindsight) to be very different kinds of action.

We are now armed with a schematic view of what ought to be visible in twelfth-century England as options for the aggrieved. We have already seen the evidence to establish the existence of option 1—feud—at least to the degree that men might conceptualize the other two options as its alternatives. In time, options 2 and 3 developed into common-law actions in quite distinct jurisdictional areas. At this stage, though, knowledge of the essential distinction between crime and tort was absent even from the *Leges Henrici Primi*. The other twelfth-century law books appear equally ignorant of the learned distinction, which first emerges in England ca. 1187–89 in a very different kind of treatise, known by the name of *Glanvill*, drawing on very different sources.[164] The earlier law books treat the available remedies for wrong in a different and all-pervasive manner.

Behind this language of complaint and wrong, one can discern the two distinct procedures of appeal (option 2) and proto-trespass (option 3). Successive Old English enactments strove to protect the king from being bothered by most such complaints. By the time of the "Leges Willelmi," in the early twelfth century, the law forbade anyone to complain to the king or bring to him any plaint ("querelam") until he had first sought and then been denied justice in the local public courts.[165]

It often seems as if the old compensation system remained fully valid well into the twelfth century. The "Leges Willelmi" held that an appellor was entitled to compensation for the head of an opponent who could not be pro-

---

163. Beckerman 1981.
164. Hyams 2000 traces this development. I have argued my own take on the character of *Glanvill* in Hyams 1982.
165. Leges Wmi 43; cf. II Cn 17: "ne gesece nan man ðonne cyng."

duced in court.[166] Its author also proclaimed the continuing validity of many Alfredian tariff payments.[167] The "Leges Edwardi Confessoris" (taking the story at least into midcentury) still obliged killers against the king's peace to make amends to their victim's kin "or suffer the life [werram]," according to the English proverb that required killers to buy off or suffer a spear in their side, "buge spere of side oðer bere!"[168] When the books were not talking of compensation, they were using the language of vengeance. When a thief of poor public reputation fails to appear and follow the appropriate procedure, "he may be avenged live or dead," and the goods are to be returned to those who claim them. His own kin are expressly warned not to interfere on his behalf,[169] for executions (which this would be) are expressly exempt from feud and attempts can be prosecuted by plaint before royal justice.[170] Yet vengeance killing is licit enough when a daughter or wife is caught in the act of adultery.[171]

None of this is yet quite like common-law actions of trespass or appeals of felony. Only in hindsight do we see the precursors of the common-law procedures. Those who bring plaints to the king (or his justices) of theft or homicide do not expect them to lead to a jury trial but rather just to the kind of old-style trial threatening punishment to life and limb, which later trespass plaintiffs are keenest to avoid. Nor are appeals confined to royal courts. Indeed, lords with full sake and soke are, we are told, entitled to exercise full jurisdiction over any appeal ("tihla" or "compellatio") concerning their men or lordship.[172] Although these are clearly not appeals "of felony" in the later sense, appellants are already bound by very similar procedural constraints. Thus an owner of stolen goods must proclaim the hue and cry or otherwise do suit before he pursues his thief. Otherwise he will be subject to *hengwite*, now understood chillingly as the penalty for hanging someone without trial. His appeal (if it comes to that) must be supported by an oath that he prosecutes "neither from hatred nor for any cause except to reclaim his rightful property," and the appeal will be resolved by some kind of oath with compurgators, not by battle.[173]

Twelfth-century remedies resist division into thirteenth-century categories. Although one can find appeals and procedures resembling the later

166. Leges Wmi 3.4.
167. Ibid., 18–19.
168. E Cf 12.6; I discussed E Cf 18 on royal pardons earlier in the chapter. Leges Wmi 7 is to the same effect adding the need for *manbot* to the victim's lord.
169. Leges Wmi 47.1–3; II Cn 26 is the source for the prohibition of feud on the thief's behalf.
170. E Cf 36 on executed thieves.
171. Leges Wmi 35.
172. *LHP* 59.17.
173. Leges Wmi 4, 14–14.3; the material phrase in 14.3 is "quod nec ex odio nec aliqua causa hoc ei imponit nisi tantum ut ius suum adipiscatur."

trespass, there is no sign that any substantive law hangs on the choice between them. No texts specify when a litigant must bring, say, an appeal rather than a plaint for damages, or even why one course might be preferable. Both options 2 and 3 offered the same opportunity to extract compensation for the wrong suffered.[174] Litigant choices seem not at this stage to have carried any of the procedural consequences that the later actions did. Men must at the time have thought and talked of both these remedies in the same or very similar terms, as petitions to a superior for redress of wrong. Some such conceptual framework persisted well into the next century.[175]

THE MEANING OF *INIURIA*

For all these reasons, the situation from which the common-law procedures later emerged may be described as undifferentiated. By focusing on the Latin words into which the literate translated their resentful clients' feelings about their wrongs, the implications become clear. The word *iniuria* was one of the most common twelfth-century ways to express wrong in Latin; it was frequently used in Anglo-Norman writ formulas and the case narratives of charters and chronicles.[176] In addition, it has two extra claims to attention. Because it was often the term of choice for draftsmen of royal writs, its history offers some insights into governmental strategies toward wrong. And it is a word much used in the central texts of Roman law, hence a candidate for law school professors to reinterpret as denoting something more sophisticated than the vernacular notions. When, therefore, we glean in the word's usage features that become important in both trespass and the crime of the early common law, we should pay attention.

Even a brief survey of iniuria in this period reveals its vast range of reference, quite as broad as our own vernacular by which we rage at our fate today. Beyond dispute, iniuria strayed far beyond the limits of the common-law classification of tort (trespass) that would in due course emerge from chancery drafting and law school debate. Men did not hesitate to identify as iniurie what we should certainly term crimes. Thus one of the midcentury legal writers holds that the king, as vicar of the king of kings, God, must defend his people "ab iniuriosis," from offenders who would harm them.[177] Indisputably, he has downward ("criminal") justice in mind, as did the Norwe-

---

174. *LHP* 59.27 forbade settlement out of court once an appeal was begun. Cf. *LHP* 24.2, 59.28; also *Glanvill* xiv.1 (172), and *Summa de legibus* LXXV.3 (Tardif 1896, 187), later.

175. See chap. 6 in this volume and Hyams 2000.

176. Another word with a (distant) future was *tort* from Old French *torture*; cf. Van Caenegem 1990–91, no. 202 (1114–16), for the Latin form. I discuss *trespas/transgressio* in chap. 7.

177. E Cf 17.

gian merchants in a tearful robbery plaint to William Rufus.[178] Land was as often the locus where wrongs were suffered and violence erupted. Thus disseizins, land invasions, illicit distraints, and other lesser infringements on land rights were also understood as wrongs[179] (as were acts harming churches and their property)[180] and made actionable within the same general category as wrongs more obviously inflicted on individuals.[181] That breach of royal property protections and confirmations could also be classified as breach of the king's peace signals both the undifferentiated conceptualization we are trying to unravel and another strand of its legacy to the future.[182]

One may deduce from the use of words like *iniuria* how contemporaries reacted to, and felt about, their perceived wrongs. Perhaps their most important challenge was to relate the perception of wrongs to the lordship by means of which one might hope to remedy them. From the vassal's viewpoint, the lord's obligation to maintain him against those who would do him wrong seemed almost the most important attribute of good lordship. In a confirmation of a tiny grant in free alms to Rielvaux during the third quarter of the century, one Yorkshire lord promised that if anyone harassed the monks or did them wrong ("injuriam"), he and his heirs would forever warrant and maintain the land to them against their adversaries.[183] The obligation flowed from the act. The expression of such obligations of good lordship is rare before this period.[184] But this must be a matter more of charter drafting than actual behavior, as clauses to similar purpose in many earlier royal documents prove.[185] Even without express guarantees of this sort, dependants could hope to move their lord to throw their greater resources into battle on their side by persuading the great man that he too was

178. Van Caenegem 1990–91, no. 143C (1095–96).
179. Ibid., no. 193 (1113); Van Caenegem 1959, nos. 42, 64, 67 (1113–28, 1087–94, 1096–97); *EYC* iv.53 (1159–71). The inclusion of wrongs relating to land rights may help to explain the later capacity to sue in trespass for various land encroachments such as breach of close.
180. E.g., Van Caenegem 1990–91, nos. 167 (1102–4), 173 (1104–7), 191 (1110–12), 223 (1121). Also ibid., 138 (1093–94), on the right to consecrate bishops.
181. One intriguing and potentially rather important case is that of the assize of novel disseizin, for which see chap. 5.
182. Van Caenegem 1959, 67 (1096–97): if anyone disseizes or does any other wrong ("iniuriam") to the monks of Durham, the sheriff is to know that they breach my peace on them and will do satisfaction to me for this breach. Alan Harding has suggested over a number of years that this association of royal protections with pleas of the crown had very far-reaching consequences, a point I consider in chap. 7.
183. *EYC* iii.1690 (1170–84); cf. *EYC* iv.50 (1158–66), xi.98 (1154–75).
184. Hyams 1987 shows why.
185. Van Caenegem 1959, 28, 31 (1092, 1087–97), and in many writs of reseizin for land, e.g., ibid., 3, 42, 64, 82, 94. For other royal acts from both sides of the Channel, see ibid. (147 n. 5) and Delisle 1909–27 (Introduction: 164–65).

wronged.[186] An allied device was to insist on the shame that accompanied the infliction of wrong in, for example, the common coupling of *iniuria* with *contumelia*.[187]

Twelfth-century complainants did not always expect their lords to initiate litigation in any court. Frequently the hope was to avoid both any further violence and the many disadvantages of a lawsuit by recourse to a lord's power and influence. Still, litigation was one possible outcome worth analyzing for itself and for hints about the more litigation-happy common-law world toward which this Anglo-Norman discourse was leading. My best guess is that contemporaries were quite comfortable understanding as plaints, or petitions for redress of wrong, all the litigation described, alluded to, or hinted at in the very scattered sources at our disposal, barring office prosecutions. An admittedly exceptional case from a few years after the Conquest illustrates the kind of "trespassory" language that was to become common. The sheriff of York was harassing Archbishop Ealdred with unwonted exactions. A direct appeal to desist only exacerbated the situation. So when Ealdred found himself in the Conqueror's presence, he seized his opportunity by refusing his customary blessing. The horrified barons read this as an intentional insult to the king. Equally shocked, William threw himself humbly at his prelate's feet. Ealdred explained that he was acting as Saint Peter's vicar in an effort to deal with a wrong done to his church's saintly patron. "He who does not fear to do injury [injuriam] to Peter's vicar," he added, "must feel Peter's power." The king first begged him to change his curse for a blessing and then ordered punishment for the sheriff and full restitution of everything taken (down to the very ropes that had bound the confiscated grain sacks). "And so from that day on," the local chronicler noted, "none of the great men around dared to inflict on him or his men any further 'injuriam . . . vel contumeliam.'"[188] The goal was to retrieve, if not to improve, the status quo ante. Once you had the king's ear, the plaint itself could be quite informal; there was no set form.[189] When physical access was difficult, men tried to do the job by putting the wrong into writing and sending it by letter, presumably a tougher task.[190] Even oral plaints delivered in person

---

186. *EYC* viii.17, 24 (ca. 1118–30, ca. 1130–38) are good illustrations from the Warenne honor. Also Round 1888, 12 (1127).

187. *EYC* iii.888, v.159 (1135–80, 1155–68); Van Caenegem 1990–91, nos. 12, 187C (1072–83, 1107–11); and the case at the following note. Classically, *iniuria* on its own also carried connotations of shame.

188. Van Caenegem 1990–91, no. 1 (1066–69), a nice example of the aggressive way petitioners needed to treat Anglo-Norman kings if they were to get a favorable hearing.

189. E.g., ibid., 236 (1110–24).

190. Ibid., 173 (1104–7), consists of letters from the bishop of Norwich.

had to be pressed with all rhetorical and other relevant skills; they did not always succeed.[191]

The particular form in which the plaint was made and argued entailed no particular set royal response. Anglo-Norman England remained far from the regulated, more nearly mechanical world of common-law writs and forms of action. Complainants were glad to gain an ad hoc remedy for their plight in, for example, an ephemeral order for restitution and compensation of the kind least likely to survive. Better still, though, was the extraction of a written privilege to guarantee continuing royal support against future wrongs. The Abingdon chronicler records an illustrative, fairly mundane case. Toward the end of the eleventh century, the house complained to William Rufus over wrongs to its customary rights in Oxfordshire, perhaps toll exemptions and the like. The king sent a writ to the sheriff, declaring that the monks were to enjoy their customs in future as well and honorably as they had in the time of King Edward and the Conqueror; that no man should do them wrong thenceforth; and that the sheriff do the abbot full right concerning his reeve and other servants who had previously wronged the monks.[192] Local notables in their shire court will have easily recalled the details of these offenses, mentioned only at the end of the writ, that had precipitated the abbot's plaint. But the rehearsal of the grievances served as a reminder to all that Abingdon enjoyed the king's grace and was not to be harassed. Royal favor was announced in a form (sealed patent) that could be produced and flourished in adversaries' faces for years to come.

Not all postulants were so fortunate. We must suspect that successful pleas more normally produced something less, an executive order for redress to the sheriff or another royal surrogate, or sometimes directly to the wrongdoer himself. The majority of extant royal writs from the century after the Conquest, and many hundreds more that have not survived, met such needs. We shall never know what proportion was obeyed. Sheriffs would not always jump to implement the royal will. They felt entitled to inquire into the justice of the royal writs they received.[193] Local politics might intervene. And the arrival of a royal writ could meet with resistance.[194] The real point of an Anglo-Norman royal writ was twofold. It announced to the

---

191. Ibid., 170 (1105), has Henry I and his queen obdurate before two hundred barefooted priests.

192. Ibid., 148 (1087–97).

193. Van Caenegem 1959 (177–81, 238–56, 272–80, 299–304) locates this "judicialization" in the final decades of Henry I's reign by reading the writ formulas literally. He takes in my view too little account of the likely responses of their addressees and the disputants themselves.

194. Van Caenegem 1990–91, no. 173 (1104–7), records that a royal writ for a Yarmouth fishermen's chapel provoked resistance "vi armata" from their rivals. Flower 1944 (90, 96) cites cases of resistance to service of royal writs from the early common law; bearers could not easily be forced to *eat* the king's writ until his chancery had begun to seal it closed, which made it bite size.

recipient's neighbors that he enjoyed royal favor, and it loaned him some portion of royal power with which to try and achieve immediate ends such as the righting of wrongs. Writs were not yet mere legal instruments. When successful, they solved problems, ended violence, and kept people out of the courts. We can seldom be sure that the real goal of the exercise was to summon the enemy to appear in court before justices able to order punishment or the payment of compensation. These occasions may be exceptional if indicative of the future. One nice case in which court proceedings did result is the writ that Abingdon Abbey obtained from Henry I against the refusal of Oxford boatmen to pay river tolls. A local court awarded the monks a full declaration of their rights, then summoned the recalcitrant boatmen and ordered them to take their due payments at once to the abbey cellarer, effectively an award of arrears or damages.[195]

CONCLUDING THOUGHTS

This chapter has established the continuing existence in the twelfth century of both a vengeance culture and its occasional employment in direct action to redress wrong. Churchmen and jurists responded to this reality in complex ways. Much that is familiar from the textbooks makes improved sense in this context. And we also see in some detail the notions of wrong through which the English converted this part of their ethics into legal action and ultimately into rights.

The procedures concerning "undifferentiated" wrong worked very differently from their thirteenth-century successors. Yet the twelfth-century materials carry ghostly hints of features familiar from the later common law, especially the precursors of those "tickets" by which thirteenth-century trespass plaintiffs claimed their day in court.[196] Some twelfth-century complainants had pleaded that they had been wronged in some fashion such as "vi et armis"[197] or in breach of the peace.[198] Or they had sought to persuade some great man that he suffered from their alleged wrong. The shame element too could be pleaded prominently. Greed for damages motivated some

---

195. Van Caenegem 1990–91, no. 191 (1110–12); the writ had apparently ordered the sheriffs "quatenus rectam justiciam inde facerent"; the venue appears to be an Oxford city court. Ibid., 167 (1102–4), is another comparable Abingdon case.

196. The tag that later enshrined the principle that some losses were not recoverable is "dampnum sine injuria." Cf. Bracton 1968–80, fols. 45b–46b, 235b (ii.140–43; iii.198–99). Britnell 1979 (93–94) suggested that it arose in the context of changes to royal market grants made at the beginning of John's reign. I wonder whether early cases of, say, the action of Nuisance, might not take this notion back into the twelfth century. For the maxim's ultimate source, the Roman law definition of "dampnum iniuria datum" remedied by Lex Aquilia, see Berger 1953 (547–48).

197. Van Caenegem 1990–91, no. 173; cf. ibid., 303, 334.

198. Van Caenegem 1959, no. 67.

then as later.[199] But these signposts to the future are most evident to historians with hindsight than they can have been at the time. They show merely that men construct new institutions from existing materials.

Yet notions change fast once the process is under way. When Robert de Lacy in 1194 granted a set of customs to his new borough of Pontefract, the language he used must have come from some law school graduate. Anyone who could successfully deny before the reeve ("pretore") an accusation that he had committed an "iniuria" or "delictum" "unjustly and without reason and within the peace" will recover damages "per forisfactum."[200] This is already the language of early trespass, a nice indicator of the direction in which thoughts about wrong were now moving.

199. In addition to the case cited at n. 195, Van Caenegem 1990–91, no. 185, discussed earlier, illustrates some older cultural imperatives.

200. *EYC* iii.1523: "Qui aliquem rectaverit de aliquo delicto in placito coram pretore, quod injuste et absque ratione et in pace illi forisfecerit, et ille negaverit injuriam vel irrationem vel pacem et quicquid dixerit versus eum bonum dedit responsum, qui negaverit injuriam vel irrationem vel pacem et non fuerit culpatus de aliqua istarum, judicabitur in curia pretoris et per forisfactum recuperabit responsum suum."

CHAPTER FIVE
COMMON LAW AND CENTRAL
ORDER IN ANGEVIN ENGLAND

Historians have long thought the reforms of Henry II and his sons marked a major transformation of legal administration and the whole process of adjudication in England. Various interpretations have almost all shared a common premise: that the decisive act was the royal provision of remedies to implement land title, notably the petty assizes, novel disseizin and the rest, plus the "action of right." In this chapter, by way of contrast, I approach the changes more through the personal perceptions of the political actors involved than has been usual. This perspective enables me to offer an alternative to the customary black-letter agenda of lawyer legal historians, one less exclusively geared to the issues that produced lawyers' law, less obviously cataclysmic *ab origine*, and less obsessed with land property and the real actions.

There is no dispute that the Angevins' fertility in the generation of new writ-based remedies for land claims was immensely influential in setting the character of the nascent common law. Writs channeled court argument along lines that did indeed compel the creation of lawyers' law; without them, no "forms of action" could develop.[1] The resulting shifts of control were indeed of some political importance to the king.[2] Questions of land title are more intimately related to law and order than is generally supposed, a fact disguised by the lawyers' categories of real property, crime, and the like. But the commitment of each king's coronation oath related very directly to law and order. The new king promised to do good justice to his people. Many who heard

---

1. The classic account is Pollock and Maitland 1898 (ii.558 sq.), with which one might compare Milsom 1985 (272–73). When someone gets around to a reconsideration of the forms of action, they will need to take account not just of the derivation from the Roman law *actio* (on which see Berger 1953, 340; and *Inst.* 4.6 pr.) but also of the fact that criminal procedures were excluded; cf. *Inst.* 4.18 pr. and Berger 1953, 340, 418, s.vv. "crimina publica," "accusatio."

2. I had rather hoped to be the one to bring the Milsomian changes in our understanding of legal change in this period into the mainstream of political and social history. A major achievement of Coss 1991a was to have made a good start on this enterprise.

him on such occasions would envision his commitment to justice in language like that of the Norman *Summa de legibus* (1236), which included among its definitions of *ius* the right to one's deserved reward, as one says of a hanged thief that he received "his proper due."[3] Ownership of the gallows on which thieves got their due was at this time a weighty issue of property rights. We should, then, lay alongside our discussions of the forms of action of civil procedure some comparable account of the legal procedures for the management of public order. Only thus can we hope to achieve a properly nuanced understanding of the sources and consequences of the common law and its birth.

The nub of the matter remains the king's claim to central control of jurisdiction. The promotion of this central model of justice was indisputably significant. The new common law certainly provided new procedures and a new legal culture but could not prevent individuals, swift to adapt to the requirements of the new system, from manipulating the new remedies toward their old goals.

The result was both more and less than the mere jurisdictional "shift of control" many now claim to find here.[4] The real Angevin achievement was to bring about a vast broadening of access to the king's law. Just how many people were equipped to take full instrumental advantage—that is, to prosecute their grudges and pursue their own gain through the common law—is unclear. Because quantifiable data are scarce even after the first plea rolls of the 1190s and totally absent from the crucial decades around 1166–76, estimates will always be largely a matter of judgment. Research certainly needs to range far beyond conventional legal history. A useful analogy is the adoption of new ways to perpetuate property dispositions in a world where the old methods were dismissed as merely private arrangements.[5] My own impression is that local power equations may in fact have changed rather little under the new common-law régime.

Henry appears to have hoped and expected otherwise. Our task here is, therefore, to evaluate a set of unintended consequences of a very conscious attempt to move in a quite different direction. Thanks to Milsom and others, we now appreciate better how profoundly the new royal remedies came to affect men's property calculations in the decades leading up to 1215. The

3. For the coronation oath, see, e.g., Stubbs 1913, 244 (Howden): "quod rectam justitiam exercebit in populo sibi commisso"; Bracton 1968–80, fol. 107 (ii.304). Tardif 1896, 6 (I.i.i.4): "stipendium meritorum, secundum quod dicitur quod latro suspensus bene habuerit jus suum." The author of the *Prose Lancelot* had said a few years earlier that "there was no lord in the world who did better justice" than Duke Esau, when he hanged a treacherous steward alongside his equally treacherous brother. *Lancelot du lac* 1991–93, ii.394: "il n'avoit adonques seignor terrien el monde qui miaux tenist jostise que li dux."
4. This key interpretational phrase comes from Milsom 1976.
5. See, on the Cockfield case, Holt 1983 (193–98, 218) and Hyams 1991a (180–81).

consequences of the real actions themselves reached far beyond matters of property. Questions of title and tenure always held the potential for violence. Many lawsuits stirred deep passions and left long resentful memories. Conversely, the roots of appeals and other "criminal" process frequently lay in competition for property.[6] These generalities become concrete when we examine the introduction of public prosecution for serious offenses through the Assizes of Clarendon 1166 and Northampton 1176. Our findings significantly improve our understanding of the implications of private-initiative prosecution of wrong, by trespass and appeal.

These "criminal" assizes and the procedures they incorporate almost certainly represent the most important royal intervention of the whole Angevin reform into English social arrangements. Through them Henry and his advisers made a firm bid for mastery of the public sphere of his realm and the high ground of public argument. What did *not* happen is significant to the argument. Few aspects of medieval English history will escape the effects of a reassessment of their character and role.

Henry's initial intention was to supplement, but not to replace, an existing system of law and order, over which the king presided but which he certainly could not, in the early 1160s, control. After Henry II's accession, the arrangements for dealing with wrong and disorder must have looked ripe for reconstruction along with so much else.[7] The avowed goal was to revert to the traditional state of affairs existing before the civil strife of the previous reign. The main responsibility for prosecution of any suspected wrongdoer had always previously rested in principle with the victim and his close kin.[8] It was a private matter in the sense that the clear ideal was for someone to put his own body behind the victim's suit. There may have been no routine way in Norman England to compel a suspect to set his own life and members at risk until such an accuser came forward to stake his too.[9] In the en-

---

6. The introduction of the distinction between crime and tort, most probably from Roman law, is central to much that follows in part 3.

7. Amt 1993 is a good recent treatment.

8. Van Caenegem 1976 sets beyond doubt the existence of prosecution at the initiative of royal officials before 1166. He cannot, however, offer any precise estimate of the comparative frequency or importance of the two approaches. More seriously, his hypothesis of a twelfth-century European trend toward office prosecutions linked to political centralization (42 sq.) raises problems at both ends of the English story. Old English reeves and judges clearly at times prosecuted thieves and others on their own initiative (see chap. 3). It is beyond belief that they lacked authority for this. Similarly, one would have expected common-law judges frequently to order inquests at the king's suit (read: in the public interest) after failed or quashed appeals. This they certainly did in the thirteenth century but only very rarely in the early years before 1215. See Groot 1983, 130–39.

9. *LHP* 64 effectively establishes the generality in the early twelfth century of the requirement that complainants offered battle or other proper suit, risking their own bodies in order to put opponents to their defense.

suing duel, the role of the king and his servants was pretty much limited to umpiring.[10] Initiative had to come from a private citizen through a public challenge. And this favored notables, the "big men," just as the general feud ethos had done. Great men might laugh the challenge of a "nobody" literally out of court. The accuser had better beware of "accidents" to prevent him from obtaining his day in court. Should he reach court, he might find himself facing some professional bruiser hired as champion and prepared to swear personal knowledge of his lord's innocence.[11] Those who set the tone in local society eagerly accepted the traditional procedures as part of their macho birthright. What could a well-meaning king do to level the playing field? Clearly, he could not always be physically present to see "fair play." Henry faced crucial questions: Who sets the local rules of adjudication? Who oversees business in the shires? And who, thus, possesses the real power? Were this rule-giver to be someone other than the king, he would possess the ability to take over any new institutions such as were introduced by Angevin reforms.[12] So soon after a damaging and inconclusive civil war, Henry was in no position to confront his baronage. He dare not face down magnates too nearly his equals in manpower. However, a possible solution was at hand in the exclusive royal duty to offer justice to all. The king was just acquiring one argument unavailable to any rival: the conflation of all inhabitants of his realm, whoever's men they might be, as "subjects" under royal authority. It is no coincidence that the justices of 1176 were instructed to take oaths of fidelity from all adults as they prepared to administer the Assize of Clarendon in its newly modified form. Henry may even have *believed* in his calling to protect men from their enemies.[13]

THE "NEW ASSIZE" OF 1166–76

By some such means, perhaps, did Henry's advisers encourage him to take in 1166 a peace initiative in the public name. Although a minutely detailed narrative of political development and legal change during the decade between

10. See below for Groot's suggestions on the appeal in royal courts during the decades before 1215. His cases may (or may not) have implications for the mid-twelfth-century position.

11. See Groot 1983, 116. But widely known loopholes permitted outsiders to assert a colorable interest in the appeal.

12. I am reminded of the old commercial slogan: "Take care that the Dubonnet she drinks comes from you!" I discuss this "penetration" of royal justice, along with the advent of "bastard feudalism," in chap. 8.

13. The curial Richard Fitzneal calls lords the "domestic enemies" of their vassals (Johnson 1983, 101). How novel this was may be doubted. But although the sub-Carolingian loyalty oath required by pre-Conquest kings of all males over twelve (the same age specified in 1176) is clearly part of the story, there seems to be no Old English term for *subject*. We need a study of Latin words *subditus*, *subiectus*, etc.

the two assizes is needed, it suffices for present purposes to consider the two assizes together as constituting a single disjuncture in administrative and legal development. This "new assize" represents a major royal intervention into matters previously covered by private remedies considered traditional, if not indispensable. It marks the ultimate origin of the grand juries and indictment that have characterized public prosecution of crime in the Anglo-American common law into the modern age.[14] Despite the admitted existence of scattered precedents for these devices, this decade of activity marks the definitive introduction into England of a system of public prosecution for what in due course, and not coincidentally, would be known as crime. It identified for supplementary public action both perceived offenses serious enough to touch the king and the common weal (pleas of the crown) and suspected offenders who might otherwise escape prosecution and punishment.

What was this "new assize" and how did it work? It started in 1166 with an unusually well recorded legislative measure, clearly framed with great care. The sensitivity with which this document instructed royal justices and sheriffs to supplement, but not to supplant, traditional private prosecutions of wrong recalls the similar care devoted contemporaneously to the creation of the assize of novel disseizin. Indeed the "new assize" could easily have emerged from the same council discussions and was possibly intended to be understood as part of the same drive toward the restoration of peace after Stephen's "usurpation" and the ensuing "anarchy." The assize of novel disseizin, although conventionally studied as a part of the common law of real property which soon absorbed and coalesced round it, may equally be viewed in terms of a wrong committed in breach of the peace and so justifying the exceptional remedy offered. The major contrast between the two assizes lies in the scale of tools employed. Where novel disseizin looked forward to delicate scalpel surgery, the Assize of Clarendon took a broad-brush approach that tarred and feathered those who needed ostracizing.

The Assize of Clarendon sought to institutionalize in twelve-man juries that concept of neighborhood reputation used in England since at least the eleventh century.[15] The jurors were to do two separate things.[16] First, they

14. The following section does not aspire to present a complete account of the assizes, just to establish their central place in the story covered by this book. I take my lead from the account in Meekings 1979–83, vol. 1, which modifies but does not quite supersede his earlier account in Meekings 1961. I mostly follow the nuanced views of Holt 1971 on our texts of the assizes and their implications. See also Hurnard 1941. Van Caenegem 1982 usefully compares the assizes with the contemporary "Grote Keure" of Flanders, although from a much more evolutionist perspective than is offered here.

15. This could use some detailed demonstration. I first made the observation in Hyams 1980 (107).

16. Here I follow Meekings 1961 (33–37, 92–97) and 1979–83 (i.94–97, 112–25), although Bellamy 1998 (20) expresses doubts.

named from their own knowledge all known rogues and villains who threatened order on their own patch.[17] That is, they named individuals who had committed any one of four categories of serious offense (expanded to six in 1176 and further thereafter), a group initially very similar to those found across the Channel in areas once under Carolingian justice.[18] Although the jury usually named the offense category, they never defined it or offered details of any specific offense, such as where or when it was supposed to have been committed. By the end of the century, the names were simply listed, preferably in writing, to assist sheriffs in finding and arresting alleged perpetrators, and the procedure was called indictment.[19] The second, more specific task concerned offenses, not offenders. The jurors answered an official questionnaire (later called the articles of the eyre) on specific offenses they knew to have been committed against the king's interest and which might otherwise have lain concealed to the king's detriment.[20] From this task of "presentment" derives the future grand jury's other name, jury of presentment.

These are two quite separate procedures performed by the same bodies of men. They may not have been started at the same time. We link them here because they so clearly were intimately associated by the time the sources begin to illustrate in detail the results of the combined legislation of 1166–76. When the jurors knew only the name of a suspicious character, they indicted him by name without any proof of a specific offense.[21] And when, as often, they could merely record the doing of nefarious acts in ignorance of the identity of those who had committed them, they presented the justices with details of the acts alone. Amid all this licensed imprecision there is considerable scope for error and omission, not to mention adjustment in the interest of friends. No wonder God's judgment (and later a trial jury) was needed to complete convictions.

Much of the historical interest of the new assize lies in the administrative arrangements for its implementation. These include an astonishing amount of written communication and record but very little lawyers' law.[22] The as-

17. Compare the later practice of indicting men as "common" (which I take to mean "public" as well as persistent) thieves, robbers, peacebreakers, and so forth.

18. Hyams 1982 (84–85) noted the vicarial character of the targets of Henry's first efforts at public prosecution. For a possible, quite recent model from Flanders, see De Gryse 1976.

19. Collas 1964 (lvii) notes the implication that the accusations were written down, but many indictments seem to have been oral and unwritten well into the thirteenth century.

20. Hurnard 1941 and Van Caenegem 1976 present different views on the way this may have been attempted before 1166.

21. Maitland 1887, 200 (1220), is an illustration.

22. The period between the two assizes was probably crucial for the triumph of pragmatic literacy in English government; Stubbs 1913 (161–81) makes the basic case. See Clanchy 1993, 62–68.

sizes are an excellent counter to the jurists' dismissal of crime as containing no "real" law, because the courts devote so much of their time to mere fact. How the sheriffs impaneled and questioned their juries, and how the justices received those verdicts, soon created new law.[23] Henry II had around him many practical men, hardened administrators who competed for attention and favor against the schools-trained lawyers and intellectuals responsible for thinking out clever legal devices like novel disseizin and the 1164 procedure for dealing with "criminous clerks."[24] Men of this ilk were surely aware of the facts of shire life and the advantages enjoyed by notables with the sheriff's ear. Perhaps they were just outmaneuvered or outvoted. Nevertheless, the law generated by the workings of the new assize came quite quickly to suit the local powers as well as the traditional situation had.

It is important not to read the story backward in the light of the later common-law code of criminal law that ultimately resulted from these events. Modern accounts understandably stress the inexorable extension of the king's peace, until it effectively covered all violence within the realm that the king cared to claim as his.[25] Arguably, this defines the direction of change. In the next chapters I examine the process of jurisdictional shuffling that split legal remedies into the borrowed Roman law categories of civil and criminal law. But that process was a long road whose end—a royal monopoly of licit violence and response to wrong—remained at best a distant goal in 1166. The effective organizing concept largely remained the ancient grab bag of pleas of the crown, which encompassed every kind of right the king might wish his justices to enforce on his behalf. Certainly, there were plenty of practical restraints on the uninhibited enjoyment of violence. Those who played that game had to beware of royal prosecution for robbery, mayhem, or homicide—capital offenses all.

Anyone shamed and resentful of his wrongs must have paid attention. Yet tenacious feud mentality still entered many calculations. The men who staffed and used the king's courts continued to enjoy a literature replete with exemplars of just vengeance, where victims of wrong took their own recourse if they could or sought assistance from others better empowered to

23. What bestows particular importance on this is the absence of any authoritative definitions of the offenses. Each group of court personnel (sheriff, jurors, justices, etc.) appeared to have its own understanding of the offenses it tried. The only control was that some of these people had experience of other jurisdictions, and even more the rare but ever-present possibility that a decision would become the subject of a plea of false judgment in a higher court, that of the king. I consider the definition of common-law crimes further in chap. 8. Equally, the administrative decisions about the circumstances in which the chancery would issue writs for a jury trial also created new law.

24. "Constitutions of Clarendon," clause 3 (Stubbs 1913, 164–65), still essentially as explicated by Maitland in "Henry II and the Criminous Clerks" (Maitland 1911, ii.232–50).

25. I discuss the expansion of the king's peace in more detail in chap. 7.

take it for them, their lords, princes, the king himself. They surely saw the king's great conflict with Archbishop Thomas Becket in this light right down to its tragic dénouement in 1170 and beyond.[26] We have seen how the feud-like moral notions underpinning personal decisions about wrong remain clearly visible in clerical discussions of sin.[27] But then self-help remained in many circumstances a licit response to violence and dispossession well into the thirteenth century.[28] Only the workmanlike skills of plea-roll clerks expunge the accompanying passions from case records and so drive them mostly from our sight.

Against this underlying continuity of reception must be placed the contemporary perception that the assizes constituted a revolutionary innovation that required substantial justification. Modern commentators do not always recognize how few contemporaries shared their applause for the law reforms. The Angevins' subjects were no Victorians; they received the novelties coolly, emphasizing the cost and intrusiveness of big government in almost American fashion.[29] Any close reading of Henry's assize texts certainly reveals an element of judicious justification very much consistent with the feeling that this innovation required some defense. There is, for example, a notable contrast between Henry II's usual care to recite assent in the first six chapters of the assize that established the new procedure and the command language into which he comfortably lapsed elsewhere in this complex document.[30]

I have drawn attention already to the traditional notion that no man should be compelled to place his life and members at risk (through corporal punishment) unless some accuser risked his body similarly through an offer of battle. Magna Carta, clause 38, indicates the continuing reverence offered this hallowed principle ("Wo kein Kläger ist, da ist auch kein Richter") into

---

26. This view of Becket's murder, the king's fury, and the need to avenge his shame comes out very clearly, for example, in the secondary, popular French account of Guernes de Pont-Sainte-Maxence 1971, ll. 5011 sq.

27. In chap. 2.

28. Sutherland 1973 (96 sq.) shows the law's ambivalence toward self-help and its efforts to tame and transform this.

29. The extracts from Ralph of Diss, quoted in Stubbs 1913 (155–56) are a fair sample of the critical ambivalence displayed by educated observers. See also Peter of Blois, letter 95 (MPL 207, cols. 298–302).

30. Compare the Assize of Clarendon, clauses 1–6, with clauses 8, 11, 14–15, 19, 22 (Stubbs 1913, 170–73), including repeated reiterations of the royal will, and note the extra care taken in 1176 to recite assent from the recent rebels around the young king (Assize of Northampton, clause 7 [Stubbs 1913, 180]). Another suggestive detail is the 1166 requirement (clause 1) that presentments should be made by *legaliores*. This may indicate men able to claim something more than mere *legalitas*, the right to make their own law, although royal draftsmen often seem to use comparative forms as a simple intensifier in the twelfth century.

the thirteenth century.[31] This may help explain the *Glanvill* author's care to distance the procedure of the new assizes of Clarendon and Northampton from the routine ones of older law.[32] The vast contemporary audience for romance will at first have seen the new public procedure pressed on them as a coward's way to deny men the ancient right to face off their accuser. Many will have deemed the assize a highly radical, even unwanted step. The draftsmen's recourse to language of *publica potestas*, with its very Carolingian resonance, reflects a feeling in the royal camp that they needed to justify and defend the new public prosecutions.[33]

This was best accomplished by invoking some notion of the public interest. The so-called Inquest of Sheriffs of 1170 provides an excellent example. Henry's draftsmen cloaked his usual driving concern to recover moneys he considered his own, and which his servants had retained unjustifiably, with a ringing declaration of the proper standards they ought to follow. Among other things, the king wanted to know of unjust assize prosecutions or releases for gain or promise, or out of love or hatred.[34] This public-interest gloss would very soon spread over the ancient appeal procedure too, at least where appellants chose to plead felony before royal justices. The king's courts were to be open to all his subjects, rich and poor, but only for reputable public purposes. Royal justice was not available for the mere prosecution of personal grudges. Thus complainants must justify their claim to the king's grace and aid with some approved purpose acceptable to his justices,[35] or risk the quashing of their suit.

A king with a conscience had to have good reasons to introduce such an innovation. Paramount was the near panic over the prevailing degree of disorder and unpeace detectable in the assize text's tone. Initially, perhaps, pre-

31. Hurnard 1941 (394 sq.), Holt 1971 (95 n. 3), and Van Caenegem 1976 (61 n. 61, 71 n. 94) give many of the pertinent references to this "traditional notion" preceding Magna Carta 1215. My friend Charles Donahue differs from Ivo of Chartres (*Decretum* vi.117) in believing that this may well have originated in Roman law. See also Chrétien 1982, ll. 4566–69: "Que ce est reisons de justise / que cil qui autrui juge a tort / doit de celui meismes mort / morir que il li a jugiee" (justice requires that he who judges another falsely should die the same death he had himself adjudged). But Jesus' remarks concerning the woman taken in adultery (Joh. viii.10) are so apposite that a search for a relevant Bible gloss looks very promising; start with gl. *Jhesus autem perrexit* ad loc.

32. *Glanvill* xiv.2 (173).

33. Assize of Clarendon, clause 1: "pro pace servanda et justitia tenenda." Later in this chapter I discuss the attempted exclusion from 1170 onward of private motives (*malicia*) from the public procedures and the extension of this principle to the ancient appeals too.

34. Inquest of Sheriffs, clauses 6, 10 (Stubbs 1913, 176–77). One could read clause 10 as referring to out-of-court settlements in private appeals or feuds; see the equivalent chapter (vii) in the version put to jurors (Morey and Brooke 1967, 523).

35. The "tickets" (as Milsom termed them) by which access was gained are to be found in both "trespass" suits and appeals "of felony"; I discuss them in chap. 7.

sentment was introduced as an exceptional remedy for an exceptionally difficult situation, a one-time exercise. It was merely "hac vice . . . pro predicta necessitate," the king explained, to reassure the monks of Durham that the 1166 supersession of their liberties was not intended as a precedent.[36] The assize was designed to target major offenders, men too powerful to be reached by normal means. The distant precedent of Æthelred's Wantage Code may conceivably have suggested this possibility.[37] The major difficulty for private prosecutions of wrong must always have been the entrenched power of some "Mr. Big"—at worst the head of organized crime in the area, at best one of the small group of notables who dominate any local society. Lesser men hardly dared confront such powers directly. They lacked the status to confront him or his followers, and they knew that to accuse the great man or his associates of any offense and then have to offer the traditional challenge of ordeal or duel was to invite the reprisals due an enemy. Without equally powerful aid, they could hardly hope to get their day in court. There was little incentive here to encourage royal advisers to urge their master to perform his royal duties. The assize therefore empowered the politically insignificant to feed accusations into the system without the need to make themselves known to their great oppressors.[38] In principle, information might even originate from paupers or women. It should follow that those indicted in the first years were wealthier and more prominent than were those indicted later on. We need a study of offenders' names from the pipe rolls (where noted) and the estimated values of their chattels to test this possibility.[39]

The Angevin think tank nudged Henry into a broad-brush approach to the problem of performing his duty to furnish such men with good justice. The texts that survive appear intended to convey only general instructions to justices. Thus, they give little indication of that conceptual precision and

36. Round 1899, 112. Hurnard 1941 (403 sq.) noted that the new procedure was not used on the 1168–69 eyre and was still distinguished as "new" a generation later. The limitation period back to Henry's accession in 1154 may also point in the same direction.

37. I do not imagine that the twelve elder thegns of III Atr 3 were expected to waste their time on petty offenders. It is tempting to connect the hypothesis that the assizes initially targeted offenders of status with the otherwise surprising absence of capital punishment in the assize. Van Caenegem 1982 (240–43) has different suggestions.

38. As Meekings 1961 (97) noted, "the essence of the eyre procedure was secrecy." Writs of prohibition "ex auditu plurium," introduced for comparable reasons a century later to facilitate action against the wishes of ecclesiastical powers, offer an appropriate analogy.

39. Serlo of Thurlaston was able to proffer ten marks after his prosecution. The Cornishman who had apparently survived the ordeal of hot iron in *Pipe Roll 6 Richard I* (174) was able to offer twenty marks to regain his lands. Proffers may be better tests than felons' chattels, whose assessments tend to underrecord value; see Hanawalt 1979, 129. The majority of thirteenth-century indictees came from the lower orders and the poor (Summerson 1985, xxviii–xxix).

law-school learning that emanate from the assize of novel disseizin (which may nevertheless have emerged from the same deliberations) and other allegedly more characteristic creations of the nascent common law. Yet it is clear enough that, just as in the better-studied petty assizes concerning property, Henry's men took care to preserve at least the appearance of traditional rights. I am still prepared to bet that royal servants sometimes rationalized early juries (tongue in cheek, perhaps) as but a new form of the judgment of God.[40]

Perhaps the initial conception of public prosecution allowed for a dual process, comparable to that which the influence of Romano-canonical procedure is said to have conferred on the petty assizes. The jury presentment would in this way supplement the right to appeal, without excluding that possibility for a later occasion. The reservation of private homicide appeals after the king had remitted his suit in a royal pardon apparently dating from the 1130s was one precedent.[41] It can be viewed as a royal declaration that what the king chooses to do with his suit must not affect the rights of the victim's kin. Henry I knew not to flout the traditional right to fight those who wronged you. His grandson was prudent enough to genuflect in a similar direction. A well-known if unique entry on the pipe roll makes this scenario plausible: After the 1166 eyre, Serlo of Thurlaston owed ten marks "to have his proof [dirationem] if he were appealed by anyone of the death with which he was indicted [retatus est]."[42] This seems to recognize the duality of rights. But if that was the initial idea, it was never permitted to crystallize into a legal right visible in later sources. If it had, the corollary ought to have been that justices exercised the option of turning aborted appeals into public prosecutions "at the king's suit." They did indeed do this in the thirteenth century whenever they deemed appropriate, but only very rarely before 1215.[43]

Henry and his advisers appear to have invested much more thought into the assizes than is generally appreciated. The royal effort extended beyond the intellectual sphere. The pipe rolls show a deplorable degree of medieval public expenditure on the building of jails as an essential prerequisite of the "stricter assize" procedure.[44] Here and elsewhere, the king was putting his

---

40. I hazarded this guess in Hyams 1981.
41. See chap. 4. See further RUMBAUD V. PRIEST.
42. *Pipe Roll 12 Henry II*, 57. Comment by Holt 1971, 95, and more generally 101 sq. As always with the compressed and laconic pipe-roll entries, other readings are very much possible. See also *Pipe Roll 23 Henry II*, 39; and Hurnard 1969, 18–19.
43. Groot 1983 (130–39) examines the pre-1215 evidence for this significant absence.
44. Pugh 1968, chap. 1. Richard FitzNeal's phrase "metu arctioris assize" (Johnson 1983, 97) may be a comment on the very recent Assize of Northampton.

own money into the project—the very reverse of the well-known tag "Justitia est magnum emolumentum." This royal expenditure is the best possible proof of the seriousness of his intent.

The existence of approvers[45]—convicted felons permitted to save their necks by appealing and then fighting their associates and any others whom they knew to be villains and offenders against the law—bolsters the argument. Those who won their duels and rid the land of a few more malefactors lived for a while, quite well, at the king's expense. He was also prepared to fund travel expenses to duel sites and (later) to train them in martial skills. The expenses for their upkeep appear on the pipe rolls alongside those for jail building. Few seem to have survived long; failure in any one of the series of duels meant death. This developmental dead end seems the most curious of all Angevin law-enforcement devices. Its origins have always been a puzzle. I know of no Continental analogues. There is no hint of anything similar in a vernacular literature crammed full of ordinary appeals. Although there is some slight evidence for a prehistory, approvers emerge into the light of Henry II's pipe rolls as an institution already fully formed. This could be a trick of survival. If the recorded pattern approximates the real story, though, we see Henry adopting a device occasionally used in the past and wrenching its potential for a purpose he and his advisers deemed important. This action comports with his habitual modus operandi in the law reforms.

LAW AND ORDER OVER LAND: THE OTHER ASSIZE

Henry's habitual modus operandi is perhaps most closely observed and much lauded in the creation of the assize of novel disseizin, that epitome of the new real actions often credited with the transition to the great common law.[46] Historians and lawyers alike class novel disseizin as a land action and include it in their books as civil, not criminal, law, property rather than violence and order. But as Henry and his advisers knew well, disseizins were themselves violent acts often leading to further violence.[47] Their suppression or control was essential to any scheme for peace in the realm. The very

45. Röhrkasten 1990, chap. 2; Hamil 1936.
46. The leading modern proponent of this is Milsom 1976. His treatment of "Countess Amicia's Case" (Milsom 1976, 45–47, 52, 54, 55, 56, 57, 62, 92, 93, 94, 95, 130, 185 n. 2, etc.), on which much of his lawyerly case hangs, may usefully be compared with mine in Hyams 1987 (494–96). Further data that has come to hand since somewhat strengthen my case for a "political" decision.
47. Sutherland 1973 was well aware of this as his index shows (s.vv. "Breach of the Peace" and "Violence"). Although Sutherland concluded that "the better keeping of the peace does not seem . . . to have been the principal object of the assize," the probability that it had originally combined presentment with individual suits did not escape his notice (ibid., 14, 28).

fact that novel disseizin apparently originated in, or very close to, the Assize of Clarendon in 1166 might have provoked more speculation about their common features than it has.[48] Only over the last generation has the hypothesis that novel disseizin had some kind of "criminal" or quasi-criminal origin approached orthodoxy.[49]

One should of course always remember that Henry of Anjou's novel disseizin rested on principles found widely in the French-speaking areas on the Continent.[50] There is nothing specifically English about it. That point conceded, I examine briefly how this new initiative may have fitted into the overall scheme of innovation in 1166. It is by now axiomatic that the essence of petty assizes such as novel disseizin lay in their borrowing from the learned laws the powerful notion of dual process,[51] which freed princes to offer newer remedies over the top of those traditionally available. How did this feature work for disseizins in 1166? The royal offering would not destroy the right of the "victim" of disseizin to bring an "appeal" plaint before an appropriate forum, just as anyone could for other wrongs (including ones about to be classified as felonies). It may itself have constituted just such a plaint. The English assize writ, as *Glanvill* first gives it more than twenty years after 1166, recites a plaint ("questus est nobis") of recent disseizin but also notoriously uses appeal language for the suit, seeking amercement but not damages from the disseizee/appellee.[52] That the earliest known Norman writ is in a quite different "praecipe" form that lacks both of these features may reflect its later date, after 1204, and much swift procedural development.[53]

These facts suggest a tentative hypothesis to explain the introduction of novel disseizin into the "undifferentiated" procedures for wrong at private initiative. We should dismiss the "appeal" language as speaking for any "criminal" origin. The required distinction between crime and tort resulted, as we shall see, from the events of 1166 themselves. The appeal-like details that persuaded scholars to presume a criminal origin for novel disseizin were even in the next century largely common to the "civil" action of trespass and are therefore less than conclusive. The initial two-stage process envisioned in 1166 could, then, have operated as follows. First, the king initi-

48. When the time comes to write the full legal narrative of Henry II's reign, the possible role of the inquiry behind the "Carte Baronum" in the same year should also receive its due.
49. Van Caenegem 1959, 283 sq.; Milsom 1981, 138–40.
50. Perrot 1910, 188–203; Strayer 1937.
51. Jouon des Longrais 1936 established this point.
52. *Glanvill* xiii.33 (167–68); and cf. ibid. xiii.38 (170).
53. *Très ancien coutumier* LXXIII.2 (Tardif 1881, 70). The second part is said to postdate the French conquest of the duchy. But there may have been some general Norman preference for the praecipe form.

ated a downward inquiry into disseizins in pursuit of his duty to do justice and keep the peace. Employing his right to require men to testify under oath as to royal rights, he then treated the findings as disclosing a wrong to him as king. This was no more than his Anglo-Saxon predecessors had done (although he was probably unaware of this), and he probably justified his actions to objectors in terms of a breach of his peace. He may have intended the assize as a one-off event and perhaps even proclaimed it as such.[54] This argument accords with the pipe-roll evidence before 1175, as Henry Mayr-Harting has pointed out to me.[55] We certainly have no reason to believe that the king and his advisers imagined any permanent abridgement of men's private rights to bring plaints for this or any other wrong. Nor is there as yet any sign of party-and-party private suits for novel disseizin. The most that an aggrieved disseizee could do at this stage was to feed information to the jurors, as many men surely did with offenses presentable under the extant Assize of Clarendon. The procedures will have looked very similar if not identical. Not until 1175–77 perhaps did the first "private" suits begin to appear, very likely as plaints spinning off from the presentments in much the way that (as I argue in chap. 7) the action of trespass itself originated a little later. This was apparently the first move in the major transformation from which the essential structure of real property law evolved in the future common law.[56] Just how long, if at all, the two procedures coexisted in a true dual process remains a matter for speculation. Certainly the *Glanvill* author included nothing of this kind in his 1187–89 account of the royal court.

A SINGLE GRAND DESIGN?

Surely we should read all the legal advances of the year 1166 as part of a single narrative, to discern fully the conscious royal initiative. Then it becomes impossible to believe that Henry II was merely offering his vassals royal assistance with the enforcement of existing custom. Once the king and his advisers had decided to extend the experiment, they were patently innovating on the grand scale, in "a nation-wide, centrally conducted operation"

54. There is little discussion of this cardinal point. On the dating of the decision, see Sutherland 1973, chap. 1, as modified by his concession to the more traditional view in Loengard 1978 (154–55 n. 28).

55. This was an oral communication. But Mayr-Harting promises a timely publication on the matter, so I leave the details to him. In the meantime, Van Caenegem 1959 (294–95) helpfully tabulates the pipe-roll evidence.

56. Cheney 1984 (12–14) assembles evidence for the kind of plaints by favored individuals possible even before 1166 and which could well have served as models. See ibid. (21–24) for her suggestions on the political means by which Henry's nobility were induced to accept some reduction in their own control of land title.

against an ever-widening group of major offenses.[57] They deliberately and consciously orchestrated an effort to engineer a "shift of control" over law and order from local powers to the king at the center.

However, the sad fact is that this royal takeover of law and order enjoyed limited success at best.[58] It proved easier to induce prelates and barons to permit the tacit redefinition in royal courts of their custom and seignorial rights than to persuade them to surrender control over their own neighborhoods. The serious offenses covered by the Assizes of Clarendon and Northampton, felonies as they were to be named, long remained legally undefined. The number of indictable offenses expanded over the succeeding decades, way beyond any initial vicarial group, without this causing any evident embarrassment.[59] We know little indeed of any pleading in royal (or any other) courts before the age of the YearBooks (from the later thirteenth century) about what actually constituted a particular offense. Definition seemed unnecessary, because all adults could be expected to "know" what murder or robbery or rape was. Thus those who controlled juries also substantially controlled the standards of order enforced at the eyre. They were able to screen indictments, suppressing perhaps some directed at their own activities, while furthering allegations against their enemies. Among these men of power one would certainly find the major offenders whom I have tentatively nominated as the assize's primary target—the very men best able to influence the composition of hundred juries and the decisions they reached. In contrast, the jurors themselves, if not actually creatures of magnates, certainly lacked the independence and status to perform their task free from local influence.

Perhaps the only way to defeat this putative unholy alliance of neighborhood power was to deploy against it a public body possessed of equivalent clout. The twelve elder thegns of Æthelred's Wantage Code may have posed similar problems a century and a half earlier. The very status that enabled them to face down their peers must also have tempted them to look after their own. The probing question "Quis custodiet custodes?" comes to mind. A century of frustrating experience of grand juries after 1166 doubtless made government all too aware that the reins were out of its hands. The

---

57. Van Caenegem 1976, 43. For this proactive Henry II, see the literature noted in n. 94.

58. Contrast Van Caenegem 1976, 75: "By welding the local juries to the central body of royal judges, the Assizes of 1166 and 1176, as enforced by the ensuing . . . eyres, solved for centuries a problem . . . urgently posed early in Henry II's reign."

59. This process of extension can be traced through the ever-lengthening articles of the eyre (Meekings 1979–83, 90–94). *Glanvill* xiv already recognizes a minimum of seven felonies. Meekings 1961 (318, index s.v. "Crimes, II") illustrates well the much wider range of indictable offenses in the thirteenth century.

problem was to create an accusing body strong enough to be independent of local influence but disinclined to go into business on its own. There was in the 1270s one further attempt to solve the problem. When Edward I initiated inquiries specifically into offenses of highborn offenders, he insisted that they be staffed by knights alone.[60] The Angevins never risked anything comparable; their efforts to restrain noble influence in the shires look fitful by comparison.

Grand juries probably picked mostly on the defenseless and the enemies of the rich and powerful. Such is often the way of the world. The suggestion can and must be tested through detailed local prosopographical study. As a working hypothesis it has, nevertheless, some suggestive and attractive features. First is the important fact that from the very inception of the assize system, the authorities struggled to keep control of "their" juries. They constantly tried to exclude illicit motives for both the preferment of indictments and the concealment of offenses, from fear or favor or in hope of gain, for love or hatred, in a word from malice.[61] And even when proper indictments reached court, the difficulties continued. The abandonment of adjudication to a trial jury permitted its members (many perhaps involved in the initial presentment) to decide on guilt and innocence largely shielded from judicial interference. So jurors could sometimes press their own agenda, whether for views of right and wrong differing from those of royal law but widely shared among their peers or simply to favor their own. The results often looked very like nullifications of the legislators' intentions, despite the best efforts of the questioning but ill-informed "outsider" justices.[62]

The phenomenon of judges questioning, if not hectoring, jurors before they would accept their verdict seems to enter the rolls during the second quarter of the thirteenth century. Here was the first step on the long road leading to Judge Jeffries and other colleagues of evil memory. Presumably, justices had learned to suspect that many juries followed their own views of justice rather than the king's laws but could seldom prove their suspicions. Small wonder that thirteenth-century eyres now began at each stop with the superficially impressive but outsider justices consulting the local notables (*buzones*) and extracting from them first thing lists of suspects for speedy ar-

60. Maddicott 1986, 13. See Jenks 2002 (5) for further recourse to knights in 1275 to purify inquisitions, in pleas *de odio et athia*.

61. I have discussed the language of malice in chap. 2, and indicated evidence of government concern into the thirteenth century in the previous section on the Inquest of Sheriffs. For further illustration, see Bracton 1968–80, fol. 185 (iii.71); Brand 2001, 242–44 (judicial oaths of 1257, 1278); Statute of Winchester 1285, clause 1 (Stubbs 1913, 464); and *Rotuli Parliamentorum* 1783, i.160a (1304), a trumped-up jury challenge "per maliciam precogitatam" to keep indicted men in jail.

62. On all this, Green 1985 (chaps. 1–3) is the authority.

rest (*privata*).[63] Their hope was to collect the malefactors and get genuine indictments against them before the locals could spirit them beyond capture. They perhaps recognized (as most modern scholars have not) their own impotence to set the local standards of public behavior and order.

A POLICY ON LAW AND ORDER?

We may wonder: Why all the effort? Why could Henry and his sons not leave the responsibility to others and content themselves with oversight of the process plus a royal cut from the proceeds? The Angevin vision of law and order emerges as substantially broader than historians have usually represented it, reaching deeply even into thinking behind the much-applauded real actions on land. The vision certainly encompassed all three "order" procedures of the future common law and possibly also the assize of novel disseizin as originally conceived. The reformers were prepared to bypass ancient appeal procedure, but so deeply was it entrenched in traditional rights that perhaps they dared not touch it too directly. The new public prosecution procedures of indictment and presentment were destined to form the future core of the criminal law, although no one will have guessed this at the time. Alongside, of equal importance but ultimately termed civil, lay the action of trespass, based on habits as ancient as the appeal but much less easily visible to the historian. Each of these ancient procedures was in effect refashioned for the also-new common law in the decades around 1200.

There are, indeed, many indirect indications that the Angevins conceived of their reforming task broadly. But the best way to establish the case is less direct: simply to investigate the implications of these very different elements in the light of the other concerns of this book. En route, we shall in turn learn more about the Angevin "shift of control" from its effects on legal remedies for wrongs.

In chapter 7 I revive an old hypothesis concerning the links between the appeal "of felony" and common-law trespass. It is necessary here to anticipate those findings with a brief, schematic presentation of the development and disentanglement of these two procedures of the early common law. The legal literature of the thirteenth century came to regard appeals of felony and trespass as quite separate remedies—the first a criminal prosecution, the other a civil action. But they had recently been twin procedures, conceptually all but indistinguishable, in an age that knew no "forms of action" anyway. And because the boundaries between the two procedures long re-

63. Meekings 1979–83, i.112 sq., and more generally i.87 sq.

mained permeable in either direction, the image should perhaps be one of "Siamese twins" sharing a single life-support system in the principle of wrong. Their common origin lay in a single right to seek a remedy for "undifferentiated" wrong by any appropriate procedural route. Once perhaps they had been, if not quite the same thing, then different ways of achieving virtually the same end of appropriate redress.

To understand why appeals eventually ended up as part of the criminal law, while trespass became almost the archetypal "civil" procedure, we must remember that we see little of English law and dispute resolution in this period beyond what the plea rolls of royal law from the 1190s on preserve to our gaze. The appeals on those rolls, to make the central point at once, represent the direct descendants of those private suits for wrong in Anglo-Saxon and Norman England that I rehearsed in chapter 3. The appeals visible on the rolls of royal courts thus form the tiny residue of what had been a far larger body of private suits once heard in the courts of lords and others all over England, and for that matter more or less everywhere in Western Christendom. The historian sees only that possibly minuscule proportion whose appellants pleaded them as "of felony" to make them the king's business. Although there were rules governing this pleading decision, the strategy of augmenting a complaint ("hyping" it) in order to obtain a royal hearing with its various consequences was already known well before 1200.[64] This contrast with the still subsisting honorable, traditional response to perceived wrong made the provision of routine public prosecution appear so radical to its critics.

The roots of the two common-law actions and their undifferentiated ancestor lie in two ancient shared premises. First comes an elemental secular, vernacular notion of wrong, long predating law schools and learned analysis.[65] This represents the layman's feeling that he is a victim who has suffered an injustice demanding vengeance. The intrinsic ambiguity of this conception should be familiar by now. The self-cast victim must proceed to decide how best to respond to the perceived injustice, through the familiar calculus of response.

The process may be analyzed in terms both of the resources available to the victim and then of his goals, his ideal redress. In neither case was consideration limited to the possibility of litigation alone. By resources I mean social status and position, the strength of the victim's potential support

---

64. Van Caenegem 1990–91, no. 471 (1171–74), is a splendid early example. Cf. Hyams 1986.
65. For the notion of elementary legal ideas, see Milsom 1985, 151 ("elementary legal ideas" involved at every stage of legal analysis) and 158 (tort not "one of the elementary particles of law, but . . . a residuary class"); also see Milsom's epoch-making study of the origins of trespass (ibid., chap. 1).

group and the willingness of his friends to support him in court and outside. Was it better for the victim to seek a judgment from God and his peers, in the form of an appeal tried by battle? Or was there more hope from his peers alone, in which case a plaint of trespass put to a jury might seem the better option? What did the victim want? Or what could he hope to achieve? If vengeance alone would satisfy him, then given that Angevin royal justice was making direct violence very risky, the option of choice was an appeal, with duel and punishment by loss of life or members to follow. The knowledge that the victim and his supporters could often hope to carry out the punishment themselves added to the allure.[66] They thus gained the great satisfaction of mutilating or hanging the enemy under the protection of the law but in full sight of a cowed and shamed opposition. Yet ensuing resentments might cause problems later, so if the preference was for greater safety, or if the victim felt that mere pecuniary compensation and a return to the status quo ante were sufficient, then a trespass plaint made better sense.

In either case, the victim had to commence by telling his story, his *conte*, his "count" as lawyers say. Appeal counts as recorded on the plea rolls are dry and formulaic. With a little imagination, though, one soon sees the affinities with the appeals of entertainment literature. Real-life appellants pleaded their plaints in emotive language designed to move their listeners in much the same way as did their literary counterparts. Their recital might tell of damage to their honor and seek honorable satisfaction for shame as well as actual loss. The major difference between counts in appeals and trespass lay in the goal sought. Appeals were the simple case, expected to lead to trial by battle, a duel between the four benches of the court. This was the finest of epic ways to settle grievances against an equal, especially if the aggrieved had greater faith in the strength of his (or a champion's) right arm than in the ability of his arguments to sway a court.[67] As feud was tamed to minimize damage within the community of a lordship or realm, appeal became the remedy of choice for the really angry or the very desperate. Men who doubted the sympathy of their lords and peers might by waging battle submit their cause to a higher authority and higher justice.

Trespass, in contrast, was a legally more sophisticated procedure, suitable for men lacking martial strength and confidence but with good access to competent legal advice.[68] Here, then, the victim worked first to convince a

66. This very important point merits greater prominence than I can give it here. Hyams 1986 (12) offers one colorful illustration. Further discussion follows in chap. 8.

67. Groot 1982 and 1983 (113) hold that jury trial was already becoming recognized as "the proper mechanism" before 1215.

68. Women could serve as a test here. The thirteenth-century rules that limited their right to appeal are well known; see Meekings 1961, 88–91; and 1979–83, i.123–25. But I know of no study of women as trespass plaintiffs or defendants, let alone a study that compared their chances for rem-

lord (under Angevin and later common law, this was always the king) to lend him aid against an enemy beyond his own powers to handle. The victim needed arguments to persuade the king (or his justice) that the wrong suffered was one deserving of remedy. The best ploy was to argue that the opponent had damaged the lord king and his honor too. This is the origin of what might be termed "tickets" of entry, the tickets, that is, by which an aggrieved person persuaded royal justices to give his plaint a hearing in their master's court.[69] The lord king should hear the plaint because (for example) the alleged wrong had been committed "against the lord king's peace" or "with force and arms." If convinced, the king tried to settle the matter in a way that would not deprive him of supporters, that is, to effect a peaceful conclusion without allowing any corporal vengeance.[70] This was no easy trick to manage, since it amounted to pronouncing a preference for one friend or vassal over another. If the case were badly handled, both might become so angry and alienated that each would defect, casting a negative example that could well affect still other vassals. A prudent lord consequently passed the buck to shelter behind the counsel of his court, which amounted to judgment by the disputants' peers. The common-law jury appears in this perspective a buffer device to protect the lord's person, by institutionalizing the counsel he received, and thereby to manage conflict within the lordship without violence. It led, logically enough, to monetary compensation—damages—without either party risking any body parts. This strategy was safe but unsatisfying for those so suffused with emotion that only vengeance would do; thus, litigant demand for appeals certainly did not cease in the early decades of the common law (as has sometimes been thought). Some always desired more than anything to harm their foes, or at least to use the threat of duel to scare them into concessions. The attractions of an allegedly more "rational" legal process were less apparent to angry litigants than to modern scholars.[71]

The main point can easily be summarized. Trespass and the appeal "of felony" at common law were both part of a history, already ancient in the late twelfth century, to tame feud. They represent two major strategies for dealing with wrong without entering the desperately dangerous world of open feud. Wronged men made choices according to what resources they possessed and what they most wanted to achieve.

---

edy against wrong through the two common-law remedies as against the previous "undifferentiated" procedures. See further Hyams 1996a, 230–31; and Hudson 1996a, 235–36.

69. The best known are the trespass formulas "contra pacem domini Regis" and "vi et armis." I discuss these in chap. 7. This image derives from Milsom 1985 (29).

70. I consider briefly the common-law rules against duels between lord and vassal or close blood relatives in chap. 6.

71. And perhaps less apparent also to such as the author of *Glanvill* ii.7 (28).

How did the incorporation of these efforts to subjugate feud into royal, public law change their form and nature? I approach the matter by way of an apparent objection to my view of the appeal. If appeals really were attenuations of feud, appellants' motives ought not to matter. Nobody should be surprised to find that those who pursue feuds, full or attenuated, do so out of strong feelings of hatred and enmity. Many would feel that some intensity of emotion was intrinsic to the process. Yet soon after 1166, cases appear in which first public prosecutions and then private appeals too were challenged by the accused on the ground that their accusers' motivation was hatred, which in turn vitiated their allegations. The evidence comes in the form of exceptional proffers recorded on the pipe rolls for the grant of a jury to inquire into the motives behind the accusation. The earliest known examples alleging hatred or envy come soon after 1176.[72] Although initially rare and expensive, the privilege of submitting appeals and indictments to special juries became increasingly routine, certainly by 1215. Appellees had an obvious interest both in delay and (often) in avoiding duel. Magna Carta came close to making jury trial, by this and other means, the appellee's right, and our writ soon became "of course" (so available to all) and familiar under the name of the writ, *de odio et athia*, "of hatred and spite."[73] Why was this route chosen by litigants and allowed by royal advisers?

The objection to abuse of the public prosecution procedures is the lesser problem. The king had already displayed concern about private abuse of his public remedy several years before the earliest writ proffers.[74] I know of no similar objection in English sources against an appeal—on the face of it a more private matter—before 1166. If anything, evidence of a previous anger or hatred may have strengthened an appeal, because it lessened the likelihood that the charges had been exaggerated.[75] Overall, the complainants' motives, though they might prevent someone serving as witness or juror,[76] were irrelevant. Any appeal could go to battle providing its appellor pos-

---

72. Hurnard 1969 (339–40) gives the early references.

73. Hurnard 1969 (app. I), the standard account, is modified in Groot 1983 (117–22). Jenks 2002 stresses the distinction between the pretrial writ itself and an interlocutory exception, subject, she thinks, to different rules. De Haas and Hall 1970 (CC 109) gives the form of the developed writ. Magna Carta 1215 (clause 36) is not specific to our writ.

74. In the Inquest of Sheriffs, discussed earlier in the chapter.

75. See *LHP* 92.14.

76. Because the rules of learned law exclude witnesses for such matters as enmity, we may take it that *Glanvill* ii.12 (32) would similarly disqualify a juror; cf. *Très ancien coutumier* VII.2, XXVII (Tardif 1881, 7, 25). The telling language of Bracton 1968–80, fol. 185 (iii.71), is a little more specific and would exclude witnesses and jurors for a really serious enmity or hatred, or close familiarity and alliance ("amicitiam") through kinship or marriage, where those involved "walk in almost the same steps" as the opposition.

sessed his *lex*, the public status that qualified him to fight his opponent in court, so long as he could support his oath with some prima facie evidence.[77]

Some see the allegation of "hatred and spite" as a fiction from the start, as just a way to raise an issue requiring local information and thus a jury trial.[78] This theory has one point in its favor. Exceptions that alleged improper motivation are never recorded in actions of trespass, which were quite as likely to have originated in hatred and spite. Trespass defendants had no need to question their opponents' motives. They had their jury without further effort and also knew that they could come to no harm in hair or hide; all they risked was money. There were soon other, more direct ways to evade battle in appeals. Yet the courts would now consider motives in appeal cases through the writ.

The allegation of hatred and spite is an odd way to request jury trial; it would have been odder still in the majority of appeals that alleged no felony and were tried away from royal courts.[79] It makes sense when an appellant struggles to jail or maim his enemy and the appellee resists as best he can.[80] The argument inevitably turns on inference. For twenty years after 1176, few actual pleas are recorded.[81] When the new royal plea rolls do start to report cases, they usually address the merits of the allegation, its truth or falsity. But the writ's wording encouraged men for once to plead their allegations of motivation in public, and extant inquisitions show how serious the investigation could be. This development helps to document the passions behind litigation.[82] It is hard to believe that the courts progressively narrowed down an option that had started as a broad, general right of challenge to appeals. In all likelihood, the pipe rolls tell something like the true story for once: jury proffers began slowly and exceptionally in the last years of Henry II, and the only ground that king and justices would at first admit was illicit motive, spite and hatred. Public opinion would not easily accept any dimin-

77. The objection that an appellor lacked *lex* is occasionally found, as in the early case cited in n. 78, but also on later occasions.

78. So Groot (1983, 117–21, 128–29), who dismisses the writ formula as lacking specific content. The possible Flemish precedent cited in n. 88 may support this view. *Pipe Roll 31 Henry I* (136), recording a proffer "ut audiretur si ille qui appellabat filium suum legalis erat," suggests that it was occasionally possible to gain a hearing for an exception to an appeal.

79. It is far from clear to me that one can assume at this date a defined concept of felony into which all appeals heard before royal justice fitted.

80. Jenks 2002 (1–2, 6) deduces from Bracton 1968–80, fol. 123 (ii.346), that one later use for homicide appeals was to get an enemy jailed for substantial periods without trial or proof.

81. Van Caenegem 1990–91, no. 471 and the later parallel case from Worcester I discussed in Hyams 1986 are both revealing of complainant choice and motive.

82. I accordingly use inquests de odio et athia for information on disputants' motives in chap. 8. Possibly this display of private enmities helped turn judicial opinion against the appeal, although Kaye 1977 has shown that the justices were quite selective and had no general policy of seeking to quash all appeals.

ution to a man's traditional right to support his accusation of wrong with his own body. We need to know why hatred justified so serious a step.

Make no mistake. To quash an otherwise plausible appeal merely because it was motivated by enmity must have been controversial. Any intelligent pleader could point to the illogicality. Everybody knew that men pursued feuds out of enmity and hatred; that was the whole point. Why should appeals be different? I can imagine a scene in some chanson de geste in which the cowardly villain tries to refuse the gauntlet because the appellant offered it out of enmity. After the uproarious laughter dies down somewhat, our hero admits the truth of the allegation with a sarcastic smirk on his face. "Yes," he says, "I'm guilty as charged. You are quite right; I do hate your guts for what you have done to me and mine. Now I am going to shame you for all to see. I shall compel you to cry craven, and then take much pleasure in seeing my friends enforce the judgment of the court *on* you by the removal of selected body parts; eyes and genitals will do nicely. Then and only then will my hatred end, as I get my satisfaction, restore my honor, and recover from the wrongs you did us!"

How can one justify so different a logic for royal courts? Four possible lines of explanation suggest themselves. Consider first learned influence from the law schools.[83] The schoolmen possibly promoted the view that the new procedures instituted by the assizes of 1166 and 1176 were public in nature and so not to be used merely for private ends that lacked a public interest component. If only for self-protection, the intelligentsia certainly broadcast the now ancient principle that, in the words of Gratian's *Decretum*, "the voice of enemies should not receive a hearing."[84] A second explanation might draw on a Christian worldview, premised on the certainty that all judgments were ultimately attributable to God. When men were sent to battle or the ordeal, for example, their fate depended on the decision of God, not men. It behooved litigants to act accordingly. This viewpoint remained too strong in the last third of the twelfth century for anyone in public life to deny or oppose openly. But the worldview of secular men and women patently also influenced political decisions. It is surely relevant, then, to notice how highly the literature they patronized rated *mesure*—that is, balanced, rational conduct and the ability to handle crises with aplomb— as a supreme virtue of courtly politics. Many contemporary literary works contrasted its practitioners with rivals, who, swept off into *desmesure* by hatred and spite, were doomed.

A fourth possibility is to seek precedents in earlier secular law. The key

---

83. This was the line I argued in Hyams 2002.
84. *Decretum* C.3.5, heading "inimicorum vox audienda non sit."

words *de odio et athia* from which the writ derives its name hint at a vernacular origin. *Athia* is not a word that one could expect to find in any text from the law schools and suggests an English provenance.[85] Knowledge of Anglo-Saxon provisions concerning the inadmissibility of malicious accusations may possibly have smoothed its way into the writ draftsmen's minds.[86] That it may nevertheless describe an import from the Continent into "Carolingian England" is a possibility worth consideration. One can imagine some Carolingian capitulary expounding the standards to be met by appellors in a way that enabled their enemies to raise a possible defense to their suits. The snag is that the experts have failed to locate any such capitulary.[87]

The nearest legal procedural parallel I have noticed comes from Flanders and dates from the aftermath of the shattering assassination of Count Charles in 1127. A new count—William Clito, Henry I's Norman nephew and rival—had succeeded in establishing himself temporarily. He soon found himself at odds with the citizens of Bruges, whose support had been crucial to his own elevation. The issue was how to deal with those who had helped some of Count Charles's murderers escape from the siege. One group of citizens, kin to men themselves killed by the offending Erembald clan, pressed William strongly to hand them over for death by precipitation over the walls, the same route by which the principals had been dispatched. The new count would have preferred to heal wounds but had to comply. The accused pleaded for their lives. They were, they said, "improperly accused, not for reasons of truth but from envy and hatred." Claiming that they were improperly accused, they besought the new count for a kind of jury trial on the rational merits of the case, "that he might deal with them by judgment of the local scabini [jurors], both on the treason charge and any other suspicion." Clito had to compromise lest the fighting break out anew more fiercely, with each side seeking its vengeance. Those who had aided the traitors after doing homage to the dead count must die. But he would receive the rest into his grace "compassionately and without judgment."[88]

85. Despite the traditional preference for translating this as "spite," Old English *hete* must be its source (*MED*, s.v. *hēte*), with the sense of intense emotion, hatred, or anger. Although it does not even figure in Niermeyer 1997, Du Cange 1733–36 (i.462–63) adduces Continental as well as English usages. *Pipe Rolls 3–4 Richard I* (110, 202), *7 Richard I* (214), and *8 Richard I* (186) already feature atia, although *invidia* and *odium* (as *Pipe Roll 24 Henry II*, 104) may be found in law school texts.

86. III Eg 4; II Cn 16; *LHP* 34.7. Some may have influenced royal advisers directly through the Latin translations of the Quadripartitus.

87. Nor could Janet Nelson suggest one.

88. Galbert 1994, chap. 88, p. 138; see the translation of Ross 1967, 260–61. It is noteworthy that Galbert's language (the key phrase is "legitime accusatos, sed causa invidiae et odii et non causa veritatis"), which may derive from an official source, raises the general issues of guilt, and right and wrong more directly than the formulation of the English writ seems to do.

The plea of the accused for a jury trial "de invidia et odio" is close enough to the later English pleas *de odio et athia* to suggest some kind of common source.

The case for a Carolingian origin retains some attractions. Distant memories of Anglo-Saxon provisions just mentioned might have favored the importation of any such Carolingian rule. But these Old English precedents must have been remote indeed to the sort of men who were advising the king in the 1160s. Prominent in their midst was the still untraced author of *Glanvill*, who never seems to have used the Old English leges or their twelfth-century adaptations and may not even have been aware of their existence.[89] He and his cohorts were more comfortable with ideas from the twelfth-century law schools, although the actual measure of their learning remains debatable.[90]

We might equally seek our precedents from Romano-canonical procedure and the two learned laws. Two principles can be found there, the one more lawyerly and novel, the other ancient and well known. First, the lawyerly innovation: a prosecution deemed public ought in principle to be limited to proper use in the public interest, which would exclude private grudges and malice in the manner already seen. A plausible Roman parallel does indeed exist. The oath of *calumnia* committed accusers to an honorable purpose and was meant to exclude malice in the sense of an evil motive.[91] This oath's underlying ideas offer us a context, which could serve as a respectable learned justification for the royal procedure. It may, however, be too sophisticated for the 1160s. Although the oath itself was probably known in England by 1200,[92] an earlier date is not impossible, despite the silence of

89. Hall, in *Glanvill*, xxxiv, notes that in contrast to the "Bracton" author (writing thirty years later), *Glanvill* shows no awareness of earlier leges.

90. I owe my caution throughout this section to kind counsel from Charles Donahue on the impossibility of knowing what works beyond the *Institutes* English draftsmen and their learned friends could possibly have known at the relevant time.

91. Berger 1953, 378–79, 534; Lemosse 1953. Donahue and Adams 1981 (43–44) offers a nice, brief account. Both litigants and advocates were required to swear that they acted without any intent of calumny, that they believed their plea just, and that they would not seek to further their cause by any improper means such as fraud or bribery. It may be worth noting that the distinction between criminal and civil causes had long ceased to be relevant to calumny. *Inst.* 2.23.12, 4.16.1, raised the matter of the oath to beginning students; another reference to the oath is De Zulueta and Stein 1990 (134). Glosses on *Dig.* 48.16.3 might conceivably provide a bridge to the minds of the reformers of 1166. The oath's twelfth-century introduction to northern Europe, including England, came by way of canonists and church courts (Brundage 1997, 795–99). The whole question would benefit from study by someone properly conversant with the two laws.

92. A Vacarian *Lectura* on the *Institutes*, probably written in the 1190s but possibly much later, comments on *Inst.* 4.18, "De publicis iudiciis," to emphasize the difference between public (= criminal) prosecutions and private (= civil) actions (De Zulueta and Stein 1990, 136–38) and could usefully be studied in conjunction with a thirteenth-century French translation in Olivier-Martin 1935 (294–98). Even the church courts are not known to have *required* an oath of calumny in England until 1237 (Brundage 1997, 793).

elementary texts like Justinian's *Institutes*. Perhaps one of Henry II's continentally trained *eruditi* drew attention to it in the course of legislative brainstorming. Or some legal expert adduced the notion a little later, either to defend the king against criticism from traditionalists,[93] or on behalf of some well-heeled and desperate client.

Such a scenario, if plausible, would imply an opposition between public and private that is not altogether new to English political culture. One might view it as a central theme in the *Song of Roland*, for instance, previously not formulated with any precision. The imposition of public standards of behavior on litigants in royal courts is an excellent indication of the complex process of Angevin legal reform.[94] Henry II wished to raise the standing of his secular justice and royal courts firmly above the occasional contempt of the schools. The *curia regis* ought not to peddle a mere blood justice, in a manner that might justify the application to it of the clerics' mocking folk etymology "curia a cruendo." The king tempered his peacekeeping with a rationality comparable to the *ius scriptum* of the learned laws.[95] His men possibly conceived of de odio et athia as an intelligent resolution of the continuing tension caused when a new ideal of public, impersonal justice learned from books and schools was compelled to acknowledge the popular, still respected, pressing private emotional need for satisfying vengeance.

But all this is very speculative. Henry's familiars cared more about enmities than for fine distinctions of the law schools. Their real concern might be simpler and more direct—the danger that, motivated by hatred, men would bring vexatious appeals in the same way that they inspired malicious indictments. As a French canonist wrote, ca. 1160, your enemy would like nothing better than to force you to offer battle and give him the chance to maim or kill you.[96] This comment was provoked by a small dossier assembled by Gratian in his *Decretum*, to establish the principle that men ought not to be permitted to accuse or bear witness against their enemies.[97] Gratian's main purpose here was to protect fellow clerics from being forced into judicial duels. But his texts were both ancient and widely known to trained lawyers and others. The principle that accusations inspired by known enmity did not deserve a hearing in court was indeed virtually self-evident.

93. For defensiveness to this kind of accusation in the Assizes of 1166 and 1176, see n. 30. Midnight oil analyses must similarly lie behind the 1164 provision for criminous clerks (Constitutions of Clarendon, clause 3, in Stubbs 1913, 164–65) and of course the assize of novel disseizin. See Herbert of Bosham's comments on Henry's legal team in *Materials* 1875–85 (iii.207).

94. I examined this more broadly in a paper presented in 1990 at Fontevraud, of which an unauthorized abstract was published as Hyams 1994. See also Brand 1992a, chap. 4.

95. See *Glanvill*, prologue (1–3).

96. McLaughlin 1952, 120.

97. *Decretum* C.3.5.2–5, 11, 13, 15, are the most relevant texts. Others dealt with the admissibility of accusations from domestics and other undesirables.

Educated English clerics and lawyers probably took it for granted in the 1160s, and expected members of the royal court to follow suit.

Now, the first signs of our writ come from proffers made by litigants to the king and reflect the minds of litigants and their advisers. Could the extension of the objection from indictments to appeals be derived in the first instance from the more practical counsel sought by fearful appellees rather than from the learned advice offered to kings? At this date, even royal advisers still recognized the need to present duels and ordeals as judgments made in the last resort by God, not man. But God made his decisions along different lines and for different reasons than might occur to the humans who had sought them. The law schools encouraged courts to direct their attention to specific acts and the way these had been committed. God operated rather differently. "His" technique of mixing law and fact in what seemed to human eyes almost haphazard ways was precisely what the new experts were out to replace.[98] "He" focused on souls and their salvation; they, on the commission of specific torts and crimes. Men who accepted divine judgment as fully just might nevertheless dislike the results. All accusers were in God's eyes sinful, but none of the accused was totally without merit either; should they repent, all could attain salvation. God's judicial unreliability thus became an awkward fact for which prudent men had to allow in their preparation for judicial ordeals and duels. They did so by making timely confession of (other) sins, courting the relevant saint through vigils at his shrine, and swearing their oaths in an appropriately defensive form of words.

One case from almost exactly the material moment, 1174, aptly illustrates their thought processes. Ailward of Westoning was fearfully facing a false accusation of theft. He consulted a priest, who explicitly advised him to exclude from his heart all anger and every provocation from hatreds, "omnem iram et incentivum odiorum." He was to seek God's mercy by suffering whatever judgment was made against him in a manner meriting divine forgiveness for his sins.[99] Extreme pride and arrogance were especially sins to avoid, and of these, unremitting anger and hatred toward an enemy appeared the clearest symptoms.[100] This mindset, faintly illogical to a modern view, was very widespread.

Another, more secular notion was as widely accepted at the time. The audience for vernacular literature, at least, believed in *mesure*, the virtue of

98. I treat the distinction between law and fact that the new law adopted in chap. 7.

99. Van Caenegem 1990–91, no. 471, at p. 508. Ailward apparently drew further consolation from the belief that his Whitsuntide baptism would protect him at the ordeal.

100. Galbert 1994 (chap. 108, pp. 153–54; trans. Ross 1967, 298–99), thoughtfully expounds its author's view of why God first spared and then executed one Lambert of Aardenburg; see Hyams 1981, 105 n. 65.

avoiding extremes in one's conduct. Men and their womenfolk knew not to permit themselves to be carried away by passion of any kind, since the consequences of this *desmesure* (when one is so moved as to virtually lose one's senses, as if one were mad) could prove disastrous for all concerned. An important episode from *La mort le roi Artu*, the last section of the Old French prose Lancelot cycle, despite its later date (ca. 1230) and Continental origin, nicely illustrates the pertinence of this secular norm. Lancelot is at odds both with King Arthur and with Arthur's nephew, Gawain. He has almost accidentally killed two of Gawain's brothers. Gawain contends that Lancelot has acted treacherously, while Lancelot tries to explain that these killings (two among many!) had happened casually and almost accidentally. Fictional onlookers, and so also we, the audience, "know" that Lancelot is in the right on this occasion. It was just "collateral damage," one of those unfortunate things that happen in wars. More than a hundred knights had seen him act quite openly.[101] A feud situation within the larger war between Lancelot and the king results all the same. Bystanders express their fear that it might escalate into one of those never-ending conflicts with terrible consequences to all concerned.[102] Confident of his basic innocence, Lancelot accepts, as he must, some liability for the deaths. Gawain is patently all but consumed by his enmity and cannot believe but that his brothers died from treachery. He has gone very obviously way over the top. After his death, an inscription on his tomb identified his major failing as "outrage" to convey just this sense.[103] While he remained alive and disputing, Yvain and the townspeople each expressed their sense of Gawain's exaggerated, obsessive pride.[104] After Lancelot had twice made the same point to Gawain,[105] his brothers tried to make him understand how so "sage" a man as Gawain could come to make so misguided a suit ("si fol apel"). Lionel declares that Gawain has grieved so deeply for his brothers that a death wish now fuels his felonious appeal. Gawain agreed; win or lose, he admits, he simply seeks "a aise ester," to gain peace in death.[106] Such men are as dangerous to their peacetime neighbors as the uncontrollable kinsman of the Old English laws or the Viking berserk. Everyone has an interest in their control or elimination.

101. As Lancelot's cousin, Bors, pointed out, *Mort le roi Artu* 1954, 145, ll. 54–65 (p. 185). It is worth noting that the author does not permit Lancelot to plead that he was acting in a legitimate public context and not from private enmity. This kind of contrast between public and private is already an important motif in *La chanson de Roland*.
102. Ibid., 90, ll. 87–88 (p. 118).
103. Ibid., 159, l. 11; 172, l. 30; 175, l. 17 (pp. 205, 220, 224).
104. Ibid., 148, ll. 76–79; 149, ll. 9–10 (pp. 193, 194).
105. Ibid., 119, ll. 117–19; 127, ll. 16–19 (pp. 160, 165).
106. Ibid., 145, ll. 54–58, 59–65; 146, ll. 50–59 (pp. 185, 187).

The handsome peace settlement Lancelot now offers is replete with reason. Intentionally designed to give Gawain what he needs for satisfaction, it far exceeds mere apology. Lancelot will publicly humble himself by becoming Gawain's vassal, along with his whole kindred. He will then go into exile as a penitent, to seek upon his return the full reconstitution of his former close relationship with Gawain and readmittance to his "compaignie."[107] King Arthur is greatly impressed by Lancelot's honorable generosity.[108] Gawain, alas, insists on his chance to kill Lancelot, and is himself killed. He is mourned as a good man gone bad.

This whole fictitious episode reveals with some clarity the kinds of consideration that could convince secular society to resist an otherwise plausible appeal, or feud. Feelings on the proper expression of hatreds, existing already before 1166, were nourished from a variety of sources. Churchgoers were uncomfortably aware that God might deny salvation to the willfully unrepentant. Their rumbling sense that government for the common good demanded the subordination of private interest was fed by an awareness of the constituent parts of malice already listed. Churchmen were ready to remind the forgetful of either point. But there was a role, too, for the rising secular ethic of restraint that was converting even royal anger into clemency and *debonereté*.[109] The ideas of the law schools served to meld these elements into a new paradigm of which emotions to display, and when.

Chance and enterprising pleaders perhaps opened the way into royal justice. The simpler case of misuse of the king's public procedure paved the way for appeal exceptions to follow. The new wave of schools-trained lawyers just beginning in this period to penetrate the common law could represent this too as the exercise of *publica potestas*.[110] All roads do not run from Rome, and the case remains uncertain. Anyone wishing to accept the royal offer must act in a similar spirit, for he who comes to public justice must have "clean hands."[111] The inquisition de odio et athia is thus perhaps best understood as stemming from a vernacular sense of what felt "right," leavened and legitimated by at least a modicum of legal training.

---

107. Ibid., 147, ll. 65–87 (pp. 190–91). The details should be compared with the accounts of peace settlements discussed in chap. 2 and the treatment of "hommage de paix" in chap. 7.

108. Ibid., 148, ll. 70–76 (p. 193). Although Lancelot's offer was less unprecedented than the king appears to think, it is notable that the multiple acts of homage offered here appear to have been intended to create new lordship.

109. Hyams 1998.

110. Turner 1985 (37–38, 95–99) collects the exiguous evidence for the schooling of royal justices before 1216. I consider *Inst.* 1.1.4, 4.18 pr., texts that should alert even beginning students to the opposition of private interest and public good, see in chap. 7.

111. One can imagine coming to a similar result without any theoretical distinction of public and private. Something along the lines of the later maxim that he who seeks equity must have "clean hands" would serve. See Walker 1980, 230. One scents a civilian source.

In any event, the writ de odio et athia enjoyed substantial use during the thirteenth century. Already before 1215, it had become one route by which appellees evaded the dangers of the duel and the potential horror of trial by ordeal.[112] The prime effect of this turn from duel to jury was to assist local powers to retain their grip over law and order on their patch. Milsom has taught us to think of the Angevin law reforms in terms of a great "shift of control" over the possession and ownership of land. More debatably, he has claimed that this shift occurred almost by accident, without any clear royal intention to produce it. I have always felt the deep implausibility of any view that assumes that Henry of Anjou would voluntarily limit himself to acting like some "altruistic automaton."[113] By no means was the other attempt at a "shift of control," around the "new assize" of Clarendon and Northampton over standards for law and order in the realm, in any sense accidental. Henry almost certainly made a far greater and perfectly conscious effort to exert control. Yet in the medium to long term, he failed.

To develop this argument would require yet another whole book. Let me content myself with a display of the kind of evidence I find persuasive. If I am right in seeing "Mr. Big," the local power-monger, as a major target of the new assize, he and his fellows will have realized this quickly, undoubtedly faster than they perceived any hidden drift in the real actions concerning property matters. But the attack was directed at the stoutest part of their defenses. The local magnates were well placed to influence the very composition and performance of the juries that were to indict them. The jurors lacked both the status and independence to carry out in the public interest the tough task assigned them. The judicial establishment and its royal controllers gradually learned the lesson over the subsequent century.[114] A best guess (before any proper social analysis of the system) is that grand juries mostly picked on the defenseless (the poor lacking patrons, vagabonds, and rootless individuals) and the enemies of the rich. Two facts illustrate this working hypothesis.

First, almost from the inception of the jury of presentment, the authorities seemed to struggle wildly and in vain to keep control of their juries. Im-

---

112. Hurnard 1969, app. I, traces the legal history. The appeal of felony soon became in effect a jury procedure in all but exceptional cases. Groot 1982 and 1983, and Summerson 1983 cover well the rise of the petty jury to meet the needs of most of the accused who wanted it.

113. The phrase is from my own review of Milsom 1976 (Hyams 1978, 859).

114. I noted one response to the problem is Edward I's appointment of high-status jurors to deal with high-born offenders earlier in the chapter. Later still, trailbaston rolls often show knights serving on the juries. But it was already hard to find enough knights for routine service on assizes, a problem the king tried to solve by distraint of knighthood.

mediately after the very first visitation of 1166, the king felt he had to charge a fresh judicial commission, the so-called Inquest of Sheriffs, to investigate illicit private motives for indictments and their suppression. As we know, the inquiry concentrated on the social emotions of "wrong"—fear and favor, love and hatred, acting for hire—in a word, malice. The royal cry for the punishment of offenders cannot have been very effective then or later. A trail of similar efforts to tighten discipline within the system runs right through the thirteenth century and nicely fills the apparent gap between Angevin judicial probity and efficiency and the alleged chaos of the late Middle Ages.[115] But local members of grand juries, and for that matter trial juries too, did more than just stymie the fine theories of the intellectuals around the king. They ground their own axes to promote their own positive views. Read sensitively, special verdicts often reveal vernacular counterviews on right and wrong, especially in regard to pleas of accident and self-defense to homicide charges. It is now abundantly evident that thirteenth-century jurors drew from the culture of their own social environment judgments on the demarcation of these defenses markedly different from the conventional opinions of the jurists and judges.[116]

Yet the assizes of 1166 and 1176 have more claim to have initiated a quiet revolution than many other events that have been awarded this accolade. Henry and his men did at least win the battle of ideas. They made a serious attempt to redefine actionable wrongs in such a way as to extend royal control over much more local conflict than before. One important consequence was to initiate a move toward that equation of royal justice with public justice, which lies at the core of our Anglo-American notion of the common law. This public justice, expounded in Latin, required some significant borrowing from Roman law before it acquired coherence. Eventually it came to include a number of legal distinctions now recognized as central to the Western view of law in general. Among them are distinctions between law and fact, and between crime and tort, which I show in chapter 7 to have proved central to the story told in this book. Roman lawyers had strongly maintained that public justice ought not be mishandled for private ends, and this led in due course to a new crime, conspiracy, encapsulating a public

115. JUST 1/1095 (Yorkshire 1294), a roll dedicated to the topic of abuse of legal process, makes a good starting point for inquiry. Sayles 1939 (liv sq.) has a brief analysis of the roll. I hope to present its evidence for the prehistory of conspiracy along with an edition. Government awareness of the problem certainly predates the changes from 1278 toward the 1305 Ordinance of Conspirators posited by Harding 1983 (94–97). See, e.g., Green 1985 (9, 25–27) and note the advice to judges of Bracton 1968–80, fols. 143–143b (ii.404–5), on the *inconvenientie* they must expect to meet when investigating indictments. The extension of the number of indictable offenses that carried mutilation or death penalties heightened tensions for jurors already before 1200.

116. Hurnard 1969; Green 1972 and 1985, esp. chap. 2. Davis 1987, chap. 2, reveals very similar patterns in late medieval France.

view of royal legal process, its proper use and abuse.[117] To put matters in these terms runs the risk of presenting legal change as a mere matter of intellectual ratiocination in the schools and the courts. But all roads do not run from Rome. Law, where life and logic meet, draws on practice and vernacular sources. This fact is nicely illustrated by the introduction of another lasting concept, traditional and non-Roman in its sources—the notion of felony. I take up all these topics in the next chapters.

117. See chap. 8.

PART III

An Enmity Culture: Writs, Wrongs, and Vengeance in the Age of the Common Law

CHAPTER SIX
WRONGS AND THEIR RIGHTING
IN THE EARLY COMMON LAW

U ntil this point, the source materials for this book have been very diverse. They have included law codes and litigation records, but all are, without exception, unofficial, that is, external perspectives on the legal system and its functioning. From the 1190s the historian enters a new world, a literature dominated by the internal viewpoint of the common law itself.[1] Now for the first time the historian can read the law's own account of litigation on the plea rolls, can study cases from original writ to final judgment through the increasingly technical documents the system itself generated for its own purposes. The royal law courts were increasingly serviced not just by judges who focused on their judicial function for a significant portion of their time and careers but also by full-time clerks who recorded the results in an internally approved manner for the internal purposes of the system.[2] Plea rolls recording the progress of cases through their various stages, hearing by hearing, have survived only from the mid-1190s, at first only in very incomplete series. It now seems certain, though, that rolls had been made since the middle of Henry II's reign and began most probably ca. 1176, when returnable writs and other technical improvements were also introduced.[3] The cumulative result was a substantial enhancement of the courts' ability to control

1. At what stage the royal courts may reasonably be deemed to have crossed some invisible watershed and merited the title "common law" with its implications of parity with the rational written law of Rome and the Church is a judgment call. The issues involved are not trivial, and I return to them in due course.

2. Turner 1985 provides the materials for an assessment of royal judges in the Angevin period. It still remains to set these data into their longer-term context, a task already much furthered by Paul Brand's continuing series of studies on Edwardian judges, of which Brand 1992a contains a number of examples. Brand 1992b (vii–viii) sets up working definitions of "professional" lawyers and a legal "profession" to serve as a starting point for terminology concerning all personnel in the legal system.

3. Brand 1992a (95–96) puts the origin of plea rolls on a more precise basis than does Clanchy 1993 (96–97). See Clanchy 1993 (91) for a brief explanation of the returnable writ. The guess that these too originated ca. 1176 is mine; surviving early examples are compatible with such a date.

their information inflow and thus the premises of court argument and the integrity of their process. The king and his advisers were making a bid for the respectability of his own legal system as a *ius scriptum* worthy to be ranged alongside the learned laws studied in the law schools. This royal law patently succeeded in attracting considerable prestige for the royal line and its people.

That very achievement presents problems to the historian. Chronicles and charters continued to be produced and to record disputes and their legal resolution. But the center of gravity of the available data inevitably shifts toward the persuasive viewpoint of the legal records themselves to transform the whole tone of the modern literature on legal development changes, and with it much of the feel of the political and administrative history. The legal records of later medieval England remain a magnificent challenge for any historian cursed with but a single working lifetime. The administrative rolls and work files that burgeoned from ca. 1199 onward fill the Public Record Office in London almost to its water line. The result flatters but often deceives. The newly available plethora of records delivers a totally new level of detail on individual disputes, on the development of the legal doctrines, and on the general pattern of dispute resolution in the royal courts. We can document for the thirteenth and later centuries the legal archaeology of doctrine and procedure with minute precision. Delusion, however, may arise from the records' tone of objective reportage and disinterested comment. The rolls and writs are themselves propaganda for the law's desired self-image, which pushed such qualities to the fore. Clerks were expected to launder out the passions of the litigants who appeared in their courtrooms, to excise these as mere noise that tended to obscure the genuine "legal" issues (a largely new idea) on which the judicial decisions were supposed to turn. They were already doing this to an impressive degree in the earliest surviving rolls of the 1190s. This reflects the stronger sense of legal relevance generated in the law schools and soon to become a core characteristic of the common-law message.[4]

Yet every plea of self-defense was capable of concealing a history of tit-for-tat rancor and violence.[5] It is easy to imagine judges insisting on the exclusion of the personal histories that might have revealed that the alleged malefactors, the perpetrators of appeals and indictments, had a good claim to be considered the true victim. Their goal was necessarily to achieve clo-

---

4. See chap. 7. Bracton 1968–80, fols. 112, 413b (ii.318, iv.285), contains a Romanist dictum to the effect that the point of writs was to tie the opposition down to an issue, which neatly illustrates this distinction.

5. Green 1972 alerted the unwary to this fictional quality of both the defenses and the ensuing jury verdicts.

sure by judgment or licensed concord. The emergence and growing success of the procedure de odio et athia by which they sought this end proclaim their insistence on clean legal issues. Thus these dryly composed plea rolls and legal records demand close critical analysis. The initial desideratum is to cross-check and supplement the information released by the courts themselves against all extracurial material that can be found. One justification for the extended case narratives in the appendix, then, is their ability to lend nuanced social and political context to lawsuits; the result is always to soften the contrast with the pre-common-law past. Many patterns traced in previous chapters now reappear, including the emergence of some very feud-like behavior (to put it at its lowest) in a sizeable minority of cases.[6] I devote the next section of this chapter to establishing this point from the earliest documented period of the nascent common law. The very casual nature of some · references reassures us that our cases are a representative sample of behavior patterns of the day.[7] I then turn to set the options (legal and extralegal) exercised by disputants in these cases into their legal context, the final, desperately slow precipitation of trespass and the appeal "of felony" as distinct procedural remedies.[8] In chapter 8 I offer a cautious generalization of the argument through a combination of some conventional nonlegal documentation for a few noble feuds with a mass of legal evidence from those exceptional common-law procedures in which motive was of the essence. This enables me to demonstrate the degree to which the urge to vengeance remained common in the thirteenth century at all social levels. In conclusion I consider briefly implications for, and from, the continuing debate on "bastard feudalism" in England.

VENGEANCE AND ENMITY ON THE EARLY PLEA ROLLS

A notable proportion of the cases recorded on the earliest plea rolls are appeals "of felony" that mostly allege acts of violence. The visible tip of a very sizeable iceberg of complaints initiated out of our sight in local courts, they gained a hearing before royal justices because they raised (so their initiators claimed) specially serious issues of violence and breach of

---

6. I hedge my bets here and do not claim to be dealing with full feud. To the extent that I can reconstruct them, many of these disputes lack the iterative (tit-for-tat) quality central to most definitions of feud. It would be possible, for example, to deny that MALTRAVERS V. TURBERVILL merits inclusion in the appendix. But all the cases there help to demonstrate the presence of a feud-like quest to avenge wrongs as a normal part of the culture.

7. *Très ancien coutumier* XCI (Tardif 1881, 101), a clear Norman feud reference already noted in chap. 2, occurs in a list of legitimate objections to land grants.

8. For convenience, I talk in the next section mostly of appeals, because that is the term found in all the literature. We are still dealing with a largely undifferentiated procedure well into the thirteenth century. I give a fuller explanation later.

the king's peace.[9] They are far from a merely random sample of the complaints the king's subjects brought against each other in his courts. Some indeed were themselves acts of malevolence and vengeance where plaintiffs cannily sought to recruit the machinery of the law onto their side of the argument.[10] Behind such suits lay calculations that tried to optimize the quest for revenge with impunity. Ideally one put one's enemy to the defense of his life and limb without risking one's own hide, an enterprise for which the new system of relatively anonymous public prosecution was admirably suited. The scarcity of public or other executioners to implement sentences of mutilation and death augmented the attractions of such a course of action. One might get to take in person from one's enemy the life or limb adjudged against him, the fullest kind of satisfaction the age could imagine.

From this perspective, much personal litigation appears fueled by that urge to wreak vengeance that is the central theme of this book. The point is not restricted to appeals and their associated trespassory procedures. Where one can discover the deeper motivations for litigation, property is almost always part of the story.[11] Because appeals sometimes ran parallel with land property actions involving the same parties within the same neighborhood, and similar or overlapping issues, one may suspect that behind the lawyers' law of much property litigation lurks the same kinds of rancor and resentment. The prominence of disputed money claims does not necessarily diminish the importance of more symbolic matters of face and honor and reputation among one's peers. Sometimes the selection of one type of procedure rather than another (suing on violence or about title) was random; more often, however, it reflected a tactical choice influenced by the counsel of friends and more or less expert advisers. One can see, especially in actions of novel disseizin with long lists of multiple defendants often headed by a lord or his officer, very comparable confrontations between principals and their support groups. We can learn from these many plea-roll

9. Examples of this are Meekings 1961, 323, 373 (1249); also see the editor's comments (ibid., 69, 87–88). Summerson 1985 (xix) suggests that most suits of country folk for personal injuries may have been in the hundred courts. Richardson and Sayles 1941, 30 (1266), is a (rather famous) plaint to a lord, in effect, a late exemplar of proto-trespass.

10. Summerson 1985 (xxxviii–xli) mentions that among the motives for appeals, he has found the following: an attempt "to embarrass, intimidate or blackmail . . . enemies," a search for better equity than that found in local courts (?), "malice, vindictiveness and greed," cheapness as against buying a writ, and a way of forcing a settlement. Gauvard 1991 (ii.754–55) calculates that about a third of her homicides turn on vengeance, although records use the words in only 13 percent of cases. Our plea rolls too may conceal many vengeance cases.

11. Examples are Stenton 1937 (1218–19), 724 (reverse result of a novel disseizin), 727, 939 (advowson suit between lords); 1940 (1221–22), 232; ibid., 427, 820, 1461, on which see the editorial comments at xxxviii–xli; and ibid., 40, 875, with editorial comments at xxxiii–xxxv. The number of cases in the appendix that turn on physical control over charters is notable. *Rogeri de Wendover* iii.22–24 is an affecting tale of the passions aroused in a son by his father's disinheritance.

records, and especially from their frequent detailed special jury verdicts, much to supplement the picture sketched below.[12]

If property and wealth represent one great source of rancor in human affairs, another even more basic motivator is sex.[13] Men are notoriously keen in this area to make the punishment fit the crime by castrating their enemy. At least one early appeal seems to stem from such a case. Alan intercepted Thomas on the high road, took him home, and had him castrated with the active assistance of his own wife. Proud to advertise their deed, they took no pains to conceal it. Thomas's appeal confirmed the main line of his story with the help of testimony from the royal sergeant responsible for order in the locality. Yet the justices acquitted Alan and actually amerced Thomas for his trouble.[14] I guess that Thomas had been sexually involved with someone in Alan's household and that Alan had set out to scare him off. Local sympathy with Alan's view is probably behind a jury nullification of the law, perpetrated for once with the justices' full complicity in the knowledge that they were following community sexual mores.[15] Cases of this kind give prominence to nonfinancial motives.

Even in cases where property or sex is obviously a central concern of one party or both, appeal records on the early plea rolls frequently contain hints of the other values at stake. Occasional references to honor and face slip past the guard, as it were, of clerks trained to exclude most evidence of litigant passion as irrelevant to or obscuring the issues. Or they copy down colorful details that take the reader beyond the courtroom and out into the real world beyond.[16] We learn, for example, how keen the killers of John Cusin were to convey their message. They cut off their victim's tongue and burned important title deeds in his face before they dispatched the poor man. Although the full purport escapes us, we may be sure that bystanders understood, and likewise those to whom they told the tale later.[17]

Here and in many other early actions, the enmities, whatever their origin, ran deep and could be of long duration. Men cited ancient hatred, "vetus

12. Sutherland 1973 remains an excellent account of the lines along which novel disseizin developed; en route it offers much telling detail pertinent to the present purpose. Illustrations include Stenton 1934, 940 (waste said to have been committed in breach of the peace); in ibid., 1057, the plaintiff may have feared to bring an appeal. The suggestion, in chap. 5, that novel disseizin originated as an early precipitation out of the pool of undifferentiated wrongs, inevitably modifies the received understandings.

13. Cf. Gauvard 1991, ii.72–73. *Très ancien coutumier* L.4 (Tardif 1881, 41), recognizes that women may maliciously accuse ex-lovers of rape out of hatred.

14. FITZLEFWIN V. HAYWARD. Other cases include Stenton 1937 (1218–19), 669 (rejected mistress on her lover's marriage), 727 (caught in bed with priest's concubine), 1045 (adulterer plans to kill cuckold); and Meekings 1961, 227 (adulterer caught in act).

15. Green 1985 (xviii–xx) explains a modern view of jury nullification in criminal cases.

16. The appeal in Stenton 1937 (734) was said to have derived from an old pub brawl.

17. CUSIN V. FITZJOHN.

odium." Appeals not infrequently refer to events five or more years back.[18] Lasting grudges leading to violent acts are unlikely to have been any secret locally, in the *patria*. It is inconceivable, for example, that the merchant communities of Dublin or Lincoln could have been unaware of some continuing "contencio et malivolentia" between prominent families in their midst.[19] Affairs of this kind fueled common gossip and were well known to the local worthies, those *buzones* who ran the local courts, and to their womenfolk. But these are the very same men who serve on juries, and this is just the kind of local knowledge that they will discuss among themselves at the start of a judicial eyre when they are deciding on their *privata* (lists of suspect names) and indictments.[20] If Richard Waver's reeve understood that his lord, in coming to stay at his Northamptonshire property, was entering enemy territory, others—quite probably the whole village—could also grasp the situation.[21] Paradoxically the very efforts to resolve enmities through public peace settlements broadcast their existence more widely; a failed peace thus actually risked exacerbating the situation. Contrary to popular view, this behavior pattern was no noble monopoly but was visible according to the evidence in virtually every social milieu, from palaces right down to village level.[22]

Ominously, in an age when men were seldom far from strong drink and always had lethal personal weapons to hand, the possibility of violence must have been omnipresent. From the quiet campus towns and suburbs in which I, and many of my historian colleagues, live today, it is hard to appreciate the prevalence of violence and enmity in the Middle Ages. Among factors that impelled men toward the violent satisfaction of even everyday grievances, hot anger and people's sense of face (if not honor in the technical sense) head the list. Furthermore, some major restraints on violence in our own world were weaker or absent. The likelihood of police action, investigation, and prosecution of peace-breakers was, even after 1166, much lower than today. The system still required a far higher degree of individual initiative from, or on behalf of, the victim, including the prompting of jury indictments, perhaps even pressing upon presentment jurors the information needed to spur them into action. Habits of obedience to law in the abstract so dear to modern respectable folk were less fully formed and weaker, and

18. Examples are CUSIN V. FITZJOHN, HILL V. FITZEUSTACE, LAUNCELLS V. FITZWILLIAM, ROSS V. TIDD, and WAVER V. ARGENTAIN.

19. The quoted words come from LE BRUN V. LONDON. MARTELL V. PARIS is a Lincoln case.

20. Meekings 1961 (92) describes their doings at the start of royal eyre visitations.

21. WAVER V. ARGENTAIN.

22. Meekings 1961 (40, and p. 260) is a relatively clear village illustration. Davis 1987 (38, 42, 70) and other students of slightly later periods agree that honor could move non-nobles too. Chap. 8 presents much evidence of enmities at the village level.

thus were correspondingly vulnerable to an instinctive feeling that response to injuries and slights should be hot and quick.

The same people who gossiped about other men's enmities surely paid attention to their own. Far more cognizant of the risks they faced than historians can ever be, they necessarily evaluated their options carefully when they found themselves, wittingly or otherwise, on the wrong end of a grudge. Any time they attended mass and contemplated taking communion, the priest would remind them of the need to ensure that they did so unencumbered by any unpardoned wrongs to other worshipers.[23] If anything of this kind came to mind, they were supposed to go straight across the nave to the person they had harmed, humble themselves before him, and seek his pardon before proceeding further. In practice, however, it was not always that simple. Let us pause, therefore, to consider the kinds of choices that someone under serious threat from his enemies had to ponder.

A power in the land might simply sit it out and wait for the attack, confident that he could beat it off, inflict further injury on his enemies, and generally profit from the situation. Leaving aside such great men, what of others more like the rest of us who are less comfortable living with fear?[24] What might they do? A first option is to leave town, at least until the heat dies down. Simon Cusin, when compelled to watch his father cut down over lunch, hid in a window alcove for safety. He then fled and for three years did not dare return for fear of the chief of the assailants, Thomas, who was "almost lord" of the *patria*.[25] Others surely felt similarly, that it was sensible to leave town for at least a while. A few may have felt that they had to move very fast or they would be caught and killed.

For the really frightened already feeling their enemies' hot breath on their necks, flight into the protection of a higher power was always attractive. In the thirteenth century, this often still meant God and a request for sanctuary at some church. But times had changed since the eleventh century, when many or most sanctuary-seekers were evading feud vengeance.[26] The ancient rules about buying time to make peace with private enemies were no longer in evidence. By far the most common reason for flight in the

23. This was the way medieval readers understood Mt. v.23. See Hyams 1992 (18–19) and also chap. 2 in this volume. Perhaps this explains the refusal of a Cornishman to take the sacrament for three years after he had quarreled with his parish priest (Summerson 1985, xlv).

24. I refer doubters again to Kadare 1990.

25. CUSIN V. FITZJOHN. Other express claims to have acted (or held back) from fear include Stenton 1937 (1218–19), 570 (dare not raise hue but went abroad) and 1022 (could not raise hue when among enemies). In Stenton 1937, 26, Alexander of Moulton's mother was inhibited from making the property disposition she said she wanted by fear of the fee's head lord who "did not love" her son. These claims to have lived in fear were sometimes disputed.

26. The rubric to Bracton's main account of sanctuary (Bracton 1968–80, fols. 135b–136 [ii.382–83]) refers to "malefactores."

thirteenth century was the threat of arrest under public justice for felony. Current procedures were directed to ensure exile after formal abjuration of the realm under the supervision of the local coroner. Some fearful fugitives confessed to crimes they had not actually committed simply to take advantage of the royal protection afforded to abjurers. Pardon proceedings later in the century provide one charming illustration. William of Bugbrooke was a chaplain in minor orders who, when on the point of being caught in the act of adultery by his lover's father-in-law, first hid in a chest. He then fled in fear for his life to a nearby church, where he was held under guard by the local tithing. The coroner arrived to order William "to come to the peace" and would not let him abjure until he had falsely confessed to stealing 8d. found in the chest. This was in 1270, and his exile continued until he managed twelve years later to get a royal pardon that authorized him to return home.[27]

INDIVIDUAL GRANTS OF PEACE

The peace to which the lascivious chaplain should have come belonged, of course, to the king. The king's peace offered to subjects under physical threat a protection less instantaneous than God's but possibly more practical. The ancient procedures for seeking a special grant of the king's peace must have been very attractive in feuding situations. The process by which the more familiar phenomenon of the king's peace swelled in the course of the twelfth century into a general peace covering all the king's subjects is important and in outline well known.[28] The survival of individual peaces alongside this general peace into the age of the common law on both sides of the Channel has been less noticed.[29] Like the ancestors of most writs, these began as favors to individual great men or their protégés. But once recorded in writing, they progressively developed into a more general civil right. The precise lines of this highly significant twelfth-century transition remain to be elucidated. Nevertheless, it is clear that seeking a grant of the peace from the king, or much more probably from some deputy (a royal justice or the sheriff), offered one a fairly routine recourse in times of perceived imminent danger. This grant might require any person by name, in a

27. *CIM* 2154 (1282). Hunnisett 1961 (45) points out that the theft William confessed to was still too petty a sum for a felony.
28. I offer a brief take on the swelling of special peaces into the universal king's peace in chap. 7.
29. The Norman *Summa de legibus* LXXI.1–2, LXXV.1–2 (Tardif 1896, 180, 186–87), talks of breach of truce ("treuga") in very comparable terms: "assecuratio facta, prestita fide corporali, quod nec per se nec per alium aliquod malum inferet huic cui dature." Cf. *Très ancien coutumier* LXX (Tardif 1881, 65–68). Yver 1928 (328 n. 5) shows this truce still in use ca. 1256. A French equivalent is the *sauvegarde royale*.

local court,[30] or before a royal justice,[31] to make or keep peace with the impetrant. An 1194 appeal case establishes the importance of the procedure. Robert Drake was in charge of the Warwickshire manor of Arrow, while his lord William de Canville was away on the king's service in Wales. A party of armed men led by local gentry came and robbed the establishment of some armor and ten marks' worth of grain. When Robert sought the king's peace for his lord, the robbers responded that "the king was in such a place [i.e., imprisoned on the Continent] that he would never see him, and that he was dead." Naturally, Robert was the one to offer proof when the appeal came before eyre justices.[32]

A grant of the king's peace could serve several different purposes, some unfortunate. While on her way to market, Alice of Ipswich overheard some men plotting the death of her husband, Elias. Thus forewarned, Elias went when he could to the shire court and duly obtained his peace grant. Three days later, he was out in the fields checking on the progress of his corn when five men (this time known characters) set upon him and knifed him so that he died (as so many were said to) in his wife's arms.[33] Elias's very act of seeking a peace may have alerted his enemies to the need for swift action and hastened his end. Publicity need not, however, always have evil consequences. It was probably the best reason to seek a formal peace. At the very least this public act served to put the parties on notice that, their intentions being known in advance, the king would take a serious view of any future vi-

---

30. In *RCR* i.231, 343, 350, 447, ii.3, and *CRR* i.101 (Sussex, 1199), Esturmi had allegedly given Trubwick the king's peace in the shire court in the course of a land dispute but then went on to make a night assault on his house. Also Stenton 1926, nos. 578, 608 (two wapentakes), 612; in the last of these, LINDSEY V. STICKNEY, it was after Osbert of Lindsey had brought a plaint in the shire against Alan that Alan waged ("vadiavit") the king's peace to him, which did not, however, prevent a further assault. Examples in the shire include Stenton 1937, 505 (suing him for debt in court christian).

31. Illustrative cases are LE BRUN V. LONDON, ROSS V. TIDD, and RUMBAUD V. PRIEST. Others noticed are *CRR* v.152–53 (Sussex, 1208), vi.115 (Yorks., 1210), xvi.1133 (Norfolk, 1239); Richardson and Sayles 1941, no. 22 (1253). Cf. also the very casual reference in Bracton 1968–80, fol. 138 (ii.388).

32. *RCR* i.51–52 (Warwicks., 1194). In addition to a plausible defense on the facts, the appellees alleged that the appeal was brought *per attiam* in the course of a land suit for Seckington by one of their number, Robert de Valle. The roll is not quite clear that Robert obtained a formal grant of peace; he may have addressed the attackers directly. But the invocation of the king's name as a defense against present danger is undeniable. Also Richardson and Sayles 1941, 1 (1224); Harding 1981, app. 1, m. 2 (1235).

33. *CRR* v.42, 49–50 (Suffolk, 1213). The appellees offered twenty marks for a jury de odio et athia, but the Ipswich bailiffs claimed the case, which therefore passed out of our sight. *RCR* ii.278 (Kent, 1199) was an appeal for robbery made after a peace grant to the appellor in a situation in which the parties agreed on the existence of an *antiquum odium* between them. In Richardson and Sayles 1941, no. 22 (Lincs., 1253), a peace was obtained first from the king's court and then at the shire "on account of various threats which [the defendant] had made, as he had heard"; the threats presaged a full-scale attack by three hundred men apparently connected with land disputes and an assize of nuisance.

olence. It would ipso facto constitute a felony. The fact of a specific grant of the king's peace was an aggravating factor for courts to consider in later proceedings.[34] We can normally expect to find references to grants of peace on the plea rolls only when the grant has proved ineffective and someone is suing for its breach. The numbers are therefore likely to have been much higher than the evidence shows, a fact that justifies the suspicion that this was a very common phenomenon in the late twelfth and early thirteenth centuries.[35] Peace proclamations may have been especially frequent at the shire court. They were indeed mandatory when a royal pardon was issued or an outlawry reversed.[36] Often they were preceded by an inquisition *de gestu et fama* to check that someone (often someone recently acquitted from a felony charge) possessed the character and local reputation to merit protection.[37]

We know very little about the mechanics by which these individual peace grants were obtained.[38] From the 1260s, one could complain to the king that a named person was threatening one's person and/or property and secure the king's special protection along with a writ *de minis* ordering the sheriff to give the impetrant the king's firm peace against this enemy. Although this procedure, available on a routine if discretionary basis, was said to be traditional, "according to the custom of England,"[39] all I know about the earlier

34. Cf. Richardson and Sayles 1941, 33 (1269).

35. If so, I wonder a little why a judicial bench that included luminaries such as Hubert Walter and Geoffrey f. Peter did not make use of it in 1200 for a dispute between the Devon baron Henry f. William Traci and Ford Abbey. Instead, Henry made a charter in which he promised "that he will behave peacefully toward the same monks and will not harass them, their men or their landholdings" (*CRR* i.155). See further *CIPM* 2296, and from the appendix to this volume, HARLOW V. LOVETOT (1287–89), HAY V. NEWCASTLE FLEMINGS (1293), and LE BRUN V. LONDON.

36. Hunnisett 1961, 68, 78–79. Hurnard 1969 (31, 59–67) explains the procedure on grant of a royal pardon. Stenton 1937 (876) is a cautionary illustration of the importance of getting the procedure right. I discussed the rule that limited pardons to the king's suit in chap. 4. *Glanvill* vii.17 (91) refers to a grant of peace "misericordie et beneficio principis" in the course of a royal pardon of outlawry.

37. Examples are *CIM* 1682–83, 1714, 1822–23, 1825 (1294–95, 1300). And see Summerson 1996 (137–38) for the similar inquests "de fidelitate."

38. This subject of individual peace grants has been little treated by historians. Richardson and Sayles 1941 (xxxvii–xxxix) does something to trace the development from Old English *grið* to common-law times. Flower 1944 (304–5) discusses a few cases among various circumstances that aggravate an offense. I do not at present see how to fit into the story the Angevin exaction from all adult males of an oath to keep the peace. For this, see Harding 1960 (87); also Stubbs 1913 (257–58) for the 1195 "Edictum Regium," which seems to direct the oaths to the purposes of something that looks very much like a formed system of public criminal justice. Critchley 1972 deals with the rather different royal grant of judicial protection.

39. De Haas and Hall 1970, CC.107–107a (mid-1260s), are the earliest examples cited and very similar to the printed register, *Registrum Brevium*, fol. 88v, 1st complete writ; De Haas and Hall 1970, R.253–54 (1318–20), are effectively identical with it. Hall shows (ibid., xlvii, lvi, cix–cx) the intimate connection in registers of writs between this writ and the trespass group. No wonder Harding 1981 (liii) calls *De minis* "the herald of trespass." This kind of protection is again to be distinguished from those treated by Critchley 1972.

situation has had to be deduced from the case records. It could be most enlightening to learn more about this unusual common-law link with the older world of private-enterprise power relations. The restoration of this resource to its proper place in the period would indisputably add important elements to our understanding of social relations in general.

RECONCILIATION RITUALS

All these options for the fearful malefactor now become potential victim must be considered context for the extremely evocative body of evidence documenting actual peace settlements made, more or less directly, between disputing parties themselves. These ensure that at least some of our cases cross the threshold from feud-like behavior into something very much like actual feud. I suggested at the outset that the generation of a private settlement resembling those treaties made between nations was a fair test for the presence of feud thinking.[40] The hope there, much as in international relations, was not merely to end enmities but to recycle them into positive amity.[41] The cases documenting the attempted implementation of these aspirations in English knightly society establish, prima facie, that the pattern was a widely accepted ideal for managing enmities and perhaps also a significant feature of English medieval life. Why else did royal justices struggle to monitor and control out-of-court peace settlements?[42]

Many desirable elements for successful peace settlements will be familiar from earlier chapters. The first requirement was to keep enemies physically separated in the hope that their rancor might cool, and so to prevent the physical confrontations that too often provoked a recurrence of violence. The device of sending the "guilty" party off on pilgrimage served this purpose,[43] with the extra advantages that the avowed and humiliatory penitential purpose of his journey offered some satisfaction to injured pride. There

---

40. In the introduction.

41. Rosenwein 1989 described this kind of recycling pattern in the relations between Cluny and her neighbors. Cf. Gauvard 1991, ii.775–86.

42. I have noted legal prohibitions of private settlements in earlier chapters. Examples of judicial action abound on the plea rolls, e.g., Stenton 1937, 766, 866, 923, 947, 979; Stenton 1940, 906 and p. 425 (with editorial comment), pp. lxii–lxiii, 923 and p. 425; Summerson 1985, 395. Some eyre rolls such as those in Summerson 1985 (cf. xl–xli) and Clanchy 1973 seem to show benches of justices with a keen interest in monitoring these settlements out of court. Cf. Meekings 1979–83, 119. I cannot detect any clear chronological trend or be sure that the differences between rolls are not primarily a matter of recording conventions. Klerman 2001 very helpfully surveys the whole question of judicial settlements of "appeals" in the thirteenth century, although unfortunately without consideration of the parallel "trespass" actions.

43. As in CHAMBERLAIN V. PATSLEY, CUSIN V. FITZJOHN. Also Stenton 1937, 944. Lancelot's peace offer to Gawain in *Mort le roi Artu* 1954, 147, ll. 65–87 (pp. 190–91), contextualized in chap. 5, illustrates many of the points that follow; cf. *Mort le roi Artu* 1954, 148, ll. 70–76 (p. 193), for Arthur's amazement at its terms.

were other ways too to soothe passions at the victim's end. Ritual submission allowed his friends a very public opportunity *not* to take the vengeance they desired. It also helped to know that the killer of their kinsman was paying for prayers to be said for the dead man's soul. The killer might even fund one of the deceased's relatives into the religious life as the best guarantee of full-hearted intercession.[44] More common were provisions for the singing of masses, other pious donations to religion, and almsgiving in general. All grants of this nature carried the added bonus of an incentive for the religious with their lasting corporate memory to remember the peace publicly and so deter any resumption of hostilities.

In the third quarter of the twelfth century, Sir Simon of Stanstead thought it wise after the death of one Julian f. William to offer a series of concessions. He promised that he would fund three masses a year for the dead man's soul, that he would feed a pauper every day of his own life, and that he would donate a small but quite valuable packet of land to the Hospitallers.[45] Simon seems to have succeeded in persuading Julian's brother and friends of his own innocence of any complicity in the killing, for the agreement provided for no compensation payments. In most cases, however, the public payment of substantial sums of money helped to douse resentment and signaled the restoration of a balance of "face" from injurers to those they had injured.

This part of the settlement process is much the best-documented element and sometimes the only one to leave any traces. The old caveats remain. Honor probably still required that unless imposed by a higher power such as the king's justice, money compensation be embedded in other acts more clearly designed to extirpate residual shame. To hit an enemy in the wallet proved a satisfying method of getting even with minimum risk of further and unwanted violence or other complications.[46]

The injured parties might want their money accompanied by a public humiliation of the injurer as well. However, this was not easily forthcoming without a balancing promise of a public pardon for the wrongdoer, prefer-

44. Examples are again CHAMBERLAIN V. PATSLEY, but also HILL V. FITZEUSTACE. *Rogeri de Wendover* iii.22–24 has a successful offer of perpetual daily masses.

45. THE STANSTEAD CONCORD. The fact that the terms of the settlement were preserved by Waltham Abbey makes me wonder if the Hospitallers did not also keep a record.

46. My student Jay Vegso pointed out to me how the changing character of the use of money in this period must have affected the advent of routine pecuniary damages. Certainly there is a big difference between the quantum of compensation payments designed to draw resources on a large scale from a feud killer and all his friends and the routine award of damages intended merely to set the victim back as he was before he received his wrong. Something similar might be said about routine recourse to fines in the modern sense as punishment. But these shifts are very long term. The inclusion in damage claims of amounts to cover shame and such remained formally present and far from a dead letter through much of the thirteenth century. This is a line of inquiry well worth pursuing.

ably in the form of some very public declaration that all wrongs to date were forgiven.[47] Solemnity was an important part of the publicity game. Especially desirable was the swearing of a public oath by one or both parties that they would "bear or carry peace" ("pacem portare") toward each other in future and, perhaps also, renounce in advance any right to sue or otherwise bring legal process against their former adversary. The more people the principals could associate with their future undertakings, the better. Multiple oath-helpers, "friends" from outside the family, and their own children became ensnared in concordats. The negotiators have their eyes firmly focused on the future and strive to maximize chances for a full and lasting peace.[48]

These provisions for the future are most needed where resentments from the past had previously run deep and long. In principle, a healing marriage agreement emblematized the ideal link between rancorous past and peaceful future. The couple's issue could at once symbolize the seamless weld of old fissures and later serve as guarantor of the new order. Unfortunately, historians still know little about noble and gentry marriages. Very occasionally, unusual documentation makes clear that some marriage (that might otherwise have been scarcely known even to genealogists) had been made for peace-weaving purposes. We owe our knowledge of one such marriage from the 1180s to the concern of monks from Byland Abbey to explain their possession of some Yorkshire lands and title deeds. There had been "great discord" between two knightly families with moorland property abutting on each other round a contested wood, whose valuable building timber both coveted. The dispute was long-lasting and carried enough potential for violence to provoke "friends and kinsmen" to mediate a detailed peace agreement sealed by the marriage of one principal, Arnold of Upsall, to the other's sister, Juliana Fossard. Only the "late" and less reliable monks' narrative reveals this. Adam Fossard's own charter made to end the "controversy" contains no hint of any marriage.[49] The extreme rarity of reference to peace marriages in this period is thus almost certainly a function of the sources and could conceal many other instances of which we can never know.[50]

Durable peace, like good justice, must be made manifest. The exchange of very visible symbols through ritual acts engaged the local community as spectators and witnesses. Peer pressure remained an important incentive for the keeping of promises. The minimum ritual act was probably the classic

47. As in MARTELL V. PARIS.
48. HILL V. FITZEUSTACE illustrates most of this.
49. UPSALL V. FOSSARD.
50. Another less clear instance is HAY OF AUGHTON V. FITZPETER. But many scholars, among them Gauvard (1991, ii.778), are skeptical about the efficacy of peace-weaving marriage alliances.

kiss of peace,[51] whose meaning must have been universally recognized and so probably formed part even of settlements that do not mention it.[52] Among much else, the kiss is, of course, a marvelous emblem of shared vulnerability and hence an earnest sign of a positive, mutually supportive relationship. This kiss on its own takes us beyond the merely negative function that provides for a simple cessation of hostilities toward a renewal of love and friendship. But the form peace settlements take is worth record and remembrance only toward the creation of a new more positive relation between the parties. So, in the Stanstead case just mentioned, the parties ended their agreement with the declaration that "in this way, Laurence [the dead man's brother] and Simon and their kinsmen became *concordes et amici* for ever, except for those [the actual killers] whom we excluded above."[53] If the italicized words present difficulties to the translator, the unmistakable intent is that hearts and minds should join so that may all live happily "ever after."

HOMAGE "FOR THE KEEPING OF THE PEACE"

This intended amity was sometimes institutionalized in a form that initially seems somewhat surprising. The aggrieved party received multiple acts of homage from members of the opposition party. The large numbers of men who sometimes accompanied the principals to perform homage alongside them require explanation. Sir Simon of Stanstead, for instance, brought with him to the peace assembly forty knights, a group described as a mix of blood kinsmen and other *amici*. These assisted him by themselves performing personal homage to his adversary, Laurence the clerk.[54] The scale of the exercise surely precludes any belief that the point was to extend lordship in any conventional manner. Those who had done homage were, however, advertising their commitment to behave like real *amici* toward their new

51. Southern 1990 (153–54) sketches the context in which other literature should be placed. See further Frijhof 1992, Offenstadt 2000 (217–20), and the literature they cite. I wish I had been able to consult Petkov 2002 for this and other purposes; it contains a full review of literature. One odd English example is the settlement between a justice and a pleader recorded in Madox 1769, i.236, n. k, cited in Brand 1992b, 63–64.

52. MARTELL V. PARIS does mention it. In 1169, Henry II had regarded the kiss as a small matter that should not be allowed to stand in the way of peace with Becket (*Materials* 1875–85, 7.79).

53. THE STANSTEAD CONCORD.

54. Ibid. The homage done to Robert de Hyl by Walter f. Eustace armed and ready for his duel in HILL V. FITZEUSTACE was said to have been six-handed. In MARTELL V. PARIS, the Lincoln citizen Martin Martell took the homage of his citizen opponent and the group that had accompanied him to court in preparation for the swearing of an oath thirty-six-handed. In 1268–69, a judge accepted the submission of a pleader who had struck him in Westminster Hall and now "supposuit se voluntati [of the judge] tam de vita et membris, quam de terris, tenementis et omnibus bonis et catallis suis" (Madox 1769, i.236, n. k, cited in Brand 1992b, 63–64). These were professional lawyers too aware of current doctrine about homage to use it in an archaic manner.

"lord" in the future. That lords, vassals, and kinsmen were regarded as the quintessential "friends" is now very well known.[55] Middle English retained the alliterative opposition between friend and enemy known, from Anglo-Saxon, in the form "friend/fiend."[56] Homages transformed the one into the other, *inimici* into *amici*, implying something much more affective than new business colleagues or casual friends. Even in the thirteenth century, homage might be refused on the ground of personal enmity or dislike.[57]

But the choice of homage as the ritual means to achieve and advertise this new friendship was complex. The physical posture struck by the homager, on his knees, head bent forward to expose naked neck, and hands between those of his new lord, is one of ostentatious vulnerability. Any primatologist will recognize here the very familiar epitome of submission behavior.[58] It is in fact the human submission ritual sometimes said to be absent from the repertoire of this highest primate.[59] Viewed with fresh eyes, unclouded by theories of "feudalism" and the like, such a ritual is as suited to peacemaking as to its more usual high medieval function of promulgating honorable relationships of dependency between men supposed to be capable of literally looking each other straight in the eyes. These acts make good sense in pardon and reconciliation scenarios. Homage constitutes a splendid visual amplification of an admission of wrong before bystanders. The ritual publicized the recipient's victory and helped to restore his "face," while at the same time it proclaimed the homagers' detachment from a hostile support group and addition to his own. The ritual's reconciliatory function could well explain homage's survival into the high Middle Ages as Western Christendom's lordship ritual of choice.[60]

We must therefore consider the deeper significance of homage and ideal *amicitia* together. All right-thinking men naturally viewed with profound revulsion violence within the kindred, that is, fratricide and parricide. In similar fashion, lord killing had been grouped among the most heinous acts, the future felonies, since Alfred's day if not before.[61] Honored in the breach though these principles sometimes were, few dared deny them. In the

55. See chap. 1.
56. *MED*, s.v. "fend" (= "fiend").
57. E.g., Stenton 1937, 1117.
58. I first made this observation in Hyams 1987, 447. What follows is developed in Hyams 2001b.
59. De Waal 1989 (43, 260–61) notes the amazing variety of human reconciliation rituals. De Waal 1996 (176–207) updates this view.
60. Hyams 1987 (448) gives references to some of the defeated competition.
61. Af El 49 singles out *hlafordsearwe* as the only bootless offense, the only offense for which compensation is never adequate. Yet Af 4–4.1 even envisions compensation for a king. See also Norðleod 1. I trust that my colleague Tom Hill (n.d.) will soon publish the fascinating paper in which he discusses these and other matters pertaining to the prologue to Alfred's law code.

decades around 1200, the act of homage consequently still advocated a powerful sentiment in favor of the bond it created and against any hostile contraventions thereof. Its echoes remained visible in contemporary law, even in England and especially in its forensic cousin across the Channel, the duchy of Normandy.

By this time, homage had come to enjoy among lawyers and those who listened to them an almost mystical aura.[62] One important consequence was the rule that no man can be at the same time lord and heir, which prevented a lord from claiming land for himself as long as it, or rather its tenant for the time being, owed him homage.[63] Even in an age most historians characterize as one where personal bonds of lordship were in full decline, the theory remained that the doing of homage established an unbreachable *amicitia* comparable to that of close blood kinship. Men had always abhorred feud between a man and his lord or close kinsman. Their revulsion extended to the stylized substitute of the judicial duel. The early common law still prohibited most such duels and their new equivalent, the grand assize.[64] These "modern" rules confirm the continued life of this evidently ancient and deep-rooted sentiment, and also indicate an ongoing desire to eliminate or refusal to acknowledge hostility within the friendship circle. These developments help us to understand why homages were still deemed an appropriate means to seal a peace agreement.

Where English sources are silent, Norman law spells out some of the consequences of this continuing theory. The Norman *Très ancien coutumier,* representing Anglo-Norman custom at the moment of the duchy's loss in 1204, contains a chapter that treats awkward cases where someone has killed, even quite unintentionally, an *amicus*, father, son, brother, vassal, or lord: a lord-killer must always die. Such was the rule even when the deed was an accident, although in that event he was spared the shaming ritual of the drawing to execution that usually accompanied death for petty treason, as later generations termed it. Likewise, the lord who killed his man lost his own life. A

62. This is reflected in the language of Milsom (1976, 139), like Maitland (Pollock and Maitland 1898, i.296–307) before him.

63. Thorne 1959 (200–201) cites the main literature on this bar. Its logic was not restricted to England but is found elsewhere in the Western French group of customs; cf. Hyams 1982, 88, for *Glanvill* vii.1 (72–73).

64. Milsom 1976 (84–85, 99 n. 4) documents from early cases the sentiment against battle between lord and man and between parties claiming from the same stock. *Pipe Roll 13 Henry II* (122) seems to be an example of a waged lord-man duel. *Glanvill* clearly holds that the grand assize (using twelve knights to determine who has greater right to land) is the formal equivalent of the duel in these matters (*Glanvill* ii.19 [36]). Milsom (1976, 80–87) treats the "upward claim" (as he labels the case where a vassal/tenant sues his lord); this did not require hostility toward the lord, since the aim was to prolong and intensify the lordship bond with him. It was even doubtful that the "action of right" lay at all between those of the same blood line, although it was certainly valid where a tenant sued to hold directly from his lord.

bond whose breach provokes such serious consequences ought to provide good protection for a former enemy.

Norman law recognized the use of the homage act in peace rituals as a separate category with its own label. The great *Summa de legibus* of ca. 1236 says that homage comes in three different manifestations. Ours is called "homagium de pace conservanda" (for the keeping of the peace) or "homagium de paga."[65] If the first title is self-explanatory, the second is not. Medieval Latin *paga*, like its close Old French cousin *paie*, comes from Latin *pacare*, "to make peace, conciliate, make a settlement." Thus, although *paga* can denote ordinary payments such as a soldier's wages, its connotation of "satisfaction" made it peculiarly suited to the compensation paid in the course of a peace settlement.[66] The author of the *Summa* explains that this kind of homage was made "in pagam concordie inter aliquos reformate," in payment for the concord now reconstructed between the parties, as when someone sues in a criminal action and "peace is restored between them." The one sued (appellee) then does homage to his opponent "to keep that peace." The *Summa* adds that the terms are just the same as in a normal homage, except that the homager adds to the standard formula "saving faith to my other lords" the extra words "and especially for the keeping of the peace."[67] The language used, as well as the purpose of the acts, reminds one of the much later procedure by which troublemakers can be bound over to keep the peace.[68]

This somewhat surprising use of homage in reconciliation rituals is so sparsely represented in the surviving documentation that most of the literature appears to have missed it.[69] Much the same is true of the peace rituals in general. Patently only a tiny proportion of concords had their terms recorded in writing at all, let alone in a form that might survive the centuries. Most are known merely from casual references elsewhere. And if we hear any details, these almost invariably concern the money and how it was to be paid over.[70] We cannot avoid asking whether similar elements were

65. *Summa de legibus* XXVII.2, 5 (Tardif 1896, 94–95).
66. Examples from the English rolls are Stenton 1934, 1298; Stenton 1940, 1143, 1462; Richardson and Sayles 1941, 35M.
67. *Summa de legibus* XXVII.4–5 (Tardif 1896, 94–95).
68. Walker 1980, 133. I am not at present aware of efforts to trace the story of "binding over" back behind Stat. 34 Edward III, clause 1 (*Statutes* 1810, i.364–65), the 1361 enactment that regularized justices of the peace. Cases like Stenton 1940, 1475 (1221), in which the justices permitted a man under indictment to find sureties that he would stand to right in the future, may be part of the story. A 1336 provision that pardoned felons must, within three months, find sureties for their good behavior is another possibility; see Bellamy 1998, 145.
69. For the exceptions, see Hyams 2001b.
70. LAUNCELLS V. FITZWILLIAM may be the best cautionary tale here. It has left many traces in the records, yet the case for a political reading still remains a matter of inference from mainly financial detail.

present in the undocumented settlements and concords too. The question is easier to pose than to answer. My own guess is that we should assume that similar elements were indeed features of at least some of the multitude of out-of-court settlements. We may reasonably suspect, indeed, that they figured routinely within the general culture.

ACTIVE PEACEMAKING BY THE KING AND OTHERS

Peacemaking had some important consequences at the summit of the system. That the king should also consider peacemaking as one of his prime tasks within the politically active nation ought not to surprise us.[71] The justices often singled out on the plea rolls those cases where they felt the need to consult the king beforehand by the tag "loquendum cum rege." Their concerns were more often political than legal.[72] Sometimes they wanted to permit or encourage concord but feared to act without prior political input from the top level. In this manner, appeals came to reach the court *coram rege* with fair frequency (a fact that has sometimes surprised scholars).[73]

But our evidence raises the suspicion that peacemaking also constituted one of the more important tasks of the Angevin chief justiciar.[74] As always, the evidence is partly inference from the justiciar's other duties, including his frequent consultation by other royal justices at work in the courts. But some type of serious role seems an inescapable conclusion from the records of a spectacular "political" case such as the batch of appeals from the southwest corner of the realm at the very start of John's reign.[75] Modern political analogies suggest that, although the clout and occasional personal interven-

71. Chap. 4 presents a little evidence on earlier kings. Richardson and Sayles 1941 (xxi, xxxvii) points out that Bracton 1968–80, fol. 107 (ii.304), glosses the Coronation Oath in terms that suggest a royal claim to a monopoly of peace-making, and Summerson 1985 (xv–xviii) marshals local evidence to show the role of the eyre in this task.

72. Turner 1968 (chap. 4; cf. ibid., 143–46) for specific royal work toward the making of concords. West (1966, 167) had thought it inevitable that at this time "consultation should more often concern administrative details rather than rules of law."

73. The suggestions in CUSIN V. FITZJOHN and LAUNCELLS V. FITZWILLIAM that the king too had suffered "huntagium" were probably intended to gain access to his court. I discuss the "tickets" for access to royal courts in chap. 7. Turner (1968, 131–32) somewhat mysteriously suggests "problems of judicial administration" as the main reason for the presence of such cases there. He attributes the size of some of the sums paid for licenses to concord simply to John's need for money (ibid., 147).

74. West 1966, the standard account, does not mention any peacemaking activities; this is a conventionally apolitical view of legal administration overall. The equally well documented study of Turner 1968 is likewise silent on this possibility.

75. I argue for a political reading of LAUNCELLS V. FITZWILLIAM. That reading is speculative and may be disputable. But the amount of organization needed to achieve the relatively satisfactory settlement of the case is beyond question. And one is driven to imagine that to get there required some personal interviews, including some knocking of heads together.

tion of the top man were essential to successful mediation, someone else did most of the drudgery on a day-to-day basis. At least during the tenure of Geoffrey f. Peter (1198–1213), the chief justiciar was that man. Fines to record concords produced in his court, the bench, always invoked his name as president even on occasions when he was physically absent.[76] We can occasionally see him in action. In 1209 Geoffrey himself ordered his bench justices to give license to concord in three out of a batch of land cases brought by the young Maurice de Gant, "as the concord has been negotiated between them."[77] And around the same time, we glimpse Geoffrey sitting alongside the king in the Tower to settle by agreement a petty case concerning a single virgate of land that happened to be situated on royal demesne.[78] When justices *coram rege* were struggling in 1200 to settle a nearly intractable appeal case, they sought from Geoffrey an explanation for its appearance before them.[79] When a Northamptonshire homicide obtained a pardon from Richard I late in the reign, perhaps on the ground that his killing had been inadvertent, Geoffrey brought back from the Continent a royal letter directing him as justiciar to help restore peace between the bearer and the dead man's kindred. The result was a very singular justiciar's writ designed not merely to ensure that the sheriff finished the job but also that he then reported back his accomplishments so that the news could be relayed to the king himself.[80] Another suit *coram rege* concerned the profitable custody of a child heir and his inheritance. Richard of Peopleton, the defendant, explained that the three-year-old was currently in the physical custody of his mother. In an earlier suit before Geoffrey as justiciar, he recounted, the parties had come to an agreement by which Richard was to pay his plaintiff, Anger of St. James, three marks per annum in order to hold the all-important lands until the child was of marriageable age, after which he was to return him to Anger to be married off in an appropriate manner. He then vouched Geoffrey to confirm his story. Not so, said Geoffrey: the parties had indeed negotiated in his presence toward a settlement ("locuti fuerunt de pace"), but they had never reached agreement because Anger had

76. West 1966, 116–17, 141; similarly, *coram rege* fines were always said to have been made in the king's presence (140). Cf. also ibid., 143, for two justices fined a hundred marks each in 1207 because they permitted an appeal between Eustace de Vesci and Richard de Umfraville to be concorded without the king's license; cf. *Pipe Roll 9 John*, 207; *Rotuli de Oblatis* 1835, 386.

77. This is *CRR* v.321; other stages to these actions are v.189, 196–97, 270, 279, 297, 317, 327–28; and of the rest of the batch, v.156, 189, 212, 215, 217, 270, 279, 280, 282, 285, 287, 322, 323–24, 325, and vi.65, 161, 235, 261. Sir Charles Clay gives the background to the case in *EYC* vi, pp. 32–38.

78. *CRR* v.324 concerning Havering, Essex, on which see McIntosh 1976, 11.

79. LE BRUN V. LONDON.

80. RUMBAUD V. PRIEST. This case provides a useful hint that the king did not always wash his hands of the affair after granting a pardon.

broken off proceedings to take counsel and never returned. They then proceeded to concord the case.[81] And in 1200, Geoffrey seems to have sent one Robert Picot to convey his license for the parties to concord yet another rather spectacular and convoluted assault case. "Concorded by [per] the Justiciar" says a note added to one roll to explain why a proffer for an inquiry de odio et athia had been canceled.[82]

There seems here a prima facie case that Geoffrey, and—one may guess—other justiciars too, saw the promotion of concord in suitable cases as a normal enough extension of their other judicial duties. This makes good sense. There were, of course, other mediators more closely associated with the immediate parties.[83] Churchmen were presumably expected throughout the period of this book to pacify their parishioners' enmities and to deploy their authority to deter peace-breakers. Thirteenth-century diocesan and provincial statutes repeatedly order parish priests to pacify their flock lest they permit the sun to set on their anger.[84] At all social levels, churchmen impressed on their flock the duty to make peace wherever possible.[85] A peacemaking role for the justiciar, as effective head of the royal judicial system, would serve as an emblem of the major change that the Angevin legal reforms had made in the otherwise relatively durable pattern of response to perceived wrongs.

THE IMPACT OF THE COMMON LAW ON THE QUEST FOR VENGEANCE

All private efforts, whether to seek or to offer either vengeance or compensation, now occurred under the shadow of a general, public system of downward justice. But I doubt that this was instantaneously all-powerful in the way historians have sometimes thought. Disputants continued on occasion to submit their disputes to private arbitration by their lords and others.[86]

---

81. *RCR* ii.167–68; *PKJ* i.3156 (Worcester, 1199).

82. *CRR* i.182, 230–31, noticed by Flower 1944, 306. Although this must have been a tale worthy of reconstruction for the appendix, I have so far failed to find anything out about the parties. One further concord licensed and possibly brokered by Geoffrey f. Peter is that for mayhem referred to in *PKJ* iii.746 (Shrewsbury eyre, 1203).

83. Thomas of Ingoldisthorp in CHAMBERLAIN V. PATSLEY and the prior of the Hospitallers in THE STANSTEAD CONCORD are obvious candidates and serve to indicate the kinds of people, powers in the locality and esteemed churchmen, most likely to have been called upon.

84. Powicke and Cheney 1964, i.64, 231, and chap. 2 here; for the excommunication of peace-breakers, see further, chap. 7. Cook 1955 (34) notes a room over one church porch used by priests for peacemaking.

85. An Episcopal charter to the town of Wells illustrates this nicely. It empowered the townsmen "ut si lis aliqua forte dampnosa . . . emerserit, liberam habeant potestatem ut adinvicem concordes fiant justicia nostra nulla inde exigente," excepting only mortal wounds and cases where one of the disputants appealed to the bishop (Shilton and Holworthy 1932, xii).

86. Richardson and Sayles 1941, 31 (1267), is one example. In ibid., 30 (1266), the lord is asked to emend a trespass. This resembles the procedures I earlier labeled proto-trespass, where seigno-

The century after the 1166 birth of indictment and the grand jury necessarily saw a sustained royal effort to deepen the ethos of obedience to the law and recourse to the courts as the main if not sole forum of adjudication for disputes.[87] Inevitably, this process impacted deeply the micropolitical dynamics and strategies of social competition. The common law of crime as administered by regular eyres even before the clear conceptual separation of crime and tort severely limited the players' freedom of action. The concept of a mortal enmity, although as familiar to Englishmen as to all who shared, for example, their Francophone reading matter,[88] never constituted a recognized defense to criminal accusations in England (as it could on the Continent).[89] Even self-defense was so narrowly defined as to demand (in principle) immediate and hot response to actual fear for one's life.[90] Thus from the inception of regular eyre visitations in the second half of Henry II's reign, anyone tempted to seek vengeance on an enemy's life knew that he was risking presentment for homicide, swiftly followed by judgment to the capital penalty of hanging. Events at the eyre moved fast, allowing no time to summon influential aid.[91] Prudent men (Bracton calls them "meticulosi") thus took to flight even after accidental or justifiable killings for which they expected pardons or acquittals. This is a far cry from a genuine ethos of blood feud expecting full publicity for a vengeance killing as a privileged, protected act.

Men who mused on their grievances privately or took counsel with their friends on how best to respond to wrong could no longer exclude royal justice from their thoughts and discussion. Of course the law was not just a nuisance. Creative use of legal resources might offer some form of revenge with impunity or at much-reduced risk. The most direct illustration of these critical litigant choices follows in the account of the separation of both trespass and the appeal of felony from the old suits concerning undifferentiated wrong. One Norfolk homicide settlement specified, for example, that the

---

rial adjudication that preceded common-law trespass must frequently have shaded into private peacemaking. Powell 1983 is the best recent general treatment of arbitration for the present purpose. But the subject has attracted much interest among other historians of England in the later Middle Ages; Rawcliffe 1984 and Beverley Smith 1991 are also helpful. Plea-roll references include Stenton 1934 (202, 1182, and ibid., 1298) and 1940 (410 and 1129), and Richardson and Sayles 1941 (94).

87. I traced one important aspect of this development in Hyams 1999.

88. See chap. 2.

89. But I showed in chap. 4 some circumstances in which the author of the *Leges Henrici Primi* thought vengeance legitimate.

90. Green 1985, esp. chap. 2, shows how jury verdicts frequently expressed a popular nullification of the definition and its rule. Green did not investigate the possibility that jurors sometimes used these means to protect avengers with whom they sympathized.

91. See Van Caenegem 1990–91, no. 553, for the speed with which a bishop must move to prevent a holiday hanging.

killer was to go and serve God in Jerusalem for seven years and was liable, if he returned sooner, to summary execution as a convicted homicide.[92] Here the threat of public justice provided a sanction to further the goal of a satisfactory peace. The reconciled killer who returned without permission risked an outlaw's death. It is similarly clear that appeals served to put one's enemies on the horns of a dilemma. Any killer who appeared to make his defense risked conviction and swift retribution. Yet if he failed to come to court, he could be outlawed and thus laid open to private retribution with impunity. In the southwestern conflict from the first weeks of John's reign already mentioned, the fact that several of the appellees were soon outlawed and so placed in this jeopardy must have helped induce their leaders to accept the terms later offered them.[93]

PATTERNS OF FEUD-LIKE BEHAVIOR

We have now examined in some detail the main lines of peace settlements to be found from the era of the early plea rolls. The evidence, even if never abundant, surely suffices to establish the survival of older patterns of peacemaking into the light of the common-law world. The next logical step is to examine whether the disputes defined by these peace treaties, as it were, possessed a feud-like nature. From the last decade of the twelfth century onward, common-law and external sources together convey a convincing picture of behavior—a definite advance beyond our guesswork for the earlier period.

House Assault
House assault, sometimes at night but often in broad daylight, was—by the invasion of an enemy's most personal, most private space—the quintessential demonstration of one's standing in the world. Angevin Englishmen (if one may so term them at this early date) already shared the sentiment later expressed by Sir Edward Coke that "a man's house is his castle, *et domus sua cuique est tutissimum refugium* [and each man's home is his safest refuge]."[94] It was characteristically from the lord's house that the feud party left on its task, returning there afterward, as if to make the point that here was where honor resided.[95] Kings recognized and exploited this salient fact. They very publicly razed, burned, or expelled the occupants from the houses of their

---

92. CHAMBERLAIN V. PATSLEY. Cf. Stenton 1940, 746 (1221).
93. LAUNCELLS V. FITZWILLIAM.
94. Cited by Rosenwein 1999, 207–8; her chap. 9 nicely expounds the medieval roots of this famous dictum.
95. I set out the evidence for this later in this chapter.

own public enemies, as if they were heretics or convicted felons.[96] This demonstrated very publicly their own capacity as kings to deal with their enemies in a fashion no ordinary man could match.

House assault is a frequent element in appeal counts, which sometimes seem to depict the kind of classic storming of an enemy's strongpoint familiar from Icelandic sagas and Old English laws.[97] These forays result not from hasty decisions made in the heat of the moment but rather from careful planning. The armed enemies who suddenly surrounded John Cusin at dinner in his own Somerset home had entered by a ruse, possibly with insider help. The ensuing events had clearly been thought out in advance and were designed to proclaim the intruders' justification for their actions. They cut out John's tongue, burned charters in his face, and then dragged him outside to behead him where all could see. We may be sure that the neighbors knew how to interpret the spectacle.[98]

Much of the action centered on the defensible entry points, through which a way had to be won. Ingress was not always as simple as it was for Cusin's assassins. Even peasant cottages had some kind of lock to secure them.[99] To break down these defenses with a successful assault carried symbolic weight: enemies might run, but they could not hide. The demonstration that the attacker paid his scores and redressed his own wrongs was very public and greatly enhanced the avenger's satisfaction, his recovery of face.

Counsel and Support Groups
Before broadcasting a message on one's neighbor's wrongs to the neighborhood, one had first to make explicit precisely what these wrongs were. Counsel with one's friends and sculpting the narrative so as to enlist the sympathy from one's necessary support group were important strategies. Perhaps the decision to attack evolved over days or weeks, having emerged from casual grumbles and consultations with friends and potential allies. But it could also be a more formal affair, held perhaps in the house of some principal—a great man—who might deliberately absent himself from the actual avenging of his alleged wrongs. We are unlikely to have much overt docu-

96. The king's common-law right to waste the houses and timber of his convicted felon is already noted in *Glanvill* vii.17 (91). Assize of Clarendon, clause 21 (Stubbs 1913, 173), had ordered in 1166 that heretics' houses be carried out of town to be burnt. See Yver 1928 (309) for comparable customs on the Continent.

97. LAUNCELLS V. FITZWILLIAM seems to have been of this type. The house assaults in THE STANSTEAD CONCORD and WAVER V. ARGENTAIN are different because the man attacked was not in his own home.

98. CUSIN V. FITZJOHN. Summerson 1985 (xxxviii) notes a clerical example of tongue extraction after death as vengeance.

99. The Bedfordshire peasant, Ailward, broke down his debtor's front door with disastrous consequences (Van Caenegem 1990–91, no. 471 [1174]). See also Stenton 1937, 977.

mentation of such scenarios at this date.[100] Thus we need to establish the fact of support groups and then note the evidence that quite frequently they set off on their violent work from an identified house, dispatched by an aggrieved leader. Then we can consider some of the implications of the overall pattern.

Support groups extending well beyond blood kindred were a constant feature of the political scenery in the thirteenth century still dominated by lords and their followings.[101] It is true that many cases concerning violent acts document the principle that blood is thicker than water. But when the draftsman of the Stanstead Concord in the third quarter of the twelfth century, for example, presents his conflict as one between two *gentes*, he goes on to distinguish between those present at the settlement ceremony as kinsmen and others simply described without qualification as *amici*. Neither kinship nor lordship can explain an ad hoc assembly of this kind. It patently included neighbors and plain-vanilla friends recruited for the occasion.[102] This was probably a fairly standard pattern. Where one possesses long lists of names, as in trespass and novel disseizin suits, most of the identifiable personnel seem to hold from the principal defendants, or their lords. That still leaves many individuals without any obvious tenurial ties of lordship, men summoned or even hired, perhaps, for the occasion. Of course the fact that the men have responded to the call to violence implies leadership that might loosely be termed lordship. One thinks here of the early-thirteenth-century Yorkshireman who liveried his retainers "as if he were an earl or a baron" and then robbed wherever he went.[103] But the few helpful plea-roll case records do not support the view that men came along because they *had* to support lords and/or kinsmen; rather, one had to induce or otherwise persuade them to participate. And this scenario was a very different matter.[104]

The very terminology of the law itself seems studiously neutral on the source of the strong-arm aid. This is the true meaning of the *vis* in the very well known phrase that defines a trespass "ticket" to the royal courts, *vi et armis*. The original implication of that formula was clearly that the defendant had committed the wrong complained of with the assistance of an armed

100. However, see earlier in this chapter for an explicit allegation that men were overheard plotting a death.
101. I discussed support groups in general terms, in chap. 1. And see chap. 8 for the behavior patterns some call "bastard feudalism."
102. THE STANSTEAD CONCORD.
103. Stenton 1937, 1149.
104. The twenty-eight men in WAVER V. ARGENTAIN belonged to at least three different lords. Active recruitment for life is the most obvious implication of Waugh 1986, even though the evidence there assembled is heavily weighted toward administrative rather than military aid to their lords. I consider the use of command language next.

support group.[105] The more official term for such a support group in common-law parlance was *forcia*.[106] After the main appeal, we frequently find subsidiary appeals *de forcia* against the principal's supporters. When writs of appeal and trespass began to appear, some of them were specifically framed for this purpose.[107] This thirteenth-century usage is notable because it is limited to appeals and actions of trespass, the constituent parts of the old undifferentiated procedure for wrong. The term *forcia* is not found in records or writs concerning the newer assize of novel disseizin, despite the obvious fact that the long lists of multiple codefendants in that action patently represent the same support group phenomenon. Thus, the language of *vis* and *forcia* was indeed a relic from an earlier vernacular world predating the common law and therefore excluded where possible from the newer forms of action.

The Principal and His Commands

Today's lawyers tend to refer to supporters of this kind as accomplices, a word that defines the principal, on whose conviction—as the main offender, the chief criminal—turns the fate of the other accused. This bespeaks a very different attitude toward criminal responsibility from that recorded in our sources.[108] The medieval principal appears much more like the man at the other end of the enmity, the perpetrator responsible for the wrong at issue, personally involved even when not physically present. Our texts use the language of command.[109] The resonances are those of some "Mr. Big" or Mafia boss who sends others out to do his dirty work for him.[110] For the medieval court, the basic tests were from whose house the assailants left on their expedition and whether they returned there afterward. By such means, appel-

105. In *CRR* v.152–53 (1208), the complainant alleged that his assailant had come against him "cum vi sua," whose names he admitted he did not know. In *CRR* v.42, 49–50 (1213), a widow accused five men of being "in auxilio et vi" to her husband's killer; in their defense the four surviving supporters denied, inter alia, "consilium et auxilium et vim." Cf. also MALTRAVERS V. TURBERVILL for a daytime house assault made by a disappointed heir "cum vi sua."

106. This sense of the word goes back at least to the ninth century. Niermeyer 1997, 448 s.v. "fortia" (meaning no. 10); *MED*, 721 s.v. "force" (meaning no. 3); *Dictionary* 1975, s.v. "fortia" (meaning no. 3); and *A-N Dict.*, 310 s.v. "force" all confirm its continuing currency. Stubbs 1913 (276; 1205 writ to summon a force against imminent invasion) suggests that the phrase "cum forcia et armis" implies a body of men *in* arms, suggesting that this was the original implication of *vi et armis*.

107. One finds from the 1220s a writ (which became "of course" after 1258) to inquire locally for the names of the *forcia* in a trespass suit (Harding 1981, xliv). Milsom 1963 (CX.20–22) is a French-language record of an "apele de force e de eide."

108. Walker 1980 (10) nicely brings out the individual, non-gang assumptions.

109. "Preceptum." Modern renderings as "instigation" weaken the point. Richardson and Sayles 1941, 9 (1226) refers to members of a support group as "fautores."

110. Geary and Freed 1994 prints a unique "hit" letter from Bavaria that, if authentic, sets the context in compelling manner. I believe that the almost contemporary parallel from *Stricker* (ll. 2419–50) virtually confirms that authenticity. See chap. 8 for further cases of contract killing.

lants sought in their counts to implicate their real or main enemy, and restore to their conflicts the ancient shape of one-on-one confrontation from which feuds usually sprang.[111]

These factors mark a further entrance of lordship into the calculation. It was always possible for men to try and enlist their lords in their quarrels. This was the goal of proto-trespass plaints, which endeavored to persuade the greater man that because his interests were involved, he should as a matter of "good lordship" pursue his man's cause as if it were his own. But traffic moved in both directions, and strife between lords was always bad news for their dependants, who were all too easily sucked in to the feuds of their betters.[112] We often see lords send men off to run the risks and wage their enmities for them. At the gentry level and above, all enmities were the stuff of local politics. By implication, then, private enmities could easily intersect local or even occasionally national political conflicts, especially in times of civil war. Amid such anarchy, some men notoriously chose their sides as an excuse to pursue their personal enemies, whereas others took their political adhesions so seriously as to provoke lasting feuds at home.[113]

Such political implications abound in certain cases from around the time of John's accession in 1199. One house assault in northern Cornwall, apparently undertaken almost as soon as news of King Richard's death reached the area, reeks of politics.[114] The scene appears to have been set some years earlier, while Count John was in disgrace after his 1194 rebellion. The owner of the house, Richard of Launcells, may have held local office around that time and was certainly identified as a Ricardian loyalist. His adversary, Henry f. William, held land of John's honor of Mortain, a dominant power in southwestern England, and can be seen quite soon after John's accession enjoying royal favor as a consequence. Although personal revenge for past insults was surely a major motive for Henry's desire to kidnap and humiliate Richard, other more obviously political issues, among them the reversal of past faction relationships and control of the royal castle of Launceston, probably played a part too. Perhaps the need to settle these old grievances impelled the king to intervene and mediate a peace settlement. But personal

111. In CUSIN V. FITZJOHN, the finger of suspicion pointed to a minor baron, William of Harptree, father of the actual assault leader, Thomas. The attackers' lord, Henry f. William, was not present at the kidnapping that provides the core of LAUNCELLS V. FITZWILLIAM. In ROSS V. TIDD, the assault party were alleged to have come from and returned to the house of Adam of Tidd. Alleged examples include Stenton 1937, 727; Summerson 1985, 114, 494 (1238), drawing a four hundred–mark fine.

112. Stenton 1940 (847) is an example, as probably are all the "de precepto" appeals; e.g., Stenton 1940 (1260), on which see Meisel 1980 (67, 72) concerning the treatment meted out to a monk found in the house of the lord's mistress.

113. Sutherland 1967 and Carpenter 1992 provide illustrations. See also chap. 8.

114. LAUNCELLS V. FITZWILLIAM.

grudges and national ambitions do not exhaust the possibilities. Hugh of Morton, one of Henry's henchmen, signaled the existence of a more complex web of relationships. Hugh pleaded that Richard's appeal was motivated by a desire for vengeance rather than a mere concern for the truth. His reasons relate to the routine of local government. He confessed—in fact, boasted—that he had previously been responsible for sending Richard's brother to the gallows and had revealed to royal justices Richard's concealment of some offense, perhaps during a spell as sheriff a few years back. There had also been ecclesiastical litigation between the two families over possession of a local church. His tales may or may not be true. They undeniably represent a plausible point of view of which further examples could be found from every shire in the land. Every time a local official committed some repressive act—and our voluminous records of these are but the tip of a vast iceberg—those at the receiving end might perceive it as tyranny, take umbrage, and conserve the memory toward some future opportunity of redress. There can have been few members of the gentry who had not, at some stage of their careers in local administration, experienced, either themselves or through their dependants, acts worth resenting, humiliations they took personally.

CHAPTER SEVEN
THE DIFFERENTIATION OF WRONGS:
TRESPASS AND THE APPEAL

T hus far, I have followed the normal conventions and referred to the cases that have provided the material for my violent tales and behavior patterns in the language of the established common law. So I have talked of either appeals or trespass. But to do so is to beg a central question. We have seen that in the twelfth century, although there were different strategies, within and beyond public courtrooms, for responding to wrongs, there was nothing approximating the separate "forms of action" of the developed common law.[1] Lawyers and their clients were, of course, well aware that their procedural choices could affect their prospects. The well advised decided whether to mount a formal appeal of felony or merely to bring a plaint of wrong, for example, on their view of the procedures and remedies potentially available to them and their opponents. But in the early thirteenth century, relatively few choices were enshrined in the sharply drafted writs that would give the common law so much of its late medieval character. To give a detailed timetable for this crucial development is beyond the scope of this book. Here I can offer only a summary account of how the common law gained its criminal appeal "of felony" and its civil action of trespass. Nevertheless, this brief sketch should make a real contribution to the larger story of legal development and political change in the century after 1166.

FIVE NECESSARY CONDITIONS FOR THE
SEPARATION OF TRESPASS AND APPEAL

I begin by outlining five premises for the necessary changes. Two are doctrinal distinctions of the learned laws, and two others are more general political and institutional shifts. The fifth, legal but non-Roman, is the origin

---

1. See chap. 4.

of the concept of felony in what was essentially to be its lasting common-law form. The common element may be that all five premises appear to have originated in the quiet revolution that attended the introduction of public prosecution as a routine part of English law enforcement in the decade or so after 1166.

The routine distinction between law and fact represents a feature of Western law inherited from Rome and injected into western European practice from the mid-twelfth century by way of the reborn law schools. The distinction between crime and tort, to which I have already referred, is a corollary. The third premise is the progressive expansion of the king's peace into national protection for all the king's subjects and all inhabitants of the realm. This notion is undeniably fundamental to the very idea of a common law, not excluding its better-known noncriminal aspects such as real property and the personal actions. The institutional provision of a lasting system of public prosecution for "crime" (as serious offenses, felonies, and much else came to be known), starting from the decade that links the two royal assizes of 1166 and 1176, is an integral part of the process. To furnish the sharp edge of this brand new public conception of crime, Angevin law turned quite naturally to a category of offense that must have seemed to contemporaries almost as ancient as Roman law. The name allotted to this—felony—had traditional resonances that conveniently provided powerful laymen with reassurance. Even the most independent-minded baron would not carp when the king offered to help him deal with betrayal by his own vassals (still the term's primary sense at the time) and other situations of comparable seriousness to him.

All five of these premises had begun to transform the way the English understood law and order well before the turn of the twelfth and thirteenth centuries. Nevertheless, to determine when these attitudinal shifts were embodied into institutional form within the system of royal justice is no easy task. To read the story backward, as to a degree the received view still does, is all too tempting. But the right questions to ask are: Which kinds of suits for wrong did the king (and his advisers) allow into his courts, from about what date, and justified by what criteria? Insofar as the questions relate to classical "forms of action," embodied from the 1160s into writs "of course,"[2] the answers are well known. Much less well integrated into the received story is the way a residual stock of wrongs with a claim to royal redress entered the common law after the first great period of writ creation was over.

---

2. De Haas and Hall 1970 (xviii–xx, xxvii–xxviii, and esp. lxiv–lxv) is the only reliable account of the availability of writs in this period and the ways in which contemporaries categorized them, including those said to be *de cursu* ("of course").

Excluded from that first rush of new writs and forms of action, they never-theless brought a greater number of ordinary men and women (and more overall business) into the royal system than did the first series of property and personal actions. These procedures crystallized late and at a leisurely pace. When one scrutinizes the records of royal justice available in bulk from the 1190s onward, it remains hard to see appeals and trespass as sepa-rate actions before the second half of the thirteenth century. The same seek-ers after justice could both sue in trespass and bring appeals on the same facts, and some even equated the two as (still) one procedure.[3] Textbook cri-teria to distinguish the two common-law actions function poorly, if at all, before the 1260s—which is also about the first time that the word *trespass* can be identified as a common-law term of art.

TWO DISTINCTIONS FROM THE LAW SCHOOLS

Such is the overall picture I see. Let us begin to argue the case with a brief exposition of the two crucial jurisprudential premises. Both, taken from Roman law, required the existence of law schools that could generate in England a critical mass of schoolmen able to deploy the thoughts of Con-tinental scholars to influence and change the vocabulary and ideas of Eng-lish secular law. The critical moment is likely to have been the 1160s, when for the first time the needs for political polemic in the Becket conflict pushed intellectuals equipped for the task to think and write about legal theory.[4]

The Distinction between Fact and Law

Ever since the thirteenth century, all Western legal scholars have taken for granted the more general of the two learned distinctions—the insistence on a clear separation of fact and law. Its most famous embodiment is a maxim very widely cited even before its incorporation in the canonists' *Sext* toward the end of the thirteenth century: "Ignorance of fact excuses; ignorance of the law does not."[5] A modern law dictionary puts the matter quite as suc-cinctly: "What A. did is a matter of fact; whether it constituted a particular

3. Richardson and Sayles 1941, cxvii, cxix–cxx.
4. Smalley 1973, *passim*, esp. 161–62; De Zulueta and Stein 1990, chap. 2, is the most useful re-cent survey of literature on studies in the learned laws at this time.
5. *VI* 5.12.13. Berger 1953 (456, 491, s.vv. "error," "ignorantia iuris") displays the Roman law roots, which basically date from *Dig.* 3.2.11.4, 22.6.9. See Boyer and Roland 1977–79, ii.193 sq., for comment; also Stein 1966, 105. Macray 1863 (191) gives from 1206 the kind of interchange between a lawyer and Pope Innocent III that publicizes the distinction beyond lawyers of the two laws.

crime or not is a matter of law."[6] But its author should perhaps have added this caveat: whether the subject of a civil complaint came within the definition of some tort was equally a matter of law. Facts are things such as time, place, identity, and what was said, done, or heard. They must be established from evidence or by inferences drawn from evidence,[7] unless conceded by a party's admission or avowal. Law comprises the substantive rules claimed to be applicable to the case, to determine some issue(s) of fact. Courts establish these rules from statutes and from precedent, which in the years around 1200 meant mostly the experience of the royal justices themselves.

This nice, clear set of linked postulates often founders today before the messy realities of life. The propositions had never posed a problem in the Early Middle Ages because they were unknown to secular law. This was not merely a matter of the disappearance of Roman law from northern Europe but a function also of God's omniscience. Men conceptualized legal proof largely in terms of God's judgment, although they sought this by a variety of means (ordeal, duel, oaths, and so forth) that could be understood in other ways too. The idea of constraining God's freedom of action in coming to these judgments must always have seemed blasphemous. Thus the older "undifferentiated" procedures for wrong that we have been considering, which sought proof by ordeal or duel, were virtually incompatible with the Roman distinction. The new-fangled jury, however, brought to the notice of the court exactly the kind of factual information to encourage its use. The conclusion that judges should rule as to the law and leave juries to act as judges of fact seems, in retrospect, almost forced. And so it was in the long run. An exceptional observer like *Glanvill* could already see in the late twelfth century that, for example, if the parties to an inheritance dispute could agree on their pedigree (fact), the court might simply apply its accustomed descent rules (the law) to determine which party took as nearest heir.[8] By this time, even intellectuals were familiar with decision-making on the basis of fact-gathering, as royal records from Domesday Book and before illustrate. But conceptual clarity took time to achieve. The most impor-

6. Walker 1980, 455.

7. It is worth noting here that the Latin substantive *evidentia*, which gives us our *evidence*, seems to have been a medieval coinage. Niermeyer 1997 (384) attributes its adoption in this sense to the twelfth century. *Dictionary* 1975– (819) and Du Cange 1733–36 (iii.118) suggest that in phrases such as "in evidentia et audientia" and "ad huius rei evidentiam" (an alternative to *testimonium*), it goes back earlier but does not get used in its later legal sense until the fourteenth century. This is the case too with the Middle English word, which seems to be unattested in any of its senses before the last quarter of the fourteenth century (*MED*, s.v. "evidence"). It is strange that a comprehensive modern study is apparently still lacking.

8. *Glanvill* ii.6 (26–27) has the assize of *mort d'ancestor* in mind. I have stated the author's view more starkly than he does.

tant reason was probably the way in which the jury was introduced into the routine of the courts through real property actions. This widespread use of juries in royal courts was very probably justified at first as a new application of the old principle of God's judgment. Brief though this stage may have been—it cannot even be directly documented—the effects were lasting. The questions put to jurors of the petty assizes were not, as is sometimes mistakenly said, clear questions of fact but ones that mixed fact with law, raising the same kinds of normative issue indeed that men had previously put to God through ordeal and duel.[9] The answers were often those blank verdicts (disseized/not disseized, guilty/not guilty, and the like) that hide the reasoning from us and had impeded substantial legal development at the time. What eventually bridged the gap between court practice and juristic ideals was the frequent perplexity of jurors about proper verdicts. Their response, often provoked by searching questions from the justices, was increasingly to pronounce "special" verdicts that told the story as they saw it, outlining the facts and leaving the hard decisions to the justices, who would then apply the law to them and deliver their judgment.[10] The timing of this information revolution has still to be determined. But its stimulus clearly came from the mysteries of seizin and land ownership that had until recently been deemed quite literally beyond human comprehension.

The Distinction between Crime and Tort

If real property provided the energy behind the emergence of the fact/law distinction, the royal duty to maintain good order fueled the adoption of the other crucial learned distinction—that between crime and tort.[11] Although patently a product of the same schools mentality, the distinction was more concrete in its legal consequences. But it was no more compatible with the kinds of undifferentiated procedure for the redress of wrong that, as we have

9. Assize writs specified in detail the questions most often put to the jurors. This was often not the case in other actions. The parties' pleading was indeed very largely directed to establishing an "issue" (of fact), which could be put to the jury. From such argument, which rapidly became very technical and is the very stuff of the YearBooks, stems much of the doctrinal development of the common law.

10. Maitland was doubtless aware of these developments when he claimed, in a characteristically guarded formulation, that the principle that jurors should speak only to the facts was "present from the first" in the jury but "long remains latent and tacit" (Pollock and Maitland 1898, ii.629–30). He also noted that the formula *maius ius* gave the lay knights of the grand assize their chance to pronounce on the law.

11. I use the modern term *tort* here, although its medieval equivalent is *trespass*. Tort represents another borrowing from French at a later period (Milsom 1985, 157–58). A formal denial of *tort e force* is the equivalent (although reversed) of *vim et iniuriam*. The Provisions of Oxford, 1258, clause 16, uses *tors* for acts of royal and other ministers demanding correction; but see the Latin of clause 1 (Treharne and Sanders 1973, 98, 106). See further Richardson and Sayles 1941, xli; *Brevia* 1951, 2 and *passim*; Kaye 1966, 2 and *passim*; Harding 1981, lvi n. 1. For earlier examples, see chap. 4.

seen, characterized English law in the twelfth century and earlier. I have suggested previously that it was unknown to English practice before the late twelfth century.[12] I certainly overestimated the ease with which one might transpose from Roman law anything like the common law's later distinction. A Roman origin seems likely all the same, if only because a very similar distinction between crime and delict also entered Continental law a little later. That, in a well-regulated legal system, legal procedures ought to be divided into criminal and civil law was evident enough to anyone capable of reading the basic *Institutes* or Vacarius's *Liber pauperum*, let alone other, more advanced texts from the *Corpus iuris civilis*. By the third quarter of the twelfth century, a fair number of well-educated Englishmen—some influential royal counselors at court—possessed such acumen. The next step was no doubt to begin using the Roman term *crimen* in some technical sense to denote serious offenses as seen from the king's new public point of view. The public prosecution from 1166 onward of a range of such offenses, soon to be called felonies, probably encouraged a few of the juristically inclined to think along some such lines.[13] The apparent, perhaps gradual assimilation of the idea that public procedures should be restricted to use for publicly proper ends may show their minds at work.[14] The result was less a slick assimilation than a botch job of the kind found frequently in northern Europe at this time, as inadequately understood Roman texts and terminology became known and influenced vernacular laws.

The first clear attempt to incorporate the Roman law distinction between criminal and civil law into the organization of secular English law, in the treatise *Glanvill* written around 1187–89, supports this hypothesis. As Milsom has observed, "Glanvill's view is not ours."[15] Its author included virtually all wrongs under the head of crime, an arrangement very different from that eventually accepted by the common law.[16] *Glanvill* influenced the writ-

12. Hyams 2000. I had learned much from Seipp 1996. But Donahue 2003 courteously showed me how complex the route from Roman to English law must have been.

13. Although Justinian's *Institutes* virtually excludes criminal law (and the word *crimen* itself) from its elementary coverage, it does at the start declare a distinction between private and public "ius," and toward the end says something "de publicis iudiciis," that is, on something that might be felt to resemble the assize procedures of public prosecution (*Inst.* 1.1.4, 4.18 pr.). Searle 1980 (70) has an early (1180s) instance of *crimen* in a clearly secular sense, on sanctuary for a "latronem vel fur aut alio crimine damnatum." Neither the "Dialogue of the Exchequer" (Johnson 1983) nor the early pipe rolls use "crime" language.

14. The reference is to the suggestion, in chap. 5, that writs de odio et athia derive in some sense from the Roman oath of *calumnia*.

15. *Glanvill* i.1–2 and bk. xiv ("De placitis criminalibus") (pp. 3–4, 171–74); Milsom 1981, 285, and cf. ibid., 402–4.

16. Donahue 2003 both shows how the Roman lawyers' view of *crimen* differed from even medieval views of crime and notes that *Glanvill* included within it the entire law of wrongs. Gauvard 1991 (i.111–16) documents the specific connotations of *crimen* and so highlights the significance of its introduction into the legal vocabulary.

ers of later law books more than the classification of doctrine and remedies in the actual system of legal administration of the author's own day. He introduced the idea to English jurists as part of his overall concern to claim for English law the status of a respectable *ius scriptum* that could bear comparison with the law of Rome. Contemporary laymen took a much simpler view that probably distinguished only between the more formal pleas and accusations (sometimes now initiated by writ) and the less formal plaints. They talked in the French vernacular about, for example, "plaintes e quereles" or "les plaiz e les clamurs."[17] This formulation patently does not address the requirements of the new public prosecution procedures.

But the system of public justice itself was slow to rethink its categories. The rolls that recorded the long arm of royal law continued long after Glanvill's time to eschew his terminology of criminal and civil. They talked first of the "pleas of the crown," a widely inclusive category of matters (not all of them legal) in which the king had a special interest. Only gradually did insiders begin to apply the ancient name of *felony* to the lengthening list of offenses that eyre jurors were to present to the royal justices. Alongside the rolls or membranes accordingly labeled "de corona" were others headed "of pleas and assizes" or something similar. When authoritative scholars refer to "civil pleas," they are apparently reading a later distinction back into the minds of the enrolling clerks.[18]

It was probably the treatise *De legibus et consuetudinibus Angliae* of Bracton that ensured the triumph of the Roman distinction over the longer term. That treatise's author, whom I shall take to be writing in the 1220s,[19] remains rather less full-hearted in his adoption of the model than one might expect. He does not follow the lead of *Glanvill*, always one of his major sources, to

17. Both of these formulations seem sufficient to cover the range of judicial work done in an Angevin royal court. The sources are Wace's *Roman de rou*, ll. 841–44 (*Roman de rou* I.92, cited in Richardson and Sayles 1941, xliii) and Marie de France's *Equitan*, ll. 195–96 (Marie de France 1978, 31). See Jocelin's claim to hold a cellarer's court at Bury "de latronibus et omnibus placitis et querelis" (Van Caenegem 1990–91, no. 648, p. 699). The clerk in Harding 1981, 430 (1256) seems to make a comparable categorization into land pleas and other wrongs.

18. Meekings 1979–83 (26, and *passim*) and Crook 1982 (3–14 and *passim*) are guides who know their rolls better than anyone and are scrupulous about the avoidance of anachronism. They follow the modern convention without ever establishing a contemporary opposition between criminal and civil business from the thirteenth-century rolls. Another common heading is "de juratis et assisis." There are also headings to indicate other types of business such as foreign pleas (held over from other counties), the making of essoins, appointment of attorneys, estreats, and plaints. See also the observations of Harding 1981 (xlii) on the distribution of civil and criminal pleas on the various sections of plea rolls.

19. For the modern view of authorship of this treatise and the stages by which it reached the present shape, the now classic study of S. E. Thorne, "Translator's Introduction" (1977), in Bracton 1968–80 (iii.xiii–lii) needs to be read against the revisions of Barton 1993 and Paul Brand in Hudson 1996b (65–89).

include the categorization among his initial definitions.[20] His extended tractate on criminal matters, though still named after the ancient pleas of the
crown,[21] is as dominated by Roman law sources as any part of the treatise.
This strategy, which did not prevent a largely faithful depiction of contemporary English doctrine, was of lasting value, for it includes a whole number
of the Roman protections from improper prosecution or conviction that we
now consider part and parcel of human rights and due process.[22] The treatise is almost entirely organized round the notion of crime as an entity distinct from civil wrongs. For Bracton, the defining characteristic of crime
was breach of the peace, with the implicit assumption that this raised a public concern.[23] The imposition of punishment in the public interest (instead
of, or in addition to, the victim's compensation) seems less central to his
concerns. Major crimes (sometimes called "crimina capitalia" in this context) certainly carried punishment to life and members,[24] whereas minor
ones had pecuniary consequences only. But these minor crimes include a
number of procedures later classified as civil, most notably trespass itself
and replevin. Still, one may see from, for example, the author's repeated
concern over the licitness of switches between criminal and civil action in
mid-suit that the line, wherever drawn, was fundamental to his thought in
the whole area.[25]

Attentive readers could not avoid hearing constantly of the differences between civil and criminal actions.[26] Those who wrote their own treatises, to
abbreviate and update *Bracton* at the end of the century, had the choice of
following his usage here or of consciously excluding it. The authors of *Fleta*
and *Britton*, both writing ca. 1290, took opposite lines, which suggests to me

20. Compare *Glanvill* i.i (Hall, 3) with the generalities of the first section of Bracton 1968–80.
The explanation is probably the absence of crime language in the *Institutes* of Justinian, from
which most of this section is taken. The main exposition of the distinction is Bracton 1968–80,
fols. 101b–102 (ii.290–91) in the tractate on actions.

21. Bracton 1968–80, fols. 115b–159b (ii.327–449).

22. Western civilization owes a great deal to the early Roman Empire, perhaps the last great
power before modern times to dedicate the minds of many of its brightest citizens to problems of
law and order. Roman jurists do not seem to have felt that criminal law lacked legal interest.

23. Bracton 1968–80, fol. 115b (ii.328), has a chief justice haranguing local notables on their
peacekeeping duties at the start of an eyre. Gaol delivery commissions later called for the sheriff
to invite by proclamation the attendance of all who wished to "show anything for the king" (Bellamy 1998, 103).

24. Bracton 1968–80, fols. 118–118b, 120b, 127b (ii.334, 340, 359).

25. The text as our printed edition has it includes different views on whether one may only
raise a civil to a criminal suit or whether any change would void the suit for variation (Bracton
1968–80, fols. 101b–102, 140b, 150b [ii.291, 396, 425]). (I am not yet clear which view represents
that of the original author.) And see ibid., fol. 145 (ii.409), emphasizing that criminal proceedings
take precedence over civil ones for the same facts.

26. Crime language is very rare on the plea rolls. *CRR* xviii.796 (1243–44, reflecting church
court practice) and Clanchy 1973, 788, 813, 843 (1248), are exceptional for the dates.

that the distinction remained even at that date incompletely assimilated into the English system.[27]

This important time lag between the perception of the learned that English law could use the twin concepts of crime and tort in the Roman fashion, and the actual assimilation of the distinction into the working life of the system, is only to be expected. Practitioners trained in the schools were the exception. To persuade royal servants of the administrative conveniences of the approach took time, and conceptual advances had to await first the emergence of the newer remedies for wrong in their common-law guise and then the analytical recognition of the changed shape of the law as a whole. Alan Harding is probably right to see breach of the peace as basic here, and to insist on a causal link with the public nature of indictment procedures and the articles of the royal eyres.[28] To this peace and the development of the various means of its enforcement, I now turn.

Expansion of the King's Peace

This phenomenon of the twelfth century is covered in all the modern books. Starting in part from those grants of special peace discussed earlier, the king's peace grew to cover all the king's subjects (as some writers were now beginning to call them) and all inhabitants of the realm. What had been a special privilege for the few was coming to be regarded as the birthright of all Englishmen.[29] One particular expansion route lay through territory crucial to the present story. Royal grants of protection by charter proliferated in twelfth-century England along with the rising volume of royal acts in general. Their effect was perhaps to convert wrongs done to grantees (in surviving acts, mostly religious houses) into pleas of the crown, injuries actionable as if done to the king himself. The simple number of such grants

27. *Fleta* 1953–83, I.xvi (i.34–35), follows Bracton (in Latin) and does not treat trespass at all. *Britton* 1983, I.xxiii–xxvii (i.97–134) expunges the language of crime and does treat trespass (in French). I treat below the little treatise *Placita Corone* (Kaye 1966), which may serve to mark an intermediate stage in developments. For usage in early YearBooks, see Seipp 1996.

28. Harding 1981, xlviii; he notes that most of the results are to be found on crown rolls (ibid., xliii).

29. Carpenter 1996 (106) is alone in seeing coverage of the whole realm achieved by 1066. If Bellamy 1998 (57–60) is right to revive Maitland's argument that homicide expanded its scope during the twelfth century to absorb the ancient notion of murder, this will have contributed significantly to the swelling of the king's peace. It must then also have heightened frustration in the victim's milieu by making all homicide unemendable and thus taking away the kin's rights of appeal.

encouraged the proliferation of specific grants of peace to resemble a general peace over all inhabitants of the realm. But equally as important for the future was the manner in which this development presaged the "tickets" by which specific contempts of royal authority authorized private complaints to royal justice.[30]

The expectation that, by such means, ordinary people could obtain justice from the king emerged by leaps and bounds. Men (and to a more limited extent, women) at virtually all social levels felt that they could seek from the king remedies for wrongs committed against them in breach of "the lord king's peace." This empowerment doubtless offered some compensation for the uncomfortable awareness that their own misdeeds too were now very much more subject to public prosecution. People grew accustomed to try and represent all wrongs they suffered as also breaches of the lord king's peace. Angevin kings and governments encouraged this.[31] Stephen Langton, the archbishop of the Great Charter, ordered his suffragans at the Council of Oxford, in 1222, to excommunicate "all those . . . who presume wrongfully [iniuriose] to disturb the peace of the Lord King and the realm, and who unjustly detain the king's rights [iura]."[32] By his time the new rules were widely understood and practiced. The aggrieved knew how to frame their complaints to get a royal hearing, and they were aware, indeed, that they must consciously avoid words of felony and allegations of breaches of the king's peace if they wished to keep their disputes out of the clutches of royal justice.[33] The far wider availability of this justice, especially through frequent eyres in the shires, fed the notion that justice was (or ought to be) available to all—the germ of a belief in the rule of law in a very strong sense.

The concept of breach of the peace focused on the king's interest, the wrong done to him. It operated mostly at a relatively low social level. It often concerned incidents that royal *familiares* regarded as too despicably trivial and dirty to warrant their time and attention. Alan Harding has suggested that this is the terrain on which trespass as an action was born.[34] He points out that Scots law, directly descended from the same twelfth-century

---

30. Harding 1966 argued for this development in Scotland. Despite several brief restatements of the insight in later publications, he has never argued the case in full for England.

31. Harding 1981 (xlv) suggests that the early royal temporary inquiries along lines similar to later commissions of oyer and terminer were particularly influential. Here and elsewhere his argument may be a little too closely tied to the chances of plea-roll survival.

32. Powicke and Cheney 1964, i.106–7; this canon, which so nicely links breach of the peace with the pleas of the crown, was repeated and developed throughout the century (ibid., i.275, 332, 387, 434, 478–79, 495, 626, 722; ii.809, 820, 849, 906, 1057, 1089).

33. Harding 1981 (xxiv) notes that changes in the judicial treatment of appeals proclaimed in effect a royal interest in much nonviolent wrong.

34. Ibid., xlix–li.

doctrinal stock as England's common law, made do with a single trespass writ, the indicatively named brieve *de pace domini regis infracta*. His implication is that breach of the peace is the fundamental plea to which all else is secondary.

Harding's contention overreaches. It is not clear that we need to privilege breach of the king's peace over other, more specific contempts. Pleas based on those "tickets" figure in cases from the very earliest plea rolls onward.[35] The argument that your wrong to me constituted also a contempt of the king's dignity patently predates the plea rolls. As we have seen, the suggestion that my injury strikes too at my lord's reputation and interests is a very ancient plea indeed,[36] easily made explicit in a form that the justices could recognize and the clerks embody in formulas on the rolls. Complainants and their counselors could choose in the late twelfth century a variety of rhetorical means to persuade the royal justices to give them their day in court. Breach of the peace, if fundamental, was never their sole argument. Specific contempts, seemingly more attractive where men could plausibly invoke them, were surely behind the first wave of trespass writs in *quare* form, which do not mention the peace at all. Not the least remarkable feature of these developments is the degree to which they embody initiatives from below. Private individuals proactively seeking satisfaction arguably fueled the process by which the king's peace spread and became universal. Beyond doubt, it was they and their advisers—not royal policy makers—who pioneered the pleading of the special contempts ("tickets") that brought so much new business into royal courts and offered so many new opportunities to ordinary folk.

Public Prosecution

Much the most prominent means by which the king strove to maintain his firm peace was through the system of public prosecution. This must have provided the main context for the separation of common-law trespass from the appeal of felony and in all likelihood the locus for the precipitation of the common-law conception of felony itself. Curiously, though, these far-reaching changes emerged, as we know, from two royal assizes that introduced hardly any explicit conceptual innovation. They appear to have treated the presented offenses as given facts that needed no definition. At first the justices assumed that their jurors shared their own understandings formed from immemorial tradition.[37] Their concern was to *extract* present-

35. E.g., Maitland 1891, 24 (1194).
36. See chap. 4.
37. I discuss the process by which crimes came into more precise definition later in this chapter.

ments, not to exclude them by narrow definition. They did not even attempt to stipulate formal rules or much in the way of procedure. There was therefore no expectation in those early eyres that the pleas of the crown would generate much lawyers' law by raising knotty points as the real actions did, with their returnable writs serving as set texts for court argument. Not until John's reign did the first trespass writs and the growing desire of royal justices to use a strict interpretation of the appeal's procedural requirements emerge as a tool of jurisdictional control.

At the same time, the establishment of grand juries and indictments as routine in the last decades of the twelfth century publicized the king's duty to provide good peace for all his subjects better and further down the social strata than ever before. On their arrival in the shire, his justices spoke of justice and peace in ways that encouraged quite ordinary folk to demand justice.[38] Because powerful individuals naturally sought to manipulate the situation to their own advantage, abuses attended the grand jury from its very inception. This opportunity for a favored few must surely have proved a source of frustration for the majority. Men hungry for redress of their own wrongs knew that the king was failing to reach the most egregious peace-breakers. The periodic opportunity to contribute to an enemy's indictment and punishment before itinerant justices pleased the king's subjects without answering all their needs. People remembered that their grandparents had done better, for they had received monetary compensation as well as the fuller, more personal satisfaction of the peace settlement. Naturally, such regret produced many complaints of wrong by and on behalf of the private "victims" in the frequent eyres at the end of the twelfth century.[39] Plaints, especially if made in the weeks immediately before the eyre (within the summons), were blessedly free from the more rigorous procedural requirements of the formal appeal of felony. It was easier to persuade the justices that you too had suffered from some wrong meriting royal remedy and compensation than to issue a formal challenge to battle. It was safer, too, since failure carried only a bearable amercement, generally half a mark.

These discussions and negotiations around juries of presentment at the eyre provide the most plausible context for the development of the future trespass action out of the inchoate procedures that I have called proto-trespass. When complainants brought their wrongs to the notice of their local juries or before the justices themselves, they often used the French

38. The chief justice was expected to give an exhortatory speech at the start of each eyre visitation on the value of good peace. Bracton 1968–80, fol. 115b (ii.328), shows what a Martin of Pateshull could make of this opportunity. See the comments of Summerson 1985, xviii.
39. Harding 1981, xlv.

word *trespas*. I shall argue that this term was uniquely suited to connote the individual's sense of his personal injury from an offense against the king's higher authority. Presentment jurors had two basic tasks. In addition to their obvious primary duty to indicate the offense and offenders against whom the justices needed to proceed, they had also to bring to the court's notice all private appeals made since the last eyre visitation. Conceivably, the later opposition of trespass and appeal began here. Some juries may have chosen, merely for administrative neatness, to label offenses not yet the subject of a formal appeal as *trespas* in order to mark these off from appeals already under way.[40] They will have understood that this usage in no way implied any substantive difference in the legal nature of the wrongs and remedies the two groups of cases treated, or even, perhaps, in the procedures to be utilized.

There are other hints that public prosecution at the eyre indeed constitutes the locus in which to seek the origins of trespass. The shape of the developed common-law civil action remained closely linked to the indictment process's criminal categories, first by its exclusion of words of felony (which inevitably implied an indictable offense not to be pursued in this exclusively private manner) but also through its criteria for royal interest. This is evident, for example, in writs provided from the 1220s to help complainants discover the names of their opponents' accomplices. Another root was provided by the rise of what has misleadingly been termed criminal trespass— in fact, privately initiated suits encouraged by the king out of a "concern for riotous and forceful wrongs."[41] The rapidly broadening range of indictable offenses in the last decades of the twelfth century further enhanced the effect.[42] The growing use of jury trial in private nonproperty suits, including those for wrong, further encouraged the aggrieved to make their plaints before royal justices now that they risked a limited sum of money (generally half a mark) rather than their own bodies.[43] Where once a man could only be put to the defense of his life and limb by an accuser who risked his own body, there were now after Magna Carta (clauses 36, 38, and 54) a variety of other ways to harm one's enemy—with a chance of winning damages from him to boot.

40. The late-twelfth-century pipe-roll data assembled by Kerr 1995 offer some confirmation of this hypothesis.

41. Harding 1981, xliii–xliv.

42. Meekings 1979–83 (i.90–94) sketches the development of the pleas of the crown through the eyre's expanding list of felonies and other articles for presentment. Cam 1921 remains the basic account of the expansion of the articles of the eyre. Harding 1981 (xxiv) suggests that indictment after, say, 1194–95 covered all *malefactores*; see Cam 1921, 92 (i.21), and Stubbs 1913, 253 (clause 7).

43. Relevant landmarks here are possibly the exclusion of hot anger appeals by the procedure de odio et athia, more certainly the end of the ordeal after 1219, and the way the king's suit increasingly intervened after the failure of a private complaint or appeal. See Harding 1981, xxxiv.

Felony

Appeals were acceptable in royal courts only when the allegation included words of felony. Conversely, trespass suits came to demand equally careful framing. They must include the proper "ticket" language to buy access to royal authority, yet at the same time exclude all words of felony, for fear that the king's interest in the punishment of villains would overwhelm the plaintiff's own pursuit of financial compensation. But whence came this felony on which so much demonstrably now turned?[44] That the voluminous literature on the origins of the common law offers no satisfactory answer to this question is remarkable. Of course the word itself is ancient and possesses a much-debated etymology, but most scholars have apparently assumed the existence of the concept of felony as ready for use in 1166. The word itself reached English from French and had no Old English cognates.[45] It does not figure in the leges prior to the *Leges Henrici Primi* in the second decade of the twelfth century.[46] That author's usage is compatible with a variety of readings that foreshadow the later common-law understanding. Very possibly, the word's primary connotation for the author related to the breach of a man's all-important obligations to his lord. This treachery constituted an offense of a quite exceptional kind in that it was the *single* circumstance that could lead to judicial battle between lord and man. As such, it was a matter of concern to the king well before Angevin times and possibly already considered in the early twelfth century a plea of the crown, as other future felonies almost certainly were.[47] Whether these other offenses, or any offenses at all, were considered as serious as treachery against a lord before the last third of the twelfth century and treated as such is impossible to establish at this stage. But indictable offenses were so treated by the end of the century, perhaps on the ground that they raised comparably profound questions of perjury and breach of trust.

Once again, the provision of public prosecution in the assizes of Clarendon and Northampton constituted, I believe, a conceptual watershed. The common-law felonies were offenses in the group considered appropriate for indictment by juries under the new assize procedure. The Northampton Assize text of 1176 groups its offenses under the general heading of

44. The hunt starts as always with Pollock and Maitland 1898, ii.464 sq.

45. The Old English *fela*, meaning "many/much," was often used as an intensifier in words like *felasynnig*, "very guilty." So it could provide some contamination in the Middle English. *A-N Dict.* documents a history of felony words congruous with the argument in the text.

46. *LHP* 43.7 (with which, contrast *LHP* 13.12, itself following II Cn 27), 46.3, 53.4, 88.14. See Liebermann 1903–16, ii.400.

47. See *LHP* 53.2. Neither *felonia* nor any other obvious reference to betrayal of a lord appears in the list of future pleas of the crown in *LHP* 10.1, which does on the other hand contain analogs to most of the early common-law felonies.

felonia, although the word had not figured at all in the received text of the 1166 assize.[48] Within a dozen years, Glanvill had largely organized his discussion of "criminal pleas" around a recognizably common-law notion of felony, from which, for example, common or garden-variety thefts were excluded.[49] By this time, the royal justices were rapidly broadening the range both of indictable offenses and of explicit public interest in crime. Private appeals heard by royal justices always allege felony from the very first extant plea rolls in the mid-1190s, although earlier appeals did not. Yet the successive articles of the eyre, which transmitted the instructions to the justices who had to implement the rules, scarcely ever use the word itself.

This characteristically Angevin recalibration of an ancient word and its associated concepts to current needs went virtually unremarked at the time. It provides an apt twelfth-century analog to the changes revealed for pre-Conquest England. The West Saxon kings of the tenth and eleventh centuries had extended the meaning of perjury to cover what they considered the most serious of the wrongs they felt they had to tackle in their own day.[50] With equal stealth, the Angevins apparently did likewise. They similarly brought into public life an equation between breaches of faith with God, secular breaches of personal faith sworn to the king and other lords, and breaches of the publicly sworn faith of adults aged twelve and over. The instructions to the justices administering the Assize of Northampton in 1176—to take within a tightly defined period "fidelitates" to the king from all who wished to remain in the kingdom without proclaiming themselves the king's enemies—is much too timely to be merely coincidental.[51]

48. Stubbs 1913, 179. Distinctions remain; you can be indicted "de murdro vel alia turpi felonia" but not "in minutis furtis et roberiis" (clause 1). There were also special rules for those caught in the act "de murdro vel latrocinio vel roberia vel falsoneria . . . vel de aliqua felonia quam fecerit."

49. *Glanvill* xiv.1 (171–73) is the main text. Other references (vii.9, 17; x.15, 17 [pp. 83, 90–91, 130, 131–32]) confirm the point. The word is notably absent from the text of the "Dialogus Scaccarii" a few years earlier still, doubtless for reasons of Latin style. Johnson 1983 (31, 97–98, 101) shows that its author followed, as one might expect, exchequer practice (for which, see Madox 1769, i.344–45), which referred to fugitives', not felons', chattels. It is also absent from the Norman *Très ancien coutumier* but emerges in the *Summa de legibus* to demonstrate that ca. 1236, Norman usage was very like England's; see *Summa de legibus* XLVII.2, LXVI.6 (Tardif 1896, 147, 166), and the various appeal forms, ibid., LXVII.6, LXIX.3, LXX.1, LXXI.3, LXXIII.1, LXXV.1 (Tardif 1896, 170, 178, 179, 180–81, 182, 186).

50. Wormald 1999, 307, as mentioned in chap. 3.

51. Assize of Northampton, clause 7, in Stubbs 1913, 180. Our text carries straight on from these *fidelitates* to the arrangements for dealing with thieves and other malefactors. At this time so soon after the 1173–74 revolt, some of those attending the eyres in question must still have been technically the king's enemies.

Inevitably, the process by which the common law divided the traditional procedures for undifferentiated wrong into a civil action of trespass and a criminal appeal of felony was prolonged. The standard tests by which one could later distinguish between the two procedures in terms of their doctrinal definitions—their procedure and consequences—do not function properly until the later thirteenth century.[52] The most important choice a "victim" had to make before seeking legal remedies against his enemy was not between different forms of action. Rather, it was whether to seek a royal hearing at all or to content himself with seeking redress closer to home. Presumably, one took the more expensive route only when local justice seemed remote, as when one's enemies dominated the hundred or shire, or when one felt the need to deploy against them the king's greater resources of process and punishment. The payoff was the threat of more severe consequences, and hence greater pressure for an outcome favorable to oneself, and even on occasion physical vengeance with impunity.

Above all, complainants had to know how to frame their suits to gain access. The famous tickets into the royal courts for trespass are at first as prominent in plea-roll records of appeals as in trespass itself. They had indeed first surfaced in suits that we should naturally classify as appeals, yet in which complainants sought and gained damages, specific relief (ending the wrong), and/or a chance to come to a satisfactory settlement. They seem already in the plea rolls of John's reign close to fully formed.[53] In the years before the first plea rolls of the 1190s, men and women already knew to exaggerate their injury where necessary, a strategy that inflated their claim to a felony and thus entitled the victor to execute a judgment on the enemy's life or members.[54] Although this "hyping" of injuries was familiar to justices,[55] they were powerless to prevent it. Nevertheless the justices' efforts probably eased the way toward the differentiation of the two procedures as they pressed the more lightly wronged to sue in "trespass." At the same time, by provoking others to greater creativity in pleading, they encouraged the development of a separate substantive doctrine for each procedure.

52. Hudson 1996a, chap. 6, is a fair sample of the textbook account.

53. Richardson and Sayles 1941, cxxv–cxxvi; Harding 1981, xxxiii. *Pipe Roll 29 Henry II* (165) might just be an early, exceptional trespassory plaint involving Jews.

54. Van Caenegem 1990–91, no. 471, is one excellent example. Cf. Richardson and Sayles 1941, cxxi, cxxiv; and for an unusually clear plea-roll example, see Hyams 1986 and *CIM* 2154 (1282).

55. Meekings 1961 (83, 86) points to the frequent practice of adding accusations of petty robbery to raise offenses against the person to felony.

The effects were slow to become evident. The imposition of later categories to such cases is of little value in the first half of the thirteenth century. Clerks showed no obvious sense of any need to demarcate the procedures from each other on the plea rolls until late in Henry III's reign. Many characteristic features that came to be regarded as distinctive to trespass were available very early. They mostly predated even the brief period around 1200 when plea-roll clerks sought to translate them into the Roman vocabulary of the schools.[56] But they do not at this stage indicate trespass rather than appeal, to use the later terminology. Litigants switched with ease from one form to the other and back. Suits called appeals were still regularly enrolled with other Common Pleas.[57]

"[T]he supposed contrast of the remedies available by appeal and by trespass" probably started only as it became, at first hard and then impossible to gain specific relief, which takes the story beyond the period of this book into the fourteenth century.[58] Appellors frequently sought damages and often succeeded.[59] In the thirteenth century the financial calculus was not as clear as later. The game was in many respects the same as before the birth of the common law: only the venue and rules had changed a little. There were more players. The poor and powerless who could afford only a minimum investment could nevertheless inflict real annoyance on relatively important enemies without paying for a writ or seeking damages. A plaint for breach of the peace was a cost-effective way to force harassing neighbors to face royal inquiry into their actions. That it proved defective or was not fully prosecuted made little difference. An additional appeal *de precepto* could put even an absent Mr. Big to his defense.[60] Writ fees, modest though these were, stimulated the bringing of such plaints by people who, if they reached a

56. Richardson and Sayles 1941 (cix–cxiii, cxvi, cxxxii) dates the Roman law enrolling fashion to the years before ca. 1212 but persuasively locate the origins of trespass talk to an earlier and English source. This must provide the essential context within which the author of *Bracton* equated appeals with the Roman *actio iniuriarum* in the (?) 1220s.

57. Richardson and Sayles 1941 (cxv, cxvii) notes that a regular trespass style of enrollment does not become routine until late in Henry's reign but that the defense by a general denial of "vim et iniuriam" (along, by that time, with the formula "deterioratus est et damnum habet") is ubiquitous by 1215 at the latest. For appeals on Common Pleas rolls, see Harding 1981 (xlii); see Clanchy 1985 (220–23) for the way the phrase "communia placita" straddled our division between civil and criminal pleas to indicate royal jurisdiction as universal or public in nature.

58. This is the view of Harding 1981, xlii.

59. Harding 1981 (xli) suggests that most of this went as fees to the clerks. Clanchy 1973, 728, 997, 1030, 1034 (1248), are appeals (997 perhaps a plaint) quashed when the justices learned that the goal was damages (emendation); in the last three, the jurors confirmed a beating (but no robbery), and the appellees were then amerced "pro transgressione." Damage awards were rare in appeals (Meekings 1961, 88).

60. See chap. 6; Harding 1981, xl. The standard amercement (fine) for withdrawal or error was half a mark, and the justices would sometimes excuse even this for a "pauper."

royal court, might well seek damages.[61] Because jury trial was almost as easily available in appeals as trespass, complainants certainly understood that they could pressure opponents with the threat of physical penalty without themselves running any real risk of "la perilouse aventure de batayles." A persistent folk memory of the old undifferentiated suits for *bot* made its own contribution to swell the volume of plaints.[62]

The first trespassory writs (*vi et armis* from the late twelfth century) were intended to assist complainants to use existing remedies for wrong by securing on their behalf the appearance of their opponents in court. Ordinary people were sometimes unable to secure the sheriff's ear, still less able to spur him into action. They needed royal assistance to compel him to attach the defendant by sureties. At first, the provision of writs hardly changed the ways that the courts understood these procedures and the rights that underlay them. Only very gradually did the constraints of an increasingly professional system begin to sharpen the choices available to litigants.[63] The boundary between the two main procedures that became trespass and appeal of felony remained extremely porous, and the cases long remained compatible with an analysis that simply saw two forms of the same set of remedies for traditional wrong.

We possibly place more weight today on the wording (appeal or trespass language) of the writs and plea rolls than contemporaries did. Many if not all of the early trespass writs developed out of appeal process in the first half of the century.[64] I should myself prefer not to talk of an action of civil trespass before the surge of new writs, during the period of Reform and Rebellion after 1258, won for trespass a place of its own in the lawyer's classification schemes.[65] If thereafter a recognizable line existed between tres-

61. Ibid., xxxviii.
62. Ibid., xli; *Britton* 1983, I.26.2 (i.123–24). Richardson and Sayles 1941, 65 (1257), is an explicit complaint at a homicide allegation brought for the purposes of extortion.
63. Meekings 1961 (82) deduces from the plea rolls that writs in "quare" form had been issued since the late twelfth century. Harding 1981 (xxxv, xl) gives from extant registers a basic account of early writs of "trespass" and "appeal"; De Haas and Hall 1970, Hib. 34; and cf. ibid., CA. 22–23. Thanks to Brand 1992a (451–56), however, we now know that the so-called "Irish Register" (Hib.) almost certainly dates to ca. 1210. Both Hib. and CA. ("some time in the 1220s") limit help with process to allegations of the classic felonies "and other pleas of the crown." Neither contains a form for use against *vi et armis* offenders, although the plea-roll "trespass" entries strongly suggest that such writs existed in the second decade of the century. De Haas and Hall 1970 (cxxxi–cxxxii) found the general absence of trespass writs before the 1260s "a little surprising" and was somewhat dismissive of the partial explanation that they were probably not yet "of course."
64. Harding 1981, xxxv; Bracton 1968–80, fol. 149 (ii.420), suggests that the invention was to counter the negligence of sheriffs and others.
65. De Haas and Hall 1970 (xlvii, lvi, cix–cxx) shows that registers of writs into the 1260s (as late as CC.) accumulated examples in a kind of rag-bag appendix. Only in Edwardian registers did trespass find its lasting place in the scheme of things.

pass and appeal, it was one by which Edward I and his advisers did not feel unduly bound. Their efforts to find effective solutions to the perceived problems of law and order led them to favor approaches that mixed public and private suits, in commissions of oyer and terminer or trailbaston that retained more than a hint of the undifferentiated procedures of the previous century.[66]

THE EMERGENCE OF *TRESPASS* AS A TERM OF ART

This story of a very gradual separation into common-law forms of action accords well with the history of the word *trespass* itself. In the longer term, trespass became the medieval antonym for pleas of the crown and then crime, used similarly as was that later French import, *tort*. The short-term history of the word's emergence and transformation is both far more complex and interesting than this brief statement implies. Milsom acutely observed that trespass as a term of art had to have developed from a vernacular sense of "wrong," in much the way and around the same time that the common law's technical understanding of *covenant* had emerged from *convencio* (and its French equivalents).[67] The insight is fundamental enough to merit full study by linguistic scholars. My suggestions here may indicate the lines along which to proceed.

The dictionaries show that the usage of French *trespas*, its Latin equivalent *transgressio*, and their cognates are not easily encompassed by a simple translation of "just wrong," in the way that Milsom envisioned.[68] We find, well into the thirteenth century, legal records using *transgressio* (and its cognates) almost exclusively for wrongs committed against the king or some other superior.[69] Such transgressions draw punishment in the form

---

66. Harding 1981, xliv–xlvii. I have learned much on all this from my own student, Amy Phelan; see Phelan 1997 and 2000.

67. Milsom 1985, 154–58.

68. Milsom 1981, 285; Milsom 1985 (154) is not quite correct about the dictionary meaning of *trespas/transgressio*. See for Old French, *A-N Dict.*, 818–19; and Tobler and Lommatsch 1925–95, 10.616–21; for Latin, Niermeyer 1997, 1038; and, for Middle English, *MED*, s.v. "trespas." I am further indebted to Dr. David Howlett of the *Oxford Dictionary of Medieval Latin from British Sources*, who kindly allowed me access to the slips for the forthcoming entries on "transgressio" and cognates. Also occasionally found at around this time are the precursors of the other lasting French import, *tort*, for which see n. 11 in this chapter.

69. In the 1256 Shropshire eyre, for example, the vast majority of the word's uses refer to default of "public" duty (e.g., Harding 1981, nos. 687/961, 750/967, 875/978, 20/982, 65/990, 672/994, 794/994), by vills (ibid., 652/940, 530/941, 456/585/955, 607–8/957, 714/963, 157/967, 770/776/969, 844/846/977, 845/978), or local officials (ibid., 621/636/950/958, 621/958, 722/964, 830–31/975, 993), or jurors (ibid., 939, 945, 947, 949, 952, 958, 972, 974, 975, 978, 990). Kennedy 1995 (149) cites in the Ely Foundation charter a clear late-twelfth-century example. *Rotuli Litterarum Patentium* 1835, 138b (1214), refers to two of the Magna Carta rebels as having "transgressi" toward the king.

of amercements recorded on the rolls and carry no implication of compensation for individuals actually harmed by the acts. This is "wrong" viewed in the same "downward" perspective in which early medieval kings constantly tried to portray their activity for the maintenance of order in their realms. The words are also frequently found in records of appeals, especially to explain the reason for an amercement.[70] Thus *transgressio/trespas* does not always translate into "wrong" understood in any private or simple sense. Where legal scholars conventionally content themselves by Englishing the words as "trespass," thereby creating a premature link with the developed common law, we might better render them by the more neutral "offense," which has the further advantage of a more crime-like connotation.[71] One is more likely to offend against a superior than an equal.

We should remember here that none of the common-law crimes received statutory definition before the very end of the thirteenth century. Until the fourteenth century, most crimes remained largely undelineated in writing outside the occasional learned treatment of a Bracton. The thirteenth-century pleas of the crown enjoyed very little of that process of minute specification that was already well under way for property rights of all kinds. The meanings of rape, arson, mayhem, and the rest were set by ancient practice, dating back to the Carolingians if not earlier. Twelfth- and thirteenth-century courts and the juries that served their various purposes were deemed to know the nature of each offense, including the permissible defenses that comprised so important a part of them.[72] Into this context of ancient customary familiarity and nondefinition, the word and original notion of trespass best fits.

By no means was customary trespass a simple notion; trespass words in both Latin and French have further connotations. The etymological implication of crossing some line remained alive throughout our period. The verbs continued to carry the possible meaning of crossing a road or

---

70. See Harding 1981, 741, 901, 613/957, 743/965–66, 721/964, 747/966, 623/862/972, 859/978, 672/994, 793/994. The phrase "pro transgressione" distinguishes these amercements from the standard ones "pro falso clamio."

71. It is hard to see the murderous attack of Clanchy 1973, 794 (1248), as a mere trespass or the purloining of the king's wreck (Stenton 1934, 687). Also Meekings 1979–83, 471 (see pp. 545–46) = Richardson and Sayles 1941, 44 (1235). See also FERNHAM V. ENGLEYS (1213–14). Meekings 1961 seems to have translated *transgressio* as "offense," since the word *trespass* does not appear, but in Meekings 1979–83 he turned to the safer translation "trespass." But a French translation of Magna Carta, clause 20, translated *delictum* by *forfait* (Holt 1974, 359). See also "Florys and Blaunchefdour" (ca. 1250), l. 1046, in Fellows 1993 (71), and the B-text of "Piers Plowman" a century later (Schmidt 1995, passus I, ll. 94–97).

72. Harding 1983 makes the point about statutory definition. Green 1985, chaps. 1–3, abundantly documents the way that judges and juries struggled to define homicide and other crimes in the thirteenth century.

traveling across country.[73] (I resist the temptation to make anything directly of the alluring possibilities presented by any Bakhtinian transgressive quality of the word.)[74] The word's flexibility is very much to the present point. The verb from which it derives can be used intransitively as well as transitively. One may simply "transgress" without specifying the line that has been crossed or the rule that is breached thereby. Similarly, the associated agent-noun, transgression/trespass, can in effect carry its object concealed within its own definition.[75] Thus one can simply accuse someone as a transgressor (or for having transgressed) and leave until later the specifics of their wrongful actions, exactly what was wrong with these and why. This usage is flexible enough to invite the speaker to inject his own sense of the breached norm without definition. It constitutes a terminology that is the very antithesis of the law school drive toward linguistic precision entailed by the introduction of the law/fact distinction. Men seriously concerned to follow the other distinction between crime and tort would hardly have introduced the trespass word, which patently ignores or obscures it. Perhaps that is why we find clerks struggling in the early plea rolls to import from the schools a more respectable Roman law vocabulary. For a while they denoted actionable wrongs by use of *delictum* or *iniuria*.[76] The more closely one examines the concept of trespass, the less comfortable it appears in the context of the emergent common law.

These facts raise several speculations on *trespass*'s rise to the status of common-law term of art. The word's initial attraction was perhaps its very imprecision, which suited the ancient undifferentiated procedure because it left the complainant's options open. I would speculate that Angevin jurors spoke of French *trespas* when discussing among themselves their obligation to present offenders for indictment before royal itinerant justices. If so, this occurred only in England and despite the availability of an English alterna-

73. *A-N Dict.*, s.vv. "trespasser," "trespassur," cites examples of ca. 1300 from the legal volumes of the Selden Society and from Britton. Niermeyer 1997 (1038) does not note usage in the literal sense of traveling through, across; perhaps he did not think of seeking it out, but the Vulgate Bible contains a number of examples, some of which are cited later in these notes.

74. For indications of where this might lead, see Stallybrass and White 1986.

75. Examples of this intransitive usage, both of the verb and of its associated nouns, are easily found in the dictionaries already cited. In Latin, the lead of the Vulgate Bible text will have been telling. See (for the verb) Gen. xxxii.31; Esd. x.10; Neh. i.8; Mal. ii.11; and (for the nouns) Ios. xxii.16; Esd. ix.2, 4, x.6; I Sam. ii.24; Isa. xxiv.16, liii.12, lix.13; Lam. iii.19. Readers did not need to be told that the reference was to sin in general and/or the breach of God's commandments. Many other verses use transitive forms of the word, including ones to denote the crossing of rivers or deserts.

76. See n. 56 in this chapter. Later usage of *iniuria* (or its French cognate *injure*) is rather different from that of the Roman lawyers, which focuses less on the act itself than the way it was done.

tive, *hearm*, with similar connotations.[77] Not even in Normandy did *trespass* become the legal term of art that the common law enshrined.[78] The term's flavor of downward justice suited wrongs under discussion because of their interest to the king and his justices. The thrust was that an offense against the king had also wronged a private individual. The word was an acceptable vernacular means to inject a delicate sense of the *publica potestas* to help justify the attempted royal takeover of law and order. Its deployment implied that the user possessed "tickets" to induce the king and his justices to notice his plaint and give it a hearing. If this is right, *trespas* may perhaps have enjoyed by 1200 a favored status that is not visible in our extant documents— that is, a lay or popular, vernacular not official, usage.

The approved internal vocabulary of the common law resulted from a complex conversation among its main actors. In this discourse, very imperfectly recorded in writing, royal clerks were perhaps at least as influential as legal practitioners and jurists. The way to establish this point is to study how common-law writs and procedures received their names, a challenge that has yet to be met. Yet the naming of writs was a serious matter,[79] an essential precondition for any efficient promotion of business within the new, royal legal system. Clerks and practitioners both needed to know what writs existed and should be used; failure to follow the correct form could now prove fatal to a suit. Labels were often chosen from some universally recognized characteristic of the action the writ initiated, frequently also from its *incipit* (first words). Thus we have writs *de recto* (of right) and of Prohibition. Eventually there are writs *de transgressione* too. But around 1200 and for a while afterward, this convention must have seemed an unpromising way to distinguish what were to be trespass writs from the many others also concerned with righting wrongs, especially as long as the word *transgressio* continued to denote primarily offenses against the king. Probably not even learned experts saw writs *de transgressione* as a useful group yet anyway. Even if some did, the label in the early thirteenth century will have seemed as little distinctive as the reference of Magna Carta, clause 34, to "breve quod vocatur Precipe" now does. It was misleading for the same reason: that it might refer to any of a number of diverse suits. The most prominent formula of early

77. Old English *hearm* survived into early Middle English with connotations that could combine notions of grief with physical damage (Hall 1960, 174; *MED*, s.v. "harm"). Other English candidates, translating *iniuria* before 1066, might have been *unriht* and *unlage* (as in Harmer 1952, 12, 114, 116). The adoption of a French word is indicative of the social climate among jurors.

78. Nor did it become so in Scotland. Both absences suggest to me that trespass language entered official vocabulary relatively late in the story, certainly after 1204, perhaps after the clerks' flirtation with Roman law language.

79. Cf. T. S. Eliot: "The naming of cats is a serious matter / It isn't just one of your every-day games."

trespassory writs, *vi et armis*, may at first have seemed more promising, and is indeed still found in professional literature from the 1250s.[80] Well before the end of the thirteenth century, however, trespass terminology is the choice of lawyers and clerks alike. This provides a chronological framework for our investigation.

The received view has held that trespass entered the common law during the second decade of the thirteenth century along with the writs in *quare vi et armis* form with which the later action was always associated but that its early appearances were mostly in the context of appeal plaints.[81] *Transgressio* cannot at this stage have been a term of art for the royal clerks. They use it sparingly in the sense of offense as explained earlier. To establish a technical term takes time. The precise moment when trespass became a term of art is hard to identify from rolls and writs. My samplings of the rolls do not demonstrate its arrival before the third quarter of the century, in the years after 1258 when the courts were faced with a flurry of newly coined trespassory writs, albeit lacking the word itself. This is the earliest time when the volume of trespass cases reached the point where some would wish to mark them off from appeals, as the headings "de transgressionibus" on some plea rolls suggest.[82]

The process by which trespass changed from denoting a very undifferentiated offense to become a specific form of actionable wrong quite distinct from felonies was equally indirect and problematic. Semantic shifts of the kind I posit cannot be mapped with precision from their written traces alone. The usage of the clerks who wrote up the plea rolls and writs of the common law will take us some distance but not the whole way. We can see, for instance, enough premature instances of apparent later usage to understand why some legal historians have assumed developmental completion.[83] It seems reasonable to fill some of the lacunae from one particular acute and

80. This can be seen from the "practitioners' aids" literature, to which Brand 1992a, chap. 3, is the most helpful introduction. *Brevia* 1951 (36–37) is the base version of "Brevia Placitata," dated ca. 1260 (ibid., xxvii). Another rather later instance is ibid., 221–22, but contrast ibid., 120, 210–12, for the "bref de trespas." A set of "Casus et Judicia" from the 1250s also twice refers to "breve quare vi" (Dunham 1950, lxxix.30–31). The later precedents of "Novae Narrationes" all use trespass words (Milsom and Shanks 1963, A34; B238, B242; C327, C331, C332A, C332C, and C332E).

81. Richardson and Sayles 1941, cxiii n. 1; Harding 1981, xxxv–xxxvi. A French translation of Magna Carta 1215, clauses 61–62, probably produced very soon afterward in Hampshire, uses *trespassement* for *excessum* and *transgressio* (Holt 1974, 362–63). Although the trespassory language in parts of these clauses is worth close examination, it does not seem that there is yet a single term of art.

82. Harding 1981 (lxxiii) notes such a heading from 1261. I cannot say whether there are earlier examples or when such headings became routine.

83. One can easily find precocious examples of the later clear common-law distinction between civil trespass and the felonies.

avid reader of plea rolls over the decade or so after 1215—the author of the treatise *Bracton*.

Bracton's author, writing soon after Magna Carta, referred to the basic notion of wrong, lying behind virtually all actions brought by individuals, in terms similar to those of his near-contemporary, the Norman author of the other *Summa de legibus*.[84] This *iniuria*, taken bodily from Roman law, denoted anything done *non iure* but was not always actionable in a royal court.[85] It is the subset of *iniurie*, which is so actionable, that he calls "transgressio." All *transgressiones* are crimes, but only some of them are major crimes, the felonies.[86] Our author is mostly interested in marking off the many *transgressiones* rated only as minor crimes from these felonies whose exposition dominates his tractate on actions. That he devotes to these civil wrongs so tiny a space shows that he did not yet see common-law trespass as either a discrete form of action or even a topic worth substantial treatment.[87] The *transgressio* is patently far from central to his thought, doubtless because trespass actions remained few in number and were still inextricably bound up with appeals of felony.

We can follow some of the century's developments in the emergence of trespass and appeal as separate remedies from the additions to *Bracton's* text made over the period.[88] These illuminate the changing manner in which men read *Bracton*. Among these readers were legal writers later in the century. By the end of the century it was possible for one of these, Britton (ca. 1290), to take a substantially different view. Liberated perhaps by his refusal to be mesmerized by the criminal/civil distinction, Britton was prepared to use trespass as a term of art in opposition to felony and covering (roughly) *Bracton's* minor crimes, and to note that its writs and procedure were distinct from those pertaining to appeals.[89] The little treatise *Placita Corone* oc-

84. See chap. 4.

85. Bracton frequently cites this definition from Justinian's *Inst.* 4.4 pr. (e.g., Bracton 1968–80, fol. 155 [ii.437]).

86. For Bracton, disseizins too are a subset of the larger pool of *iniurie*; e.g., Bracton 1968–80, fols. 163b, 164b (iii.23, 26). Summerson 1985, 528 (1238), was a case of violent house-breaking and abduction across a county line. Yet the jurors reported that the intention was only to disseize (an assize was proceeding concurrently) "and not out of felony."

87. In contrast to the bulk of the tractate (at least Bracton 1968–80, ii.334–60, arguably 334–437) devoted to felony, minor crimes get only ibid., ii.437–38. See generally ibid., ii.347, 372, 378, 390, 436, 446.

88. A nice example is the *addicio* to Bracton 1968–80, fol. 127b (ii.359), which Woodbine thought might be from the original author, whom he calls Bracton (ibid., i.386). The main text denies that there can be outlawry in any civil suit. The *addicio* says it may be awarded also in any trespass against the peace. This mirrors an actual change in mesne process dated by Sutherland 1967 (486–87) to ca. 1250 but possibly starting some years earlier. Thorne sets out his understanding of the *addicio* (Bracton 1968–80, ii.xxx).

89. Britton 1983, I.xxii.11, I.xv.2, I.xxvi.2 (i.105, 116, 123).

cupies an intermediate position in the middle of the century between *Bracton*, which he probably had not read, and Britton. Its author saw his task essentially as the description of appeals of felony. He describes these as lying against trespassers, probably in the simple sense of offenders.[90] He also carefully distinguishes between two possible outcomes. Where an appellee was convicted by battle or by a jury on which he had put himself, the consequence was life or members "according to what the *trespas* is" and at the discretion of the justices. If, however, the conviction came after the appeal had been quashed as defective, on an inquest concerning the king's peace, the consequences were pecuniary only, in the form of damages to the appellor plus a payment to the king "pur le trespas."[91] This is not trespass as a term of art, certainly not as a discrete form of action. Readers of this very knowing handbook named after the pleas of the crown seem—to judge from the number of surviving manuscripts—to have found this still acceptable at the beginning of Edward I's reign. We remain at a stage where most lawyers were still satisfied to concern themselves with offenses against a victim and against the king himself, seen perhaps as an individual power rather than as the personification of a state-like public entity.

But this is not the full story. In such a legal system, labels and entities do not coincide until time has passed. Most of the evidence for the actual terms used comes from the plea rolls themselves. Plea-roll clerks labeled their cases as helpfully as they could to fill their own need of easy retrieval, without in the first half of the century ever approaching a consistent specification of "trespass" as a discrete action. There is nothing special about their many references to "placitum de transgressione," which just meant "a plea *concerning* a trespass," or maybe even "concerning an offense." Their readers (mostly themselves and colleagues in any event) knew this to be a shorthand to help them find other entries relating to the same litigation. They will have become accustomed, as modern researchers must also, to finding that the same case received different labels in different plea-roll entries. They were not yet seeking "a plea *of* trespass," even though they could, if asked, have told how significantly the pleadings and substance of these trespass cases (as we call them) could now differ from anything raised in appeals of felony. Trespassory actions now frequently raised issues of property title, the ownership of chattels, and the like, that were never allowed to surface in appeals. They increasingly contain overt lawyer's law, which in appeals, if al-

90. Kaye 1966, 1, 25. The author's "working hypothesis" for a date of 1274–75 (ibid., xiv–xviii) is debatable on his own evidence, and in any event covers only Group I MSS representing an intermediate stage of the text. His own conclusion that "the state of legal practice . . . is that of the 1240s" tallies with my own samplings and suggests an origin in Henry III's reign.
91. Ibid., 6, 27.

lowed at all, was concealed behind procedural argument. What would in time be two separate actions, although already sometimes very different in character in the 1230s and before, had yet to be labeled as such.[92]

If, therefore, we place somewhere in the third quarter of the century the birth of *trespass* as term of art and form of action,[93] we thereby merely mark a conceptual advance in the way the system as a whole was understood by its players. It portends no great doctrinal change in either of the new actions. It may, however, signal a decisive step toward the common law's irreversible acceptance in principle of the distinction between crime and tort.

Let me summarize the case for nominating this watershed in what was obviously a protracted process of change. The critical test for the technical usage of the law is clearly that of the writ. Forms of action are about writs. Only around this time did writs of trespass, although not yet "of course," nevertheless reach a critical mass sufficient to encourage the compilers of registers to regard them as a discrete group.[94] This must be regarded as a necessary precondition to the emergence of a new form of action. Far more trespass writs were now issued, so that they come vastly to outnumber appeals brought with words of felony under their stricter procedural rules. Royal clerks too would sometimes now group these cases "de transgressionibus" together less formally on special sections of their plea rolls. The courts too began to conceptualize the various types of contempt to which they gave a hearing as different kinds of breach of the same undivided king's peace. Gradually, the different wrongs they had long been hearing under various tickets began to crystallize into a single broad, though still vague, group of remediable wrongs. Even more gradually, the conceptual existence of these actionable wrongs as an entity began slowly to render other senses of the chosen term *trespass* peripheral at least in lawyers' discourse.

92. Plea rolls of the 1240s show a very mixed usage, sometimes resembling that of the modern textbooks but often much looser. *CRR* xviii (1243–45) has about fifty references to *transgressio* by name but many more "trespass" cases. Among them are two also labeled as appeals (ibid. 796, 938, 1148, 1727), and one on the excommunication of an attorney in an action of right (ibid., 902, 1836).

93. This is compatible with the expert view of Meekings 1961 (82–83) based on a still unmatched knowledge of plea rolls and other contemporary legal sources, and before him of Sayles 1936 (xxxviii–xl).

94. For discussions of the writs in this chapter and the last, see "Writs, Trespass" in the index.

CHAPTER EIGHT
WAS THERE AN ENMITY CULTURE IN THIRTEENTH-CENTURY ENGLAND?

C hapters 6 and 7 have established two important facts about medieval England. The first is somewhat surprising: feud-like enmities survived into the age of the common law and remained visible at least in the first two decades of surviving plea rolls. The second finding, perhaps a consequence of the first, concerns the two common-law remedies that faced each other across the divide between criminal and civil law, crime and tort. The process by which these forms of actions developed out of similar but inchoate remedies for undifferentiated wrong that preceded them extended far longer than one might have thought. Taken together, these facts raise a number of questions about the remainder of the thirteenth century and also (although this is beyond the scope of this book) about the period after 1300.

A number of items are needed to complete the picture. The laundering of passions from the common law's internal records was never full or universal. Thus there remain certain areas in which litigant motives are more readily documented because they were pertinent to the legal issues in certain types of procedure. One of these, the writ de odio et athia, has already been discussed. Others, such as commissions of oyer and terminer and of trailbaston, merit notice here because they fit awkwardly into a crime/tort distinction still struggling for acceptance among jurists in the latter part of the thirteenth century. Although we tend to group them with crime because they deal with violent disorder, contemporaries persisted with the language of trespass. The stories told by inquisitions de odio et athia refute any idea of an exclusive association of enmity and feud, however understood, with the nobility and its peculiar conception of honor. Their evidence establishes the reality of urges to vengeance down to the level of village and (probably) town society. It thus appears to constitute the kind of general cultural pattern to which I alluded at the outset.[1] One may therefore suspect that the will to avenge a perceived wrong, to get even with an enemy, may feature in virtually any kind of litigation on the rolls. From this premise one might proceed, as I do cursorily, to seek anecdotal and other information about noble enmities, in order to test the hypothesis that we should regard them as an unexceptional part of the warp and weft of thirteenth-century politics. The suggestion is not that all politics was enmity but that recognized enmities were one of the routine features of social and political life. If this is acceptable, the argument reaches a point very close to the conclusions of other recent investigators into the origins and meaning of "bastard feudalism." I therefore conclude with a brief summary of the debate on this matter, to see how its findings might advance the overall argument.

SOCIAL EMOTIONS IN THE COURTROOM

Let us begin with litigants' motives. The historian can often deduce these by analysis of the cause of action or from the way juries and others tell the underlying story. Much that legally untrained litigants and other speakers said in court about the reasons for the actions that brought them there is, of course, lost to us.[2] The plea rolls seldom record anything like dialog and mostly state deceptively simple fact and argument. Sometimes that argument supplies the information. For pleadings to be informative about emotions and motive, the law governing the case must permit, or better still require, discussion of them. In the procedure de odio et athia, for example, the writ in its classic form demanded of jurors whether someone was being accused "by hate and spite or because he is guilty, and if by hate and spite by what hate and what spite."[3] A jury so charged could not avoid consideration of motives, and many of them responded by producing stories of great interest.

Juries must often have often been in a position to recount circumstantial tales that have not come down to us. But the court would not always let them tell their tales. Special verdicts of the kind we desire are rarely

1. Gauvard 1991 (ii.719, 743, 765–66) makes a similar point. Brooks 1933 (27) argued that many town group enmities deserved the feud label. The Cinque Ports invite special investigation here. Their conflict with Yarmouth, characterized by exceptional "spirit and bitterness," also passes the peace treaty test (ibid.). Their private war with Norman rivals precipitated the Anglo-French war of 1294–97 (Powicke 1962, 644–45).

2. The revealing confrontations between a very angry Henry III and Peter de Rivaux, and between Earl Warenne and Alan de la Zouche (on which see Kaye 1967, 374–75; and Hyams 1998, 121–22), are quite exceptional because of their political nature.

3. De Haas and Hall 1970, CC 109. This phrase, here quoted from a register of the 1260s, is already present in the earliest surviving exemplar of 1236 (Hurnard 1969, 348).

recorded among the pleas of the crown, even for homicides. Bracton's treatise suggests that courts even in the first half of the thirteenth century did give a hearing to testimony concerning motives now unavailable to us. The author's admonition that justices investigate whether homicides were committed "without premeditated hatred but moved by sorrow of the heart," echoing canon law, may seem more reforming ideal than actual reportage of practice.[4] But Bracton hints that the courts of his day were indeed interested in motive. When he explains, for example, that to be culpable, a homicide must be willed (again taking his cue from learned law), he glosses this as meaning "from anger or hatred or for the sake of gain."[5] He and his colleagues in the legal system were aware that the countryside was alive with enmities. So he envisions a false appeal of rape brought out of hatred of the man's new girlfriend or wife, and permits an accused to challenge jurors with whom he had mortal enmities or who were out to get his land. Jurors should themselves be warned not to conceal any offense from love, hatred, or fear. He further admonishes judges to examine the evidence carefully lest, as he puts it, people say that Christ is crucified and Barabas freed.[6] It seems likely that judges were already directing juries to distinguish, for instance, killings in hot blood from ones committed with what would later be called "malice aforethought."[7] Almost none of this is apparent in the brief plea-roll entries, which contain few good stories, and little indeed about a killer's motives beyond the obvious formulas. The value of Bracton's testimony here is to alert us to what the records do *not* tell us. He thus encourages us to generalize from the exceptional cases that do directly document the passions behind the acts that brought offenders into court.

These exceptions mostly exist where the law made motives a central issue. Writs that directly seek such information are rare indeed. This leaves an awkward gap in the evidence, which the historian can only fill from the less formal plaints exempt from some of the routine restraints of the writ system.[8] In the early rolls, trespass complainants routinely claim redress not merely for actual loss but also for shame suffered. Their pleas end with a declaration such as that they would not have suffered such

4. Bracton 1968–80, fol. 120b (ii.340–41): "sine odii meditatione immo cum motu dolore animi"; see also ibid., fol. 155 (ii.438): killing culpable if premeditated and willed "ob iram et cupiditatem."
5. Ibid., fol. 121 (ii.341).
6. Ibid., fols. 123, 137, 143, 143b, 148 (ii.343–44, 386, 404–6, 416). Cf. *Britton* 1983, I.xxv.9 (i.122).
7. Green 1985, 56, 122; Bellamy 1998, 58–60, 61, 64; Kaye 1967, 373–77. Also Davis 1987 (16, 36–37) for similar evidence on "chaude colle" in France. Bracton (as mentioned earlier) wants from his courts a good deal more close investigation than the courts can be seen to give.
8. Richardson and Sayles 1941 furnishes a number of good illustrations.

shame for a thousand marks.[9] But such pleas become increasingly rare in the king's courts after the first decades of the thirteenth century and eventually disappear altogether. The reasons are obscure, although in view of what we have learnt about trespass's lack of conceptual autonomy in the early common law, it seems likely that the availability of writs de odio et athia was influential here as well as with appeals proper. At least the result is clear: trespass pleas seldom reveal the emotions or passions behind the dispute.

The dramatic expansion of trespass in the years after 1258 and through the change of regime on Henry III's death in 1272 may have been pivotal. Edward I chose on his return from crusade to adopt many of the reformist ideas from the period of disturbances. In the first decade of his reign, he took or permitted a whole series of steps that invited his subjects to bring their grievances before his judges or himself. The rising tide of parliamentary petitions, of commissions of oyer and terminer, and perhaps the inquiries recorded in the Hundred Rolls ought all to be seen alongside the continued rise of trespass, including a number of new types of writ, as part of the same process of reconstruction.[10] The pattern is promising for our purposes, because the underlying rhetoric is the ancient one of a special plea on the reasons why the king ought to take up an individual's wrong as his own.

The dearth of rolls recording proceedings of oyer and terminer commissions is particularly unfortunate. This hybrid process combined, as Richard Kaeuper in particular has shown, the language of trespass (wrong and redress) with an insistence on the model of central, royal justice. The writs conferred substantial power to dictate the ground rules of the lawsuit on men who were often demonstrably after vengeance. Edward's government had clearly signaled its intention to restrict use of the commissions to cases of "heinous trespass," with exceptions only where specially approved by the king.[11] The market, however, had other ideas. Private individuals soon saw the potential of oyer and terminer for harming their enemies; the king and his ministers seldom bothered to impede them.[12] The procedure's great attractions were the power to nominate one's own judges and the very heavy

9. Beckerman 1981 studies both the shame element in early plaints and the process by which it came to disappear from common-law records, while surviving in some local courts.

10. Maddicott 1986 gives an excellent account of Edward's period as a new broom and may be supplemented by Hershey 1995 on the boost that Hugh Bigod's special eyres of 1258–59 and after gave to process by plaint. Maddicott 1986 (14–16) nicely characterizes the 1275 Statute of Westminster I as Edward's "coronation charter."

11. Kaeuper 1979, 741, 747.

12. Ibid., 742–43, 749–50, 752–53.

odds in favor of success.[13] All in all, the middling classes, who were by 1300 obtaining many of the commissions for "local gentry quarrels," found that oyer and terminer commissions enabled them to enjoy for their private purposes "the delights of managing the king's justice . . . in their own locality."[14] The implication that oyer and terminer commissions evidence widespread pursuit of enmities through law still needs to be tested by comparison of the cases against those of the routine common law with which they were habitually contrasted.[15] It is always hard to distinguish unjustified instrumental use of the system from its "real" business of righting genuine wrongs, which may lurk behind the most ostentatious enmities. But the prima facie case here is eminently plausible.

Kaeuper's picture has its paradoxical side. The rise in the later thirteenth century of oyer and terminer and associated procedures such as trailbaston coincided with the maturation of a royal legal system that was just beginning to call itself a "common law," in emulation of the impartial, public, and universal pretensions of the *ius commune*. Most scholars believe that by this time men could no longer comfortably regard open violence in pursuit of their private interests and quarrels as legitimate or justifiable.[16] But received opinion also sees widespread apprehension at the time that the mechanisms for the maintenance of order had proved inadequate. Edward I's reign consequently saw changes in the responsible agencies and institutions that can be paralleled only from the period of the Angevin reforms themselves.[17] The worsening disorder of the fourteenth century, often involving the private pursuit of enmities, shows that this great legislative effort, like its predecessor, enjoyed limited success. Much recent scholarship, intensively mining archival materials, has tended correspondingly to soften the traditional contrast between the relative order of the thirteenth century and the allegedly unrestrained noble violence of the later Middle Ages.

ENMITY IN THE COUNTRYSIDE

In the light of these general considerations, I now consider eyre rolls and the records of inquisitions de odio et athia. These show a full panoply of hatreds and acts of vengeance. Paradoxically, we know more about enmities

13. Ibid., 752, 755–64, 771–73.
14. Ibid., 751, 777, 780, 782.
15. Ibid., 767, 777; see ibid., 781, for Edward II's manipulative use of his own common law against enemies.
16. McFarlane 1973 (115) hedges his judgment with a "most of the time." Cf. Brand 1978, 92: "Violence to the person was still for many people in late thirteenth-century England well within, or only just outside, the perceived range of socially acceptable behaviour, even if it was outside the king's peace."
17. Kaeuper 1979, 737–38.

that showed themselves in legal action, appeals, and indictments than we do about ones that led directly to actual violence.

The cases certainly confirm that the *patria* was inevitably aware of lasting enmities. Juries frequently attribute acts to ancient hatred.[18] On one occasion their explanation that a killing was "due to a great enmity that was in existence for a long time" was confirmed by the killer's confession at his abjuration of the realm.[19] Other cases hint at feud-like elements. Chance meetings could prove dangerous, as when a man who happened to be carrying a spade killed an enemy whom he encountered in a wood. On the other hand, a man who, with his wife and mother, killed three people in the course of a burglary "odio antiquo" may have premeditated his house assault.[20] Deep-seated enmities were on occasion palpably evident in court. They could persist after an enemy's death. When Remigius of Easthall was found drowned on Eastbourne beach and the jury tried to brand him a suicide, it eventually emerged that the locals held him in such "great hatred" that they had resisted his burial in their churchyard. But Remigius had apparently fallen off his horse into the sea by accident.[21]

We are seldom treated to the root reasons for these long-term enmities. Often the explanations we do have concern sex. A common pattern is that of the woman slighted. Richard de Loges, "a ruthless, vicious" royal forester, had Margery de Wymbury as his live-in lover for many years but would not marry her even after she sued him in the rural chapter. Her relatives naturally hated Richard for this, and when Margery went off to live in Ireland, they had him falsely indicted for her death.[22] A Cornish husband warned away from his house the cleric who was having an adulterous affair with his wife. He was said to hate the couple. When the lover was found dead, it was the husband whom the wife accused.[23] William seduced, so it was said, a young woman and kept her living with him against her father's will. Perhaps the couple had wanted to marry but were unable to obtain consent. But when a convenient death of natural causes occurred elsewhere, the girl's mother accused William of homicide.[24]

---

18. E.g., JUST 1/569, m. 9d (1247–48); JUST 1/1051, m. 7d (1268); JUST 1/186, ms. 5, 20 (1281–82). The perception of ancient hatred (more than twenty years) in GRAY V. PORTER (1232) may have been much stronger on one side than the other. Kaye 1967 (376–77) notes that this kind of evidence works against pleas of self-defense or misadventure. Examples are *CIPM* 1904, nos. 2097 (in which the jurors reported that there had been no previous enmity "but rather brotherly love"), 2109, 2286. *Très ancien coutumier* LXX (Tardif 1881, 65) lists among ducal pleas of the sword ones "de assultu de veteri odio."

19. JUST 3/85, m. 19 (1278).

20. JUST 1/736, m. 28 (1272); JUST 1/778, m. 44 (1256).

21. JUST 1/909A, m. 28d (1248).

22. C 144/12, no. 10 (1274), on which see Coss 1991a, 229–34.

23. C 144/12, no. 20 (1274).

24. C 144/17, no. 37 (1277).

Such stories surely engaged local interest among drinkers in village taverns.[25] Villagers knew the reasons behind violent acts that enlivened the dullness of rural life far better than we can. The occasions when they proclaimed these in court, through an inquisition de odio et athia perhaps, give us precious glimpses into the dynamics of interpersonal relations. Thomas married twice. John, the son of the first marriage, hated his stepmother Juliana, so he assaulted her. Her own son, Robert, struggled to protect her against his older half-brother. When John died, his relatives procured indictments against Juliana and Robert, even though there was no evidence of foul play.[26] The strong feeling displayed on occasions of this sort begins to explain the care with which some custom could specify the inheritance rights in the families of men who had married more than once.

Property disputes often spawned hatred and violence. Nine villagers of Colney, Norfolk, rented a meadow together. Roger and his brother perhaps thought they had some claim to the land. They were at any rate in the habit of going there to cause damage, until the renters caught them in the act and beat them up. When someone killed Roger and fled a couple of years later, his kin at once appealed the Colney nine because of their well-known hatred for the dead man.[27] Other cases show men accused of killings because of litigation over withdrawn land grants and leases, the shaming takeover of some common of pasture, previous assaults and disputes over such matters as a horse sale, and (frequently) distraints and impoundings of animals.[28] The late C. A. F. Meekings, the paramount authority on these thirteenth-century rolls and inquisitions, summarized the scope of the disputes they recorded as covering "the everyday processes of a mainly rural society."[29] Taking my cue from Meekings, I suggest that enmities could sometimes permeate the furthest corners of rural life.

For the most part the quest for vengeance appears as a one-off affair. But this view reflects the snapshot nature of the sources, and one may reliably interpret the very existence of the legal record as evidence for a short series of tit-for-tat feud-like responses. Contract killings and attempts to take vengeance for, or by, legal executions exemplify the point. I have noticed two occasions where the system caught up with someone trying to escape responsibility for blood vengeance by getting others to do the job for him. Walter hated William for unknown reasons, and "wishing to be avenged

25. See also C 144/2, no. 15 (1267) and, for an oyer and terminer brought against an earl by his discarded mistress in 1320, Kaeuper 1979, 768 and n.

26. C 144/8, no. 43; 34, no. 3 (1278).

27. C 144/4, no. 6 (1272).

28. The examples cited are C 144/1, no. 6 (1248); 2, no. 9 (1262); 17, nos. 1, 19–20 (1277); 10, no. 32 (1273); 15, no. 21 (1276); 18, no. 25 (1278); 25, no. 9 (1285); and JUST 1/569A, m. 6 (1268).

29. Meekings 1961, 73.

[vindicari] on him," paid Steven the clerk to beat him up. William died. Both men were indicted and hanged.[30] Robert granted Richard a piece of land but later ousted him. An assize of novel disseizin merely exacerbated the conflict between the two men. Robert persuaded his brother and another man to kill Richard; he waited with his greyhounds in a nearby wood for them to do the deed, then took the killers off home with him. He pleaded his clergy but was handed over to the bishop as a convicted killer.[31] Others probably committed similar crimes without prosecution.

Men inevitably sought to use the law for their own purposes. The opportunity to take vengeance with impunity—that is, by using the law's own machinery to effect the killing—inevitably attracted some. This was one motive behind the fraudulent appeals and indictments noted earlier. Sometimes, in the wild north at least, men took a more direct and satisfying route. One such occasion arose in the course of a bitter dispute in Newcastle-upon-Tyne between some of the local merchants and a group of Flemings. Two of the foreigners cornered Richard Hay in a lethal skirmish. Richard, though seriously wounded, fought back and killed one of his attackers. The Flemings' response was to raise the hue and thereafter to drag their dying enemy from his house and have him beheaded under color of a rather hasty court judgment.[32] Another Northumbrian case has one Maurice le Skot compelled to behead a homicide.[33] In both of these cases, the executioner was a stranger, patently chosen to distance the avengers from their act, a further indication that most people considered open blood vengeance very risky.

The existence of even a few cases of judicial vengeance must have fed cynicism about the supposed impartiality of the king's law. It is not surprising, then, that we still find people trying by whatever means they could to avenge executions duly carried out in proper form. When a number of "malefactors and disturbers of the lord king's peace" were executed as felons "for the conservation of the king's peace," Agnes, sister to one of them, tried to appeal those responsible and succeeded so far as to secure a hearing at king's bench.[34] A young man, Richard, stole from Hugh's goods. Hugh brought his appeal and had Richard hanged as a thief in the earl of Leicester's court. By so doing he earned the hatred of Richard's kinsmen, who, "wishing to avenge themselves on the said Hugh," had the sheriff jail him

30. JUST 3/85, m. 3d (1276).
31. JUST 1/569A, m. 6 (1268). LE BRUN V. LONDON and Brand 1992b, 184 n. 100.
32. HAY V. NEWCASTLE FLEMINGS (1293).
33. JUST 1/653, m. 12 (1293), cited in Hurnard 1969, 127. The court was notably careful to check the facts of the story in this case; Maurice had to await the royal grace in jail.
34. KB 26/204, m. 26d (1270–71), cited in Hurnard 1969, 205.

for the death of a third party.[35] The fact that convicts and their friends could conceive of vengeance against those whom they considered responsible must have weighed on the minds of jurors considering whether to indict or convict more often than we can know. Convicts for whom the thought of vengeance after the event proved incomplete consolation might still hope that their friends would rescue them en route to the gallows.[36]

Executions of convicted criminals are often highly charged events. One modern palliative, the official impersonality of the execution process, was largely lacking in medieval England. Few areas possessed anything like a professional hangman. Even mere passersby might be pressed into service. Possibly accusers and their friends sometimes got to carry out the job themselves.[37] It is not too surprising that some convicted criminals were so terrified by the prospect of what was "commonly a messy business, unskillfully carried out" and quite liable to be botched, that they committed suicide or dropped dead on the spot.[38]

People who tried to pay off their scores directly by bringing their own appeals against their enemies thereby put themselves at risk. That the initial proceedings in the shire court unequivocally proclaimed their identity may have prompted opponents to respond in violent ways, a fact that goes some way to explain the high proportion of appeals brought by women,[39] whose failure incurred at worst a money amercement. One could also achieve the same end of putting the enemy's life and limb at risk in a cost-effective manner by procuring his indictment. All indications are that this was extremely common and quite well known to the authorities, who were inclined, however, to emphasize the overall public interest in bringing all suspects into court.[40] The many cases I have noticed prominently feature resentments at

35. C 144/2, no. 9 (1262). Note that the earl in question was Simon de Montfort.
36. Some of the rescues mentioned by Summerson 1999 (126, 130–31) may reflect local feelings that particular individuals did not deserve to die, although there is little evidence of principled opposition to the death penalty as such (ibid., 125–26, 133); see Chobham 1968 (422) for summary approval of judicial executions. Others doubtless represent the efforts of the victim's friends. Richardson and Sayles 1941, 36 (1225), and Summerson 1999, 125 (1255), are two clear examples.
37. Chobham 1968 (432–33) seems to take it as normal that executioners were compelled to act and might include men unlucky enough to be found on the road. They, but not those who performed for gain, might purge their sin through confession. Summerson 1999 (127–29) assembles evidence for the different ways various communities organized their executions. He suggests that the *carnifices* of some twelfth-century accounts may have been actual butchers, as was the case in early modern Germany. The urban instances furnished by Bateson 1904 (55, 73, 76) are likely to indicate a general pattern in the period before the emergence of the common law; e.g., in twelfth-century Preston, when anyone was justiced for theft or "de aliqua infidelitate, ille qui sequitur faciet justiciam." Hyams 1986 (12) describes one case where the accuser's friends apparently got to carry out a mutilation. GIROIE V. MONTGOMERY reflects earlier mores.
38. Summerson 1999, 133.
39. Examples are C 144/1, nos. 3, 9 (1236, 1252).
40. Bellamy 1998 (21–25, 47) suggests this as an explanation for the rise of procedure by (true) bill. Jurors were not at this stage subject to conspiracy charges (ibid., 31). See also Musson 1996,

rural distraints and impoundings of beasts,[41] and prolonged enmities. After a narrow escape from a *contencio* at Appleby Fair, Adam was ambushed on the way home. His assailants meant business. One of them "falsely and maliciously" accused him of two murders, an accusation strengthened with the authority of the Beverley town seal.[42]

This abundant evidence supports the conclusion that mortal enmities were an absolutely normal feature of rural life. I am confident that a more comprehensive search would confirm my samplings. We can now understand why churchmen were so quick to scent the urge to vengeance behind their parishioners' displays of the sin of anger. This explains why Thomas of Chobham chose to illustrate the difficulties presented by the seal of confession with an exemplary tale of vengeance killing. I do not suggest that life in the thirteenth-century English countryside was subject to constant violence and an inordinate flood of homicides; rather, lethal argument was a ubiquitous possibility. The very mundane nature of so much evidence for enmities serves to underline another important point. Vengeance does not have to be associated with some concept of noble honor in the way that older theories of feud have tended to suggest. Anger, resentment, and the fear of losing face are sufficient to spur humbler men to seek revenge in appropriate circumstances.

ENMITY AND FEUD AMONG THE NOBILITY

The nobility was certainly not exempt from these mundane human emotions; great men, after all, possessed the most face to lose. Did this common-law culture that hid and transformed, but could not repress, the urge to vengeance permit the survival of direct action by nobles, perhaps even feud in the sense that we have understood it in this book? A number of respected historians writing about thirteenth-century England believe that it did, and they do not hesitate to label a number of sometimes spectacular noble rivalries as feuds. Candidates for this treatment include the relationships between the Lord Edward and Robert de Ferrars, earl of Derby, from the 1250s, Earl John de Warenne and Alan de la Zouche in 1270, and the

---

176–79. Even the exceptional 1294 Yorkshire investigation into conspiracy on JUST 1/1095 focuses more on those who rigged juries than simply served on them; cf. Sayles 1939, liv.

41. C 144/17, nos. 45, 48 (1277); 27, no. 13 (1286–87), displaying the rivalry of two separate hundreds; 32, no. 18 (1300); 33, no. 19 (1302). Also JUST 1/497, m. 28d (1280–81), cited in Hurnard 1969, 370.

42. C 144/17, no. 8 (1276–77). Another example is the case of Robert and Juliana noted earlier in this chapter, of enmity between the families of a man's two successive wives (C 144/18, no. 43; 34, no. 3).

earls of Gloucester and Hereford especially in the 1290s.[43] The list could readily be lengthened from the chronicles, and further extended to cover more of the lesser baronage down into gentry by a careful examination of plea-roll cases of rape/abduction and novel disseizin among others.[44] The terms in which contemporaries debated their foreign relations—especially, in Edward's case, his relations with the Welsh and Scots—are also emotionally charged and in many ways palpably feud-like.

However, proof that even the clearest of these enmities merit the label of feud in our sense is another matter. It is not easy to find the type of peacemaking associated with feud,[45] because by Edward I's reign, the final resort to private warfare was rare. Old formalities for peacemaking had not fallen into total desuetude. The character of the century's two civil wars—the rebellion against John after the quashing of Magna Carta in 1215, and especially the disturbances of the period of reform and rebellion following the 1258 Provisions of Oxford—attest to this fact.

Civil wars tend to be much more emotionally charged than foreign ones, as the adage "Grass soon grows over a battlefield; under a scaffold, never" reminds us. Local and national enmities interact in civil strife. Men often chose their loyalties in national conflicts on grounds of local loyalties, to fight with friends and against enemies.[46] This pattern probably explains many of the alignments visible during the first years of the infant Henry III's reign.[47] Indeed, in 1258–67, personal enmities were commonly subsumed into the national conflict.[48] Chroniclers' tendency to describe political con-

43. Golob 1984, chaps. 7–8, the best guide, shows how the Ferrars family nursed its enmities well into the fourteenth century; see also Carpenter 1990 (284) and Maddicott 1994 (322–24). I sketched the spectacular confrontation in Westminster Hall between Warenne and La Zouche in Hyams 1998 (121–22). Prestwich 1988 (348–51) outlines the Gloucester–Hereford enmity with references to the literature.

44. As I suggested in Hyams 1992, 16.

45. In JUST 1/954, m. 63d (1262, Warwicks. eyre) it was attested that a man had been pardoned for homicide a decade earlier (C 66/64, m. 8) under the routine condition that he make peace with the deceased's kin and that he had actually done so. There being nobody else present wishing to sue, he was therefore given a full acquittal. Cf. Hurnard 1969, 183 n. 4.

46. The appendix of cases includes illustrations from widely separated dates.

47. The literature around Magna Carta naturally emphasizes political interests vis-à-vis the king; cf. Carpenter 1990, chaps. 1–2, or Turner 1994, 221–24, 227–30. Holt 1961 (67) thinks intrafamily feuds "probably exceptional," but Matthew Strickland has remarked to me that the king's relations with the Braose family and Matilda de Briouze might repay study in this light.

48. Sutherland 1967 is a clear case to point. See also Coss 1991a (277–79), and n. 63 in this chapter for the Cinque Ports and Yarmouth. Brand 1978 nicely illustrates the evidentiary problem. It recounts the stormy relationship of two minor barons from a large body of evidence thrown up by multiple litigation. It includes a great deal of violence, including several killings (and one incidental tit-for-tat set of revenge assaults related to civil war loyalties between Oldcotes and Furnivall [67–68]). Brand believes the two principals were initially "on good terms" but then "fell out" and into a dispute that outlived them both (70, 71, 74). Their stakes were by their own terms high and must have involved equally high emotions. Yet the sources, alas, contain not a word of this. Also, Hunt 1997, esp. 25–29; Page 2000, 31–33; Carpenter 2000, 45–47.

flicts in very personalized terms to meet the demands of their own readers is notable. They portray individual actors such as the king and the Lord Edward, Simon de Montfort, and Gilbert de Clare of Gloucester, facing each other as men with private interests, personal strengths, and weakness underpinning their political goals. Modern scholars returning to these narrative sources have softened an older picture that strained to find constitutional principles behind almost all political action. Some have felt licensed to use the language of feud.[49] They see here more acrimony than the generalized "bad temper" with which Sir Maurice Powicke famously dismissed the political passions of the day to a previous generation.[50] Their point is certainly not to suggest that feuding or personal enmities can "explain" all or even most of the great events of high politics. But this view does supply elements missed by older historians and presents accounts in terms closer to those of contemporary participants. The fact that actors and bystanders were so often inclined to depict the politics of the day in terms of personal enmities has to be significant.

Edward and Simon emerge as especially polarizing figures. Each possessed a fierce sense of his own rights and placed full importance on maintaining face and public reputation. The leitmotif of John Maddicott's excellent biography of Montfort is that his personal ambitions and interests constantly interfered with his political idealism. His case was extreme but not atypical. Edward too was slow to accept apologies for insult and wrongs. Once roused, neither man could be satisfied by anything less than vengeance or a genuine personal reconciliation involving persuasive humility from his adversary. In their retinues and affinities, each had the means to seek this satisfaction through his own resources, even before Edward became king. The striking fact, almost unique for the thirteenth century, that about thirty of Montfort's followers died with and around him at Evesham testifies both to his ability to gain and keep affection and the strength of the passions on the battlefield.[51] Montfort, as a new man, had had to construct his affinity largely from scratch. Perhaps his experience of feuds worthy of the name during his time in Gascony helped to sensitize him to the need for loyal support.[52]

Around these principals, contemporaries framed the issues in party terms. For the reformers it was very much a case of with us or against us. By brand-

49. E.g., Maddicott 1986, 3–4, 8–9; 1994, 151, 215, 218, 263, 309. See Knowles 1959 (ii.116) on the way that "acrimonious feelings" were aggravated at the end by the Dictum of Kenilworth.

50. Powicke 1947, ii.119.

51. Maddicott 1994, chap. 2, esp. 59 sq., 342, 350. See Page 2000 (26–27) for Richard of Cornwall's affinity.

52. Maddicott 1994, 110–14.

ing opponents of the Provisions of Oxford in 1258 as "mortal enemies" in the required communal oath, the reformers were buying into a familiar enmity culture. The deliberate echo of this sentiment, at the moment of their triumph in 1264,[53] strengthens our sense that enmity discourse was general and that the enmities were both lasting and involved kith as well as kin.[54] Henry III was said to have recalled in 1259 the deadly hatred with which the English had pursued his father in 1215, and he angrily promised to respond in hostile kind.[55] Later he threatened to treat the rebels besieged in Kenilworth Castle as public enemies unless they surrendered forthwith; clearly, he intended to make them an exception to the normal rules of mercy in the conduct of hostilities.[56] Finally the dispatch, after Evesham, of Montfort's head and testicles to Lady Mortimer attested to the deep loathing she and others felt toward the arch-rebel,[57] and it prepared the way for the 1271 murder of Henry of Almain at Viterbo in Italy by Simon's son, Guy de Montfort.

The king's nephew, Henry, a tireless fighter in the disturbances, doubtless was an acceptable substitute for his first cousin, Edward. The opportunistic act was immediately stigmatized as the indisputable taking of vengeance that it was. Up to that moment, the king seemed willing to treat Montfort's family with the generosity customarily expected after noble rebellions. This abruptly ceased. The king now pursued "remourseless justice," and, when in 1273 Edward discovered that Guy was close by his road through central Italy, he almost set out to hunt Guy down. Had he done so, the talk would surely have been of vengeance—what at this distance we would justifiably label the tit for tat of successful feud. It was not to be. Instead, a papal bull effectively outlawed Guy and brought him to offer penance and accept an absolution from the pope, which doubtless helped him with his God but cut no ice with Edward.[58]

Edward could hardly be as obdurate with all rebels or the country would never have recovered its peace. In 1267 he and his father had faced the usual challenge of governments after a rebellion: how best to reabsorb the ex-rebels without depriving supporters of their anticipated reward. The pope

53. Treharne and Sanders 1973, 100 ("enemi mortel"), 254 ("inimici capitales"). Assize of Northampton 1176, clause 6, had ordered the arrest of anyone unwilling to swear fidelity to the king "tanquam inimicus domini regis" (Stubbs 1913, 180).
54. See Knowles 1959 (i.47–48) for the king's nomination of Eyville as his "capitalis inimicus." Also Maddicott 1994 (263) for the French king's perception of the rancor between the parties.
55. Paris 1872–83, v.732.
56. *CPR* 1258–66, 488, with comment Knowles 1959, ii.29. See Treharne and Sanders 1973 (336) for "Dictum de Kenilworth," clause 39.
57. Maddicott 1994 (344) curiously only calls this "almost symbolic."
58. I follow the account of the events in Powicke 1950 (chap. 4) and 1947 (ii.606–12), while drawing my own conclusions. The quoted words come from Powicke 1950 (72).

had already urged clemency on the king in 1265.[59] It is generally agreed that the Dictum of Kenilworth met the need well enough, exacting harsh but in most cases bearable terms according to the extent of their guilt.[60] But readmission to normality required two separate acts.[61] The former rebel needed first to reenter the king's peace, so that he was no longer liable to be attacked on sight as an outlaw unprotected by the king's peace. This purged him of *his* enmity against the king.[62] It did not restore royal favor or friendship. That could not follow until the king chose to remit his rancor, in the formal terms recorded in their dozens on the rolls. This second step was essential for all, no exceptions. Even after the earl of Gloucester had negotiated terms for his own men, they still had to remit their own personal rancors against royalists and seek for themselves a full reconciliation with the king. This was no mere matter of form; many Londoners left town for fear of the king's continuing anger against them in 1266.[63] This public ending of rancor was not just an artificial device dreamed up for the occasion. Rather all parties drew upon their common knowledge of effective peacemaking procedure to maximize the chances that the result would amount to something more than a temporary cessation of hostilities, that a new and much needed *amicitia* might follow.[64]

BASTARD FEUDALISM IN THE THIRTEENTH CENTURY?

I have managed to this point happily to avoid all mention of feudalism. I have found feudal models and discourse to be at best unnecessary to the understanding of medieval English society and culture, at worst a highly distorting force.[65] I concede that a concept called "bastard feudalism" necessarily assumes some previously defined model of feudalism, from which the

---

59. Hyams 1998, 123.

60. See on this in addition to Maddicott 1986, Knowles 1982 and 1986.

61. Knowles 1959, ii.57 sq.; cf. Hyams 1998, 122–23.

62. Bracton 1968–80, fol. 132b (ii.372), suggests the kinds of resonance in the act. Restoration of peace to an outlaw, he said, meant that he might now "ire . . . et redire et de novo contrahere," but this only restored what was the king's to give, i.e., his peace. The former outlaw thus regained his legal rights and returned to a normality that might require him to answer private suits.

63. Knowles 1959, ii.51. Henry assured the men of the Cinque Ports (who had supported Montfort [Brooks 1933, 36–37]) that he was "willing to show mercy and grace rather than vengeance," providing they submitted (*CPR* 1258–66, 488). For his similar message the same day to the defenders of Kenilworth, see text at n. 56 in this chapter. *CPR* 1247–58, 57 (1250), shows that the procedure was not confined to civil wars.

64. In 1264, the baronial reformers had prudently insisted that Edward remit "all sense of wrong [iniuriam] and rancor" to their party, explicitly so that none of them would be harmed in future for their activities during the disturbance (Treharne and Sanders 1973, no. 40 at end, p. 300). Similar language (concerning the remission of rancor due inter alia to the commissions of *transgressiones*) occurs again during the 1297 crisis (Prestwich 1980, 154–56; 1988, 427).

65. I have said as much on other occasions; see Hyams 1986 (483 n. 200), 1991b, and 1997.

bastard form is a decline or deterioration. I shall ignore these contentious matters of terminology and simply concentrate on the social relations denoted by those who use the phrase.[66] Their disagreements as expressed in recent debates on the subject bear closely on the central themes of this book, especially the contentions of this chapter on the existence of a culture of enmity and vengeance in thirteenth-century England.

The late Bruce McFarlane presented the formerly received view of bastard feudalism half a century ago in a classically concise article.[67] In it he posited a society in which, by 1300, "the tenurial bond," essential to any feudalism worthy of the name, "had been superseded as the primary social tie by the personal contract." This constituted "something essentially different while superficially similar," bastard in the dictionary sense of "having the appearance of, resembling." The transition arose toward the end of the thirteenth century, when Edward I for the first time systematically extracted from his tenants-in-chief paid service in place of what they owed by reason of tenure. In their turn, the great barons recruited by subcontract the fighting men they needed to fill their agreed quotas. These subcontracts, often made (unlike royal contracts) for the life of the parties, transformed the social body. By 1400, every great man had recruited a retinue through agreements recorded in writing. Moreover, "over and above his indentured retinue . . . a great man . . . was the patron and paymaster of a swarm of hangers-on." Few or none of these ties was exclusive to a single lord; multiple lordship was normal but without any equivalent of the old liege lordship to declare priorities. And McFarlane was fully aware that ties created by indenture were not unbreakable. Yet he did not decry the results. Bastard feudalism was for him a reasonable response to England's lack of good governance caused by the political inadequacy of several of its fourteenth- and fifteenth-century kings. Indeed he thought it constituted a noble, private-enterprise "steadying influence" on society as a whole, not obviously inferior to that more direct monarchical government of the preceding period, covered in this book.

One may easily translate McFarlane's hypothesis into terms germane to the present argument. The traditional picture implies relatively effective royal governance in the twelfth and thirteenth centuries that progressively usurped adjudication of wrongs from private to public authority. Then at some later date, this governance somehow failed; the world of private enmi-

<hr>

66. The main contributors to the debate are Coss 1989 and 1991b, Bean 1989, Carpenter 1991 and 2000, Crouch 1991, and Hicks 1995. All modern thought in this area began from the magisterial McFarlane 1945.

67. McFarlane 1945. The further developments McFarlane made in the remaining twenty years of his life and his students and others thereafter are not my concern here.

ties returned and captured the political stage. The ethics of good lordship now, once more, committed a lord to take wrongs done to a vassal or retainer as committed against his own honor; thus, he felt compelled to act on their behalf. McFarlane's followers deferred this reversion to a world more ostentatiously dominated by lordship until sometime in the fourteenth century, with the tacit implication that an accompanying vengeance mentality may have been similarly deferred. But revisionists are tempted by a much earlier date, justified in part by concerns comparable to those of this book.

In Peter Coss's constructive reappraisal, the years around 1258 figure strongly.[68] There are for Coss two keys: the control of one's patch, *patria*, through the possession of an effective retinue,[69] and the shift from a lordship organized around land tenure to one of contractual relationships. The shift, he believes, resulted from the magnates' reaction to Angevin kingship, more specifically to the Angevin legal reforms. He has in mind, I think, especially the real actions and other property procedures of the early common law, whose new remedies must, he feels, have struck many barons as evidence that the king was aggressively seeking to detach dependants from their lordship. Real though the risks were, both Angevin barons and some recent scholars probably exaggerate the actual impact on private lordship. Coss finds abundant active lordship still in the thirteenth century, implemented either against or through the new common-law modes.[70] But to continue to exercise real power, magnates had to adapt to the new situation. They felt compelled to seek extra leverage in their own shires, so subverting existing balances of power. They also experienced enough apprehension at the threat to their own position to search actively for more support and pay for it by new forms of protection and clientage. Thus from the time of the disturbances, Coss suggests, recourse to retainer contracts of various kinds (mostly at first not in indenture form) began to change the whole nature of local and then national politics.

Coss may take too rosy a view of the common law. The Angevin model of central, downward justice exercised in the public name looks most attractive through the law's own internal records. But we must as always compare as-

68. Coss 1989, 1991b.
69. See CUSIN V. FITZJOHN.
70. The disintegration of the honor in the later twelfth century has perhaps become a prematurely received truth. See, e.g., Thomas 1993, chap. 1 and *passim*. This position has been lent theoretical plausibility by the legal development schema of Milsom 1976, with its postulate of a far-reaching "shift of control" from lords to the king and his justice. But Sutherland 1973, chaps. 2–3, to name but one source, contains ample witness of active seignorial action continuing into the thirteenth century, and Carpenter 2000 marshals plenty of evidence to show "the continuing reality of the exercise by lords of power within their fees" (as Paul Brand carefully put it in a letter cited ibid., 44 n. 66) although not, in my view, to document that centrality of "feudal" tenure that he seeks to prove.

pirations with the actualities, which could differ significantly. Coss high-lighted the need for renewed research on the ability of the magnates in the thirteenth century to exercise effective power on their own behalf, whether directly through the common law itself or by circumventing it, for example, by arbitrations.[71]

The challenge was soon accepted. Critics argued for greater continuity across the "point of fracture" Coss had seen in 1258, and they supported their position by noting the existence of affinities and retinues back into the twelfth century and thus before the common law and the Angevin re-forms.[72] The informative discourse in twelfth-century charters can docu-ment the arrangements between lord and retainer in more detail than any other sources until the advent of the indentures on whose evidence the tra-ditional view of bastard feudalism was largely based.[73]

But the brief "magnates' peace" in Stephen's reign already exemplified the strengths and weaknesses of this private enterprise alternative.[74] In times of real upheaval, the very great tend to feel that they have the most to lose, and consequently they make their own defensive arrangements, including the recruitment of fighting men. The potential was certainly there from at least the 1140s. A fair number of twelfth-century affinities have now been uncov-ered and presented for examination,[75] and the evidence will surely accumu-late now that we have license to look for it.[76] Household knights were in any case virtually ubiquitous through the Middle Ages,[77] and certainly they were featured in most castles from the Conquest onward. They too were there not because of any tenurial obligations but rather in the hope of future re-ward for their martial utility.

To discern serious structural discontinuities in England between 1150 and, say 1600, is becoming harder. Throughout this long period, noble houses rose and fell, prospered and disappeared, according to their ability to adapt to changing circumstances, especially perhaps innovations in government.

71. Several studies of the decade before Coss wrote had highlighted the wide occurrence of noble arbitration in the later Middle Ages and, to an extent, earlier too. Powell 1983 and Rawcliffe 1984 give the main references; also Beverley Smith 1991 for Wales, and Offenstadt 2000 on ritu-als used.

72. Carpenter 1991 and especially Crouch 1991.

73. I have examined the development of the less helpful but much more widespread common-place diplomatic of the thirteenth-century charter and suggested links with contemporary legal change in Hyams 1992.

74. Davis 1990, 111–14; Crouch 2000, chap. 13; see Powicke 1947 (397–98, 406, 408) for com-parable treaties from the 1258–67 period. Henry I must similarly have used his money to rally sup-port before 1100.

75. Examples include Crouch 1990, 133–34, and chap. 6, esp. 157 sq.

76. Brown 1950 (204–8) is one example of the kind of evidence that is out there. McFarlane 1945 (162) already pointed out a royal contract from as early as 1213.

77. As Hicks 1995, 23, 103 noted.

From this perspective, the distinguishing feature of the century after 1066 is the abundant supply of land available for ambitious men to exploit and use in their recruiting.[78] Ambitious lords in all areas must at some stage have felt challenged to maintain the following they felt they needed without permanently depriving themselves of demesne lands. There were limits to the number of retainers they could board in their own household and the length of time they could keep them there. Demands for further reward came as the retainers aged. Contractual retaining in return for some kind of payment was an obvious answer. The first hard evidence in the form of actual written agreements comes from the 1220s, for the most part because of litigation in royal courts. This somewhat weakens the case for explaining the rise of explicit agreements as a response to royal legal innovations, which may have played a lesser role in popularizing retainers.

How much earlier than the thirteenth century might interested parties have created similar agreements? Two factors were possibly determinative: monetary liquidity that enabled lords to offer pecuniary rewards, and awareness that they could not continue to grant out land indefinitely without destroying their own patrimonies. The fact that twelfth-century England was still a substantially regional economy suggests that the practice may have begun in a few more advanced lordships and spread from there. The returns to the *Carte Baronum* of 1166 demonstrate that much of the sub-enfeoffment by the king's tenants-in-chief dates from the middle third of the twelfth century. Those inquiries hint at another danger of granting out too much land—the possibility that the king would raise the effective tax burden of the lordship by levying service or its equivalent on the surplus. This will have been a wake-up call to any great lord slow to see the advantages of the contractual alternative. Thus the recognition that land was fast becoming a nonrenewable resource, and the early spread of contract retaining as one possible solution to the dilemma, may well have been contemporaneous.

The shift came in Stephen's reign, a classic period of poor governance and civil war that highlighted the desirability of having military support at one's beck and call. We learn of the measures taken by the very great from the treaties they made at this time. Lesser brethren too will have appreciated the need to cultivate their network of near-equals (their affinity, to use the later term) and buttress it as they could with fighting men as retainers. This chronology accords with the earliest affinities so far noticed coming from

78. Waugh 1986 (814–17) makes the point well; see also Crouch 1990, 163: "Society still had not got over the expectations raised by the great binge of land patronage under the Norman kings."

the 1140s—about the period when English support groups emerge from their lords' castles but not yet into written record and commitment. I doubt there was any substantial break in the development of nontenurial retaining (bastard feudalism, if you will) between the mid-twelfth century and the end of the period covered in this book. Neither the birth of the common law itself in the decades around 1200,[79] nor Coss's "point of fracture" in the mid-thirteenth century, seems more than a minor kink in an established line of development.

The most intriguing aspect of the whole debate on bastard feudalism concerns the extent to which one may regard the establishment of durable affinities and personal retinues as ensuring the availability of support groups for use in physical competition. Scott Waugh was careful to note that only two among his corpus of early retaining contracts mentioned military service, that defining staple of traditional land enfeoffments.[80] But silence is seldom conclusive. It would be extremely legalistic to believe that these first contracts set down in writing everything that was expected of the two parties. It is true that the remarkable willingness of parties to sue in royal courts for the enforcement of these agreements distinguishes them from holders of the better-known indentures of the fourteenth century. Possibly the reduction of these obligations into writing had the temporary consequence of making retainers appear more like matters of business than honor. But our evidence comes mostly from agreements that failed.[81] When lords sought out likely recruits and put them on retainer, they surely did not expect their new men to "work to rule." Nor did the new retainers cease to hope for further benefits. The written texts expressed a minimum view of the parties' obligations. They surely hid an expectation that something more affective was at least possible in the relationship of lord and man. The earl of Gloucester called his retinue an *amicitia* in the 1260s.[82] The minimum requirement to offer counsel and aid in the lord's hour of need, unrestricted as to venue, accordingly licensed expectations of further service in hall and courtroom. The written agreements were most probably understood to

79. Waugh 1986 (812–18) suggested ca. 1200–1275 as the crucial period.
80. Ibid., 822.
81. See McFarlane 1945 (173) for the absence of litigation in the fourteenth century. Waugh 1986 (818–19) may be set against the changes I studied in Hyams 1992. Brand 1978, a dispute about something very close to a failed retainer contract, is informative about some of the many ways in which the different parties might understand their relationship and its implications. More successful agreements would never have left such voluminous documentation and might leave no trace at all.
82. Examples are KB 26/185, m. 13d (William de Tracy) and C 47/14/6, no. 6 (1270), cited in Knowles 1959, 91–92.

continue customary practices of earlier times,[83] when men felt committed by both honor and advantage to respond swiftly to their lord's summons. Nothing, of course, is automatic when lives are at risk, but the commitment was surely intended to parallel a kinsman's. Writing, however, introduced a new factor into the equation. Some retainers, a minority perhaps, now felt that the rise in court practice of close reading of writs (along lines akin to today's strict constructionists) licensed them to decline obligations unspecified in the text. Hence, from the 1220s, cases reveal retaining to us.

With that caveat, it seems reasonable to assume that thirteenth-century noblemen could, like their ancestors, summon support groups to their aid for the purposes of taking or resisting vengeance. Prosopographical study of the plea rolls' long lists of defendants to assizes of novel disseizin could test, and will probably confirm, the plausibility of the assumption. This ability of magnates and others to muster physical force, when taken together with the substantial degree of violence visible on legal records, must refocus our thoughts on the problem of order in the shires. I have suggested that those who framed the public prosecution system of the Angevin assizes in the 1160s and 1170s had been aiming to wrest from local notables for the crown the capacity to set the acceptable levels. Even in failure, this attempt significantly altered the local power balances. The king's intent to challenge the control of local power-mongers over their various spheres of influence had been declared. But the limited success of the royal effort, and especially the process of jury nullification that so stymied it, supports the view of bastard feudalism as a continuous extension from earlier forms of power-mongering, including the maintenance of dependants in their lawsuits.[84]

The exercise of power within and outside the royal courts remains a rich subject for research. One excellent test is the ability of an ordinary John Citizen to sue the great men about him. David Carpenter's contention that "small men could sue magnates" will remain unconvincing until confirmed from the plea rolls.[85] Given that some areas had no resident magnates anyway, the investigation will have to be detailed enough to make some very local calibrations. For the moment, I can only say that enabling suits against the great appears to have been intrinsic to the original purposes of the Angevin law reforms. Most scholars would now accept that suits against lords were basic to the invention of the assize of novel disseizin and other property remedies in the last third of the twelfth century. But the authorita-

83. Stacy 1999 (29–31) gives one early-twelfth-century example. Cf. Hicks 1995, 45, 51, 91; even peasants were likely at times to feel they had to fight on their lord's behalf.
84. Crouch 1991.
85. Carpenter 1991, 181; Carpenter 1996 (116–21) does not make a very strong case.

tive view that the Angevins achieved a genuine "shift of control" in property adjudication that severely limited seignorial power over their own lordships now looks an exaggeration.[86] The system of public prosecution initiated at around the same time was a step in the same direction. Indictments proved vastly more effective at exposing homicides than did appeals. Since royal justices had to inquire into all suspicious deaths on their eyre visitations, all feud killers now risked the gallows, however exalted their lordly patrons.[87] Lesser offenses were probably not so comprehensively scrutinized. Even from the long labor pains of trespass, there is no good evidence to encourage the belief that complainants of low status were operating on a basis of equality with the great and powerful.

At best, one might apply to the thirteenth-century common law that most cynical of twentieth-century legal aphorisms, that "the law is like the Ritz Hotel, open to rich and poor alike." But proof of inequality before the law does not establish magnate penetration into the early common law. The bastard feudalism debate has assumed, rather than defined, the existence of magnates whose power and capacity to make instrumental use of royal courts for their own purposes differ from that of others not just in degree but in kind. We need to define first the group of men with such extraordinary resources that they were capable of dominating royal law. Only then can we determine whether, when, and how they actually did so.

That effort will not be easy.[88] The common law's own records were never designed to record the kind of information most needed. There are of course certain exceptions, in particular the crime of conspiracy, notoriously the first to be given statutory definition.[89] The acts that initially shaped this crime were very largely abuses of legal process and are therefore directly relevant. Contemporaries sometimes listed them under three heads. Maintenance was the use of one's power and influence in support of another's lawsuit. Champerty was the support of a plea in return for some share of the spoils, for example, by sharing the expenses. And embracery was interference with jury recruitment or function to procure a verdict favorable to one side.[90] This trio of offenses remains specifically prohibited in England to this day. Remarkably, all three had been considered part of good lordship in

86. See n. 70 in this chapter.

87. But influential men still tried to conceal murders. Those in two cases from the late 1280s are known only because of the inquiry into judicial corruption; Tout and Johnstone 1906, 53–61 (HARLOW V. LOVETOT in the appendix), 81–84.

88. The need to set the picture from the system's own internal records like the plea rolls against all available external sources of information is worth stressing.

89. Harding 1983 is the authority here. See also Sayles 1939, liv sq. A note in a fourteenth-century register of writs, cited in Jenks 2002 (7), denies that the writ lies against "indictatores."

90. Sayles 1939 (lv, lvii) defines the first two, on which see also Brand 1992b (121–22); and Walker 1980 (399) defines embracery.

the twelfth century. Men had then expected their lords to maintain them in their suits and to help with costs where necessary. Their charters had often promised as much. We can occasionally see great men actively telling jurors how to testify,[91] and thus we must presume that they made their wishes felt orally on many other undocumented occasions too. The fascinating story of the degeneration of good lordship into abuse deserves detailed exposition. The criteria for proper behavior in the law courts were under particular scrutiny during the years of reform and rebellion after 1258.[92] Perhaps that was again a turning point. But there are other indications that many remained very attached to the legitimacy of noble influence, despite the weight of learned authority behind the model of impartial law. It was said in the decades around 1300, for example, that unless indicting jurors were exempted from prosecution for conspiracy, few villains would ever be brought to book for their crimes.[93]

Pending fuller study, I am most impressed by the *absence* of thirteenth-century evidence for magnate ability to flout the law directly in the spectacular manner sometimes evident in succeeding centuries. I know of only a few cases where the addressees treated royal writs with ostentatious contempt, as when they were broken into pieces in open court,[94] and no instances of assault or kidnapping of royal justices as sometimes happened in the fourteenth century.[95] Presumably men confident in their ability to control events in the courts felt no need to act so blatantly. They worked more through their social contacts with the royal justices, by hospitality and bribery,[96] or by retaining them in their service.[97] They could also deploy their superior resources to secure lengthy delays or other procedural advantage on their lawyers' advice. The almost inexhaustible supply of evidence for the corruptibility of every kind of royal official can serve as a list of further means of control over the operations of the king's courts.[98] But most of

91. Van Caenegem 1990–91, no. 470, is one of two illustrations I noticed in Hyams 1981 (119 n. 54).
92. See Hicks 1995, 119, 124.
93. Bellamy 1998, 34; cf. Harding 1983, 93–97, and Musson 1996, 194–95.
94. Neither of the two cases Flower 1944 (90, 96) cites from 1211 involved a magnate. Nor do the very different instances in Prestwich 1988 (414) and Powicke 1947 (63, 531); Treharne and Sanders 1973, 328–29 (Dictum of Kenilworth, clause 17).
95. Stones 1957 gives the best-known instance. For *The Tale of Gamelyn* later in the fourteenth century, see Kaeuper 1983.
96. Brand 1992a (152–55) sketches the size of the bribery problem by the time Edward I started to try and control it. Hospitality expenses are sometimes openly recorded in accounts; Meekings 1961 (13) cites those of the bishop of Winchester.
97. Maddicott 1978 assembled the basic evidence about the retaining of justices by private individuals; for senior court clerks, see Brand 1992a, 184–87.
98. Cam 1930, pt. 3, based on the royal inquiries of 1274–76, is only one of many classic works to present very adequate illustrative material. JUST 1/1095, ms. 1–2, a 1292 inquiry into conspiracy and maintenance in Yorkshire, is a suggestive source.

those active in the work again appear to be relatively ordinary people, influential locally but hardly prominent on the national scene. If magnates were the controlling influence, one can only say that they were remarkably successful in keeping their names off the record. This accords with the pattern of users of oyer and terminer commissions as studied by Richard Kaeuper. Magnate influence is always useful and everywhere apparent, but it is far from paramount.

No compelling case has yet been made for any large-scale magnate penetration of the common law in the thirteenth century. It is hard to tell whether the dominant pattern really is one of aristocratic penetration of the common law and a half-successful effort to exclude it. What is evident can be better described as evasion from justice rather than a takeover. By the late thirteenth century, litigants at all social levels were striving to make instrumental use of the courts in their own favor. In such an atmosphere, royal clerks and ministers were probably better placed than magnates to penetrate the king's law. They enjoyed a number of procedural favors and other advantages. They knew both court personnel and ground rules from the inside, and could on occasion present themselves as acting in some sense in the king's name.[99] By comparison, magnates as a group, however defined, possessed no exceptional powers over cases that concern their interests. They too normally had to work through ministers whom they despised but needed.

SOME CONCLUSIONS

England's thirteenth century, like all centuries, witnessed both continuity and change. Into its first decades, men and women pursued their enemies in ways that continued to draw upon the ritual acts and notions traditionally associated with feud. Enmities still satisfied the peace-treaty test and called forth peacemaking up to the highest levels of the kingdom. Soon, however, the evidence and probably the actual patterns too fade from sight.

This is very much the time of the common law's emergence into full activity at center stage. Prosecution of enmities through legal process had long been as much part of the same familiar pattern of redress for wrong as the more spectacular direct action. The common law now offered in its new forms of action fresh channels for the same old urges. The wronged were now counseled to appeal felonies, or to sue plaints and writs of trespass for any wrongs that could be squeezed into shape acceptable to the king's justice. Or they sued under heads that privileged motives like property loss

99. See, for examples, Tout and Johnstone 1906 and Brand 1992a, chap. 8.

over any underlying hatreds and resentments but yet served their purpose by harming those who had wronged them.

The powerful also demonstrated their influence by deploying, when necessary, support groups always at their disposal to oust interlopers on lands they claimed as theirs and to avenge acts they deemed to shame them. People of all social classes killed and were killed. But sensible counselors now rarely pressed for the ultimate satisfaction of a life for a life. During the period of a flourishing eyre system that brought royal justice into the shires as a solemn, periodic part of normality, the king's men managed to keep themselves informed of virtually all unnatural death and to deter concealment along with most efforts at private settlement out of court. For these reasons, overt feud action, whether for blood or money, became so much rarer—a feat to be accounted no small success for the king and his law. As we have seen, blood vengeance may never have been as familiar a feature of English life as in some Continental societies. It had never, for instance, been allowed as a legitimate defense to homicide in England. Even proof of "hot blood" was used in England primarily to depict the behavior of the deceased in a light to justify the killer's plea of self-defense.

Nevertheless, the king's justices were fully aware that their courtrooms seethed with hatreds that they, as outsiders, could seldom understand properly. They knew that many of the killers and other assailants who appeared before them had acted from passions that could be both deep-seated and, in the view of the countryside, justified. Hence the justices struggled to control jurors out to nullify the letter of the law. Direct confirmation reaches the rolls only where exceptional procedures concerned themselves with motive. One could seek indirect evidence almost anywhere on the plea rolls—civil pleas not excluded—where external sources throw light on the real-world relations behind the lawsuit.

Resentment at wrong, then—the urge to seek direct, visible, and physical satisfaction for acts that shamed or otherwise harmed one—never disappeared in the thirteenth century. Men and women listened attentively in their leisure hours to tales of laudable vengeance taken on villains on behalf of the wronged of all descriptions, and they took special pleasure from justice meted out on behalf of wronged and marriageable maidens. They certainly also recounted their personal experiences, both triumphs and failure, in terms as similar to the literary models as they could make them. It is disappointing that they left so few of the private letters and other papers to set these tales in writing as later generations would. The transition from the efforts of effective kingship to control order directly from above to a much less centralized machinery of social control in the later Middle Ages is important in all kinds of ways to the development of the English polity. There is no good reason, though, to confuse political and administrative change with cultural change. Our sources do not reveal that the *mentalité* and *imaginaire* of the English underwent any extraordinary or accelerated transformation during the decades around 1300. Wrongs remained wrongs, which people felt entitled to redress by whatever means they could find, and where none seemed feasible or appropriate, they nursed their rancors and bided their time.

APPENDIX
Case Narratives

This appendix of case narratives (given in alphabetical order) is intended to keep the main text clear of digressions and long footnotes that would further disturb the flow of argument. These are pièces justificatives. But the narratives below also represent some central premises and contentions of this book. For the historian, these narratives convey the most salient aspects of lawsuits and other disputes: their dynamics. Only through analysis of the minutiae revealed from all available sources of information about the parties and their continuing social relations (including extracurial information whenever possible) can this dynamic be re-created. The narratives that follow are my best endeavor to make historical sense of scattered, imperfect, and sometimes very technical source material. They are often speculative because I pose questions the texts were not composed to answer and were indeed sometimes designed to conceal. Because each is open to alternative readings, I give references. But the contingencies of interpretation exposed here exist equally in conventional footnotes. All these narratives, intended to reveal the basis for generalizations that arise, have helped to form the arguments of this book. Often the case stories that emerge reveal patterns that might remain unsuspected without this detailed treatment.[1] Some indisputably deserve translation from the cautious, abbreviated scholarly style I use here into more emotive language suited to the drama of the underlying stories.[2] All raise issues that currently resonate in radical legal scholarship and in source criticism, since the very manner of storytelling—with concomitant bias—affects decisions.[3]

---

1. One example from my first effort at this technique in Hyams 1987, app. II (490 sq.), is a plausible political reading of "Countess Amicia's Case" (494–96). A legal reading of this case is highly germane to the central theses of Milsom 1976. My alternative reading would require some serious rethinking of Milsom's argument.

2. Noonan 1972 is a marvelous model here; it contains a series of novels awaiting authors.

3. Cf. Kathryn Abrams, "Hearing the Call of Stories," *California Law Review* 79 (1991); Patricia Williams, *The Rooster's Egg* (1995); Peter Brooks and Paul Gewirtz, eds., *Law's Stories: Narrative and Rhetoric in the Law* (1996); and Janet Malcolm, *The Crime of Sheila McGough* (1999).

ÆTHELWOLD, SAINT V. LEOFSIGE (LATE TENTH CENTURY)

Blake 1962, ii.11, pp. 84–86 = "Libellus Æthelwoldi," chapter 11

Bishop Æthelwold of Ely set out to acquire for his church the desirable estate of Downham, Cambs., in a complex multifaceted deal (*conventio*) involving an exchange of another property of his and other estates, Oundle and Kettering in Northants., also destined for Peterborough Abbey. After Edgar's death, the vendor Leofsige f. Brixius (on whom see Blake 1962, xii–xiii, xv) and his wife broke the pact and sought to recover their land through an offer of a portion of the purchase price. Ely had enough witnesses to defeat them. But around the same time, Leofsige seized Oundle and Kettering, whose fields then lay untilled for two years. This surely represents the *reaflac* (land-theft) of the laws. Fortunately, the Lord God saw how great *injuriae* and tribulations afflicted his servants of Peterborough and took pity. At a *generale placitum* in London, Æthelwold "in ius protraxit" and pleaded the "injuriam et rapinam" against Leofsige to regain by judgment the lands for Peterborough. The court ordered the thief to repay the bishop for his losses and previous protection; further, as required by II Cn 63 of those who committed *reaflac*, Leofsige had to make amends to the king with his *wergeld* for the violence. The cautious bishop renewed the plea to attain a further sworn judgment at Northampton from the whole folk returning the two estates to Peterborough.

Leofsige's death around this time did not stay the bishop's drive for redress. Ealdorman Æthelwine of East Anglia (for whom, see Blake 1962, 79 n. 7) held a *placitum* at Wansford, Northants., for the men of East Anglia, which adjudged that Leofsige's widow and sons must still pay for the *rapina* as if the perpetrator were still alive. It assessed the bishop's damages at over £100. The widow, a good person (unlike her dead husband), humbly, but with support from powerful friends, implored the bishop to commute her share of the royal payment to 100s. for the two hides at Downham. He kindly accepted this and agreed to remit the case against her provided that she paid the money within eight days at Ely. Apparently, she succeeded in doing so. This whole proceeding looks as much proto-trespass as appeal.

ANON V. ÆLFNOTH, ÆLFRIC, AND ÆTHELWIN (995)

Wormald 1988, 54 = Sawyer 1968, 883, from Stevenson 1858, i.394–95 (992–95); trans. *EHD* I, no. 117
Comment: Stenton 1955, 76–78

Æthelred's diploma, granting to his *miles* Æthelwig (reeve or sheriff of Bucks.) an estate at Ardley, Oxon., explains with exceptional clarity how the land came into the king's hands. Three brothers were living together on the land as co-lords. One of their men, Leofric, was caught in possession of a stolen bridle. The brothers took up their man's cause and rallied to his defense. Two brothers died in the ensuing fight, and the third, Æthelwin, barely escaped along with the thief to sanctuary in St. Helen's Church, Abingdon.

The royal reeves of Buckingham (Æthelwig) and Oxford, along with many men, surrounded the church. They also gave the two dead brothers honorable burial. When Ealdorman Leofsige (of East Anglia?) heard this, he hurried to the king's presence to protest, accusing the reeves of acting unlawfully. Apparently, his point was that the brothers, being in breach of their peace oaths, were as perjurers thereby excluded by the laws from Christian burial. But the king sympathized with Æthelwig (and conceivably with the dead men too), permitted the bodies to remain where they were, and passed the estate onto Æthelwig (the reeve?) in perpetual inheritance.

BALLIOL V. CRICLESTON (1217–18)

Stenton 1937, 570; cf. ibid., 902
Comment: ibid., xlvi

Late in December 1208, as was later said, Gilbert of Hook was so maltreated in the course of a night assault on his house that he died. His young nephew, Robert de Balliol, fled in fear, not daring or knowing how to raise the hue. He traveled abroad (to Ireland and Poitou), returning only when the civil war broke out. He began the appeal for his uncle's death against William of Crigglestone and his two brothers at the very first shire court session after peace was declared (1217) (Parker 1921, 41, no. 27).

William denied Robert's story. The truth, he claimed, was very different. Elenard, a family servant, had killed William's father, and William had brought a homicide appeal against him for the deed. Elenard was thus an enemy of William's kindred. But Robert had at one time been with him and now, said William, brought the present appeal for love of Elenard. William offered half a mark for an inquiry de odio et athia and also pointed out that Robert had not appealed within the year normally allowed.

The court chose to interrogate the presentment jury that was already on hand. Its members denied that Gilbert had been wounded at all or his house broken into. They further reported that Gilbert had been seen riding to the shire court after the supposed date of his death and had never himself brought any appeal concerning the alleged assault. Robert had had opportunities in time of peace to bring his appeal had he so wished. The appeal failed, and Robert was amerced.

There is undoubtedly more to discover about the relations between these two families. One might start from *EYC* i.511–12, viii.190–91.

BISHOP WALCHER'S MURDER (1080)

Symeon of Durham 1882–85, i.114–19 ("Historia Dunelmensis Ecclesie," chaps. 23–24), ii.208–11 ("Historia Regum"); Thorpe 1849, ii.13–16
Comment: Offler 1968, 2, 45–47; Gransden 1974, 115–16, 143–50; Kapelle 1979, 137–41, 270 n. 73

The Norman Conquest provoked movements of people into, out of, and within England for at least a generation after 1066. The Lotharingian Walcher was one among many foreign beneficiaries of the regime change. When the king had Walcher consecrated bishop of Durham in 1071, he also entrusted him with the earldom of Northumbria, taken from the rebellious Waltheof. The new bishop-earl attracted a coterie of other foreigners eager to share in the spoils. The Durham monks remembered him fondly for his deep attachment to Saint Cuthbert and care for the saint's property. But they deplored his inability to restrain his followers from excesses, which included killings of prominent local nobles as well as property invasions. They saw this avarice as the root of the tragedy. The chroniclers' xenophobic talk seems to have real substance. For all his English blood, Ligulf himself must have seemed very foreign; his noble descent had brought him lands all over the country (cf. Ellis 1833, ii.181, for possible references). He read the signs that Norman adventurers threatened landowners in the south and so moved his whole household—possessions, family, followers, and all—to some Northumbrian estates, largely, so the monks believed, on account of his deep devotion to Saint Cuthbert. The decision seemed prudent. Ligulf moved easily between his rural estates and his townhouse in Durham itself. He connected with his fellow Cuthbert devotee, Bishop Walcher, whose counselor he became, most likely as an adviser in lawsuits. But this undue favoritism to an outsider caused resentment.

Ligulf fell foul of Leobwin—from his name, another Englishman—who had so risen in Walcher's service that the bishop rarely moved in either episcopal affairs or those of the earldom without seeking his opinion.[4] Leobwin's pride was so piqued by his rival's success that he tried to thwart all Ligulf's moves. This *invidia* reached the stage of public threats and shaming words in the bishop's presence. One day, after a very harsh put-down from Ligulf, Leobwin approached the bishop's close kinsman, Gilbert, who ran

---

4. The chronicler may intend a distinction between Ligulf's "consilium" and Leobwin's "arbitrium." Perhaps the first was the legal expert, the other more a political adviser. At the fatal confrontation, the bishop had consulted Ligulf on "legalia et recta."

the earldom. He had been wronged, publicly shamed. He implored Gilbert to avenge him by killing Ligulf as soon as possible. Gilbert agreed and assembled a group of episcopal knights to do the job. The band traveled by stealth of night, caught Ligulf and his entourage unawares on one of his manors, broke in, and killed almost everyone. This is the classic feud attack, by night into the opponent's private space, but on this occasion without formal advance warning.

When the news reached the bishop, he threw his cap and cowl onto the ground in despair, telling Leobwin that his deceit and lack of judgment had ruined them: "you have killed me and you and the whole of my following with the sword of your tongue."[5] That he apparently knew at once who was behind the killing is itself instructive. Hurrying to his castle, the bishop sought to minimize the damage. Messengers were dispatched round Northumbria to proclaim that Walcher was not in on the murder and had indeed outlawed the killer and his associates. Concurrently, other representatives quickly contacted the dead man's kin, agreed on a mutual truce, and fixed a day to meet near a rural church to negotiate a full peace settlement with the restoration of *amicitia*. The foreign-born bishop experienced no difficulty in discovering the proper procedure, much along the lines of II Em. The bishop went to the meeting in person. That mistake cost him his life. Unwilling to negotiate out in the open, he took his small band of followers and advisers into the church. Negotiators shuttled between the parties without achieving a settlement. Ligulf's friends were sure the bishop had ordered the killing. They knew that Leobwin had received Gilbert and his men after the killings "familiariter et amicabiliter." But the bishop too had received Gilbert back into his favor and household. Walcher, struggling to save himself, dispatched Gilbert to meet the waiting mob "to satisfy the enemies' fury." The Norman knights made their confession and followed Gilbert out, vainly hoping that they might fight their way through the mob. The sole survivors were two English thegns (*ministri*) spared by kinsmen outside. The cathedral dean, Leofwine, had to die too, so the narrator says, because he had repeatedly given Walcher bad advice against them.[6] Now it was the turn of Leobwin, "the main progenitor of the whole calamity." He, however, would not go softly into that dark night. The villain lacked the courage to die a good death. He absolutely refused the bishop's order to exit the church and accept his fate. Bishop Walcher went to the church door to plead for own his life—to no avail. Lacking any other options, he pulled his

---

5. This may be an allusion to Old English law, or the laws in question may reflect a common image.

6. Here and elsewhere in the text, the word used is *insilium*, a calque for Old English *unræd*. This most unusual usage signals the ultimately Old English nature of the tale.

cloak over his head, darted through the door, and met the swords of his en-emies. Only Leobwin remained inside the church. The besiegers called him out in vain, then torched the church. Leobwin still refused to budge. Not until he was already half burnt did he emerge to reap the reward of his wickedness. It took several days for normality to return to the area. The killers pursued any of the dead bishop's men who dared to show themselves outside Durham Castle; meanwhile, the monks sailed downriver to recover their spiritual father's corpse without, significantly, any talk of martyrdom or sanctity.

Such was the saga told in Worcester and Durham.[7] It ends at this point, with the abrupt observation that, in revenge for these detestable deaths, King William wasted Northumbria during the next campaign season. "His-toria Dunelmensis Ecclesie" tells us that it was in fact Odo of Bayeux, not William, who harried the region.[8] Although Kappelle rightly seeks an ap-propriate political context for the events, our informants tell their tale in terms of individual and group vengeance. They lament the inhumanity and bestial cruelty of the killings.

CAUDEL, IN RE WILLIAM (1248–49)

Meekings 1961, no. 40 and p. 260

Startley hundred (Wilts.) presented five men before the itinerant justices for having given William Caudel his mortal wound in 1248. Two of the five had already fled; the jurors asserted their guilt, and they were outlawed. The other three accused were Simon atte Berne and his two sons, John the hay-ward and Henry. The previous August a royal writ de odio et athia had been procured on their behalf to keep them from jail. The jurors reported that William Caudel had died because of a quite separate dispute involving only one of the two fugitives; Simon and his sons were innocent. Their indict-ment had a different explanation. A dog, taken from a mill belonging to a friend of the Atte Berne family, reappeared in the house of the dead man's

7. The base account must surely be local and very likely English in origin. The original may well have been composed in Old English. Scholars agree that the Durham "Historia Regum" is at this point following "Florence" (that is, John) of Worcester. The two texts are identical, word for word, with a single major divergence. Where Florence inserts an account of Ligulf's visions of Saint Cuthbert, the "Historia" explains Ligulf's local connections. Florence probably obtained his material from Ealdred, bishop of Worcester before he became archbishop of York. On the other hand, the "Historia" could well be reporting local Northumbrian information; these very details were in fact reworked in twelfth-century Durham (Offler 1968, 2, 45–47). In other words, even if the Worcester account is primary, as the experts instruct us, the story itself has to be both local and quickly known elsewhere.

8. Kapelle 1979 (270 n. 73) may be wrong to dismiss "Historia Dunelmensis Ecclesie" as vague. I suspect that a chapter has dropped out of our text between the present chapters 23 and 24. If the lost chapter described the murder of Ligulf, the account could have been both independent and to the point.

uncle, Philip. From this relatively trivial incident arose a series of clashes between the two parties at ale-drinkings ("cervisias") and elsewhere. When Philip's men had wounded Henry atte Berne in a tavern, John had brought an appeal against them, which exacerbated the rancor between the parties. Henry survived this incident but not the next one; he was certainly dead by the time of the eyre, when another man was accused and cleared of his death. This string of violent clashes, while not obviously a feud in any formal sense, reflects village enmity of feud-like character.

CHAMBERLAIN V. PATSLEY (1207–8)

CRR v.182, 244–45 (Norfolk)

In the fall of 1207, Herbert of Patsley struck Drew Chamberlain a heavy blow over the head with his bow in Rainham, Norfolk; Drew's brains poured out. Then, "not content" with this, Herbert proceeded to stab him in the heart with a knife "so that he died." Through the restrained plea-roll Latin looms an act of some vernacular passion. The next year, Drew's brother John appealed Herbert of the homicide, and the parties were preparing for a duel by the time proceedings came before royal justices.

Thomas of Ingoldisthorp, a local notable who had served on several grand juries alongside a Patsley kinsman, was one of two men to accept responsibility for Herbert pending the duel and to guarantee his appearance on the day. He probably used the delay to mediate a settlement between the parties. He now took responsibility for the heavy fine (40m.) for the royal license to settle. The terms were as follows: Herbert was to go to Jerusalem within forty days, to serve God in the Holy Land for seven years to the benefit of the deceased man's soul. Should he return within that period, he was liable to execution as a convicted homicide—a strong inducement to keep his word. In addition, Thomas would pay for one of the dead man's kinsmen to become a monk or canon at a local monastery by Michaelmas. He was also to pay the Chamberlain family 40m. by installments before the succeeding August. Sunday, July 27 (a week or so after Herbert's final departure), was fixed for both the first payment and the presentation of the Chamberlain candidate for the religious life. If all went as planned, the occasion must have been quite notable. Eight local knights stood surety for Thomas's proffer to the king and also perhaps for the settlement itself.

COTENTIN V. CORNWALL (1138)

Orderic vi.494, 510–14

Hostilities between Normandy and Anjou were natural opportunities to settle scores. This Norman act of vengeance occurred during one of many breaches of a two-year truce agreed between Stephen and Geoffrey of Anjou. Roger, vicomte of Cotentin, was one of the two justiciars Stephen had left in Normandy to keep his peace there. Reginald, natural son of Henry I and later earl of Cornwall, pressed fiercely from the Angevin side. Roger resisted effectively until he fell into an ambush mounted by jealous rivals. They cut his throat, despite his desperate pleas for mercy. Afterward, as order broke down entirely, the two armies met at Isle-Marie. In the heat of battle, Roger's partisans ("quidam de parentibus et amicis") thought they saw "the place and time for revenge." They drew their swords against their own side, took Roger's assassins by surprise, and killed them. The result was a victory for the hated Angevins. This is an occasion when private loyalties ostentatiously took precedence over public duties to a king-duke. Orderic's citation of Mt. xxvi.52 ("He who takes the sword shall perish by the sword")[9] seems not to disapprove this personal view of events.

CUSIN (MONACHUS) V. FITZJOHN (1196–1201)

RCR ii.245; *CRR* i.194, 395; *Pipe Roll 3 John*, 31–32; *Rotuli de Oblatis* 1835, 126–27

One fine afternoon in the latter part of Richard I's reign (ca. 1196), John Cusin was dining as usual in the security (as he thought) of his own home at Babington (Somerset) when seven men led by Thomas, son to William f. John, a feared local figure, burst into the room. They had bribed or talked their way through the gates ("per seductionem") in an obviously preplanned raid. They seized John by his feet, dragged him into a bedroom, dumped him on a bed, and brought in firebrands, with which they burned him about the mouth and set his beard alight. They then pulled his tongue out under his chin, "linguam ei extraxerunt sub mento," which, I fear, means that they cut his tongue off and placed it on his chest. Then they ransacked the house, broke open chests containing valuables, and seized charters from the present king and his father (among others). After displaying one of King Richard's charters and another from an unidentified archbishop before John, they then burnt them in the poor man's face. (This act was later noted specially as "ad huntagium Regis," thus justifying royal interest in the case.) Only after all these assaults did they take John outside and cut his head off with William Basher's ax. (I did not make this name up, though one entry does spell it "Boscher"!)

These assailants knew precisely why they had come. One can but wonder what horrible things John had said to make them want to cut out his tongue and how these remarks could have related to the charters they then burned

9. Could Orderic have known the line taken in the Ordinary Gloss on Mt. xxvi.51–52? It advises patience but prophesies vengeance for those like the Jews, who seek it for themselves.

in his face. These were patently not ordinary robbers but men determined to make a point not merely to the dying man but for themselves and to all around who saw what they did or heard the tale afterward.

The story comes from one of those eyewitnesses. Simon Cusin, John's son and a clerk, had been serving his lord and father at table. When the attackers had broken in, he fled in fear for his own life and hid in a window recess; from this vantage point, he could see all the atrocities. As a cleric, he was after all expected to shed no blood. He it was who eventually brought the decisive appeal in the Easter term of 1200 against Thomas and his six associates (Mr. Basher among them), and also against Thomas's father William f. John, who had allegedly sent them to do the job. (There had apparently been an earlier flawed suit, from which Thomas claimed acquittal.) But Simon had done nothing for three years after the incident, not even when the eyre justices were in the area and Thomas was available to be sued.[10] Simon explained that he had not dared stay in the area to press his suit, "from fear of the power of Thomas who was almost lord of the whole area." (The Latin word used is *patria*.) The absence of any reference to an indictment for John's death seems to corroborate Simon's version of the story. Confident of his reputation among potential jurors, perhaps, Thomas willingly sought trial by a jury of that same *patria* (since Simon as a clerk could not offer battle) and was remanded in his own father's custody.

The case never reached trial. The Fitzjohn party had influence aplenty with the new king. Successive adjournments (not all recorded on extant rolls) deferred the hearing into the Hilary term of 1201, by which time Thomas had offered the king £100 for license to concord on behalf of all eight men appealed by Simon Cusin. Thomas was to give Simon 10m., half paid on the spot (indicating that the deal was made in advance) with the rest payable a few weeks later at Easter by the hand of Hugh de Neville—a great man indeed—chief forester and royal intimate. He was also to make one monk for the soul of Simon's father. In return, Simon was to quitclaim Thomas and all his men from further responsibility for the killing.

William f. John and his son must have been powerful and influential figures in the southwest. William of Harptree (seven miles north of Wells, Somerset) was a younger son of a former seneschal of Normandy (ob. 1198) who had been a magnate under Henry II. His English lands had included at least twelve fees held of the honor of Bath and seven more from the Montacute honor in the county of Mortain (Hall 1896, i.219). Most of the inheritance went to the oldest brother, Henry de Tilly, with whom William had to make terms around this time, ca. 1200 (*Rotuli Normanniae* 1835, 7–9; *Rotuli*

10. Dating this is a bit of a problem; cf. Crook 1982, 58–59.

Chartarum 1837, 75b), but who then abandoned England after 1204. Our William's estate, perhaps somewhat less than he had once hoped, was still substantial, with holdings in Bucks. and Northants. as well as Somerset, where they included a tenement in Babington (*Rotuli Litterarum Clausarum 1833–34*, i.58). He was, like his father, a major tenant of Count John's Mortain honor (*CRR* xi.1516) and doubtless was an early supporter. In 1194, after John's revolt, he had had to pay Richard I 100m. to regain the king's peace and his own lands (*Pipe Roll 6 Richard I*, 193). After John's accession, the king was twice at Harptree (*Rotuli Chartarum* 1837, 157b, 169b [9–6–1205, 9–16–1207]), and in 1207 helped William raise his ransom after being captured on royal service (*Book of Fees* 1920–31, 373). Thomas was dead by 1214 (*CRR* vii.237). William was accused in 1220 of masterminding a similar assault during the civil war.[11]

DURHAM SANCTUARY BREACH (EARLY TWELFTH CENTURY)

Rayne 1836, chaps. 60–61, pp. 119–21

A young episcopal servant was killed at Durham. The perpetrator fled to sanctuary with Saint Cuthbert in the cathedral "where he could have had the remedy of peace." The dead youth's loving friends promptly sought to avenge the death. Although temporarily restrained by the church whose peace they dare not break, they set a strict armed guard around all exits. They refused to let food in (but the monks supplied it anyway) or the killer out (for any reason, even to relieve himself), and harassed him until he retreated to the saint's tomb. With the bishop on their side, the besiegers were confident of their revenge, sanctuary or no, and reconnoitered with swords beneath their cloaks while the monks ate their evening meal. Six of them attacked while the killer was at prayer before the altar of the Holy Cross and wounded him severely in the head and throat. Some monks threw the attackers out in the nick of time. The news provoked a loud "clamor vulgi" by Saint Cuthbert's admirers, who extinguished a candle before the altar and trampled on the altar cloth to humiliate the saint into striking at his enemies; they even tried in vain to remove the fugitive to safety. When the bishop was informed, he absolved the wounded fugitive, reconciled him with the church, presumably by the assignment of penance, and formally remitted his own anger (as the dead man's lord). With the saint's aid, the man recovered with unexpected speed. Reginald, the storyteller, sees here an indication that the saint had turned evil into good; the would-be avengers had

11. This is Gurnay v. Fitzjohn; *CRR* ix.244–46, 348–50; x.215, 317–18; *Pipe Roll 5 Henry III*, 92 (Somerset, 1220–22).

helped their enemy by presenting him with the penitential suffering to release him from the consequences of his own misdeed.

But the sacrilege itself remained to be punished. The attacker laughed off his actions and, on Saturday evening, started to ride out of town and escape retribution. But Saint Cuthbert blinded him so that, with everyone watching, he could not find the gates. Although his friends urged him to flee for his life, his horse would only carry him to a nearby village, where, the next morning (Sunday), he was arrested and flung into a dungeon in irons so heavy that he soon died. The saint had avenged his own wrong.

EARL UHTRED'S FEUD (ELEVENTH CENTURY)

Symeon of Durham 1882–85, i.215–20 ("De obsessione Dunelmi"); ibid., ii.382–84 ("De Northymbrorum Comitibus"); ibid., ii.147–48, 196–200, 208–11 ("Historia Regum")

Comment: Hart 1975, 143–50; Kapelle 1979, 14–49, 127, 134–37; Fleming 1991, 47–49; Morris 1992; and now Fletcher 2002 (whose findings I was unable to take into account)

Æthelred II recognized Uhtred as earl of Northumbria in the lifetime of his father, Waltheof I, and added York to the earldom. The context reveals the king's need for a young, effective warrior in the north, an area with many Danish inhabitants of dubious loyalty. Perhaps Uhtred had exercised power before his formal investment; he celebrated a major victory over the Scots (1006?) by displaying many heads on the walls of York. His marriage to the bishop of Durham's daughter, Egfrida, had brought him a dower of half a dozen Durham estates. Now, however, he repudiated Egfrida, duly returned her dowry, and married Sige, the daughter of a rich York citizen, Styr f. Ulf. As Kapelle remarks, this connection strengthened the royal party in the north. The marriage alliance was allegedly made on condition that Uhtred kill his father-in-law's enemy, Thurbrand, surnamed Hold, perhaps the leader of York's Danes and a kind of local king's reeve. Uhtred was joining, maybe politicizing, an existing enmity. Whether Uhtred tried to perform his obligation, we are not told. But he probably did.

The marriage with Sige seems to have been childless; perhaps she died. King Æthelred then gave in marriage to Uhtred his own daughter Ælfgifu, to solidify his party loyalties further. When Cnut invaded, he sought Uhtred's military assistance, promising to confirm his earldom, properly augmented of course. Uhtred refused and proclaimed his loyalty to his current lord, his (new) father-in-law, and benefactor, but added a significant modifier, "as long as he shall live." Æthelred did die. Uhtred then (1016) traveled south to negotiate terms with Cnut. En route, Thurbrand Hold ambushed his party and killed Uhtred and his entire Northumbrian entourage, said to number forty. Our principal account believes that Cnut authorized this act and even furnished his own warriors for the purpose. Cnut then replaced Uhtred with a Norwegian earl of York but allowed Uhtred's brother, Eadulf Dudel, to succeed to the Northumbrian earldom (1016–?1019).

Ealdred, Uhtred's son by his first wife Egfrida, soon inherited both the Northumbrian earldom (ca. 1019–38) and the feud. He killed Thurbrand, "his father's killer," and entered into a period of open hostilities with Thurbrand's son, Carl. Eventually, mutual *amici* mediated a settlement ("concordia") with terms for the restitution of mutual *amor*. The terms apparently included some kind of brotherhood ritual and a joint penitential pilgrimage to Rome. Peace must have seemed close and possible. Unfortunately, bad weather prevented the start of the Rome trip, and the halcyon moment passed. After a feast at his hall in Ealdred's honor, Carl had his guest killed in a nearby wood, where a stone cross still marked the spot half a century later. As a subscriber to some of Cnut's charters, he could doubtless rely on royal protection.

The earldom moved out of the direct Bambergh line. First Eadulf, a son of Uhtred's second marriage (1038–41), and then the Danish Siward (1041–55) became earls of Northumbria. Siward, who had Eadulf killed, then married Ealdred's daughter, Ælfflæd, doubtless partly, as Kapelle suggests, "to appease local feelings," but also to strengthen his claims to lands and legitimacy. There may also have been other gestures toward Uhtred's family (Kapelle 1979, 29, 43–44). "Justice waited until the 1070s," when Waltheof II (earl 1072–75), great-grandson to Uhtred through Ealdred's daughter, avenged Ealdred's death in appropriate fashion. He caught Carl's sons feasting in the house of the eldest brother near York and killed the brothers (save one, spared as a good man, and another who was fortunately absent), and the grandsons too. This chilling act was the last recorded in our principal source. Whether it was the end of the feud, or if Uhtred's line came to regret Waltheof's mercy, is unknown.

Durham had not, however, recovered the lost dowry lands. Earl Siward had successfully claimed these by the hereditary right of his wife and used them to dower her. The feud obligation then passed to their son Waltheof. The lands lost much of their value in the course of further violence ("werra surgente") between Uhtred's descendants and those of Egfrida's second marriage to a Yorkshire thegn, Kilvert f. Ligulf. When our account was written, some lands remained with the Northumbrian earls, some with Kilvert's progeny, and a few had even returned to Saint Cuthbert and his monks.

These facts explain the composition of the misnamed "De obsessione

Dunelmi," our principal source. Some Durham monk wrote this account, almost certainly after the death of Earl Waltheof II in 1075. The author seems to have been familiar with sagas and feud lore, but as a monk, he may have disapproved of vengeance. He comments on Earl Uhtred's gloating display of defeated Scots' heads: "sicut tunc temporis mos erat." He was primarily interested in the recovery of his house's estates from Uhtred's line. The feud, secondary to the property descent, was presented only as essential background.

Kapelle (1979, 24, 31 n. 9: "There was no northern blood feud") notwithstanding, this seems as clear a blood feud as one can find. The main text's interest in property holdings probably excludes other relevant events and ends the account prematurely. However, it contains another feud-like episode—the account of Earl Eadwulf's return of some Lothian territory to the Scots, from fear that they would take vengeance for the deaths and shame involved in Uhtred's victory of 1006 (see Kapelle 1979, 21 sq., on this). The admixture of private enmities with local and even national politics is exemplary. All the accounts (including "De Northymbrorum Comitibus") may go back to an earlier lost text on the earls.

FERNHAM V. ENGLEYS (1213–14)

CRR vii.46, 94, 165, 177, 214 (Essex, 1213–14); cf. *CRR* vii.26; viii.2
Comment: Turner 1968, 132

This case is clearly labeled an appeal concerning a breach of the king's peace, apparently some kind of assault or entry into Elias of Fernham's houses. It troubled the justices that Gilbert Anglicus (Engleys) was Elias's lord,[12] and they sought guidance from the king, through Chief Justiciar Peter des Roches (West 1966, chap. 6). Gilbert gave the king 100s. for the acquittal "de illa transgressione" of his seven men imprisoned in the Fleet "pro transgressione quam ipsi fecerunt de domibus Elye de Fernham et aliis iniuriis ei factis." His incarceration had been embarrassing. (He had defaulted on jury service to which he had been nominated in a Devon assize of novel disseizin.) Elias had himself been jailed for appealing his lord. He later paid the king 3m. from the 50s. damages paid him by Gilbert. Gilbert was a substantial landholder in the southwest as well as Essex (*Book of Fees* 1920–31, 394, 436, 713, 745, 770, 776, 1161), and his sureties included the sheriff of Cornwall and various other southwestern notables. Here *transgressio* is used for two separate offenses, Elias's appeal of his lord, and Gilbert's original assault on his man.

---

12. For the rule against duels between lord and man, see chap. 6.

Stenton 1926, 773–75 (Lincoln eyre)
Comment: ibid., lix

Alan Hayward abducted Thomas f. Lefwin on the high road and carried him off to his house. Thomas was robbed and beaten, breaking a small bone in his arm. Alan's wife, Emma, then allegedly cut off one of his testicles; one Ralf Pilate detached the other. The unfortunate man was then dumped unceremoniously back onto the road where he had been intercepted. The ritual nature of the wounding and the perpetrators' patent interest in publicizing their deed are obvious.

Thomas followed the proper procedures (hue, view of wounds, and so forth), leading to an abortive appeal against Alan for broken bones. Because of this, when his fresh appeal for breach of the peace against Alan (but none of the others) came before the justices at the Lincoln eyre, Alan had to offer 2m. for judgment. The justices questioned the hundred sergeant, who confirmed the essential details of the story; he had viewed the wounds and had then visited Alan's house, where he found the knife and a testicle bowl. Nevertheless, the justices quashed Thomas's appeal, amerced him, and formally declared Alan quit of any offense.

The editor surmised that Thomas had been sexually involved with some woman in Alan's household—maybe a daughter—and that Alan and his family had intended to teach him a lesson and warn him off. The neighbors must have sympathized with this taking of vengeance, as perhaps also did the justices.

FRAWIN OF CORNWALL V. SONS OF TOKI (CA. 1100)

Padel 1984, 20–27

This tit-for-tat killing bears all the marks of a cause célèbre of its day. All England should be weeping, not just Cornwall, it was said later. Yet Padel had to reconstruct the outlines from a few scraps, a laconic aside in Geoffrey of Monmouth's "Prophecies of Merlin," itself requiring contemporary elucidation (including the remark just cited) (*Pipe Roll 31 Henry I*, 159–60; and *Book of Fees* 1920–31, i.441 [Gloucs. account for 1235 aid]).

Osulf, who in 1066 had held nine manors and lost them all by 1086, was killed by Toki's sons, ca. 1100, and well before 1130. The sheriff, Frawin, led a group of avengers, six of whom who were still paying a set of royal fines in 1130. Henry I seems to have treated the incident severely. Frawin still owed more than £50, plus a further 300m. to get his land back. He and his supporters, all apparently Cornish or English, nevertheless prospered from the Norman Conquest. Geoffrey calls Toki's sons "frankigene" (i.e., French-born) and seems to harbor a latent sympathy for the way Oswin's friends had made the Normans pay for their deed. Padel suggests a context within some anti-Norman revolt, which would certainly explain why the king treated it so seriously.

GIROIE V. MONTGOMERY (CA. 1030–93)

Orderic ii.24; iii.134–36, 160; iv.294

Comment: Chibnall, in *Orderic* ii.24–25 n. 3; Searle 1988, 166–69, 179–85; Bennett 1998, 130–33

Giroie had been an early benefactor of Saint Evroul but was dead by ca. 1030. Count Gilbert of Brionne saw an opportunity to expand his lands at the family's expense and moved against Giroie's young sons. They, however, mustered an effective support group that pursued the count back to his own territory; they were able to take the town of Le Sap. The duke intervened to persuade Count Gilbert to let them keep it "for a firmer peace." This held for a few years, but the count tried again and was murdered for his pains. Many of the disputed lands later came into the hands of Roger de Montgomery, who held them for a quarter century, during which time the Giroies nursed their hated for Roger's cruel wife, Mabel. (Orderic blames her for the loss of their paternal inheritance.) One night in 1077, Hugh and three of his brothers caught her relaxing in a bath inside one of her castles and beheaded her to avenge their patrimony. The brothers escaped, and many local people applauded the "savage killing." The Montgomery clan retained thoughts of vengeance. They suspected Hugh Giroie's old friend, William Pantulf, of complicity, because of his long *malivolentia* against Mabel, who had deprived him of a castle. This may explain William's withdrawal to Apulia, a plausible retreat for a man in fear for his life. On William's return, Earl Roger and his sons invaded his lands and sought to kill him. William fled to sanctuary at St. Evroul, fiercely protesting his innocence and offering proper legal purgation, which his enemies refused to accept, even though they could produce no convincing evidence of guilt. The matter was resolved only by William's submission to a hot iron ordeal before a royal court at Rouen. The Montgomerys attended, fully armed and ready to execute the judgment personally. But God cleared William, to the accompaniment of hymns of praise sung by all Orderic's fellow monks. Robert Giroie was still allegedly meditating vengeance against his enemies in 1092–93.

GRAY V. PORTER

JUST 1/62, m. 2 (Bucks. crown pleas, 1232)

Roger Gray must have been quite young and very impressionable on the day when, just outside the Buckingham city gates, William le Porter struck his grandfather (also called Roger) a fierce and mortal blow on the head. Gray claimed to remember the events quite clearly at his appeal twenty-three years later. He also asserted that he had appealed once earlier, when he was first of age, although neither the coroners nor the shire court could remember this. He offered no satisfactory explanation for the subsequent delay. His mother had not chosen to appeal; his father could not do so, because he had been in Scotland at the time of the event and thus was not an eyewitness. William emphasized the negligence and suggested that Roger was only appealing now to counter his own wounding suit. In any event, the old man had remained alive ten years after his alleged killing. There were two counterappeals. These concerned a recent incident in which William le Porter came across Roger and William Gray grazing their horses on (his?) meadow grass. Roger had jumped up, shouted at him, and then launched a crossbow bolt, which had broken William's "ratleure" along with two of his teeth. William Gray had pursued him to the door of his own house and struck him with a sword. Roger pleaded exemption from any duel as a maimed man, although the court could see no evidence for this other than broken teeth. His appeal was held null. The ensuing jury inquiry *pro pace* found that Roger had indeed shot William le Porter, and that William too had wounded him in the head. The court ordered both to be arrested.

Whatever the truth of the matter, Roger had harbored his grudge from youth into middle age and made his bid for vengeance through the courts.

HARLOW V. LOVETOT (1287–89)

Tout and Johnstone 1906, no. 12, 53–61
Comment: Brand 1992a, 192–93

Two rival claimants competed for the wardship of Peter de Perevile's heir and lands in Matching, Essex. John f. Hubert of Harlow contended that Peter had assigned the wardship to him while still alive, and was first to take possession. But Gilbert f. William of Dunmow came on Saint Margaret's Day (July 20) in 1287, and took control with a force of more than sixty men armed ready to fight. John at once made his plaint to the sheriff at the shire court. There he secured an order that the coroner and two other shire officials should check the site and, should the story prove true, remove Gilbert's force ("vim"). But Gilbert's men refused to move. One of them shot and nearly killed the coroner, who thereupon raised the hue, summoning the neighborhood to assist him. Gilbert's men resisted. One of those who responded to the hue, a cousin of John's named Richard f. William, was killed at the coroner's feet. The posse arrested Gilbert and twenty-six of his followers. An inquest quickly established who had committed the actual killing—Clement of Cookham (or rather, as it later emerged, Clement's cook, John le Keu). The two were taken to Chelmsford and handed over to the sheriff as peace-breakers.

What happened next is disputed, but John's version was later confirmed in most details. Gilbert's *amici* approached the sheriff and persuaded him to bail Gilbert under manucaptors to guarantee his later appearance for trial. Because it was illegal for homicide suspects to be bailed in this way, they promised the sheriff 10m. for his help in acquitting Gilbert of the felony. They paid 7m. on account and promised the coroner £10 to record falsely on his roll that the accused had surrendered to the peace before the killing took place. Now free pending trial, Gilbert was further able to arrange for a friendly judge, John de Lovetot, to try the homicide at the gaol delivery. The justice's price for this favor was 20m., and Gilbert also had to pay the judge's clerk, Henry of Guildford, another 100s. for his services as intermediary. Lovetot then impaneled a jury that deliberately (and improperly) included biased men, friends and relatives of the accused. At various times Gilbert also had John f. Hubert summoned to Colchester, then to Saffron Walden, and into jail for a time. One of his stratagems was to have a jury stacked with John's enemies indict him for abetting the (allegedly) false appeal for Richard's death. He then allowed John no chance to defend himself before compelling him to choose between prison and a 40s. fine *pro transgressione*, that is, for the abetting offense of which the jury ultimately cleared him. Lovetot denied knowledge of the money until put to his oath. A jury agreed that he had proceeded "otherwise than he ought." Thus through gifts (bribes?), so John of Harlow later asserted, the murder was concealed.[13] As a consequence, John suffered great damage.

The abetting charge must have been very plausible. In essence, an outsider successfully instigated and procured legal action. Although there are no signs of any homicide appeal over Richard's death, the guilty man, le Keu the cook, was in fact indicted. John was said later to have instigated the charge. Some of the earlier jurors thought this justified the charge, but others felt that *abbettum* was not to be adjudged in such a case—a rare but interesting glimpse at the legal discussions sometimes carried on inside a criminal jury.

Once Gilbert had saved himself from the immediate threat of jail on a capital charge, he brought an assize of novel disseizin against John f. Hubert for ejecting him from the wardship and lands at Matching. Gilbert later ad-

---

13. The use here of the word *murdrum* is worth noting in view of the dispute about the prehistory of the murder/manslaughter distinction in homicide cases. Cf. Kaye 1967; Bellamy 1998, 57–62.

mitted the main corruption charges against him. He had a legitimate reason to be at Matching, namely, the wardship claim. Then once the hue and cry arrived, Richard was killed. Fearing his own indictment for the felony, Gilbert promised the coroner 20m. to keep his name out of the indictment. He was indeed jailed overnight until he connived with the under-sheriff so that he and his close kin were not locked in with the rest. Once again he tried to get Lovetot as his judge, but unsuccessfully (as the justice was about to cross the Channel on crown business). Under questioning, Gilbert further admitted that he had offered to let Lovetot's clerk have the disputed lands at Matching for his help in keeping out of jail. But because he realized he could not warrant them (guarantee title), he openly promised the clerk 100s. to aid him by the best means he could.

HAY (HAGGE) V. NEWCASTLE FLEMINGS (1293)

JUST 1/651, m. 21d (gaol delivery before Hugh of Collingham and colleagues)
Cited: Hurnard 1969, 310

Conflict arose in Newcastle between Richard Hagge of Lindsey and two Flemings from Ypres, one Peter and Walter Coksy (aka Utrekyn). The two Flemings had been the attackers, two on one. They wounded Richard with their swords. He then fought back and struck Peter a mortal blow with his knife; then, also mortally wounded, he had himself taken into a nearby house. Soon, with night falling, John Jakes, the dead man's cousin, came to the house with a hue and cry to which the borough coroners, bailiffs, and under-bailiffs had all been summoned along with many others—the jurors named thirty-three men! Four men—Jakes, Walter Coksy, Clapkyn of Ypres, and one William Thorald—dragged the dying Richard out of the house and to the place where Peter's corpse lay. The coroners asked him if he had killed Peter. The dying Richard could hardly whisper his responses. He first asked if Peter were indeed dead. If so, he admitted, he must have killed him in self-defense with no other hope of preserving his own life. But the coroners wished to avenge Peter's death and ordered Richard beheaded under cover of a judgment ("sub colore iudicii"). So John Jakes twisted a piece of wood through Richard's hair and in this way held his head still, while an unknown pauper (whose name nobody could discover) performed the actual beheading. Such is the basic tale told by the jury of presentment to royal justices intent on delivering Newcastle jail.

John Jakes, under arrest for the deed, was now produced in court. He explained that the other dead man, Peter, was his cousin; he had therefore beheaded Richard to avenge his cousin's death, claiming that he was acting to execute a felon, and so not feloniously. The jury on which he put his case "for good and evil" confirmed his motive as vengeance and had heard Richard say that he had acted only in self-defense. Only after the justices had carefully checked that Richard's self-defense plea met the law's rather strict standards did they sentence Jakes to be hanged for feloniously beheading Richard "racione vindicte."

Next the court turned to the city officials responsible for keeping the law. Both coroners pleaded clergy and were claimed by the local dean. The jury, proceeding in the usual manner, nevertheless found them guilty of ordering the death. Their chattels were confiscated, and then they were handed over to the bishop. Attention next turned to the bailiffs and under-bailiffs. One bailiff admitted he had been present but denied consenting to the execution; he had quickly left the scene. He still had to make fine for not actually prohibiting the deed. The other bailiff's defense was that he could not hear the words spoken by the moribund Richard and thought he had confessed. He was therefore acquitted of the felony but still made to fine, because being present as bailiff, he ought to have ascertained the facts and prevented the felony. One under-bailiff had similarly to fine for being present, even though the jury said he did not consent. The case against the remaining under-bailiff was stronger. He had, according to the jury, pronounced judgment at the coroners' command and so actually ordered the execution. He did so even though he too claimed not to have heard the supposed confession. His fine was lower than his colleague's.

Thirty-one local citizens were also arrested for aid and assent. Although cleared of the felony, the court still ordered their temporary custody until all except some paupers had made fine for sums that ranged from twenty pence to several pounds. One who had fled after the death lost all his goods as a fugitive for felony.

The next business was the outlawry of William Thorald and the two Flemings, Walter Coksy and Clapkyn of Ypres. They had fled across the Scots border at Berwick. William had absconded with a lot of money and goods. John de Hedon, Newcastle's royal bailiff, had set off at once in pursuit and caught up with the two fugitives in Berwick Castle in the presence of its Scottish constable. He demanded their bodies, and the next morning a fearful William took the king of Scots' peace. Negotiations followed between the two sheriffs, Hugh Cobyon of Northumberland and Richard Fraser of Scottish Berwick, who prevaricated on the ground that he was new and did not know the relevant custom. After due consultation, the Scots formally refused to return the fugitives. The Northumberland shire court confirmed that in such cases, fugitives were permitted to remain freely unless they were under formal felony accusation, as in this instance. The English court's judgment confidently recited that "the Lord King of England is the

Lord of Scotland's superior" and had received judgment of the felons' chattels before their escape; therefore, the king of Scotland was bound in faith to assist and not impede the English king to keep his rights. "We must therefore speak about this with the lord King."

The court was not yet done. John le Flemyng, accused of knowingly harboring John Jakes, pleaded clergy. Learned discussion as to whether his bigamy removed his claim to clerical status produced diverse opinions, until someone uncovered the relevant, recent statute on the subject, whereupon John was compelled to answer as a layman. The jury cleared him on the tenuous ground that he did not know that Jakes's deeds had been felonious. Then the court pressed the city itself. Testimony was received that Jakes had been living openly in Newcastle until the justices' arrival, without anyone arresting him. Nobody, the court said, could be ignorant of so notorious a felony carried out in full sight of the whole people. For this "trespass" the justices fined the town £200.

The protagonists were all men of substantial means and position in Newcastle. If Richard was Richard de la Hay, he belonged to a draper family that had produced a recent bailiff. William Thorald rode off to Scotland on a horse worth 40s. and took with him £20 worth of goods. Jakes himself was said to have possessed more than £4 in goods and to have held a shop and other property in the borough as well as lands worth nearly 50s. per annum from the king. The size of the various fines extracted from participants attests to Newcastle's commercial prosperity at this time. The justices' determination to hold strictly to account all responsible for the illegal act of vengeance thus remains very impressive.

HAY OF AUGHTON V. FITZPETER (1195–1211)

EYC ii.1130; cf. ibid., 1129 (1180–1200)

The double marriage agreement made by William f. Peter of Goodmanham and Thomas (II) Hay of Aughton, Yorks., in the last years of the twelfth century was intended to bring to a mutually satisfactory conclusion a long series of financial dealings between their two substantial landholder families. Thomas's grandfather, Roger f. Alfred, had held two of the Fossard fees among other parcels in Henry II's reign (*EYC* ii, p. 423), and William f. Peter was able to found a Gilbertine priory at Ellerton (Clay 1973, 40–41). But William's grandfather, William f. Anketin, had amassed debts to the king and certain *regales* amounting to 60m. or more. In order to persuade Roger f. Alfred to pay these off for him, William the grandfather was forced to gage some of his lands into the possession of the Hays. This landed debt was still an issue in our William's day. He made a *conventio* with Emma Hay,

Roger's daughter, which carried a cost. William confirmed to Emma her right to retain the gaged lands for her lifetime, peacefully and unmolested. In return for this life tenancy, she gave him a mill at Goodmanham, plus six bovates of land there and elsewhere, together with an acknowledgment of the debt's full discharge. The pair swore and gave faith to each other that they would observe their agreement in full. But Emma's son, Thomas, was neither a party nor a witness to this agreement and may have had different plans. Meanwhile, the death of William (II) Fossard ended the Fossard lordship over both families. Richard I's familiar, Robert of Thornham, obtained the Fossard heiress from his king with her considerable lands, and married her in 1197 (*EYC* ii, pp. 328–29).

Soon afterward, William made a further concord with Thomas. Our copy represents Thomas's quitclaim, reciting under his seal the discharge of the debt and gage in his mother's time. (There was probably a parallel document made and sealed by William on his side of the bargain.) In return, so Thomas said, William gave to his own nephew, William of Burland, six bovates of land in Goodmanham with Thomas's daughter, Emma (II). He also gave five bovates that had been the head messuage (residence) of Emma (I) to Thomas's eldest son, Roger, with William of Burland's sister, Christina. Although both of these endowments are described as being in free marriage—implying, at least in later law, that they created no new lordship—they were subject to forinsec service to the king. Heading the long list of witnesses was Alan of Wilton, steward to Robert of Turnham—suggesting that the agreement was possibly made and brokered in the lord's court, where, Thomas might have had some advantage (*Rotuli de Oblatis* 1835, 105).

HILL V. FITZEUSTACE (1219)

CP 25 (1)/212/6/39 (fine from Suffolk eyre, Bury, June 19, 1219)

The fine tells us only about the settlement and nothing of the previous enmities and events that made it necessary. Robert de Hyl's appeal against Eustace's sons, Walter and William, had reached the point where Robert and Walter were armed and ready for their duel when the parties reached agreement. Walter did Robert homage, six-handed, apparently on the spot. This unusual wording (which is more common in definitions of oaths) implies that the brothers had brought with them supporters, perhaps to cheer them on in the duel but ready also to support their oaths or (as actually happened) to contribute public submissions on their behalf. The six men then swore, in words that bound their children ("cum progenie sua"), to "carry peace" ever thereafter to Robert and his progeny; furthermore, they would never bring any appeal or plaint ("querimoniam") against them "for any rancor in word or deed" previously existing between them. In response Robert and his children too swore in the same terms to the Fitzeustaces. Although no money changed hands at the time, the settlement imposed (excluding all right to appeal or maneuver further) a 40m. penalty on anyone from either side who broke its terms.

KITTISFORD V. WOODLAND (1258)

C 144/4, no. 46

Augustine de la Wodelonde acquired by escheat a house on a ferling of land in "Clipewille," Somerset, after the heirless death of its previous owner, Thomas of Clipewille. Richard de Kittisford, a man of some means (Landon 1923, 180, 182), claimed this land as his wife's inheritance; he produced a charter from Adam, parson of Kittisford, and impounded Augustine's animals he found there. Augustine and his friends several times rescued these beasts or had them released through the sheriff. Doubtless there was some violence. The parties concurrently sued each other for almost a year in Somerset shire court. Then Richard, having by this time conceived a "magnum odium et atya," came and assaulted the house before dawn on May Day with twenty-two men. They forced Augustine and his companions to flee, whereupon Augustine raised the hue "with mouth and horn." One of the assailants, William of Kiddisford, pressed William de Hurtston (perhaps Augustine's brother) so hard that he could escape only by hitting his attacker a mortal blow. He alone was guilty, said the subsequent jury de odio et athia. Richard nevertheless appealed his other enemies, Augustine, John de la Pouleshull, and William his brother.

LAUNCELLS V. FITZWILLIAM (MAINLY 1199–1201)

RCR i.373; PKJ i.3074, 3263, 3291; RCR ii.244; CRR i.238, 255–56, 267, 278–79; Rotuli de Oblatis 1835, 78, 103, 106–7; PKJ i.3372; CRR i.384, 386, 397, 437–38, 440; PKJ ii.124 (Devon/Cornwall, 1199–1201). Also Pipe Roll 2 John, 223–24; 3 John, 190, 192, 222; 4 John, 170, 251; 5 John, 75, 78; CRR ii.313; Rotuli de Oblatis 1835, 235, 259–60 (1204–5)

Comment: Flower 1944, 314–16

Richard of Launcells's house in northern Cornwall suffered a violent springtime assault, probably in 1199. A large number of gentry from a wide area of the southwestern counties broke in and violently took various items of value, going so far as to pull rings off their owners' fingers. Robbery was not their main purpose. They compelled Richard to make a solemn promise that he would surrender himself to their lord, one Henry f. William, at his house on a given day. He was also to travel there on a nag ("runcinus") selected, Richard later alleged, specifically to dishonor him.

By the Easter term of that year, Richard had a whole series of appeals under way in the royal courts and had already obtained the outlawry of several of his enemies. (These outlawries suggest that some of the appellees regarded their chance of going to the gallows to be high enough that they dare not appear to answer the charges.) The appeal pleadings reveal that an old enmity, involving large and valuable landholdings among several counties, lay behind the incident.

Although the origins of this *vetus odium* are never directly stated on the rolls, the political overtones of the story are evident. That the incident occurred during the interregnum after Richard I's death (April 6) but before John's coronation (May 27) is already significant. One case entry placed it "straight after king Richard's death" (*Pipe Roll 4 John*, 78; *CRR* ii.313), as if the royal demise had prompted action. The lord John was still in Normandy at the time. Perhaps for this reason, the first appeals plead breaches of the ducal (not the king's) peace. That several appellees failed to appear at the first recorded hearings is normal. But some had already been outlawed, and their land taken into the king's hand by the Easter term (Easter Sunday being April 18), after some unusually swift action. Concerns were voiced at later stages that the case should be determined by normal procedures, "according to the law and custom of the king's court" (*Rotuli de Oblatis* 1835, 103; *Pipe Roll 3 John*, 222). This may suggest that the Fitzwilliam party feared they might fall foul of royal anger, leading to some extraordinary royal order. Indeed, the king did take a personal interest in the dispute. One issue concerned control of the royal castle at Launceston (fifteen or so miles south of Launcells), which Henry f. William was later said to have wished to take over "to the lord king's shame [huntagium]." One of the appealed men, Thomas of Dunham, pleaded as his alibi that he had gone to Launceston on that day to swear his fidelity to the new king.

The context of the dispute was the effect of the change of kings on the local political situation in north Cornwall and the western portion of Devon. Most of the main protagonists were deeply involved in local politics and administration; they inevitably knew each other well from meetings of the shire court and eyre. They had multiple—hence sometimes conflicting—loyalties to their betters, the king and other national players, and their local attachments. Here as elsewhere, local enmities could determine alignments in national events and vice versa.

Henry f. William had close links to John before his accession, through holding some lands as tenant of Count John's honor of Mortain (*Book of Fees* 1920–31, i.394, 436). At the 1201 Launceston eyre, he was able to plead the king's service to excuse himself from four apparently separate assizes of novel disseizin (*PKJ* ii.146; cf. ibid., ii.443, 464 [= 505], 477, 521). One of these plaintiffs, Robert de Heriz, offered 80m. for seizin of land allegedly taken "by reason of the king's service." Henry countered with an offer of £100 to have the king's grace in order to defend that appeal against him and to recover the obviously substantial lands of which he had been disseized "by reason of that appeal," apart from those given to Robert de Heriz (*Pipe Roll 1 John*, 182, 186; *2 John*, 220–21). Henry even had another go at the lands after Robert's death.

Richard of Launcells, also a man of means, was thought to be capable of frustrating hostile lawsuits. In 1201, a hundred jury was amerced for making "a stupid presentment" regarding a homicide that had already been before the justices three times on the widow's appeal (*PKJ* ii.370). Henry Summerson has suggested to me that Richard may also have been a Ricardian loyalist sheriff after the fall of John in 1194. If so, Richard's death and John's accession appeared to Henry and his followers to afford an opportunity to settle old political scores that had previously been repressed. We may imagine the atmosphere at Launceston Castle on that day when Thomas of Dunham and others went to swear their fealties to the new king. Rumors about John's accession and the fate of Arthur of Brittany must have swept through the crowd. The type of grievances they recounted to each other are illustrated by the plea de odio et athia of one appellee, Hugh de Morton (below). Henry's party had perhaps overestimated its clout with the new regime. His men had to reckon with the shire's willingness to follow rules that threatened their life and limb with outlawry. Almost inevitably, their hopes for an acceptable settlement focused on the king.

Some such hypothesis helps to explain the complex course of the half dozen associated appeals brought by Richard and his friends: more than thirty entries on the printed rolls relate to this dispute. In the Michaelmas term of 1200, two of the appeals (neither of them involving Richard in person) reached the point (wager) where the parties had committed themselves to duel. The justices quashed three other appeals, so that the appellees went free and Richard was in mercy. Despite this, Richard and some of his adversaries were given a day to hear judgment coram rege a few weeks later. The king then ordered the justices to send the two live cases coram rege "because he wish[ed] to see them" (*RCR* ii.244; *CRR* i.238, 267). Some historians have seized upon this transfer as an indication of John's prurient interest in duels (Turner 1968, 95–96), a black mark against his character. However, subsequent proceedings entirely refute such a reading of the case.

Hugh de Morton was an appellee summoned to hear his judgment from the king *after* acquittal. His defense, more fully reported than the others, helps to establish the context for the whole affair. He went beyond a general denial of all Richard's charges; indeed, he himself alleged that the appeal against him was brought "per attiam et per vetus odium" on three separate grounds.[14] Hugh had been with the hundred sergeant on the occasion when he arrested Richard's brother, "such a man that neither could nor should [be permitted to] dwell in the area," and was responsible for sending him to the gallows. On another occasion, Hugh had informed the royal justices of a plea of the crown previously concealed by Richard, and the justices had subsequently amerced Richard. And Richard had once tried to revoke his grant of a church in his gift to Hugh's nephew, who then had to obtain papal letters against him.

Such factional hostility was exactly the type of conflict a new king needed to resolve—either by a political decision favoring the loyalist party over their enemies or by brokering a peace settlement. The complex and expensive settlement that ensued was undoubtedly negotiated with the king's knowledge, which explains why he "wished to see" the cases before him, to exercise his mediation skills. The plea-roll clerks merely record (*CRR* i.386, a damaged, incomplete roll) that at the hearing coram rege in the Hilary term of 1201, Richard came into court and withdrew from his suit against Henry f. William, quitclaiming his adversaries on behalf of himself and his heirs. Henry was to pay to him the 20m. that the king had expected as an amercement. This was done "coram rege and by the consent of the Lord King." Hearings nevertheless continued into Easter term, probably in part to clear up the details of the whole dispute, including the subsidiary appeals.

Most of the appellees paid handsomely for their settlement. (They would have been liable to death or mutilation if the appeal had succeeded.) Henry f. William had himself to proffer £100 for the concord, and to regain the king's grace and love on condition that he stood to right against (i.e., satisfied the claims of) anyone who appeared against him on the matter.[15] Richard of Launcells was to receive 100m. from Hugh of Staddon and Richard of Dunham plus 40m. (damages?) for his chattels. Three county locals (one of them sheriff at about this time) guaranteed with the pair that "no evil will happen through them or by their counsel or will to the said Richard

14. This plea de odio et athia is discussed in chap. 5.
15. *Rotuli de Oblatis* 1835, 106–7; *Pipe Roll 2 John*, 223; *Pipe Roll 3 John*, 190. He still owed Richard 20m. in 1204, perhaps from this (*Pipe Roll 2 John*, 223–24; *Rotuli de Oblatis* 1835, 235, 259–60). In 1205, Henry conceded coram rege that the sheriff might levy 7m. still owing to Richard (with a third going to the king for his help in collection) from this fine from his chattels and rents (*Rotuli Litterarum Clausarum* 1833–84, i.24; *Pipe Roll 4 John*, 170).

de Lancells" or to his men who had gaged that duel on his behalf.[16] Overall the king received at least 145m. (nearly £100) in amercements. Richard too was supposed to receive substantial sums within the year but predictably had trouble in collecting his money. The delay may have suited the king, since it both sustained the standoff between the two parties and brought Richard back to offer him money for help in collecting his payments.

Much of this account must remain speculative. Nevertheless, there can be little doubt that we are glimpsing, through a glass darkly, the type of dispute an entertainment writer might have chosen to describe in feud terms. Read in conjunction with the other contemporary cases, the tale reveals just a little of the interplay between personal rancor and politics at both the local and national levels.

LE BRUN V. LONDON (1200)

RCR ii.172–73 = *PKJ* i.3169; *Rotuli de Oblatis* 1835, 66 (Dublin, 1200)
Comment: *PKJ* i.78–79. Much information courtesy of Paul Brand.

This was a "contencio et malivolentia" between two Dublin merchants, William Le Brun and Warin of London, who must have known each other very well. By the 1190s, they were both middle-aged men with adult children; both were members of the same local community and had ongoing social relations,[17] with frequent business contacts and, doubtless, some competition. Their enmity appears to have been long-lived. Sometime in the early 1190s (ca. 1192–94, while William Pipard was justiciar), William went to the Dublin county court—exceptionally here in Ireland the main royal court for the English settlement—and obtained (as was later said) a promise of the king's peace from Warin and four other named associates.

Sometime later William was summoned to Dublin Castle by the royal justiciar. After his business was done, when he and four close kinsmen had started home, they found waiting on the bridge outside the castle four men later named in the appeal, together with a fifth man whom they had never

---

16. *Rotuli de Oblatis* 1835, 78, 103, 106–7; cf. *Pipe Roll 3 John*, 192, 222. If the fine roll editor were right in dating the original proffers to 1200, this would be evidence that the settlement had been prepared well ahead of the hearing before the king.

17. The murdered man had been in Ireland at least since 1173–76 (Gilbert 1889, 369–70). He figured on the roll of free citizens (Connolly and Martin 1992, 113), was known to have made a number of small donations mostly consisting of Dublin rents to local monasteries, and frequently witnessed other men's grants in the decades before his death. Warin of London was likewise a regular witness to Dublin charters of the late twelfth and early thirteenth centuries; he may be the Warin who owes 6s. (Connolly and Martin 1992, 7). The two men sometimes witnessed together (as in Gilbert 1889, 369–70; Brooks 1936, 135–36, 267–68), and Warin also attested alongside his appellor, William's own son, Owen (Brooks 1936, 49, 92, 179), one of which may postdate the killing. The other three appellees can all be found witnessing deeds of the same general nature, in each other's company and sometimes alongside William or Owen le Brun.

seen before or since. This one was carrying an ax; he barred their way and struck William a blow that knocked him into the moat. Two of William's companions descended to help their lord; the other two raised the hue and chased after the malefactors. But Warin was there to receive the assailants, and he let the killer out through a locked gate to which he (alone) held the key, then re-locked it to hamper the pursuit. The noise of the hue reached the justiciar and Ralf Morin, so that they and others saw what happened— including the "hatchet" man still carrying his ax. William died three days later.

Such was the four kinsmen's story, told in the spring of 1200 when they brought an appeal coram rege for William's death. They named the men who had gaged peace to William on the previous occasion (although one was now dead) and accused Warin of having ordered the deed and harboring the killer afterward, wickedly and against the peace which all had gaged. William's son Owen was in a position to bring the case to the king's notice.[18] He may have been the one to secure a hearing before the king. Each appellor offered proof by battle against one of the opponents.

Warin denied the story word for word in the required manner and side-stepped any risk of battle by pleading that he was a maimed man with a broken leg. His colleagues likewise put in their denials and then offered 60m. for an inquiry as to whether they had ever gaged the peace in the way the appellors claimed. The breach of a special peace, if confirmed, aggravated their offense and risked angering the king. The court permitted all but Warin to defend themselves by battle; Warin was to undergo the ordeal of the hot iron. The parties were given a date several weeks off, on May 8, before the king wherever he was. The threat of these unpleasant proofs encouraged the appellees to come to terms, and sure enough Warin and two of his colleagues made substantial proffers (twenty ounces of gold are mentioned) for license to concord Owen's homicide appeal. We can assume that the terms of this settlement involved the payment of comparable sums to the complainants, although no details have survived.

LINDSEY V. STICKNEY (1202)

Stenton 1926, nos. 612, 1031 (Lincoln eyre)
Comment: ibid., l–li

Osbert de Lindsey had built a house on his free holding in Stickney. Alan of Stickney came there with a retinue ("cum vi sua") one day and demanded

---

18. Owen was a clerk who started in the service of Archbishop John Comyn (Brooks 1953, xvi, 14, 16; Brooks 1936, 209). He moved into royal service (*Rotuli Litterarum Clausarum* 1833–84, i.12, 72), probably by 1204, and rose to be a chamberlain of the Irish exchequer (ibid., 526).

lodging. Perhaps Osbert was slow to welcome him, but the consequences were violent. Alan leveled the house by cutting through the middle of the posts holding it up. Osbert was wounded and robbed of some money. He brought a plaint at the shire court, whereupon Alan gaged (vadiavit) him the king's peace. Later, when Osbert's mother died, Alan returned to the house and found Osbert inside with his niece, who had just inherited the old lady's land. He broke in, threw all their people out of the house, and wounded Osbert on the arm in the process. This was Osbert's story at his appeal before the itinerant justices. Before they could come to judgment, however, the parties entered court together and placed themselves on the king's mercy "for license to concord," a slightly unusual move. Alan's amercement was assessed at 6m., and Osbert's at 20s. (= 1½m.). The same three local men acted as sureties for the payments of both parties. Several participants can be identified as substantial landowners within the earldom of Chester.

MALTRAVERS V. TURBERVILL (1199–1202)

CRR i.219, 271, 273, 332, 356, 380–81, 393, 441; ii.37 (Dorset, mostly coram rege)

The summer of 1199 undoubtedly marked a turning point in the life of John Maltravers, a younger son of the father whose name he shared. John senior lay sick (mortally, as it turned out) at his house in Woolcombe (near Melbury Bubb, Dorset, close to the Somerset border and Yeovil).[19] When the younger son, John junior, came with a couple of followers to see the old man on the octave of Saint John the Baptist (June 30), he found Walter de Turbervill in his way. With five others, Walter chased after young John, and cornered his two friends in the cowshed, where one, Simon Blund, was "killed and hanged [*sic*]." The elder John died soon after. But a charter was nevertheless made in his name granting the house with its three (or four) carucates of land (a respectable half knight's fee) to his wife, Alice. Medieval deathbed grants were always suspect, for the obvious reason that they were likely to be the product of undue influence on a weakened mind. Although the dying man's eldest son and heir, Walter, confirmed the grant by his own charter, he may not have been able to arrange the public transfer of physical control (livery of seizin), which the law required in such cases.

John junior perhaps understood the reasons for the attack. His filial visit may even have been an unsuccessful effort to forestall the dissipation of his inheritance hopes. He may have been the youngest of the old man's sons. Or

19. John senior had held a knight's fee in Yeovil on which there had been a concord in the court of King John while he was count of Mortain, another indication of John's considerable influence in the southwest before his accession. Cf. Chadwyck-Healey 1897, no. 293 (1225).

there may be other reasons why they, but not he, had received portions while the father was still vigorous. Any residual uncertainty about his situation disappeared when Walter de Turbervill swiftly married the widow Alice. On Saturday, August 7, John was back at the Woolcombe house, ostensibly perhaps to claim as his expected inheritance the house and its half fee of land. (The youngest son, or hearth-child, sometimes received his father's home as a customary portion.) He found Walter in possession and at home. Whether he knew already that he was not to have "his" property or learned this only on arrival, we do not know. But the house was torched, and many of its contents lost. According to Walter's tale in court later, he escaped from the burning house and, upon finding John outside, realized that John and his force ("cum vi sua") were responsible. Walter claimed that six of his men were killed that day. Some of John's companions at the house-burning had already been outlawed in the shire court at the suit of Walter's associate, Robert de Lit, concerning a suit for £5-0-11d. Walter's own appeal specified that he had lost in the fire charters to the value of £100, adding that, on top of all this, John and his companions had taken such other chattels as they wished.

In due course, John junior initiated several lawsuits of his own relating to these events. He brought an assize of mort d'ancestor against Walter and Alice for his father's half fee at Woolcombe. To meet this claim, the couple produced in court the deathbed charter and its confirmation. John's case seems to have been the obvious one, that Alice had had her grant drafted as pleased her but had entered the land while it was in her custody anyway, that is, without proper livery of seizin before John senior's death. John junior would not answer as to the charters until he had obtained his seizin, since they related to the right and so ought not to stand in the way of an assize that sought only his father's seizin.[20] Successive adjournments deferred judgment until a day shared by the appeals. He also sued the couple, apparently at the same time, for detinue of two royal charters that ought to have been in Alice's custody and five hauberks apparently needed for the discharge of royal service obligations. These were the essential symbols of his birthright. Walter and Alice defended each charge. Alice had indeed had the charters, but they were lost when the house was burnt down. As for the hauberks, there had only been the one that the old man had given to another of his sons along with £10 worth of land seven years before he died. To this John responded that Walter should accept responsibility for the char-

20. The hearing (Oct. Michaelmas, 1200) is recorded on three rolls, and the entries from two of these are printed in *CRR* (i.271, 356). Neither makes the actual plea fully clear, so I have combined them to make the best sense I could.

ters since he admitted they were lost while in his possession; he went on to assert that his father had previously taken all five hauberks on one Welsh expedition, in fulfillment of his tenurial obligations. At a later hearing, Walter first tried to gain further delay, then left without the court's permission and consequently lost the case by default. John's appeal against Walter (whose circumstantial detail reads like a trespass plaint) was accompanied by two others brought by associates against two of Walter's henchmen for their share in the *maleficium*. All three rather unusually obtained a hearing coram rege. Walter, after the usual general denial of all charges, went on to deny proper summons (he was not given a day to answer, apparently a plea for time to prepare his defense) and offered 40s. for a jury of the countryside. The justices adjourned proceedings until mid-Lent for judgment; they also requested to know from the chief justiciar, Geoffrey f. Peter, how the case came before them. Successive adjournments then took it into the Michaelmas term of 1201, when the parties requested, and were granted, a further adjournment into Hilary 1202 and a license to concord. And that is the last we hear of the matter.

MARTELL V. PARIS (1200–1202)

PKJ i.3250; *CRR* i.292–93, 382; *PKJ* i.3352, 3419; *CRR* i.425; *Pipe Roll 3 John*, 18. Cf. Stenton 1926, 249, 1056 (p. 182); *Pipe Roll 5 John*, 99 (Lincs., coram rege and eyre)

Martin Martell and Peter f. John of Paris were prominent Lincoln citizens. Martin accused Peter of breaking and entering his house at Canwick just a mile south of the city. Peter and his cohorts had assaulted and robbed him of a large sum of money (either 47m. or 67m.) and the title deeds of his lands. This was but one incident in a continuing dispute. Peter's defense recalled that a previous appeal on the same facts had been settled by royal license on terms by which each of the appellees had to wage his law thirty-six-handed. But when he arrived on the day as arranged, with his large company ready and prepared to swear their oaths, Martin quitclaimed them and went on to take their homages, exchange with each the kiss of peace, and pardon them "all his ill will that he had held toward them." Martin admitted that this had happened but added that he was appealing now precisely because Peter's side did not keep the bargain. That admission killed Martin's case; the court held his appeal null and amerced him. This did not end the matter, whose stakes seemed so high to parties inevitably in regular contact with each other in the public life of the city. The citizens of Lincoln as a body are recorded on the 1201 pipe roll as having offered 700m. and seven palfreys for the confirmation of their liberties granted by the king "in order that they should be quit of Martin Martell's appeal for breach of the peace." And Martin's request at the eyre "to have his charters heard" was probably also related to the same affair.

RICHARD, BASTARD SON OF DUKE ROBERT CURTHOSE, DEATH OF (1100)
Orderic v.282

Orderic leaves anonymous the "certain knight" whose shaft accidentally killed Richard the Bastard while hunting in the New Forest. He at once fled in great distress to Lewes Priory and escaped the expected "double vengeance" of the royal youth's kinsmen and friends by becoming a monk there and expiating his guilt for the killing with monastic penance. He certainly seems to have expected violent retribution from their "rancor," which the claim of accident ("casu") might not suffice to prevent.

ROSS V. TIDD (1194–99)
Maitland 1891, 35; *RCR* i.29, 57–58 (Lincs.); cf. *Pipe Roll 3 John*, 13

These two substantial Lincolnshire families had been at loggerheads for some years before this lawsuit emerged. An earlier lawsuit may have been either symptom or cause of the enmity. In the course of this dispute, angry words were spoken. Adam of Tidd (Tydd St. Mary) had twice, according to William de Ross, threatened him that he would not long enjoy his father's fine arms and buildings. This disturbed William enough for him to have persuaded royal justices at the trial to formally proclaim the king's peace between the parties. Nevertheless, an armed assault occurred in which houses of the father (Richard) were burned down, his reeve and others from the house were killed, and the family's weapons were seized. William brought against Adam, three of his brothers, and his stepfather, Hamo Dot, an appeal that eventually reached the royal justices at Westminster. (It was already in progress in 1194, when Adam assembled an impressive group of eighteen manucaptors from the top levels of county society to guarantee his appearance in court.) The assault party had, William claimed, come from, and returned to, Adam's house. Adam had planned the deed along with Hamo and others, even if he did not personally participate. Adam denied all, adding that he had in any event given peace only to William and not to the others involved. He also offered the king 10m. for a jury of two shires on the issue of whether the appeal was brought out of hatred (de odio et athia). Since no verdict is known, the parties may possibly have come to an agreement, of which there are conceivable traces on the pipe rolls (e.g., *Pipe Roll 3 John*, 13).

Stenton 1930, 64, 66 (Northampton eyre, 1202)

Comment: ibid., xxv; but not noticed in Lady Stenton's 1948 discussion of justiciars' writs, *PKJ* i.5–33; not apparently noticed by Hurnard 1969 or De Haas and Hall 1970, lxvi–lxx.

Hugh, son of Walter the priest of Grafton Regis, in Cleyley Hundred, Northants., was responsible for the death of Roger Rumbaud at some undetermined date late in Richard I's reign. This seems undisputed; whether the circumstances constituted culpable homicide is less clear. Roger's sister Lucy, and/or his brother(?) Robert, duly appealed Hugh of the deed at successive county courts until he was outlawed. Hugh never appeared to defend himself. Instead, he took steps to obtain a pardon from the king, probably Richard I, whom he had to pursue abroad for the purpose. (Or perhaps he was already serving in the army.) Only then dare he return home to brandish his pardon and a writ from the justiciar to the sheriff ordering his readmission to the (king's) peace.[21]

We are now in 1198 or later, since the justiciar was Geoffrey f. Peter. The wording of his missive is very revealing. He had, he says, received a written order from the king "in auxilium ad pacem reformandum inter ipsum [H.] et parentes interfecti," to help make peace between the parties. So, he says, he now orders the sheriff first to implement that help to Hugh, then to report back by letter what he has done, "quoniam tenemur illud domino Regi significare," since he has to keep the king informed. Clearly, both the king and justiciar thought themselves under a duty to promote peacemaking in the kingdom even at the village level; the parties involved were by no means important people, nor obviously exceptional in other ways.

Hugh's two documents were read aloud at a full meeting of the shire, which then directed him to find sureties to guarantee that he would in future remain within the king's peace. He went off promising to do this but never returned, as he should have done, to give the court the sureties' names. One may guess that he was unable to find anyone prepared to stand surety for him, local sentiment was against him, and he was felt to be guilty of wrongful homicide, as ordinary people understood the matter. But perhaps fear or sympathy for the Rumbauds dissuaded potential guarantors. Certainly, the dead man's kin appears to have been caught napping, absent

21. This is no routine writ, certainly no writ "of course." Royal property (a hunting lodge?) in Grafton Regis may explain the king's interest. Perhaps the fact that these letters are not strictly a writ explains their neglect. The authorization "per breve domini Regis de ultra mare" contrasts with writs authorized by an ordinary royal justice.

from court on this occasion. When they realized that Hugh, their enemy, had returned to the area, Robert Rumbaud came to the very next court with one Geoffrey f. Turstan, who declared that he would appeal Hugh of the death should he ever see him. Geoffrey's interest is easily explained. He had himself fled after Roger's death, for which flight (and possible criminal involvement) the same jurors presented him to the eyre. Not surprisingly, Hugh did not appear in court.

The circumstances of Hugh's readmission to the peace were explained to the angry Rumbaud family. The shire then decided to commission a hundred sergeant to find Hugh and produce him at a later court. Hugh was pretty obviously at risk again, quite possibly as much from Rumbaud vengeance as any royal action (so Stenton 1930, xxv). He made himself scarce so that the sergeant had to report he could not find him. Geoffrey ostentatiously produced himself all prepared to begin his appeal. The shire gave Hugh a further chance at the following court, with the same negative result. When this procedure had been repeated at the third court, the shire pronounced that since Hugh was unwilling to appear to the king's peace, he should once again bear the wolf's head, be deemed an outlaw.

At the next eyre in 1202, the hundred jury included an account of the matter among their presentments. A double outlawry for the same deed must have looked highly irregular to the justices. They questioned the shire representatives, who told the story reproduced above. Ought the justices to believe it? They remained suspicious and suspended judgment on the coroners and hundred jurors. They must have been very aware both how easily the locals might concoct a plausible story in order to protect their friends, and how difficult it was for outsiders from Westminster to be sure of the facts of such an affair.

The case documents a stage in the developing common-law treatment of homicide pardons at which the kin's rights seem still ominously close to blood vengeance.

ST. EVROUL V. L'AIGLE (1136)

Orderic vi.458–62

L'Aigle partisans pursued the abbey of St. Evroul and its men for gain even—to Orderic's horror—in Whit week. The townsmen seized twelve of those responsible (out of thirty) and hanged them from an oak tree. The infuriated L'Aigle party came together to avenge their fellows by attacking the town of St. Evroul. The monks feared they would be the next target. They tearfully sought to excuse themselves with the attackers, and offered justice and due compensation for the crime, as they termed it, of hanging the seven attackers. But L'Aigle men were now so blinded by fury that they refused and instead threatened to knock the monks off their horses. Lacking all reverence for God, they started to take vengeance on the innocent monks and their dependants. But the direction of the wind changed, thereby saving the monastic church from fire, and the L'Aigle side began to lose. Orderic took this as a sign of God's judgment on them and on their lord, Richer, for turning against his godparents, the monks. His deduction—that when heavily armed men fight against the simple and defenseless, they risk not merely defeat but opprobrium and derision—was apparently shared by some of the attackers, who were so shamed by taunts from the opposition that they broke down and publicly repented of their actions. The fact that God might be expected to punish men who sought wrongful vengeance was thus widely enough accepted as to play a part in the politics of such disputes.

STALWORTHMAN V. RUNTON HOLM (1261–69)

JUST 1/569A, m. 30 (Norfolk eyre, 1268–69); *CPR 1266–72*, 252 (8/18/1268)
Cited: Given 1977, 44

Trinity Sunday in late June of 1261 was fair time in Stow (Bardolph?), doubtless provoking a festive air of excitement and much drinking. Many villagers, taking their ease in a nearby field, were disturbed by the sudden appearance of John Loveday and his wife, shouting that they had been threatened by the men of Shouldham and pleading for assistance. Close upon their heels came John Stalworthman, exclaiming, "Where is that traitor, John Loveday? He's dead if I find him." Upon hearing this threat, Loveday tried to hide himself and his wife in the crowd. But Stalworthman pursued them, shouting and pushing people out of the way with his ax. One of those he hit (in the head) was Gregory ad Pontem. Gregory's father, Nicholas de Ponte, saw his son go down and rushed over to his aid. Finding himself hemmed into a corner and despairing of escape, so he later claimed, he hit Stalworthman in the head with his own ax and killed him.

Adam Stalworthman's daughter Beatrice appealed one Henry f. John of Runton Holm of the premeditated killing of her nephew, John, and accused eleven others of aiding the killer. A jury later acquitted Henry at the 1268–69 eyre. But Beatrice had not been idle in the meantime. The trial jurors told the justices that, abetted by the dead man's brother, Richard, she had accepted more than £11 to abandon the appeal. The circumstances surrounding this concord recall the feud settlements of an earlier age. Such deals were certainly illegal, and the court ordered her arrest. Her accomplice came in and made fine for 4m.; then she too fined for 1m., an indication of how local opinion rated what was presumably a family initiative. Finally, Nicholas de Ponte of Wiggenhall obtained his royal pardon on the justices' report that he had acted in self-defense.

THE STANSTEAD CONCORD (CA. 1150–78)

Ransford 1989, no. 368

One may deduce from the concord (our sole evidence) that the precipitating event in this story was an attack by armed men on a house in the manner of those found in appeal cases on the early plea rolls a generation later and discussed in chapter 6. Among four men killed was Julian f. William. His brother, a clerk called Laurence, may or may not have initiated a formal appeal for his death. The settlement Laurence made with Sir Simon of Stanstead just names Simon's brother as one of the actual killers. This document reflects an occasion that patently involved kin groups on either side and enmeshed a fair number of the local gentry as well.

Sir Simon promised to have three masses celebrated each year for Julian's soul, to feed one pauper on every day remaining in his own life, and to donate a small packet of land and meadow to the Hospitallers in perpetual alms, free from both secular service and any claims from his own heirs. He then did homage to the cleric, Laurence, along with forty knights (some of them described as his kinsmen, others as unqualified *amici*), and swore a carefully drafted oath. This stated that (1) he had not killed Julian with his own hand; (2) he had not come to the "hospicium" where the brothers then dwelt to cause their death; and (3) when he heard of Julian's death, "he was more saddened [condoluit] by the news than joyful [letatus]." (The wording chosen implies that he shared the pain of the dead man's kindred and felt no inclination to gloat over them. It evokes the passions roused by the killing, including the fear of being shamed among the victim's friends.) He then promised "in the hand" of the prior of the Hospitallers in England, on behalf of both himself and his whole party ("gens"), that he would observe the terms of the peace. I imagine that he made this undertaking on his knees or in some previously agreed pose of submission and humiliation. However, when Laurence made a similar promise for his side (again "gens"), there was a significant addition: he expressly excluded from the amnesty all who had actually committed the homicide. The fact that the document then names the alleged killers—among whom was Sir Simon's own brother—suggests that he would have been unable to make this peace had he been an accomplice. Clearly, Laurence's friends expected to take physical vengeance on any killers who fell into their hands. There is no sign that any of those involved paid the slightest attention to either royal justice or any public officials. The final sentence before witnesses are named expresses the positive outcome of the deal: "In this way, Laurence and Simon and their kinsmen became *concordes et amici* for ever, except for those whom we excluded above."

The settlement seems to have been effective. Both principals lived on into the 1220s (Ransford 1989, nos. 318, 367, 370, 378), by which time Waltham possessed a substantial interest in the village, still known as Stanstead Abbots, and the whole Wanchy fee (from which Simon held) there. Laurence had been on pilgrimage to Jerusalem (1184/1201), conceivably with the Third Crusade.

The document remains unique. Private agreements not concerning landed property are indeed rare. Laymen seldom recorded their peace settlements in writing without stern clerical pressure. And if they did, only the very great possessed safe places in which to preserve documents (cf. CUSIN V. FITZJOHN above). But few churchmen would bother much about such a document once the immediate crisis had passed; unlike title deeds, they had no cash value for the house's saint. This one was passed over by two early cartulary compilers before gaining inclusion in a fourteenth-century cartulary, more than a century after the event. It shows signs of careful drafting, possibly by someone with a schools training (witness the phrase "plus inde condoluit quam letatus est"). One possibility is that Prior Roger acted as mediator and helped settle the peace terms, whereupon he or one of his Hospitaller scribes composed the text too. But Waltham was much closer to Stanstead (seven miles), probably already eyeing property there, and so perhaps happy to offer a convenient archive in which to conserve the all-important concord in the absence of any nearby Hospitaller house. The document's very survival is fortuitous.

TOSNY V. BEAUMONT (CA. 1030–63)

Orderic ii.40, 90, 92, 104–6, 124; iii.88; iv.212–17
Comment: Douglas 1964, 85; White 1940, 87; Chibnall 1984, 195; Searle 1988, 185–89; Fletcher 1989, 78–79; Bennett 1998, 135–36

Orderic never tells this story directly; instead, he alludes to it obliquely in a manner favorable to the Tosny side as friends of his own abbey and themselves founders of Conches. Robert (junior) de Grandmesnil had entered St. Evroul shortly after 1050, lamenting the "dangers of secular warfare" by which his father and others had died fighting bravely against their enemies. The death of his father, alongside Roger de Tosny and his sons, sometime around 1040, had prompted Robert to choose the monk's higher form of warfare. But his decision did not end the enmities. According to Orderic, Earl Roger of Montgomery and Mabel his wife took advantage of disturbed times after the French king's death to plot against the life of Roger (II) de Tosny; in the early 1060s, they brought to Duke William unsupported accusations against de Tosny and his close associates. Orderic's own abbot, implicated for injudicious words spoken in private against the duke, fled from fear that the duke's *malivolentia* would lead to physical retaliation against him and his kin. Another who went into exile at this time was Arnold d'Echaffour. He avenged the wrong of his expulsion and effective disherison over three years by harrying the area, including his own old castle at Lieuvin and even St. Evroul. This became a full *werra* waged with the help of Arnold's Giroie kinsmen and other men summoned from various regions. Duke William could not afford such disorder in the midst of his own campaigns against Brittany and Maine. Powerful voices among his barons counseled him to recall the exiles and broker a peace that presumably suited all participants.

UPSALL V. FOSSARD (CA. 1183–1203, ? 1183–89)

EYC ix.81–82

Arnold of Upsall and Adam Fossard were substantial gentry who held abutting lands in the North Yorkshire moors. Friction between them arose from conflicting claims to common rights in Killingwith wood, which lay between their properties. We know about their "magna discordia" both from the narrative memorandum of a monk of Byland (the house that, in the long term, was to acquire all the disputed land and more) and from Adam's charter made close to the time of its settlement. The argument seems to have been about timber for building rather than mere firewood. In this kind of rough country, suitable trees were quite rare and valuable enough to provoke strong feelings and even violence. Only some element of real conflict in the woods can explain the mediation of *amici* and kinsmen needed to achieve the settlement. The terms were as follows: Each was responsible for conserving growing trees "in good peace" until some were needed for building purposes. They could only give or sell wood by mutual consent. This "concord" was made "on the moor" in the presence of William de Stuteville, their common lord, four knights, and many others. William, a baron who served three kings at different times as (among other offices) sheriff of more than one county and, between 1188 and 1194, as a royal justice (*EYC* ix.9–12), was clearly one of the *amici*. He was cousin to Adam's wife, who had made the peace. The occasion was, indeed, probably understood as a meeting of William's (honorial) court. His heir, acting as lord, later confirmed the settlement by charter (*EYC* ix.60, ?1224–33).

Adam's sealed charter, preserved in the Byland archive, should be supplemented from the monks' own account, compiled with the help of oral memories. Originally Arnold and his men were supposed to have only pasture rights in the disputed wood but only took wood there "per eschapiam," meaning (I think) that Adam neither knew nor approved. The memorandum reveals a marriage agreement unmentioned in Adam's charter.[22] For making his peace settlement, Arnold was to receive Juliana, Adam's sister, as his wife, and Adam endowed the marriage with full rights of common in the wood over everything save timber, for which the couple still needed his license. "And all these things were brought to closure amicably and in peace," the narrative recounts, and the two principals "lived to the end of their lives in great peace and love."

Two final comments: Neither William de Stutevill, for all his connections, nor anyone else appears to have felt the need for any royal confirmation of the deal. Second, neither of these documents would have survived had the property and its title deeds not passed to the monks of Byland.[23]

WARIN OF WALCOT (MID-TWELFTH CENTURY)

Stenton 1940, no. 390
Comment: ibid., lxv–lxvi

This remarkable story was so unexpected in context that the plea-roll clerk did not allow enough space on his roll and had to struggle to find room. It emerged from an action of right, as the quite exceptional special verdict of a grand assize at the Coventry eyre of 1221.

Warin of Walcot was initially an honest knight errant ("miles . . . itinerans et probus") in the Warwickshire of Stephen's reign. One night he came to stay at the house of Robert of Shuckburgh, on the eastern edge of the county, a few miles south of Rugby, near the Leicestershire border. There he met his host's daughter, the (presumably) fair Isabel, and in true romance style, fell in love with her and sought her hand. Alas, neither Robert nor his son and heir, William, approved the match. Our hero was not deterred. He left the house, only to return soon after with a whole mob of supporters, who abducted Isabel by force against her will (so we are told), without assent from either herself or her father.[24] Warin held his prize a long time, while earning his living as a robber. The couple may be said to have lived as man

22. There probably was also a charter under Arnold's seal, now lost (because deposited with Adam and not at Byland), which may have differed significantly from Adam"s.

23. Adam seems to have held land in socage of Byland for some time before this incident and later released it to the monks (Greenway 1972, xl n. 5 and nos. 42, 362).

24. The only doubt that the story was one of nonconsensual abduction comes in the jurors' description of Warin's earlier behavior. They say he "adamavit et captavit" her, which may imply that he had won her heart. But they may have been fans of romance too and were reporting some seventy years or more after the event.

and wife, since a son was born and named Warin after his father. (The jurors of 1221 were uncertain that they were ever married, which may represent an imposition in hindsight of the then new Alexandrine marriage rules.) Stephen died and the new king, Henry II, proclaimed his peace. This was not good news for Warin. He could not abandon his trade as a robber, even when this became far less lucrative and he fell into poverty. Complaints about the knightly bandit reached the king ("auditis de eo clamoribus"), who ordered his arrest. Unsurprisingly, the first attempt to take him failed. Warin fled to a marshy area north of Shuckburgh and kept his liberty there for a while. Captured at last, he was brought before the king himself at Northampton to receive his day in court coram rege. We hear of no defense. The king consulted his barons in proper manner before delivering a sentence that sent Warin to the pillory, where he died.

With Warin dead, Isabel could return to her father's house. Doubtless she had no alternative. Our narrative strongly implies that her welcome was dependent on her having been an unwilling victim of abduction. In time, a more acceptable suitor, a local man called William, sought her hand, was approved, and duly received her in marriage along with a modest dowry of four virgates of land. The plaintiff (demandant) of our action of right, Henry, was the legitimate issue of this union. With the principal actors long since dead, his opponent was Robert f. Warin, the errant knight's grandson and Henry's half-nephew. That Henry sued the writ suggests that Robert had taken possession of at least part of the land. The grand assize jurors explain why Robert had put his case on them: Isabel had survived her (second?) husband, William. While he still lived, however, she had persuaded him to grant jointly with herself half a virgate from their small estate to Robert, her grandson by her (first?) husband Sir Warin. The jurors were nevertheless sure that Isabel had died in seizin of the whole four virgates, which she held (they report) first as her dowry and then, after her husband's death, as her inheritance, since he had no other heir except her. That too is a trifle mysterious, since Henry can only be suing on the basis that he was his father's heir.

When facts like these reach a grand assize, the jurors can be excused for declining to do their duty and rule who had greater right to the disputed land. This assize merely narrated the facts as it saw them and left the court to make the decisions. In the event, the parties saved the justices the trouble by concording on terms that seem to confirm the plausibility of the whole story. Robert f. Warin abandoned his claim in return for 5m. plus confirmation of his right to the half virgate. Maybe this was the extent of the whole dispute. Normally in such cases, somebody had to pay the king for license to concord. On this occasion, however, the justices gave their permission free, "for God," deeming both parties to be too poor.

Lady Stenton, author of *The English Woman in History* (1957), remarked upon the "surprising fact" that one finds such a "fresh account of a love story" in such a source. Modern readers may find it equally surprising that Lady Stenton did not think to consider the abduction as the rape of an unwilling virgin, though that is how the story is told. The whole tale would look and feel very comfortable in one of the contemporary romances whose ambiguities have been explored by feminists of a more recent vintage (e.g., Gravdal 1991). Yet there could be a love story here; perhaps the jurors colored their version to exclude Robert f. Warin's claim to the whole four virgates. We shall never know.

Two points should interest legal historians. We are presented, in proceedings coram rege from the early years of Henry II, with some kind of appeal plaint quite explicitly described as being against the new king's peace, and leading to a judgment of life and members. But we hear of no accuser prepared to set his life at risk in proof of the accusations. Was this was an "office" prosecution, pursued by the itinerant king himself? Perhaps such prosecutions helped to provoke the thoughts that culminated in the Assize of Clarendon in 1166, with its innovative system of public prosecution. The second noteworthy point is the sentence itself. Was the pillory imposed because the king hesitated to judge a free man to death in such circumstances, or was it perhaps understood as a concealed death sentence?

WAVER V. ARGENTAIN AND MENTMORE (1194)

Maitland 1891, 18–20; *RCR* i.60, 100; cf. *RCR* i.6

The Waver family derived their toponymic from Cesters Over (near Monks Kirby, Warwicks.), an estate held from the Camvilles within the honor of Mowbray (Greenway 1972, 263 [10]; cf. ibid., 81, 192). Night was already falling by the time that Richard de Waver and his entourage reached his Northamptonshire property in the village of Byfield (Wardon Hundred). He had expected to lodge with his reeve, Robert Thwerteful, and may have been anxious to reach shelter in the knowledge that old enemies, the Argentain family, lived nearby. But Robert demurred; he could not offer him hospitality because his entire household was deeply engaged in brewing beer that night. Robert then diverted him to a neighbor's house. Richard asked for white sheets for the bed, but the reeve said that his were elsewhere; he offered (he later said) to go and get them. In fact he sent word of Richard's arrival to the brothers Argentain, "whom he knew to be [his lord's] enemies." Richard was awakened in the middle of the night by Argentain's arrival—a party of twenty-eight in all. The group included men of at least three different lords, Robert de Nevill, Robert Capun, and Hugh de Herdeberg. They wounded Richard (in the shoulder), as well as several of his men, and killed two people (one, his nephew). The attackers took away the corpses—in sacks provided by a helpful villein.

In a murder appeal, the first step was to show the bodies to the coroner. Obviously, Richard could not do so. His first effort to bring an appeal was rejected by a jury. Richard then successfully complained to the justiciar that this inquisition verdict had been fraudulent, due to bribery. He was granted a royal order to arrest the appellees, from which followed the proceedings whose record provides most of our details.

The enmity can be traced back at least to the start of the reign and the preparations for the Third Crusade. Richard, a cleric in deacon's orders, did not go, but his (elder?) brother, William, did. And William died in the process. William's preparations for the crusade affected relations with the Argentain family in two different ways.

First, he had had to make respectable dispositions for the safety of his wife and her land during his expedition. William's wife, Maud, was an heiress in the royal gift. William had paid 220m. for her hand. The way Richard told the story later, William had committed her with her lands into the custody of her kinsman, Reginald of Argentain. He requited this trust by breaking many of the rules governing such custodies. He wrongfully took for himself 150m. worth of produce from the land and then, without royal license, married off Maud (by that time a widow, I hope) to his own brother Roger. Reginald told a different tale. He claimed to have taken the land on a crusading lease, which would imply a loan (toward traveling expenses?) to William as lessor, repayable on his safe return. It was not he but his lord, Robert de Nevill, he said, who gave Maud to Roger. Richard was in any event already suing Roger for Maud's abduction and his intrusion into her land, in what reads from the roll like a trespass plaint. Roger's defense denied that Maud was a royal ward, confirmed his brother's story, and summoned his lord Robert de Nevill to confirm the story as his charter warranty required.

Richard also remembered William as having deposited his warhorse with Henry of Mentmore, another of the 1194 appellees, and now sued to get it back, pledging all his property that he would convict William of unjust detinue. But Henry claimed that he had only exchanged a trotting nag ("runcinum trotantem") for a palfrey. His point—that William wanted a mount more suitable for the journey—makes more sense than abandoning an expensive warhorse that would be needed for battle.

Were these two disputes alone sufficient to explain an enmity worth a murderous night attack? The different lords of the two sides are, very likely, also part of the story. The litigation certainly includes at least four appeals carried over from the shire, plus two other plaints that look more trespassory in nature. Even in the appeals, Richard evaded the risks of battle by pleading his clerical status, with his disability (mayhem) as an additional excuse. This would have compelled his opponents to undergo either an ordeal or battle against the vigorous kinsmen of those who had been killed. They met the threat by adding to their general denial a defense as against an excommunicate, which may imply yet further proceedings earlier in a church court. All this litigation had two effects: to fan the flames of enmity, and to ensure that everyone in the area understood what was happening.

BIBLIOGRAPHY

Abels, Richard P. 1988. *Lordship and Military Obligation in Anglo-Saxon England.* Berkeley: University of California Press.

Abu-Lughod, Lila, and Catherine A. Lutz. 1990. "Introduction: Emotion, Discourse, and the Politics of Everyday Life." In *Language and the Politics of Emotion*, edited by L. A. Abu-Lughod and C. A. Lutz, 1–23. Cambridge: Cambridge University Press.

Ælfric, Abbot of Eynsham. 1967–68. *The Homilies of Ælfric: A Supplementary Collection.* Edited by J. C. Pope. Early English Text Society, o.s. 259–60. London: Oxford University Press.

Althoff, Gerd. 1990. *Verwandte, Freunde, unde Getreue: Zum politischen Stellenwert der Gruppenbindungen im früheren Mittelalter.* Darmstadt: Wissenschaftliche Buchgesellschaft.

——. 1992. *Amicitiae und Pacta: Bündnis, Einung, Politik und Gebetsgedenken im beginnenden 10. Jahrhundert.* Hanover: Hahnsche Buchhandlung.

——. 1997. "Das Privileg der *deditio*: Formen gütlicher Konfliktbeendigung in der mittelalterlichen Adelsgesellschaft." In *Spielregeln in der Politik im Mittelalter*, 99–125. Darmstadt: Primus.

——. 1998a. *"Amicitiae* [Friendships] as Relationships between States and People." In *Debating the Middle Ages: Issues and Readings*, edited by Barbara H. Rosenwein and Lester Little, 191–210. Malden, Mass.: Blackwell.

——. 1998b. *"Ira Regis:* Prolegomena to a History of Royal Anger." In *Anger's Past: The Social Uses of an Emotion in the Middle Ages*, edited by Barbara H. Rosenwein, chap. 3. Ithaca, N.Y.: Cornell University Press.

Amt, Emilie. 1993. *The Accession of Henry II in England: Royal Government Restored, 1149–59.* Woodbridge, U.K.: Boydell.

Anglo-Norman Dictionary. 1992. Edited by William Rothwell, Louise W. Stone, and T. B. Reid. London: Modern Humanities Research Association.

Attenborough, F. L. 1922. *The Laws of the Earliest English Kings.* Cambridge: Cambridge University Press.

Augustine. 1958. *Questiones in Heptateuchum.* Edited by I. Fraipont. Corpus Christianorum, Series Latina, 33. Turnholt: Brepols.

Axelrod, Robert. 1984. *The Evolution of Cooperation.* New York: Basic Books.

Axelrod, Robert, and Robert O. Keohane. 1986. "Achieving Cooperation under Anarchy: Strategies and Institutions." In *Cooperation under Anarchy*, edited by Kenneth A. Oye, 226–54. Princeton, N.J.: Princeton University Press.

Axtmann, Roland. 1993. "The Formation of the Modern State: The Debate in the Social Sciences." In *National Histories and European History*, edited by Mary Fulbrook, 21–45. Boulder, Colo.: Westminster Press.

Baldwin, John W. 1970. *Masters, Princes, and Merchants: The Social Views of Peter the Chanter and His Circle.* 2 vols. Princeton, N.J.: Princeton University Press.

Barlow, Frank. 1983. *William Rufus.* London: Methuen.

Barraclough, Geoffrey, ed. 1988. *The Charters of the Anglo-Norman Earls of Chester, c. 1071–1237.* Record Society of Lancashire and Cheshire, vol. 126. Chester, U.K.: Record Society of Lancashire and Cheshire.

Barrow, Julia. 1999. "Friends and Friendship in Anglo-Saxon Charters." In *Friendship in Medieval Europe*, edited by Julian Haseldine, 106–23. Sutton: Stroud.

Bartlett, Robert. 1998. " 'Mortal Enmities': The Legal Aspect of Hostility in the Middle Ages." T. Jones Pierce Lecture. Aberystwyth: University of Wales Press.

Barton, J. L. 1993. "The Mystery of Bracton." *Journal of Legal History* 14: 1–142.

Bates, R. H. 1983. "The Preservation of Order in Stateless Societies: A Reinterpretation of Evans-Pritchard's *The Nuer.*" In *Essays in the Political Economy of Rural Africa*, chap. 1. Cambridge: Cambridge University Press.

Bateson, M., ed. 1904. *Borough Customs.* Vol. 1. Selden Society, vol. 18. London: Bernard Quaritch.

Bean, J. M. W. 1989. *From Lord to Patron: Lordship in Later Medieval England.* Manchester: Manchester University Press.

Beckerman, John S. 1981. "Adding Insult to *Injuria*: Affronts to Honor and the Origins of Trespass." In *On the Laws and Customs of England: Essays in Honor of Samuel E. Thorne*, edited by Morris Arnold, Thomas A. Green, Sally Scully, and Stephen D. White, 159–81. Chapel Hill: University of North Carolina Press.

Bede's Ecclesiastical History of the English People. 1969. Edited by B. Colgrave and R. A. B. Mynors. Oxford: Clarendon Press.

Bellamy, J. G. 1998. *The Criminal Trial in Later Medieval England.* Toronto: University of Toronto Press.

Bennett, Matthew. 1998. "Violence in Eleventh-Century Normandy: Feud, Warfare and Politics." In *Violence and Society in the Early Medieval West*, edited by Guy Halsall, 126–40. Woodbridge, U.K.: Boydell.

Benoît de Sainte-Maure. 1998. *Le roman de Troie.* Edited and translated by Emmanuèle Baumgartner and Francoise Vielliard. Lettres Gothiques. Paris: Livre de Poche.

Beowulf and the Fight at Finnsburg. 1950. Edited by F. Klaeber. 3d ed. Boston: Heath.

Berger, Adolf. 1953. *Encyclopedic Dictionary of Roman Law.* Transactions of the American Philosophical Society, n.s., vol. 43, pt. 2. Philadelphia: American Philosophical Society.

Bessinger, Jess. 1978. *A Concordance to the Old English Poetic Records.* Ithaca, N.Y.: Cornell University Press.

Beverley Smith, Llinos. 1991. "Disputes and Settlements in Medieval Wales: The Role of Arbitration." *English Historical Review* 106: 835–60.

Bezemer, Kees. 1997. *What Jacques Saw: Thirteenth-Century France through the Eyes of*

Jacques de Revigny, Professor of Law at Orleans. Ius Commune, Sonderheft 99. Frankfurt am Main: Klosterman.

Bible Moralisée: Codex Vindobonensis 2554, Vienna, Österreichischen Nationalbibliothek. 1995. Edited by Gerald B. Guest. London: Harvey Miller.

Black, Donald. 1989. *Sociological Justice.* New York: Oxford University Press.

Blake, E. O., ed. 1962. *Liber Eliensis.* Camden Society, 3d ser., 92. London: Royal Historical Society.

Bloch, Marc. 1961. *Feudal Society.* Translated by L. A. Manyon. Chicago: University of Chicago Press.

Boehm, Christopher. 1984. *Blood Revenge: The Enactment and Management of Conflict in Montenegro and Other Tribal Societies.* Philadelphia: University of Pennsylvania Press.

———. 1985. "Execution within the Clan as an Extreme Form of Ostracism." *Social Science Information* 24: 309–21.

The Book of Fees. 1920–31. Edited by H. Maxwell-Lyte. 3 vols. London: H. M. Stationery Office.

Bosworth, J., and T. N. Toller. 1973. *An Anglo-Saxon Dictionary.* Oxford: Oxford University Press.

Bourdieu, Pierre. 1977. *Outline of a Theory of Practice.* Translated by Richard Nice. Cambridge: Cambridge University Press.

Boyer, Laurent, and Henri Roland. 1977–79. *Adages.* Vols. 2 and 3 of *Locutions latines et adages du droit français contemporain.* 3 vols. Lyon: L'Hermès.

Bracton, Henry de. 1968–80. *De legibus et consuetudinibus Angliae.* Edited and translated by George Edward Woodbine and Samuel E. Thorne. Cambridge, Mass.: Harvard University Press.

Bradley, S. A. J., trans. 1982. *Anglo-Saxon Poetry.* London: Everyman's Library.

Brand, Paul. 1978. "Oldcotes v. d'Arcy." In *Medieval Legal Records: Edited in Memory of C. A. F. Meekings,* edited by R. F. Hunnisett and J. B. Post, 64–113. London: H. M. Stationery Office.

———. 1990. " 'Multis Vigiliis Excogitatam et Inventam': Henry II and the Creation of the English Common Law." *Haskins Society Journal* 2: 177–222.

———. 1992a. *The Making of the Common Law.* London: Hambledon Press.

———. 1992b. *The Origins of the English Legal Profession.* Oxford: Blackwell.

———. 2001. "Ethical Standards for Royal Justices in England, c. 1175–1307." *University of Chicago Law School Roundtable* 8: 239–79.

Brevia Placitata. 1951. Edited by G. J. Turner and T. F. T. Plucknett. Selden Society, vol. 66 for 1947. London: Bernard Quaritch.

Britnell, R. H. 1979. "King John's Early Grants of Markets and Fairs." *English Historical Review* 94: 90–96.

Britton. 1983. The French text reissued, with an English translation, introduction, and notes, by Francis Morgan Nichols. 2 vols. Holmes Beach, Fla.: Gaunt. Original edition, Oxford: Clarendon Press, 1865.

Brooke, Z. N. 1931. *The English Church and the Papacy.* Cambridge: Cambridge University Press.

Brooks, Eric St. John, ed. 1936. *Register of the Hospital of St. John the Baptist without the New Gate, Dublin.* Dublin: Stationery Office.

——. 1953. *The Irish Cartularies of Llanthony Prima and Secunda.* Dublin: Stationery Office.

Brooks, F. W. 1933. "The Cinque Ports' Feud with Yarmouth in the Thirteenth Century." *Mariners Mirror* 19: 27–51.

Brown, Keith M. 1986. *Bloodfeud in Scotland, 1573–1625.* Edinburgh: John Donald.

Brown, R. Allen. 1950. "Framlingham Castle and Bigod, 1154–1216." *Proceedings of the Suffolk Institute of Archaeology* 25: 127–48. Reprinted in R. Allen Brown, *Castles, Conquest and Charters* (Woodbridge, U.K.: Boydell, 1989), 187–208.

Brundage, James A. 1995. *Medieval Canon Law.* London: Longman.

——. 1997. "The Calumny Oath and Ethical Ideals of Canonical Advocates." *Proceedings of the Ninth International Congress of Medieval Canon Law, Munich, 13–18 July 1992.* Monumenta Iuris Canonici, ser. C, Subsidia, vol. 10. Vatican.

Brunner, Otto. 1992. *Land and Lordship: Structures of Governance in Medieval Austria.* Translated by Howard Kaminsky and James Van Horn Melton. Philadelphia: University of Pennsylvania Press.

Bullough, Donald. 1991. "Friends, Neighbours and Fellow-Drinkers: Aspects of Community and Conflict in the Early Medieval West." First H. M. Chadwick Memorial Lecture, Department of Norse and Celtic, Cambridge University, Cambridge, U.K.

Calendar of Inquisitions Miscellaneous (Chancery). 1916. Vol. 1. London: H. M. Stationery Office.

Calendar of Inquisitions Post Mortem and Other Analogous Documents Preserved in the Public Record Office. 1904. Vol. 1. London: H. M. Stationery Office.

Calendar of Patent Rolls. 1901–. London: H. M. Stationary Office.

Calin, William. 1962. *The Old French Epic of Revolt.* Geneva: Librairies Droz and L. Minard.

Cam, Helen M. 1921. *Studies in the Hundred Rolls.* Oxford Studies in Social and Legal History, vol. 6. Oxford: Clarendon Press.

——. 1930. *The Hundred and the Hundred Rolls.* London: Methuen.

Campbell, Anne. 1993. *Men, Women and Aggression.* New York: Basic Books.

Campbell, James, general ed. 1982. *The Anglo-Saxons,* by James Campbell, Eric John, and Patrick Wormald. Oxford: Phaidon. Reprint, London: Penguin, 1991.

——. 1986. *Essays in Anglo-Saxon History.* London: Hambledon Press.

——. 1995a. "The Late Anglo-Saxon State: A Maximum View." *Proceedings of the British Academy* 87: 39–65.

——. 1995b. "The United Kingdom of England: The Anglo-Saxon Achievement." In *Uniting the Kingdom? The Making of British History,* edited by Alexander Grant and Keith J. Stringer, 31–47. London: Routledge.

Carpenter, D. A. 1990. *The Minority of Henry III.* Berkeley: University of California Press.

——. 1991. "Comment 2." *Past and Present* 131: 177–90.

——. 1992. "English Peasants in Politics, 1258–67." *Past and Present* 136: 3–42.

———. 1996. "Kingship and the Maintenance of Peace: England in the Twelfth and Thirteenth Centuries." In *England and Germany in the High Middle Ages*, edited by Alfred Haverkamp and Hanna Vollrath, 105–25. London: Oxford University Press and the German Historical Institute.

———. 2000. "The Second Century of English Feudalism." *Past and Present* 168: 30–71.

Cartularium Monasterii de Rameseia. 1864–93. Edited by William Henry Hart and Rev. Ponsonby A. Lyons. 3 vols. Rolls Series. London: Longman.

Chadwyck-Healey, Charles E. H., ed. 1897. *Somersetshire Pleas (Civil and Criminal), from the Rolls of the Itinerant Justices (Close of the Twelfth Century–41 Henry III)*. Somerset Record Society, vol. 11. London: n.p.

Cheney, Mary. 1984. "The Litigation between John Marshall and Archbishop Thomas Becket in 1164: A Pointer to the Origin of Novel Disseisin?" In *Law and Social Change in British History*, edited by J. A. Guy and H. G. Beale, 9–26. Royal Historical Society Studies in History, no. 40. London: Royal Historical Society.

Chibnall, M. 1984. *The World of Orderic Vitalis*. Oxford: Oxford University Press.

Chobham, Thomas de. 1968. *Thomae de Chobham Summa Confessorum*. Edited by Rev. F. Broomfield. Analecta Medievalia Namurcensia, 25. Louvain: Éditions Nauwelaerts.

———. 1988. *Summa De Arte Predicandi*. Edited by Franco Morenzoni. Corpus Christianorum, Continuatio Medievalis. Turnholt: Brepols.

Chrétien de Troyes. 1982. *Yvain*. Edited by M. Roques. Les classiques français du moyen age. Paris: Librairie Honoré Champion.

The Chronicle of Walter of Guisborough. 1957. Edited by Harry Rothwell. Camden Society, vol. 89. London: Royal Historical Society.

Clanchy, M. T. 1985. "Magna Carta and the Common Pleas." In *Studies in Medieval History Presented to R. H. C. Davis*, edited by Henry Mayr-Harting and R. I. Moore, 219–32. London: Hambledon Press.

———. 1993. *From Memory to Written Record: England, 1066–1307*. 2d ed. London: Blackwell.

———, ed. 1973. *The Roll and Writ File of the Berkshire Eyre of 1248*. Selden Society, vol. 90 for 1972–73. London: Selden Society.

Clay, Sir Charles. 1973. *Early Yorkshire Families*. Yorkshire Archaeological Society, Record Series, vol. 135. Wakefield: Yorkshire Archaeological Society.

Cockayne, O., ed. 1864–66. *Leechdoms, Wortcunning and Starcraft in Early England*. 3 vols. Rolls Series. London: Longman.

Collas, John P. 1964. "Problems of Language and Interpretation." In *Year Books of Edward II: 12 Edward II, Parts of Easter and Trinity, 1319*, edited by J. P. Collas, xiv–cxxviii. Selden Society, vol. 81. London: Selden Society.

Comaroff, John L., and Simon Roberts. 1981. *Rules and Processes: The Cultural Logic of Dispute in an African Context*. Chicago: University of Chicago Press.

Connolly, P., and G. Martin, eds. 1992. *The Dublin Merchant Guild Roll, c. 1190–1265*. Dublin: Dublin Corporation.

Cook, G. H. 1955. *The English Medieval Parish Church*. London: Phoenix House.

Cooper, Alan. Forthcoming. "The Rise and Fall of the Anglo-Saxon Law of the Highway." *Haskins Society Journal*.

Corpus Iuris Canonici. 1879. Edited by Emil Friedburg. 2 vols. Leipzig: Bernard Tauchnitz. Successive parts include *Decretum, X*, and *VI*.

Corpus Iuris Civilis. 1967–73. Edited by P. Krueger and T. Mommsen. 3 vols. Berlin: Weidmann.

Coss, Peter R. 1989. "Bastard Feudalism Revised." *Past and Present* 125: 27–64.

———. 1991a. *Lordship, Knighthood, and Locality: A Study in English Society c. 1180–c. 1280*. New York: Cambridge University Press for Past and Present Publications.

———. 1991b. "Reply." *Past and Present* 131: 190–203.

———, ed. 1980. *The Langley Cartulary*. Dugdale Society, vol. 32. Stratford-upon-Avon: Dugdale Society.

Cowdrey, H. E. J. 1970. "The Peace and Truce of God in the Eleventh Century." *Past and Present* 46: 42–67.

Cox, J. C. 1911. *The Sanctuaries and Sanctuary Seekers of Medieval England*. London: George Allen.

Crane, Susan. 1986. *Insular Romance: Politics, Faith and Culture in Anglo-Norman and Middle English Literature*. Berkeley: University of California Press.

Critchley, J. S. 1972. "The Early History of the Writ of Judicial Protection." *Bulletin of the Institute of Historical Research* 45: 196–213.

Crook, David. 1982. *Records of the General Eyre*. Public Record Office Handbooks no. 20. London: H. M. Stationery Office.

Crouch, David. 1986. *The Beaumont Twins: The Roots and Branches of Power in the Twelfth Century*. Cambridge: Cambridge University Press.

———. 1990. *William Marshall: Court, Career and Chivalry in the Angevin Empire, 1147–1219*. London: Longman.

———. 1991. "Comment 1." *Past and Present* 131: 165–77.

———. 1994. "A Norman *Conventio* and Bonds of Lordship in the Middle Ages." In *Law and Government in Medieval England and Normandy: Essays in Honour of Sir James Holt*, edited by George Garnett and John Hudson, 299–324. Cambridge: Cambridge University Press.

———. 2000. *The Reign of King Stephen, 1135–1154*. New York: Longman.

Curia Regis Rolls . . . Preserved in the Public Record Office. 1922–. 18 vols. to date. London: H. M. Stationery Office.

Daniel, Walter. 1950. *The Life of Ailred of Rievaulx*. Translated by F. M. Powicke. Nelsons Medieval Texts. London: Thomas Nelson and Sons.

Darlington, R. R., ed. 1928. *The Vita Wulfstani of William of Malmesbury*. Camden Society, n.s., 11. London: Royal Historical Society.

Davies, R. R. 1969. "The Survival of the Bloodfeud in Medieval Wales." *History* 54: 338–57.

Davis, Natalie Zemon. 1987. *Fiction in the Archives: Pardon Tales and Their Tellers in Sixteenth-Century France*. Stanford, Calif.: Polity Press.

Davis, R. H. C. 1990. *King Stephen, 1135–1154*. 3d ed. London: Longman.

Day, David. 1999. "Hwanan sio fæhð aras: Defining the Feud in Beowulf." *Philological Quarterly* 78: 77–95.

de Gryse, Louise M. 1976. "Some Observations on the Origin of the Flemish Bailiff (bailli): The Reign of Philip of Alsace." *Viator* 7: 243–94.

De Haas, Elsa, and G. D. G. Hall, eds. 1970. *Early Registers of Writs.* Selden Society, vol. 87. London: Bernard Quaritch.

Delisle, Léopold, ed. 1909–27. *Receuil des actes de Henri II, roi d'Angleterre et duc de Normandie, concernant les provinces françaises et les affaires de France.* Revised by Élie Berger. 4 vols. Paris: Librairie Klingsieck.

De Waal, Frans. 1989. *Peacemaking among Primates.* Cambridge: Harvard University Press.

——. 1996. *Good Natured: The Origins of Right and Wrong in Humans and Other Animals.* Cambridge: Harvard University Press.

De Zulueta, Francis, and Peter Stein. 1990. *The Teaching of Roman Law in England Around 1200.* Selden Society, supplementary ser., 8. London: Selden Society.

Dictionary of Medieval Latin from British Sources. 1975–. Edited by R. E. Latham. London: Oxford University Press for the British Academy. Appearing in fascicles.

Dictionnaire de droit canonique. 1935–65. Edited by R. Naz. Paris: Letouzey et Ané.

Dictionnaire des lettres françaises: Le moyen âge. 1992. Edited by R. Bossuat et al. Rev. ed. edited by G. Hasenohr and M. Zink. Paris: Fayard/Pochotèque.

Dobson, E. J. 1956. "The Word *Feud.*" *Review of English Studies* 7: 52–54.

Domesday Book. 1975–92. Edited by John Morris. 38 volumes. Chichester: Phillimore.

Donahue, Charles, Jr. 2003. "The Emergence of the Crime-Tort Distinction in England." In *Conflict in Medieval Europe,* edited by Peter Gorecki, 219–28. London: Ashgate.

Donahue, Charles, Jr., and Norma Adams, eds. 1981. *Select Cases from the Ecclesiastical Province of Canterbury, c. 1200–1301.* Selden Society, vol. 95 for 1978–79. London: Selden Society.

Douglas, David. 1964. *William the Conqueror: The Norman Impact upon England.* London: Eyre and Spottiswoode.

Douie, Decima L., and Hugh Farmer, eds. 1961–62. *Magna Vita Sancti Hugonis.* 2 vols. Nelsons Medieval Texts. Edinburgh: Thos. Nelson and Sons.

Duby, Georges. 1968. "The Diffusion of Cultural Patterns in Feudal Society." *Past and Present* 39: 3–10.

——. 1983. *The Knight, the Lady, and the Priest: The Making of Modern Marriage in Medieval France.* Translated by Barbara Bray. New York: Random House.

Du Cange, Charles Du Fresne. 1733–36. *Glossarium ad scriptores mediae et infimae latinitatis.* 6 vols. Paris: C. Osmont.

Dunham, W. H., Jr., ed. 1950. *Casus Placitorum.* Selden Society, vol. 69. London: Selden Society.

Eadmer. 1884. *Historia Novorum.* Edited by M. Rule. Rolls Series. London: Longman.

Earle, J., and C. Plummer, eds. 1892–99. *Two of the Saxon Chronicles Parallel.* 2 vols. Oxford: Clarendon Press.

Early Yorkshire Charters. 1914–65. Edited by W. Farrer and C. T. Clay. 13 vols. Yorkshire Archaeological Society, Record Series, extra ser. Edinburgh: Ballantyne, Hanson.

The Ecclesiastical History of Orderic Vitalis. 1969–78. Edited by Marjorie Chibnall. 6 vols. Oxford: Oxford University Press.

Ellickson, Robert C. 1991. *Order without Law: How Neighbors Settle Disputes*. Cambridge: Harvard University Press.

Ellis, Sir Henry. 1833. *A General Introduction to Domesday Book*. 2 vols. London: Record Commission. Reprint, London: Muller, 1971.

Elton, G. R. 1972. *Policy and Police: The Enforcement of the Reformation in the Age of Thomas Cromwell*. Cambridge: Cambridge University Press.

English Historical Documents. Vol. 1, *c. 500–1042*, 1979. Edited by D. Whitelock. 2d ed. Vol. 2, *1042–1189*, 1953. Edited by D. Douglas and G. Greenaway. London: Eyre and Spottiswoode.

Epp, Verena. 1999. *Amicitia: Zur Geschichte personaler, sozialer, politischer und Geistlicher Beziehungen im Frühen Mittelalter*. Monographien zur Geschichte des Mittelalters, Band 44. Stuttgart: Anton Hiersemann.

Evans-Pritchard, E. E. 1940. *The Nuer*. Oxford: Clarendon Press.

Fajans, Jane. 1985. "The Person in Social Context: The Social Character of Baining 'Psychology.'" In *Person, Self, and Experience: Exploring Pacific Ethnopsychologies*, edited by Geoffrey M. White and John Kirkpatrick, 367–97. Berkeley: University of California Press.

Farrer, William. 1923–25. *Honors and Knights' Fees*. 3 vols. London: Spottiswoode, Ballantyne.

Feet of Fines. CP 25, Public Record Office, London.

Fellows, Jennifer, ed. 1993. *Of Love and Chivalry: An Anthology of Middle English Romance*. London: J. M. Dent/Charles Tuttle.

Fichtenau, H. 1957. *The Carolingian Empire*. Translated by P. Munz. Oxford: Blackwell.

Flamborough, Robert of. 1971. *Liber Poenitentialis*. Edited by J. J. Francis Firth. C.S.B. Studies and Texts, 18. Toronto: Pontifical Institute of Medieval Studies.

Fleming, R. 1991. *Kings and Lords in Conquest England*. Cambridge: Cambridge University Press.

———. 1995. "Oral Testimony and the Domesday Inquest." *Anglo-Norman Studies* 17: 101–22.

———. 1998. *Domesday Book and the Law: Society and Legal Custom in Early Medieval England*. Cambridge: Cambridge University Press.

Fleta. 1953–83. Edited by H. G. Richardson and G. O. Sayles. Selden Society, vols. 72, 89, 99. London: Bernard Quaritch.

Fletcher, Richard. 1989. *The Quest for El Cid*. Oxford: Oxford University Press.

———. 2002. *Bloodfeud: Murder and Revenge in Anglo-Saxon England*. London: Penguin.

Flower, C. T. 1944. *Introduction to the Curia Regis Rolls, 1199–1230 A.D.* Selden Society, vol. 62 for 1943. London: Bernard Quaritch.

Forey, A. J. 1985. "The Emergence of the Military Orders." *Journal of Ecclesiastical History* 36: 175–95.

Foster, Charles Wilmer, and Kathleen Major, eds. 1931–73. *The Registrum Antiquissimum of the Cathedral Church of Lincoln*. 12 vols. Hereford: Lincoln Record Society.

Frank, Robert H. 1988. *Passions within Reason: The Strategic Role of the Emotions*. New York: W. W. Norton.

Frantzen, A. J. 1983. *The Literature of Penance in Medieval England*. New Brunswick, N.J.: Rutgers University Press.

Frijhof, Willem. 1992. "The Kiss Sacred and Profane: Reflections on a Cross-Cultural Confrontation." In *A Cultural History of Gesture*, edited by Jan Bremmer and Herman Roodenburg, 210–36. Ithaca, N.Y.: Cornell University Press.

Fuhrmann, H. 1973. *Einfluss und Verbreitung der Pseudoisidorischen Fälschungen*. 3 vols. Schriften der Monumenta Germaniae Historica, 24. Stuttgart: Hiersemann.

Galbert of Bruges. 1994. *De Multro, Traditione et Occasione Gloriosi Karoli Comitis Flandriarum*. Corpus Christianorum, Continuatio Medievalis, 131. Turnholt: Brepols. (Ross 1967 is a translation of this work.)

Garnett, George. 1986. "Coronation and Propaganda: Some Implications of the Norman Claim to the Throne of England in 1066." *Transactions of the Royal Historical Society*, 5th ser., 36: 91–116.

Garnier, Claudia. 2000. *Amicus amicis, inimicus inimicis: Politische Freundschaft und fürstliche Netzwerke im 13. Jahrhundert*. Anton Hiersemann Monographien zur Geschichte des Mittelalters, vol. 46. Stuttgart: Hiersemann.

Gauvard, Claude. 1991. *"De grace espécial": Crime, état et société en France à la fin du moyen âge*. 2 vols. Paris: Publications de la Sorbonne.

Geary, Patrick J., and John B. Freed. 1994. "Literacy and Violence in Twelfth-Century Bavaria: The 'Murder Letter' of Count Siboto IV." *Viator* 25: 115–29.

Gibbs, Marion, and Jane Lang. 1934. *Bishops and Reform, 1215–72: With Special Reference to the Lateran Council of 1215*. London: Oxford University Press.

Gilbert, John T., ed. 1889. *Register of the Abbey of St. Thomas, Dublin*. Rolls Series. London: Eyre and Spottiswoode.

Gillingham, John. 1992a. "The Beginnings of English Imperialism." *Journal of Historical Sociology* 5: 392–409.

——. 1992b. "Conquering the Barbarian: War and Chivalry in Twelfth-Century Britain." *Haskins Society Journal* 4: 67–84.

——. 1994. "1066 and the Introduction of Chivalry into England." In *Law and Government in Medieval England and Normandy: Essays in Honour of Sir James Holt*, edited by George Garnett and John Hudson, 31–55. Cambridge: Cambridge University Press.

Giraldus Cambrensis. 1861–91. *Opera*. Edited by J. S. Brewer, J. F. Dimock, and G. F. Warner. 8 vols. Rolls Series. London: Longman.

Given, James B. 1977. *Society and Homicide in Thirteenth-Century England*. Stanford, Calif.: Stanford University Press.

Gluckman, Max. 1955. *Custom and Conflict in Africa*. Oxford: Blackwell.

Goebel, Julius, Jr. 1937. *Felony and Misdemeanor*. Vol. 1. London: Humphrey Milford. Reprint, Philadelphia: University of Pennsylvania Press, 1976.

Goering, Joseph. 1992. *William de Montibus (c. 1140–1213): The Schools and the Literature of Pastoral Care*. Studies and Texts, 108. Toronto: Pontifical Institute of Medieval Studies.

Goering, Joseph, and Daniel S. Taylor. 1992. "The Summulae of Bishops Walter de Cantilupe (1240) and Peter Quinel (1287)." *Speculum* 67: 576–94.

Golob, P. E. 1984. "The Ferrars Earls of Derby: A Study of the Honor of Tutbury (1066–1279)." Ph.D. dissertation, Cambridge University.

Goody, Jack. 1983. *The Development of Marriage and the Family in the West.* Cambridge: Cambridge University Press.

Gorringe, Timothy. 1996. *God's Just Vengeance: Crime, Violence, and the Rhetoric of Salvation.* Cambridge: Cambridge University Press.

Gould, Roger V. 2000. "Revenge as Sanction and Solidarity Display: An Analysis of Vendettas in Nineteenth-Century Corsica." *American Sociological Review* 56: 682–704.

Gransden, Antonia. 1974. *Historical Writing in England, c. 550–c. 1307.* London: Routledge and Kegan Paul.

Gratian. 1879. *Decretum Magistri Gratiani.* Edited by Emil Friedburg. Leipzig: Bernard Tauchnitz.

Gravdal, Kathryn. 1991. *Ravishing Maidens: Writing Rape in Medieval French Literature and Law.* Philadelphia: University of Pennsylvania Press.

Green, Judith A. 1986. *The Government of England under Henry I.* Cambridge: Cambridge University Press.

Green, Thomas A. 1972. "Societal Concepts of Criminal Liability for Homicide in Medieval England." *Speculum* 47: 669–94.

———. 1985. *Verdict According to Conscience: Perspectives on the English Criminal Trial Jury, 1200–1800.* Chicago: University of Chicago Press.

Greenway, D. E., ed. 1972. *Charters of the Honour of Mowbray, 1107–1191.* British Academy Records of Social and Economic History, n.s., 1. London: Oxford University Press.

Groot, Roger D. 1982. "The Jury of Presentment before 1215." *American Journal of Legal History* 26: 1–24.

———. 1983. "The Jury in Private Criminal Prosecutions before 1215." *American Journal of Legal History* 27: 113–41.

Grosseteste, Robert. 1987. *De Decem Mandatis.* Edited by R. C. Dales and E. B. King. Auctores Britannici Medii Aevi, 10. London: British Academy.

Gruter, M., and R. D. Masters. 1986. "Ostracism as a Social and Biological Phenomenon: An Introduction." *Ethology and Sociobiology* 7: 149–58.

Guernes de Pont-Sainte-Maxence. 1971. *La vie de Saint Thomas Becket.* Edited by Emmanuel Walberg. Paris: Librairie Honoré Champion.

Haddan, A. W., and W. S. Stubbs. 1869–78. *Councils and Ecclesiastical Documents Relating to Great Britain and Ireland.* 3 vols. Oxford: Clarendon Press.

Hall, David. 1989. "The Sanctuary of St. Cuthbert." In *Saint Cuthbert, His Cult and His Community,* edited by Gerald Bonner, Claire Stancliffe, and David Rollason, 425–36. Woodbridge, U.K.: Boydell.

Hall, Hubert, ed. 1896. *The Red Book of the Exchequer.* 3 vols. Rolls Series. London: Eyre and Spottiswoode.

Hall, J. R. Clark. 1960. *A Concise Anglo-Saxon Dictionary.* 4th ed. Cambridge: Cambridge University Press.

Halsall, Guy. 1998a. "Violence and Society in the Early Medieval West: An Introductory Survey." In *Violence and Society in the Early Medieval West*, edited by G. Halsall, 1–45. Woodbridge, U.K.: Boydell.

——, ed. 1998b. *Violence and Society in the Early Medieval West*. Woodbridge, U.K.: Boydell.

Hamil, F. C. 1936. "The King's Approvers: A Chapter in the History of English Criminal Law." *Speculum* 11: 238–58.

Hanawalt, B. A. 1979. *Crime and Conflict in English Communities, 1300–1348*. Cambridge: Harvard University Press.

Harding, Alan. 1960. "The Origins and Early History of the Keeper of the Peace." *Transactions of the Royal Historical Society*, 5th ser., 10: 85–109.

——. 1966. "The Medieval Brieves of Protection and the Development of the Common Law." *Juridical Review*, n.s., 11: 115–49.

——. 1975. "Plaints and Bills in the History of English Law, Mainly in the Period 1250–1350." In *Legal History Studies 1972*, edited by Dafydd Jenkins, 65–86. Cardiff: University of Wales Press.

——. 1981. *The Roll of the Shropshire Eyre of 1256*. Selden Society, vol. 96 for 1980. London: Selden Society.

——. 1983. "The Origins of the Crime of Conspiracy." *Transactions of the Royal Historical Society*, 5th ser., 33: 89–108.

Harmer, F. E. 1952. *Anglo-Saxon Writs*. Manchester: Manchester University Press.

Hart, C. R. 1975. *The Early Charters of Northern England and the North Midlands*. Leicester: University of Leicester Press.

Hart, W. H., and P. A. Lyons, eds. 1884–93. *Cartularium Monasterii de Rameseia*. 3 vols. Rolls Series. London: Longman.

"Havelok the Dane." 1966. In *Middle English Verse Romances*, edited by Donald B. Sands, 55–129. New York: Holt, Rinehart and Winston.

Head, T., and R. Landes, eds. 1992. *The Peace of God: Social Violence and Religious Response in France around the Year 1000*. Ithaca, N.Y.: Cornell University Press.

Hemingi Chartularium Ecclesiae Wigorniensis. 1723. Edited by Thomas Hearne. Oxford: Sheldonian.

Herlihy, David. 1991. "Family." *American Historical Review* 96: 1–16.

Hershey, Andrew H. 1995. "Success or Failure? Hugh Bigod and Judicial Reform during the Baronial Movement, June 1258–February 1259." *Thirteenth Century England* 5: 65–87.

Heyn, Udo. 1997. *Peacemaking in Medieval Europe: A Historical and Bibliographical Guide*. Claremont, Calif.: Regina Books.

Hicks, Michael. 1995. *Bastard Feudalism*. New York: Longman.

Hill, N. G. 1937. "Excavations on Stockbridge Down, 1935–6." *Papers and Proceedings of the Hampshire Field Clubs and Archaeological Society* 13: 247–59.

Hill, Thomas D. N.d. "Satan, Judas, and the Formation of the West-Saxon State: Myth and Exegesis in the Prologue to Alfred's Laws." Unpublished.

Hilton, R. H. 1975. *The English Peasantry in the Later Middle Ages*. Oxford: Clarendon Press.

Hollister, C. Warren. 1962. *Anglo-Saxon Military Institutions on the Eve of the Norman Conquest*. Oxford: Oxford University Press.

Holt, J. C. 1961. *The Northerners*. Oxford: Clarendon Press.

———. 1971. "The Assizes of Henry II: The Texts." In *The Study of Medieval Records: Essays in Honour of Kathleen Major*, edited by Donald A. Bullough and R. L. Storey, 85–106. Oxford: Oxford University Press.

———. 1974. "A Vernacular-French Text of Magna Carta, 1215." *English Historical Review* 89: 346–64.

Howlett, Richard, ed. 1884–89. *Chronicles of the Reigns of Stephen, Henry II and Richard I*. Rolls Series. London: Longman.

Hudson, John. 1994. *Land, Law, and Lordship in Anglo-Norman England*. Oxford: Clarendon Press.

———. 1996a. *The Formation of the English Common Law: Law and Society in England from the Norman Conquest to Magna Carta*. London: Longman.

———. 2000. "Court Cases and Legal Arguments in England, c. 1066–1166." *Transactions of the Royal Historical Society*, 6th ser., 10: 91–115.

———, ed. 1996b. *The History of English Law: Centenary Essays on "Pollock and Maitland."* London: British Academy and Oxford University Press.

Hunnisett, R. F. 1961. *The Medieval Coroner*. Cambridge: Cambridge University Press.

Hunt, John. 1997. "Families at War: Royalists and Montfortians in the West Midlands." *Midland History* 22: 1–34.

Hunt, Tony. 1989. "Anglo-Norman Rules of Friendship." *French Studies Bulletin* 30: 9–11.

Hurnard, N. M. 1941. "The Jury of Presentment and the Assize of Clarendon." *English Historical Review* 56: 374–410.

———. 1949. "The Anglo-Norman Franchises." *English Historical Review* 64: 289–322, 433–60.

———. 1969. *Pardon for Homicide before A.D. 1307*. Oxford: Oxford University Press.

Hyams, P. R. 1978. Review of *The Legal Framework of English Feudalism* by S. F. C. Milsom. *English Historical Review* 93: 856–61.

———. 1980. *King, Lords and Peasants: The Common Law of Villeinage in the Twelfth and Thirteenth Centuries*. Oxford: Clarendon Press.

———. 1981. "Trial by Ordeal: The Key to Proof in the Early Common Law." In *The Laws and Customs of England: Essays in Honor of Samuel E. Thorne*, edited by M. Arnold, T. A. Green, S. Scully, and S. D. White, 90–126. Chapel Hill: University of North Carolina Press.

———. 1982. "The Common Law and the French Connection." *Anglo-Norman Studies* 4: 77–92, 196–202.

———. 1985. "Deans and Their Doings: The Norwich Inquiry of 1286." In *Proceedings of the Sixth Congress of Medieval Canon Law, 1980*, edited by Stephan Kuttner and Kenneth Pennington, 619–46. Monumenta Iuris Canonici, ser. C, Subsidia, vol. 7. Vatican: Biblioteca Apostolica Vaticana.

———. 1986. "The Strange Case of Thomas of Elderfield." *History Today* 36: 9–15.

——. 1987. "Warranty and Good Lordship in Twelfth-Century England." *Law and History Review* 5: 437–503.

——. 1991a. "The Charter as a Source for the Early Common Law." *Journal of Legal History* 12, no. 3: 173–89.

——. 1991b. "Heinrich Mitteis and English Constitutional History." In *Heinrich Mitteis nach hundert Jahren (1889–1989): Symposion anlässigdes hunderten Geburtstages in München am 2. und 3. November 1989*, edited by P. Landau, H. Nehlsen, and D. Willoweit, 61–70. Munich: Verlag der Bayrischen Akademie der Wissenschaften.

——. 1992. "Feud in Medieval England." *Haskins Society Journal* 3: 1–21.

——. 1994. "Henri II comme juriste, eut-il une politique de réforme?" *Cahiers de Civilisation Médiévale* 37: 85–89.

——. 1996a. "Maitland and the Rest of Us." In *The History of English Law: Centenary Essays on "Pollock and Maitland,"* edited by John Hudson, 215–41. London: British Academy and Oxford University Press.

——. 1996b. "What Did Edwardian Villagers Understand by Law?" In *Medieval Society and the Manor Court*, edited by Zvi Razi and Richard Smith, 69–102. Oxford: Clarendon Press.

——. 1997. "The End of Feudalism?" *Journal of Interdisciplinary History* 28: 655–62.

——. 1998. "What Did Henry III of England Think in Bed and in French about Kingship and Anger?" In *Anger's Past: The Social Uses of an Emotion in the Middle Ages*, edited by Barbara H. Rosenwein, chap. 5. Ithaca, N.Y.: Cornell University Press.

——. 1999. "Rogues and Respectable Folk in Common Law and *Ius Commune*: Due Process versus the Maintenance of Order in European Law." In *The Moral World of the Law*, edited by Peter Coss, 62–90. Cambridge: Cambridge University Press.

——. 2000. "Does It Matter When the English Began to Distinguish between Crime and Tort?" In *Violence in Medieval Society*, edited by R. W. Kaeuper, 107–28. Woodbridge, U.K.: Boydell.

——. 2001. "Feud and the State in Late Anglo-Saxon England." *Journal of British Studies* 40: 1–43.

——. 2002. "Feudalism and Homage: A Judicious Separation." In *Die Gegenwart des Feudalismus*, edited by Natalie Fryde, Pierre Monnet, and Otto Gerhard Oexle, 13–49. Göttingen: Veröffentlichungen des Max-Planck-Instituts für Ge-schichte.

——. 2003. "Nastiness and Wrong, Rancor and Reconciliation." In *Conflict in Medieval Europe*, edited by Peter Gorecki, 201–18. London: Ashgate.

Inquisitions de Odio et Athia. C 144, Public Record Office, London.

Jaeger, C. Stephen. 1999. *Ennobling Love: In Search of a Lost Sensibility*. Philadelphia: University of Pennsylvania Press.

Jenks, Susanne. 2002. "The Writ and Exception *de odio et atia*." *Journal of Legal History* 23: 1–22.

Jessopp, Augustus, and Montague Rhodes James, eds. and trans. 1896. *The Life and Miracles of St. William of Norwich by Thomas of Monmouth*. Cambridge: Cambridge University Press.

John, Eric. 1966. *Orbis Britanniae*. Leicester: Leicester University Press.

Johnson, Charles, ed. 1983. *Dialogus de Scaccario*, by Richard Fitz Nigel. Corrected ed. Oxford Medieval Texts. Oxford: Clarendon Press.

Jolliffe, J. E. A. 1955. *Angevin Kingship*. London: Adam and Charles Black.

Jones, George Fenwick. 1963. *The Ethos of the Song of Roland*. Baltimore: Johns Hopkins University Press.

Jordan Fantosme's Chronicle. 1981. Edited by R. C. Johnston. Oxford: Clarendon Press.

Jouon des Longrais, F. 1936. "La portée politique des réformes d'Henri II en matière de saisine." *Revue Historique de Droit Français et Étranger*, 4th ser., 15: 540–71.

Justices Itinerant. Assize rolls and coroners' rolls. Public Record Office, London.

Justinian. 1967–73. *Digest*. In *Corpus Iuris Civilis*. Edited by P. Krueger and T. Mommsen. 3 vols. Berlin: Weidmann.

——. 1967–73. *Institutes*. In *Corpus Iuris Civilis*. Edited by P. Krueger and T. Mommsen. 3 vols. Berlin: Weidmann.

Kadare, Ismail. 1990. *Broken April*. New York: New Amsterdam Press.

Kaeuper, R. W. 1979. "Law and Order in Fourteenth-Century England: The Evidence of Special Commissions of Oyer and Terminer." *Speculum* 54: 734–84.

——. 1983. "An Historian's Reading of 'The Tale of Gamelyn.'" *Medium Ævum* 52: 51–62.

Kapelle, W. C. 1979. *The Norman Conquest of the North: The Region and Its Transformations*. London: Croom Helm.

Kapuscinski, Ryszard. 1983. *The Emperor: Downfall of an Autocrat*. San Diego: Harcourt, Brace, Jovanovich.

Karl der Grosse, von dem Stricker. 1857. Edited by Karl Bartsch. Quedlinburg: Basse.

Kay, Sarah. 1995. *The Chanson de Geste in the Age of Romance: Political Fictions*. Oxford: Clarendon Press.

Kaye, J. M. 1967. "The Early History of Murder and Manslaughter: Part I." *Law Quarterly Review* 83: 365–95.

——. 1968. "The Sacrabar." *English Historical Review* 83: 744–58.

——. 1977. "The Makings of English Criminal Law: The Beginnings—A General Survey of Criminal Law and Justice down to 1500." *Criminal Law Review*, 4–13.

——, ed. 1966. *Placita Corone or La Corone Pledee devant Justices*. Edited by J. M. Kaye. Selden Society, suppl. series, vol. 4. London: Bernard Quaritch.

Kemp, Brian. 1968. "The Berkeley Hernesse." *Transactions of the Bristol and Gloucester Archaeological Society* 87: 96–110.

Kennedy, Alan. 1995. "Law and Litigation in the *Libellus Æthelwoldi Episcopi*." *Anglo Saxon England* 24: 131–83.

Kerr, Margaret. 1995. "Angevin Reform of the Appeal of Felony." *Law and History Review* 13: 351–91.

Keynes, S. 1980. *The Diplomas of King Æthelred the Unready, 978–1016: A Study in Their Use as Historical Evidence*. Cambridge: Cambridge University Press.

——. 1990. "Crime and Punishment in the Reign of King Æthelred." In *People and*

Places in Northern Europe, 500–1000, edited by I. Wood and N. Lund, 67–81. Woodbridge, U.K.: Boydell and Brewer.

———. 1992. "The Fonthill Letter." In *Words, Texts and Manuscripts*, edited by M. Korhammer, 53–97. Cambridge: Cambridge University Press.

Keynes, S., and M. Lapidge, eds. and trans. 1983. *Alfred the Great: Asser's Life of King Alfred and Other Contemporary Sources*. Harmondsworth: Penguin.

King, Edmund. 1992. "Dispute Settlement in Anglo-Norman England." *Anglo-Norman Studies* 14: 115–30.

"King Horn." 1966. In *Middle English Verse Romances*, edited by Donald B. Sands, 15–54. New York: Holt, Rinehart and Winston.

Klerman, Daniel. 2001. "Settlement and the Decline of Private Prosecution in Thirteenth-Century England." *Law and History Review* 19: 1–65.

Knowles, Clive H. 1959. "The Disinherited, 1265–1280: A Political Study of the Supporters of Simon de Montfort and the Resettlement after the Barons' War." Ph.D. dissertation in 4 vols., University of Wales.

———. 1982. "The Resettlement of England after the Barons' War, 1264–67." *Transactions of the Royal Historical Society*, 5th ser., 32: 25–41.

———. 1986. "Provision for the Families of the Montfortian Disinherited after the Battle of Evesham." *Thirteenth Century England* 1: 114–27.

Le lai d'Haveloc. 1925. Edited by Alexander Bell. Manchester: Longmans and Manchester University Press.

Lancaster, Lorraine. 1958. "Kinship in Anglo-Saxon Society (7th Century to Early 11th)." *British Journal of Sociology* 9: 230–50, 359–77. Reprinted in abbreviated form in *Early Medieval Society*, edited by Sylvia Thrupp (New York: Appleton-Century-Crofts, 1967), 17–41.

Lancelot du lac. 1991–93. Vol. 1, translated by François Mosès. Vol. 2, translated by Marie-Luc Chênerie after the edition of Elspeth Kennedy. Lettres gothiques. Paris: Livre de Poche.

Landon, Lionel, ed. 1923. *Somersetshire Pleas (Civil and Criminal)*. Vol. 2, *From the Rolls of the Itinerant Justices (41 Henry III to the End of His Reign)*. Somerset Record Society, vol. 36 for 1921. London: Somerset Record Society.

Langmuir, Gavin I. 1984. "Thomas of Monmouth: Detector of Ritual Murder." *Speculum* 59: 820–46.

Laughlin, J. Laurence. 1876. "The Anglo-Saxon Procedure." In *Essays in Anglo-Saxon Law*, by Henry Adams, Henry Cabot Lodge, Ernest Young, and J. Laurence Laughlin, 183–305. Boston: Little, Brown.

Lawson, M. K. 1993. *Cnut: The Danes in the Early Eleventh Century*. London: Longman.

Leach, E. R. 1961. *Rethinking Anthropology*. L.S.E. Monographs on Social Anthropology, 22. London: Athlone Press.

Leges Henrici Primi. 1972. Edited by L. J. Downer. Oxford: Clarendon Press.

"The Leges Willelmi." 1903–16. In *Gesetze der Angelsachsen*, by F. Liebermann, 1:492–520. Halle: Max Niemeyer. This refers to the Latin, not the French, text.

Lemosse, Maxime. 1953. "Recherches sur l'histoire du serment de calumnia." *Tijdschrift voor Rechtsgeschiednis* 21: 30–54.

Le Patourel, J. 1976. *The Norman Empire*. Oxford: Clarendon Press.

Lewis, Andrew D. E. 1982. "Trespass and Iniuria." In *Anglo-Polish Legal Essays*, edited by W. E. Butler, 93–115. New York: Transnational.

Leyser, Karl J. 1979. *Rule and Conflict in an Early Medieval Society: Ottonian Saxony*. Bloomington: Indiana University Press.

———. 1982. "Ottonian Government." *English Historical Review* 97: 721–53. Reprinted in Leyser, *Medieval Germany and Its Neighbours* (London: Hambledon Press, 1982), chap. 4, 62–101.

———. 1987. "The Angevin Kings and the Holy Man." In *Saint Hugh of Lincoln*, edited by Henry Mayr-Harting, 49–74. Oxford: Clarendon Press.

"Liber Sextus." 1879. In *Corpus Iuris Canonici*, edited by Emil Friedburg, pt. 2. Leipzig: Bernard Tauchnitz.

Liebermann, F. 1903–16. *Gesetze der Angelsachsen*. 3 vols. Halle: Max Niemeyer.

Little, Lester K. 1993. *Benedictine Maledictions: Liturgical Cursing in Romanesque France*. Ithaca, N.Y.: Cornell University Press.

Loengard, Janet. 1978. "The Assize of Nuisance: Origins of an Action at Common Law." *Cambridge Law Journal* 37: 144–66.

Loyn, H. R. 1974. "Anglo-Saxon Kinship." *Anglo Saxon England* 3: 197–209.

Lutz, Catherine A. 1988. *Unnatural Emotions: Everyday Sentiments on a Micronesian Atoll and Their Challenge to Western Theory*. Chicago: University of Chicago Press.

Lynch, Joseph H. 1998. *Christianizing Kinship: Ritual Sponsorship in Anglo-Saxon England*. Ithaca, N.Y.: Cornell University Press.

Macfarlane, Alan. 1978. *The Origins of English Individualism*. Oxford: Blackwell.

Macray, W. D., ed. 1863. *Chronicon Abbatiae de Evesham*. Rolls Series. London: Longman.

Maddicott, J. R. 1978. *Law and Lordship: Royal Justices as Retainers in Thirteenth- and Fourteenth-Century England*. Past and Present, suppl. 4. Oxford: Past and Present Society.

———. 1986. "Edward I and the Lessons of Baronial Reform, 1258–80." In *Thirteenth-Century England*, edited by P. R. Coss and S. D. Lloyd, 1:1–30. Woodbridge, U.K.: Boydell.

———. 1994. *Simon de Montfort*. Cambridge: Cambridge University Press.

Madox, Thomas. 1769. *The History and Antiquities of the Exchequer of the Kings of England, in Two Periods*. 2 vols. London: Owen and White. Reprint, New York: Greenwood Press, 1969.

Maitland, Frederic William. 1911. *The Collected Papers of Frederic William Maitland*. Edited by H. A. L. Fisher. 3 vols. Cambridge: Cambridge University Press. Reprint, Tokyo: Logos, 1975.

———, ed. 1887. *Select Pleas of the Crown (A.D. 1200–1225)*. Selden Society, vol. 1. London: Selden Society.

———. 1891. *Three Rolls of the King's Court in the Reign of King Richard the First, A.D. 1194–1195*. Pipe Roll Society, vol. 14. London: Wyman and Sons.

Mansfield, Mary. 1995. *The Humiliation of Sinners: Public Penance in Thirteenth-Century France*. Ithaca, N.Y.: Cornell University Press.

Marie de France. 1978. *Lais*. Edited by A. Ewert. Oxford: Basil Blackwell; original edition, 1944.

Martindale, Jane. 1995. " 'His Special Friend?' The Settlement of Disputes and Political Power in the Kingdom of the French (Tenth to Mid-twelfth Century)." *Transactions of the Royal Historical Society*, 6th ser., 5: 21–57.

Mason, Emma. 1990. *St. Wulfstan of Worcester, c. 1008–1095*. Oxford: Blackwell.

———, ed. 1988. *Westminster Abbey Charters, 1066–c. 1214*. London Record Society Publications, vol. 25. London: London Record Society.

Mate, Mavis. 1973. "The Indebtedness of Canterbury Cathedral Priory, 1215–95." *Economic History Review*, 2d ser., 26: 183–97.

Materials for the History of Thomas Becket. 1875–85. Edited by James Craigie Robertson et al. 7 vols. Rolls Series. London: Longman.

Mayr-Harting, H. 1965. "Henry II and the Papacy, 1170–1189." *Journal of Ecclesiastical History* 16: 39–53.

McFarlane, K. B. 1945. "Bastard Feudalism." *Bulletin of the Institute of Historical Research* 20: 161–80.

———. 1973. *The Nobility of Later Medieval England*. Oxford: Clarendon Press.

McGee, J. Sears. 1976. *The Godly Man in Stuart England: Anglicans, Puritans, and the Two Tables, 1620–1670*. New Haven, Conn.: Yale University Press.

McGuire, Brian Patrick. 1988. *Friendship and Community: The Monastic Experience, c. 350–c. 1250*. Kalamazoo, Mich.: Cistercian Publications.

———. 1994. *Brother and Lover: Ælred of Rielvaux*. New York: Crossroad.

McIntosh, Marjorie Keniston. 1976. "The Privileged Villeins of the English Ancient Demesne." *Viator* 7: 1–34.

McLaughlin, Terence P., ed. 1952. *The Summa Parisiensis on the Decretum Gratiani*. Toronto: Pontifical Institute of Medieval Studies.

Meekings, C. A. F., ed. 1961. *The Crown Pleas of the Wiltshire Eyre, 1249*. Wiltshire Archaeological and Natural History Society, Records Branch, vol. 16 for 1960. Devizes.

———. 1979–83. *The Surrey Eyre of 1235*. 2 vols. Surrey Record Society, vols. 31, 32. Guildford: Surrey Record Society.

Meisel, Janet. 1980. *Barons of the Welsh Frontier: The Corbet, Pantulf, and Fitz Warin Families, 1066–1272*. Lincoln: University of Nebraska Press.

Middle English Dictionary. 1952–. Edited by Hans Kurath, Sherman M. Kuhn, and Robert E. Lewis. Ann Arbor: University of Michigan Press; and London: G. Cumberledge, Oxford University Press. Also consulted at http://ets.umdl.umich.edu/m/med/.

Migne, J.-P., ed. 1844–64. *Patrologia cursus completus*. Series Latina. Paris: Migne.

Miller, W. I. 1983. "Choosing the Avenger: Some Aspects of the Bloodfeud in Medieval Iceland and England." *Law and History Review* 1: 159–204.

———. 1990. *Bloodtaking and Peacemaking: Feud, Law, and Society in Saga Iceland*. Chicago: University of Chicago Press.

———. 1999. "In Defense of Revenge." In *Medieval Crime and Social Control*, edited by Barbara A. Hanawalt and David Wallace, 70–89. Minneapolis: University of Minnesota Press.

Milsom, S. F. C. 1958. "The Origins of Trespass." In *Studies in the History of the Common Law*, chap. 1, 1–90. London: Hambledon Press.

———. 1976. *The Legal Framework of English Feudalism*. Cambridge: Cambridge University Press.

———. 1981. *Historical Foundations of the Common Law*. 2d ed. London: Butterworths.

———. 1985. *Studies in the History of the Common Law*. London: Hambledon Press.

Milsom, S. F. C., and Elsie Shanks, eds. 1963. *Novae Narrationes*. Selden Society, vol. 80. London: Bernard Quaritch.

Monasticon Anglicanum. 1817–30. By Sir William Dugdale. 6 vols. in 8. London: Longman, Hurst, Rees, Orme and Brown. Reprint, Farnborough, U.K.: Gregg International, 1970.

Moore, Sally Falk. 1978. *Law as Process: An Anthropological Approach*. London: Routledge and Kegan Paul.

Morey, Adrian. 1937. *Bartholomew of Exeter, Bishop and Canonist*. Cambridge: Cambridge University Press.

Morey, Adrian, and C. N. L. Brooke, eds. 1967. *The Letters and Charters of Gilbert Foliot*. Cambridge: Cambridge University Press.

Morris, C. J. 1992. *Marriage and Murder in Eleventh-Century Northumbria: A Study of the "De Obsessione Dunelmi."* Borthwick Paper, no. 82. York: Borthwick Institute of Historical Research, University of York.

Morris, W. A. 1910. *The Frankpledge System*. New York: Longmans, Green.

La mort le roi Artu: Roman du xiiie siècle. 1954. Edited by Jean Frappier. Geneva: Librairie Droz.

Muir, Edward. 1993. *Mad Blood Stirring: Vendetta in Renaissance Italy*. Baltimore: Johns Hopkins University Press.

Musson, Anthony. 1996. *Public Order and Law Enforcement: The Local Administration of Criminal Justice, 1294–1350*. Woodbridge, U.K.: Boydell.

Myers, Fred R. 1979. "Emotions and the Self: A Theory of Parenthood and Political Order among Pintupi Aborigines." *Ethos* 7: 343–70.

Nelson, J. 1986. " 'A King across the Sea': Alfred in Continental Perspective." *Transactions of the Royal Historical Society*, 5th ser., 36: 45–68.

Niermeyer, J. F. 1997. *Mediae Latinitatis Lexicon Minus*. Leiden: Brill.

Noonan, John T., Jr. 1972. *Power to Dissolve: Lawyers and Marriages in the Courts of the Roman Curia*. Cambridge: Harvard University Press.

O'Brien, Bruce. 1996. "From *Morðor* to *Murdrum*: The Preconquest Origin and Norman Revival of the Murder Fine." *Speculum* 71: 321–57.

———. 1999. *God's Peace and King's Peace: The Laws of Edward the Confessor*. Philadelphia: University of Pennsylvania Press.

Offenstadt, Nicolas. 2000. "Interaction et regulation des conflits: Les gestes d'arbitrage et de la conciliation au moyen âge (xiii–xv siècles)." In *Les rites de justice: Gestes et rituels judiciaires au moyen âge occidental*, edited by R. Jacob and C. Gauvard, 201–28. Paris: Lasjoud d'Or.

Offler, H. S. 1968. *Durham Episcopal Charters, 1071–1152*. Surtees Society, vol. 179. Gateshead.

Offutt, Chris. 1997. *The Good Brother*. New York: Simon and Schuster.

Olivier-Martin, Félix, ed. 1935. *"Les Institutes" de Justinien en français, traduction anonyme du XIIIe siècle*. Paris: Receuil Sirey.

Oye, Kenneth A. 1986. "Explaining Cooperation under Anarchy: Hypotheses and Strategies." In *Cooperation under Anarchy*, edited by K. A. Oye, 1–24. Princeton, N.J.: Princeton University Press.

Padel, O. J. 1984. "Geoffrey of Monmouth and Cornwall." *Cambridge Medieval Celtic Studies* 8: 1–27.

Page, Mark. 2000. "Cornwall, Earl Richard, and the Barons' War." *English Historical Review* 115: 21–38.

Paris, Matthew. 1872–83. *Matthæi Parisiensis, monachi Sancti Albani, Chronica majora*. 7 vols. Edited by H. R. Luard. Rolls Series. London: Longman.

Parker, John, ed. 1921. *Feet of Fines for the County of York from 1218 to 1231*. Yorkshire Archaeological Society, vol. 62. Leeds: Yorkshire Archaeological Society.

Perrot, Ernest. 1910. *Les cas royaux*. Paris: Rousseau.

Petkov, Kiril. 2002. "The Kiss of Peace: Ritual, Self, and Society in the High and Late Middle Ages." Ph.D. dissertation, New York University.

Phelan, Amy. 1997. "A Study of the First Trailbaston Proceedings in England, 1304–7." Ph.D. dissertation, Cornell University.

———. 2000. "Trailbaston and Attempts to Control Violence in the Reign of Edward I." In *Violence in Medieval Society*, edited by Richard W. Kaeuper, 129–40. Woodbridge, U.K.: Boydell.

Philpott, Mark. 1993. "Lanfranc's Canonical Collection and 'the Law of the Church.'" In *Lanfranco di Pavia e L'Europa del Secolo XI*, edited by Giulio d'Onofrio, 131–47. Italia Sacra, vol. 51. Rome: Herder.

———. 1994. "The *De iniusta vexacione Willelmi episcopi primi* and Canon Law in Anglo-Norman Durham." In *Anglo-Norman Durham*, edited by David Rollason, Margaret Harvey, and Michael Prestwich, 125–37. Woodbridge, U.K.: Boydell.

Pinker, Steven. 1997. *How the Mind Works*. New York: W. W. Norton.

Pipe Roll Society. Various dates. London: Public Record Office. The society's editions of royal pipe rolls are cited by the regnal year of the king.

Pleas before the King or His Justices, 1198–1212. 1948–49, 1966–67. Edited by D. M. Stenton. 4 vols. Selden Society, vols. 67–68, 83–84. London: Bernard Quaritch.

Pollock, F., and F. W. Maitland. 1898. *The History of English Law before the Time of Edward I*. 2d ed. 2 vols. Cambridge: Cambridge University Press.

Powell, Edward. 1983. "Arbitration and the Law in the Later Middle Ages." *Transactions of the Royal Historical Society*, 5th ser., 33: 49–67.

Powicke, Frederick Maurice. 1947. *Henry III and the Lord Edward*. Oxford: Clarendon Press.

———. 1950. "Guy de Montfort (1265–71)." In *Ways of Medieval Life and Thought*, 69–88. London: Odhams.

———. 1962. *The Thirteenth Century*. 2d ed. Oxford: Clarendon Press.

Powicke, Frederick Maurice, and C. R. Cheney, eds. 1964. *Councils and Synods with*

Other Documents Relating to the English Church, II, A.D. 1215–1313. 2 vols. Oxford: Clarendon Press.

Prestwich, Michael. 1988. *Edward I.* London: Methuen.

———, ed. 1980. *Documents Illustrating the Crisis of 1297–98 in England.* Camden, 4th ser., 24. London: Royal Historical Society.

Pugh, R. B. 1968. *Imprisonment in Medieval England.* Cambridge: Cambridge University Press.

———. 1983. "The Duration of Criminal Trials in Medieval England." In *Law, Litigants and the Legal Profession,* edited by E. W. Ives and A. H. Manchester, 104–15. Royal Historical Society Studies in History, no. 36. London: Royal Historical Society.

Radcliffe-Brown, A. R., and Daryll Forde, eds. 1950. *African Systems of Kinship and Marriage.* London: Oxford University Press for International African Institute.

Ransford, Rosalind, ed. 1989. *The Early Charters of the Augustinian Canons of Waltham Abbey, Essex, 1062–1230.* Woodbridge, U.K.: Boydell.

Rawcliffe, C. 1984. "The Great Lord as Peacemaker: Arbitration by English Nobles and Their Councils in the Later Middle Ages." In *Law and Social Change in British History,* edited by J. A. Guy and H. Beale, 34–54. Royal Historical Society Studies in History, no. 40. London: Royal Historical Society.

Rayne, James, ed. 1836. *Libellus de Admirandis Beati Cuthberti Virtutibus,* by Reginald of Durham. Surtees Society, vol. 1. London: J. B. Nichols and Son.

Registrum Brevium tam originalium quam judicialium. 1687. Printed Register of Writs. London: Atkins.

Reuter, Timothy. 1991. "Unruhestiftung, Fehde, Rebellion, Widerstand: Gewalt und Frieden in der Politik der Salierzeit." In *Die Salier und das Reich, 3: Gesellschaftlicher und ideengeschichtliche Wandel im Reich der Salier,* edited by S. Weinfurter, 297–325. Sigmaringen: J. Thorbecke.

Reynolds, Andrew. 1999. *Later Anglo-Saxon England: Life and Landscape.* Charleston, S.C.: Tempus.

Richardson, H. G., and G. O. Sayles. 1941. *Select Cases of Procedure without Writ under Henry III.* Selden Society, vol. 60. London: Bernard Quaritch.

———. 1963. *The Governance of Medieval England from the Conquest to Magna Carta.* Edinburgh: University of Edinburgh Press.

Riggs, Charles H. 1963. *Criminal Asylum in Anglo-Saxon Law.* Florida Monographs in the Social Sciences, 18. Gainesville: University of Florida Press.

Riley-Smith, Jonathan. 1984. "The First Crusade and the Persecution of the Jews." *Studies in Church History* 21: 51–72.

Riley-Smith, Louise, and Jonathan Riley-Smith. 1981. *The Crusades: Idea and Reality, 1095–1274.* London: Edward Arnold.

Robarchek, Clayton, and Carole Robarchek. 1998. *Waorani: The Contexts of Violence and War.* Fort Worth, Tex.: Harcourt Brace.

Robertson, A. J. 1925. *The Laws of the Kings of England from Edmund to Henry I.* Cambridge: Cambridge University Press.

———, ed. 1956. *Anglo-Saxon Charters.* 2d ed. Cambridge: Cambridge University Press.

Rogeri de Wendover Liber qui dicitur Flores historiarum ab Anno Domini MCLIV Annoque Henrici Anglorum regis secundi primo. 1886–89. Edited by Henry G. Hewlett. 3 vols. Rolls Series. London: Eyre and Spottiswoode.

Röhrkasten, J. 1990. *Die Englischen Kronzeugen, 1130–1330.* Berliner Historische Studien, vol. 16. Berlin: Duncker and Humblot.

Rollason, D. W. 1982. *The Mildrith Legend: A Study in Early Medieval Hagiography in England.* Leicester: University of Leicester Press.

———. 1983. "The Cults of Murdered Royal Saints in Anglo-Saxon England." *Anglo-Saxon England* 11: 1–22.

Le roman de Rou de Wace. 1970. Edited by A. J. Holden. 3 vols. Paris: Picard.

Le roman de Thèbes. 1995. Edited and translated by Francine Mora-Lebrun. Lettres Gothiques. Paris: Livre de Poche.

Rosaldo, Michelle Z. 1984. "Toward an Anthropology of Self and Feeling." In *Cultural Theory: Essays on Mind, Self, and Emotion,* edited by Richard A. Shweder and Robert A. Le Vine, 137–57. Cambridge: Cambridge University Press.

Rosenwein, Barbara H. 1989. *To Be the Neighbor of Saint Peter: The Social Meaning of Cluny's Property, 909–1049.* Ithaca, N.Y.: Cornell University Press.

———. 1999. *Negotiating Space: Power, Restraint, and Privileges of Immunity in Early Medieval Europe.* Ithaca, N.Y.: Cornell University Press.

Ross, J. B. 1967. *The Murder of Charles the Good.* Rev. ed. New York: Harpers Torchbooks.

Rotuli Chartarum in Turri Londinensi Asservati. 1837. Edited by Thomas Duffus Hardy. Vol. 1, pt. 1. London: Record Commission.

Rotuli Curiae Regis. 1835. Edited by Sir Francis Palgrave. 2 vols. London: Record Commission.

Rotuli de Oblatis et Finibus in Turri Londinensi Asservati Tempore Regis Johannis. 1835. Edited by Thomas Duffus Hardy. London: Record Commission.

Rotuli Litterarum Clausarum in Turri Londinensi Asservati. 1833–34. Edited by Thomas Duffus Hardy. 2 vols. London: Record Commission.

Rotuli Litterarum Patentium in Turri Londinensi Asservati. 1835. Edited by Thomas Duffus Hardy. London: Record Commission.

Rotuli Normanniae in Turri Londinensi Asservati. 1835. Edited by Thomas Duffus Hardy. London: Record Commission.

Rotuli Parliamentorum. 1767–77. 6 vols. London.

Round, J. H., ed. 1888. *Ancient Charters, Royal and Private, Prior to A.D. 1200.* Pipe Roll Society, vol. 10. London: Wyman and Sons.

———. 1899. *Geoffrey de Mandeville: A Study of the Anarchy.* London: Longmans, Green.

The Ruodlieb. 1985. Edited by C. W. Grocock. Chicago: Bolchazy-Carducci.

Russell, M. J. 1959. "Hired Champions." *American Journal of Legal History* 3: 242–59.

Saint Cuthbert, His Cult and His Community. 1989. Edited by Gerald Bonner, Claire Stancliffe, and David Rollason. Woodbridge, U.K.: Boydell.

Sawyer, P. H. 1968. *Anglo-Saxon Charters: An Annotated List and Bibliography*. London: Royal Historical Society.

——. 1987. "The Bloodfeud in Fact and Fiction." In *Tradition og Historieskrivning*, edited by Kirsten Hastrup and Preben Meulengracht Sorensen, 27–38. Acta Jutlandica 63, no. 2. Aarhus: Aarhus University Press.

Sayles, G. O., ed. 1936. *Select Cases in the Court of King's Bench under Edward I*. Selden Society, vol. 55. London: Bernard Quaritch.

——. 1938. *Select Cases in the Court of King's Bench under Edward I*. Selden Society, vol. 57. London: Bernard Quaritch.

——. 1939. *Select Cases in the Court of King's Bench under Edward I*. Selden Society, vol. 58. London: Bernard Quaritch.

Schmidt, A. V. C. 1995. *The Vision of Piers Plowman: A Critical Edition of the B-Text*. 2d ed. London: Everyman.

Schneider, Reinhard, ed. 1968. *Kapitularien*. Historische Texte/Mittelalter, 5. Göttingen: Vandenhoeck and Ruprecht.

Scholz, Bernhard W. 1966. "Eadmer's Life of Bregwine, Archbishop of Canterbury, 761–764." *Traditio* 22: 127–48.

Searle, Eleanor. 1980. *The Chronicle of Battle Abbey*. Oxford Medieval Texts. Oxford: Clarendon Press.

——. 1988. *Predatory Kinship and the Creation of Norman Power, 840–1066*. Berkeley: University of California Press.

Seipp, David J. 1996. "The Distinction between Crime and Tort in the Early Common Law." *Boston University Law Review* 76: 59–87.

Shilton, Dorothy O., and Richard Holworthy, eds. 1932. *Wells City Charters*. Somerset Record Society, vol. 46. London: Somerset Record Society.

Shippey, T. A. 1976. *Poems of Wisdom and Learning in Old English*. Cambridge: D. S. Brewer.

Short, Ian. 1992. "Patrons and Polyglots: French Literature in Twelfth-Century England." *Anglo-Norman Studies* 14: 229–49.

Sims-Williams, Patrick. 1998. "The Uses of Writing in Early Medieval Wales." In *Literacy in Medieval Celtic Societies*, edited by Huw Pryce, 15–38. Cambridge: Cambridge University Press.

Singer, Peter. 1981. *The Expanding Circle: Ethics and Sociobiology*. New York: Farrar, Straus and Giroux.

Sklute, J. 1990. "*Freothuwebbe* in Old English Poetry." In *New Readings on Women in Old English Literature*, edited by H. Damico and A. H. Olsen, 204–10. Bloomington: Indiana University Press.

Smail, Daniel Lord. 1996. "Hatred as a Social Institution in Medieval Society." *Speculum* 76: 90–126.

Smalley, Beryl. 1973. *The Becket Conflict and the Schools: A Study of Intellectuals in Politics in the Twelfth Century*. Oxford: Basil Blackwell.

——. 1987. *The Gospel in the Schools, c. 1100–c. 1280*. London: Hambledon Press.

Solomon, Robert C. 1990. *A Passion for Justice: Emotions and the Origins of the Social Contract*. Reading, Mass.: Addison-Wesley.

Southern, Sir Richard. 1990. *Saint Anselm: A Portrait in a Landscape*. Cambridge: Cambridge University Press.

Squire, Ælred. 1969. *Ælred of Rievaulx: A Study*. London: S.P.C.K.

Stacy, N. E. 1999. "Henry of Blois and the Lordship of Glastonbury." *English Historical Review* 114: 1–33.

Stallybrass, Peter, and Allon White. 1986. *The Politics and Poetics of Transgression*. Ithaca, N.Y.: Cornell University Press.

Statutes of the Realm. 1810. 8 vols. London: Record Commission.

Stein, Peter. 1966. *Regulae Iuris: From Juristic Rules to Legal Maxims*. Edinburgh: University of Edinburgh Press.

Stenton, Doris Mary. 1964. *English Justice between the Norman Conquest and the Great Charter, 1066–1215*. Memoirs, 60. Philadelphia: American Philosophical Society.

———, ed. 1926. *The Earliest Lincolnshire Assize Rolls, A.D. 1202–1209*. Lincoln Record Society, vol. 22. Lincoln: Lincoln Record Society.

———. 1930. *The Earliest Northamptonshire Assize Rolls, A.D. 1202 and 1203*. Northamptonshire Record Society, vol. 5. Lincoln: J. W. Ruddock and Sons.

———. 1934. *Rolls of the Justices in Eyre, Being the Rolls of Pleas and Assizes for Lincolnshire, 1218–19, and Worcestershire, 1221*. Selden Society, vol. 53. London: Bernard Quaritch.

———. 1937. *Rolls of the Justices in Eyre, Being the Rolls of Pleas and Assizes for Yorkshire in 3 Henry III (1218–19)*. Selden Society, vol. 56. London: Bernard Quaritch.

———. 1940. *Rolls of the Justices in Eyre, Being the Rolls of Pleas and Assizes for Gloucestershire, Warwickshire and Staffordshire, 1221, 1222*. Selden Society, vol. 59. London: Bernard Quaritch.

———. 1952–67. *Pleas before the King and His Justices, 1198–1202*. 4 vols. Selden Society, vols. 67–68, 83–84. London: Bernard Quaritch.

Stenton, F. M. 1955. *The Latin Charters of the Anglo-Saxon Period*. Oxford: Clarendon Press.

———, ed. 1920. *Documents Illustrative of the Social and Economic History of the Danelaw*. British Academy Records of the Social and Economic History of England and Wales, 5. London: Oxford University Press.

———. 1922. *Transcripts of Charters Relating to Gilbertine Houses of Sixle, Ormsby, Catley, Bullington, and Alvingham*. Lincolnshire Record Society, vol. 18. Horncastle: Lincolnshire Record Society.

Stevenson, Joseph. 1858. *Chronicon Monasterii de Abingdon*. 2 vols. Rolls Series. London: Longman.

Stewart, Frank Henderson. 1994. *Honor*. Chicago: University of Chicago Press.

Stones, E. L. G. 1957. "The Folvilles of Ashby Folville, Leicestershire, and Their Associates in Crime." *Transactions of the Royal Historical Society*, 5th ser., 7: 117–36.

Strayer, J. R. 1937. "Le bref de nouvelle dessaisine et le 'commun' en Normandie à la fin du xiiie siècle." *Revue historique de droit français et étranger*, 4th ser., 16: 479–88.

Stubbs, W., ed. 1913. *Select Charters of English Constitutional History*. 9th ed. Revised by H. W. C. Davis. Oxford: Clarendon Press. Reprint, 1957.

Summerson, H. R. T. 1983. "The Early Development of the *Peine Forte et Dure*." In

Law, Litigants, and the Legal Profession, edited by E. W. Ives and A. H. Manchester, 116–25. Manchester: Royal Historical Society.

——. 1996. "Maitland and the Criminal Law in the Age of *Bracton*." In *The History of English Law: Centenary Essays on "Pollock and Maitland*," edited by John Hudson, 115–43. London: British Academy and Oxford University Press.

——. 1999. "Attitudes to Capital Punishment in England, 1200–1350." *Thirteenth Century England* 8: 123–33.

——, ed. 1985. *Crown Pleas of the Devon Eyre of 1238*. Devon and Cornwall Record Society, n.s., 28. Torquay: Devonshire Press.

Sutherland, D. W. 1966. "Mesne Process upon Personal Actions in the Early Common Law." *Law Quarterly Review* 82: 482–96.

——. 1967. "Peytevin v. La Lynde." *Law Quarterly Review* 83: 527–46.

——. 1973. *The Assize of Novel Disseisin*. Oxford: Clarendon Press.

Symeon of Durham. 1882–85. *Symeonis Monachi Opera Omnia*. Edited by Thomas Arnold. 2 vols. Rolls Series. London: Longman.

Tardif, Ernest-Joseph, ed. 1881. *Le très ancien coutumier de Normandie*. Pt. 1, vol. 1 of 3 vols. Rouen: Société de l'histoire de Normandie.

——. 1896. *La summa de legibus normannie in curia laicali*. Vol. 2 of 3 vols. Rouen: Société de l'histoire de Normandie.

Tavris, Carol. 1989. *Anger: The Misunderstood Emotion*. Rev. ed. New York: Simon and Schuster.

Thomas, Hugh M. 1993. *Vassals, Heiresses, Crusaders and Thugs: The Gentry of Angevin Yorkshire, 1154–1216*. Philadelphia: University of Pennsylvania Press.

Thomas, Mestre. 1955–64. *The Romance of Horn*. Edited by M. K. Pope. 2 vols. Anglo-Norman Text Society, 9–10, 12–13. Oxford: Basil Blackwell.

Thorne, Samuel E. 1959. "English Feudalism and Estates in Land." *Cambridge Law Journal*: 193–209.

Thorpe, Benjamin, ed. 1849. *Florentii Wigorniensis Monachi Chronicon ex Chronicis*. 2 vols. London: English Historical Society.

——. 1865. *Diplomatarium Anglicum Ævi Saxonici*. London: Macmillan.

Tobler, Adolf, and Ernest Lommatsch, eds. 1925–95. *Altfranzösisches Wörterbuch*. Berlin: Weidmann/F. Steiner Verlag.

Tout, T. F., and H. Johnstone, eds. 1906. *State Trials of the Reign of Edward the First, 1289–1293*. Camden Society, 3d ser., 9. London: Royal Historical Society.

The Treatise on the Laws and Customs of the Realm of England Commonly Called Glanvill. 1993. Edited by G. D. G. Hall. Oxford Medieval Texts. New York: Oxford University Press. Original edition, Nelsons and Selden Society Medieval Texts, London: Nelsons, 1965. This volume is cited by book, chapter, and page numbers of the 1993 edition.

Treharne, R. F., and I. J. Sanders, eds. 1973. *Documents of the Baronial Movement of Reform and Rebellion, 1258–1267*. Oxford: Clarendon Press.

Turnbull, Colin M. 1973. *The Mountain People*. London: Jonathan Cape.

Turner, Ralph V. 1968. *The King and His Courts: The Role of John and Henry II in the Administration of Justice, 1199–1240*. Ithaca, N.Y.: Cornell University Press.

———. 1985. *The English Judiciary in the Age of Glanvill and Bracton, c. 1176–1239.* Cambridge: Cambridge University Press.

———. 1994. *King John.* London: Longman.

Tyerman, C. J. 1988. *England and the Crusades, 1095–1588.* Chicago: University of Chicago Press.

Van Caenegem, R. C. 1959. *Royal Writs in England from the Conquest to Glanvill.* Selden Society, vol. 77 for 1958–59. London: Bernard Quaritch.

———. 1976. "Public Prosecution of Crime in Twelfth-Century England." In *Church and Government in the Middle Ages: Essays Presented to C. R. Cheney on His 70th Birthday*, edited by C. N. L. Brooke, D. E. Luscombe, G. H. Martin and D. Owen, 41–76. Cambridge: Cambridge University Press.

———. 1982. "Criminal Law in England and Flanders under King Henry II and Count Philip of Alsace." In *Diritto e Potere nella Storia Europea: Atti in honore Bruno Paradisi*, 1:231–54. Florence: Leo S. Olschki.

———. 1990–91. *English Lawsuits from William I to Richard I.* Selden Society, vols. 106–7. London: Selden Society. Case numbers are cited for this volume, with pages given in parentheses where appropriate.

Van Houts, Elizabeth M. C., ed. 1992–95. *The Gesta Normannorum Ducum of William of Jumièges, Orderic Vitalis and Robert of Torigni.* Oxford Medieval Texts. Oxford: Clarendon Press.

Vecchio, Silvana. 1989. "Il decalogo nella predicazione del xiii secolo." *Cristianesimo nella Storia* 10: 41–55.

Victoria History of the County of Oxford. 1907. Vol. 1, edited by L. J. Salzman. London: Oxford University Press.

Walker, David M. 1980. *The Oxford Companion to Law.* Oxford: Clarendon Press.

Wallace-Hadrill, J. M. 1962. *The Long-Haired Kings.* Methuen: London. Reprint, Toronto: MARTS, 1982.

———. 1971. *Early Germanic Kingship in England and on the Continent.* Oxford: Oxford University Press.

———. 1988. *Bede's Ecclesiastical History of the English People: A Historical Commentary.* Oxford: Oxford University Press.

Waugh, Scott L. 1986. "Tenure to Contract: Lordship and Clientage in Thirteenth-Century England." *English Historical Review* 101: 811–39.

Wells, John Edwin, ed. 1907. *The Owl and the Nightingale.* Boston: D.C. Heath.

West, Francis. 1966. *The Justiciarship in England, 1066–1232.* Cambridge: Cambridge University Press.

White, Geoffrey H. 1940. "The First House of Bellême." *Transactions of the Royal Historical Society*, 4th ser., 22: 67–99.

White, Graeme J. 2000. *Restoration and Reform, 1153–1165: Recovery from Civil War in England.* Cambridge: Cambridge University Press.

White, S. D. 1986. "Feuding and Peacemaking in the Touraine around the Year 1100." *Traditio* 42: 195–263.

———. 1989. "Kingship and Lordship in Early Medieval England: The Story of Sigebehrt, Cynewulf and Cyneheard." *Viator* 20: 1–18.

——. 1996. "Clotild's Revenge: Politics, Kinship, and Ideology in the Merovingian Bloodfeud." In *Portraits of Medieval and Renaissance Living: Essays in Memory of David Herlihy*, edited by Samuel K. Cohn Jr. and Stephen A. Epstein, 107–30. Ann Arbor: University of Michigan Press.

——. 1998. "The Politics of Anger." In *Anger's Past: The Social Uses of an Emotion in the Middle Ages*, edited by Barbara H. Rosenwein, 127–52. Ithaca, N.Y.: Cornell University Press.

White, T. H. 1954. *The Bestiary: A Book of Beasts*. New York: Putnam.

Whitelock, Dorothy, ed. 1963. *Sermo Lupi ad Anglos*. 3d ed. London: Methuen.

Whitelock, D., M. Brett, and C. N. L. Brooke. 1981. *Councils and Synods with Other Documents Relating to the English Church*. Vol. 1 in 2 parts. Oxford: Clarendon Press.

Wightman, W. E. 1966. *The Lacy Family in England and Normandy*. Oxford: Clarendon Press.

Woodbine, George E., ed. 1910. *Four Thirteenth Century Law Tracts*. New Haven, Conn.: Yale University Press.

Wormald, Jenny. 1980. "Bloodfeud, Kindred and Government in Early Modern Scotland." *Past and Present* 87: 54–97.

Wormald, Patrick. 1977a. "*Lex Scripta* and *Verbum Regis:* Legislation and Germanic Kingship from Euric to Cnut." In *Early Medieval Kingship*, edited by P. H. Sawyer and I. N. Wood, 105–38. Leeds: School of History, University of Leeds.

——. 1977b. "The Uses of Literacy in Anglo-Saxon England and Its Neighbours." *Transactions of the Royal Historical Society*, 5th ser., 27: 95–114.

——. 1986. "Charters, Law and the Settlement of Disputes in Early Medieval England." In *The Settlement of Disputes in Early Medieval Europe*, edited by W. Davies and P. Fouracre, chap. 8. Cambridge: Cambridge University Press.

——. 1988. "A Handlist of Anglo-Saxon Lawsuits." *Anglo Saxon England* 17: 247–81.

——. 1992. "Domesday Lawsuits: A Provisional List and Preliminary Comment." In *England in the Eleventh Century*, edited by C. Hicks, 61–102. Stamford, U.K.: Paul Watkins.

——. 1994. " 'Quadripartitus.' " In *Law and Government in Medieval England and Normandy*, edited by G. Garnett and J. Hudson, 111–47. Cambridge: Cambridge University Press.

——. 1995. "Leges Edwardi: The Textus Roffensis and Its Content." *Anglo-Norman Studies* 17: 243–66.

——. 1996. "Maitland and Anglo-Saxon Law: Beyond Domesday Book." In *The History of English Law: Centenary Essays on "Pollock and Maitland,"* edited by John Hudson, 1–20. London: British Academy and Oxford University Press.

——. 1997. "Giving God and King Their Due: Conflict and Its Regulation in the Early English State." In *La Giustizia nell'alto medioevo (Secoli ix–xi)*, 549–90. Settimane di studio del centro Italiano di studi sull'alto medioevo, 44, 11–17 April 1996, Spoleto. Spoleto: Presso la Sede del Centro.

——. 1999. *The Making of English Law: King Alfred to the Twelfth Century*, vol. 1, *Legislation and Its Limits*. Oxford: Basil Blackwell.

Wrangham, Richard, and Dale Peterson. 1996. *Demonic Males: Apes and the Origins of Human Violence*. Boston: Houghton Mifflin.

Wright, Robert. 1994. *The Moral Animal: Evolutionary Psychology and Everyday Life*. New York: Vintage.

Yver, Jean. 1928. "Interdiction de la guerre privée dans le très ancien droit normand." In *Travaux de la semaine de droit normand tenue à Guernesey du 26 au 30 mai 1927*, 307–47. Caen: Caron.

INDEX

Abingdon 139n, 152–53, 268
Abjuration of the realm 97n, 135–36
Accomplices 213, 228, 283, 300. *See also*
  Words: abettum
Action, forms of 152, 155, 216–18, 239–42
Actions and procedures. *See* Appeals "of
  felony"; Grand assize; Land disputes: Suits;
  Mort d'ancestor; Novel disseizin; Nui-
  sance; Oyer and terminer; Proto-trespass;
  Right, action of; Trailbaston; Trespass
Adultery 148, 193n, 196
Æthelred II, king of Wessex 26–27, 31,
  75–76, 84–85, 102n, 164, 169, 268, 277
Æthelstan, king of Wessex 27, 81–82, 91n,
  95, 99
Æthelwig, abbot of Evesham 124
Æthelwold, bishop of Winchester 106n, 268
Affinity. *See* Retainers
Ailred of Rielvaux 51n, 124–25
Ailward of Westoning 181
Alan de la Zouche 243n, 251–52
Alcoholic drink 30, 76, 91, 140, 194, 248,
  273, 300
Alexander, bishop of Coventry and Lich-
  field 50
Alfred, king of Wessex 80, 85, 96, 98–100,
  103, 144n, 148
Amercement 93, 113–15, 232n, 235, 292
Amicitia 20, 26 83, 132, 139, 143, 175n, 204,
  255, 260, 271, 304. *See also* Friendship
Angevin law reform 224–30
Anglo-Saxon Chronicle 75
Anselm, St., archbishop of Canterbury 125
Appeals "of felony" xvii, 103–5, 146–48, 157,
  165, 167, 171–74, 176, 184n, 191, 207, 210,
  247, 250, 262, 268–69, 273, 279–82, 287–93,
  296–300, 306–8; de precepto 232; as feud
  tamed 174–75, 191; differentiation from
  trespass 231–34; for hot anger 228n
Appleby, Westmoreland 251
Approvers 166
Aquinas, Thomas 25
Arbitration 83–84, 209n, 258. *See also* Peace-
  making
Ardley, Oxon. 268

Aristotle 51n
Arrow, Warwicks. 197
Aughton, Yorks. 286
Augustine, St. 47–48, 53, 56
Axelrod, Robert 16–21, 65

Babington, Somerset 274
Bakhtin, Mikhail 236
Balance, restoring the 53, 65
Banleuca 96
Barbarian 112–13, 115n
Bartholomew, bishop of Exeter 42n.
Bartlett, Robert 57n
Bastard feudalism xix, 243, 255–64
Bath 275
Bathing 281
Battles: Brémule 128; Evesham 253–54;
  Mortemer 129
Baudri of Dol 120
Bedding 306
Beowulf 74–75, 81n
Berwick, Scotland 285–86
Beverley, Yorks. 135, 251
Bible xxiv, 44–48, 236n. *See also* Glossa Or-
  dinaria to Bible
Binding over to keep peace 205
Bourdieu, Pierre 7
Bracton 145–56, 209, 222–24, 232n, 239–40,
  244
Brand, Paul 257n
Bruges 178
Buckingham 269, 281–82
Burton Abbey 143
Bury St. Edmunds, Suffolk 121, 222n
Buzones (notables) 170, 194
Byfield, Northants. 306
Byland Abbey 201, 303–4

Campbell, James 72, 98n
Camville family 306–7
Canon law xxiv, 179–80, 244, 246; dual
  process 165, 167; *Sext* 218. *See also* Gratian; Roman law
Carolingian capitularies 41n, 86, 178; influence 178–79; vicariae 160, 169

40–41, 139, 163, 170, 18, 244; malice (*see* Words: malitia); nasty passions 38–39, 42, 44; outrage 182; pride 44, 64, 181; rancor 54–55, 64, 130, 190, 199, 255, 273, 297; rhetoric of xvi, 37–38, 59, 66–67; scripts 60; sorrow 63; visual signs of 49, 62–63. *See also* Motives of litigants and disputants; Shame

Enemies 17, 25, 27, 42–43, 109; mortal 57–59, 61, 66–67, 209, 244, 251, 254. *See also* Words: inimicitia, inimicus

Enmity. *See* Feud; Emotions: hatred

Essoins 58

Eucharist 52, 64

Eve, daughter of 58

Evesham, Worcs. 124, 253–54

Execution cemeteries 81, 99

Executions 5, 156, 248–50; feud for 81; performed by non-professionals 141, 173, 192, 249–50, 284–85; rescues 250

Exile x, 5, 65, 77, 195–96, 199, 303. *See also* Pilgrimage

Eyre 265; articles of 224, 228 n, 230

Fairs 251, 300

Fealty. *See* Fidelity oaths

Feasting 26 n, 91

Feelings. *See* Emotions

Felony 146, 160, 163, 166, 169, 171, 176, 196 n, 197–98, 205 n, 217, 221–22, 225–28, 228–31, 233 n, 239, 264, 284–85; subset of trespass 239

Feud x–xii, xv–xvii, 50, 57, 111, 113, 243, 251–55; analogy with international relations 33 n; anecdotes 75–77, 131–32; definitions 8–9, 13; divine 44 n, 78, 123; holy 119–20; language 128; lords as principals 213–14; need to publicize 11, 66, 80; peace in the, theory of 14–16, 51 n, 72, 82, 87–92; peace treaty test of 13, 199, 264; situation within war 182; strong and weak views of xii, 8 n, 19; the word 66. *See also* House; Words: inimicitia, inimicus

Feudalism 80 n, 203. *See also* Bastard feudalism

Feud-like behavior xviii, 33, 191, 199, 210–15, 248–50

Fines 207 n

Fidelity oaths 99–100, 107, 158, 230, 254 n, 289

Fight or flight reaction 37 n

Flanders 159–60, 178–79, 249, 284–86

Ford Abbey 198 n

Forfeiture 80–81, 99

Fossard family 201, 286–87, 303–4

Frank, Robert 21 n.

Frankpledge. *See* Tithings

Friendship xvi, 12, 21–32, 42, 83, 87–91, 93, 102, 104 n, 106, 201, 203–4, 301–2; best 56; plain-vanilla 21–23, 29–30, 91, 212. *See also* Amicitia

Galbert of Bruges 178 n

Geoffrey f. Peter, chief justiciar 198 n, 207–8, 296, 298–99

Geoffrey of Anjou 274

Gerald of Wales 42 n.

Germany x, 99 n

Gilbert de Clare, earl of Gloucester 252–53, 255, 260

Gilbert, count of Brionne 281

Gilds 10 n, 28–29, 81, 88, 90–91, 98 n

Gillingham, Jon 112

Giroie and family 281

Glanvill 117, 147, 163, 168, 179, 219, 221–22, 230

Glossa Ordinaria to Bible xxiv, 25 n, 44–47

Goading 11, 60, 76

Goodmanham, Yorks. 286–87

Gospels 25

Grafton Regis, Northants. 298

Grand assize 204, 220 n, 304–5

Grand jury xvii, 159, 160, 169–70, 184–85, 227–28, 269, 273; knights on 170; privata for 171, 194

Gratian 41–42, 118, 180

Gregory the Great 48

Hall, Derek xix

Harding, Alan 150 n, 224–25

Harlow, Essex 282–84

Harptree, Somerset 275–76

Havering, Essex 207 n

Helmstan 91 n, 102 n

Hemming 124

Henry f. William 214, 288–91

Henry I 85, 118, 129 n, 131, 134–38, 152–53, 165, 258 n, 280

Henry II, king of England 42 n, 60, 137, 143 n, 155, 189, 209, 275, 305–6; not an altruistic automaton 184

Henry III, king of England 58 n, 240 n, 243 n, 245, 252, 254

Henry of Almain 254

Herbert of Bosham 180 n

Hereford, Earl of 252

Herfast, bishop of Thetford 121

Hexham 135

Hill, Thomas D. 74 n, 84 n

Homage 140 n, 178; peace 202–6, 287–88, 301

Honor 11, 61–62, 79, 88, 173, 193, 200, 242, 251; duel of 4

Horses 189, 289, 307

Hospitallers 200, 208 n, 301

House assaults 4, 58 n, 85 n, 139, 197 n, 210–14, 269, 270, 274–76, 279, 297, 301, 306–8

Howlett, David 234n
Hubert Walter, archbishop of Canterbury
  and chief justiciar 198n
Hue and cry 85n, 97–98, 148, 195n, 249,
  280, 282, 284, 288, 293
Hugh Bigod 245n
Hugh de Neville 275
Hugh, St., bishop of Lincoln 125
Human rights 222
Humiliation of saint 276
Hundred Rolls 245
Hundred sergeant 291, 299
Hyping a complaint 172, 231

Indictment xvii, 43n, 159–60, 164, 169–71,
  180–81, 194, 222, 224, 227, 228–29, 247,
  249, 262–63, 275, 283–84, 290, 299
Innocent III, pope 218n
Inquests: de bono et malo 285; de fidelitate
  198n; de gestu et fama 198; de pace 282;
  at the king's suit 157n. See also De odio et
  athia
Ipswich 197
Ireland 247
Isidore of Seville 41
Ivo of Chartres 163n

Jail 93, 165, 176, 223n, 249n, 283–84
Jews 120, 231n
John de Lovetot 283–84
John, king of England 153n, 206, 214, 227,
  231, 276, 289–91
Joliffe, J. E. A. 39–40.
Judges 41, 57, 157n, 218–20, 244–45;
Juries 159, 160, 165, 169–70, 174, 175–76,
  184n, 219–20, 222, 228, 233, 243–44, 250,
  262–63, 275, 282–83, 285; information
  sources 168; issue for 220n; knights on
  170, 184n; nullification 170, 193, 265; spe-
  cial verdicts 220, 243. See also Grand jury;
  Inquests
Justice 45n; biblical sense of 44–45; down-
  ward 13, 87, 106–9, 149, 235, 257; good
  156n; royal, penetration of 158n
Justices, royal 143, 183n, 189, 196–97, 199n,
  202n, 206, 227, 244, 262–63, 265, 275, 280,
  283, 297, 303, 305; bribery of 263, 307; as
  outsiders 170, 265; retaining of 263n
Justiciar, chief 206–8, 279, 292–93, 296, 307;
  Writs 207, 298. See also Geoffrey f. Peter;
  Hubert Walter, Peter des Roches

Kaeuper, Richard 245–46, 264
Kapelle, W. C. 278–79
Kenilworth, Dictum of 253–55, 263n
Kent, princes of 89
Kettering, Northants. 268
Keynes, Simon 86
Killing, contract 132, 213n, 248–49, 270–71

Killing, secret. See House assaults
Killingwith, Yorks. 303
Kinship xvi, 4, 6–7, 9–10, 14, 21–25, 28, 32,
  41–42, 52, 75, 89, 120, 131, 175n, 212;
  brother 24n; foster-kin 28, 91; killings
  within 54, 74, 88, 107, 203; spiritual 28,
  91. See also Troublemakers, control or expulsion of
King, access to 26–27, 93–94, 102, 133, 147,
  156
King's peace 56, 82–83, 94, 133–34, 138n,
  150, 161, 168, 191–93, 196, 217, 224–26, 232,
  249, 255, 279, 297–98; special (grið)
  94–95, 134, 196–99, 224–25, 255, 292–94,
  297–98
Kings. See Æthelred II; Æthelstan; Alfred;
  Charlemagne; Edgar; Edmund; Edward
  I; Edward II; Edward the Confessor; Edward the Martyr; Henry I; Henry II;
  Henry III; John; Louis VI; Richard I;
  Stephen; William I; William II Rufus
Kiss of peace 201–2, 296

Lacy family 131, 154
Land disputes: suits 150, 155; and distinction
  between law and fact 220
Launceston, Cornwall 214, 289–90
Law and fact, distinction between 181, 185,
  217–20, 236
Laws. See Canon law; Common law; Roman
  law
Lawyers 189n, 237
Le Sap, Normandy 281
Legal distinctions. See Crime and tort; Law
  and fact; Public and private
Legal ideas, elementary 172n
Legal writings 140, 144; Brevia Placitata
  238n; Britton 223–24, 236n, 239–40; Fleta
  223–24; Grið 92n; "Leges Edwardi Con-
  fessoris" 136, 148; "Leges Willelmi"
  ("Leis Willelme") xxiii, 147–48; Norman
  Summa de Legibus 145–46, 156, 204–5,
  230n, 239; Norman Très ancien coutumier
  204, 230n; "Novae Narrationes" 238n;
  Placita Corone 224n, 239–40; Swerian
  104n; Wer 83, 143n. See also Bracton;
  Glanvill; Leges Henrici Primi
Leges xiii, xvi, xxi, 10n, 41, 72, 78–87, 99,
  102, 104, 108, 115, 129, 136, 138, 164, 169,
  179, 229; manuscripts of 83n, 86n, 118n
Leges Henrici Primi xvii, 104, 116–19, 129,
  137–45, 147, 229
Legislation: assizes of Clarendon and
  Northampton xvii, 40, 157–63, 165n, 167,
  169, 180n, 184–85, 226, 229–30, 254n,
  306; Constitutions of Clarendon 161n,
  180n; Edictum Regium 198n; Inquest of
  Sheriffs 40–41, 163, 185; Provisions of
  Oxford 252, 254; Statute of Westminster I

209–10, 214–5, 227, 252n, 272–73, 278, 287–88, 293–94, 298, 300–302, 304; humiliation in 200–201, 301; licenses to concord for 206n, 207n; offers 75; rituals 199–205; rule against unlicensed 93n, 199
Shadow of the future 18–20, 102–3
Shame 11–12, 36, 44n, 52, 62, 139, 145, 151, 153, 173, 192, 200n, 206n, 244–45, 274, 279, 289, 301
Sheriff 151–52, 160–61, 196–97, 215, 223n, 233, 249, 268, 279–80, 282–85, 288, 291, 303; bribery 283
Shift of control 156, 169, 171, 184–6, 257, 262
Shuckburgh, Warwicks. 304–5
Simon de Montfort 250n, 253–55; Guy, son of 254
Simon of Stanstead 200, 202, 301–2
Sins and virtues, cardinal 35–36, 43n, 48–50. *See also* Emotions: pride; Tongues: sins of
Siward, earl of Northumbria 278
Social control 7; royal action for 80
Solomon, Robert 38–39, 66
St. Augustine's, Canterbury 122
St. Cuthbert 131–32, 270
St. Edmund 121
St. Evroul 125–26, 281, 299, 302
St. Peter 151
St. William of Norwich 120
Stanstead, Herts. 200, 301–2
Startley, Wilts. 272
State xii, 71–73, 101; maximalist and minimalist views of 72–3, 78–87, 101, 106
Stenton, Lady (D. M.) 58n, 298, 306
Stephen, king of England 131, 137, 258–59, 274, 305
Stephen Langton, archbishop of Canterbury 225
Stickney, Lincs. 293–94
Storytelling ix, 6, 38, 61, 76, 173, 243, 267
Stow Bardolph, Norfolk 300
Strickland, Matthew 252n
Subjects 158
Summerson, Henry 290
Summons 101
Support groups 4, 9–10, 23n, 32, 89–90, 92, 106, 142, 211–13, 261, 265, 295, 306–7; force 212–13; at lord's command 213–14, 232, 282–84, 295
Sureties 99, 115, 205n, 273, 294, 298
Sutherland, Donald 166n, 239n

Ten Commandments 25, 46–49, 54; tablets of the law 47; the Lord's 124
Thegn 138; average 101–2; king's 102n
Theodore, archbishop of Canterbury 77n
Thomas (f. William) FitzJohn 274–76
Thomas of Chobham 45n, 48–58, 251
Thomas of Elderfield 58
Thomas of Ingoldisthorp 208n, 273

Thomas of Monmouth 120
Thorne, Samuel E. 239n
Thurbrand Hold 76–77, 277–78
Tickets 152–53, 163n, 206n, 225–26, 229, 231, 237, 241, 274; breach of the peace 153, 168, 174, 191–93, 223, 239n, 280, 306; vi et armis 153, 174, 212–13, 233. *See also* Hyping a complaint
Tit-for-tat strategy 20, 33
Tithings 28–29, 88, 92, 115
Tongues 211, 274; sins of 41n
Torture 52
Tosny family 302–3
Trailbaston 184n, 234, 242
Trees, falling from 142–43
Trespass xvii–xviii, 36, 42, 53–56, 60, 126, 145, 149–51, 154, 168, 171–73, 176, 191, 198n, 212, 244–45, 262, 264, 296; "criminal" 228; differentiation from appeal 231–34; heinous 245; naming of 227–28. *See also* Proto-trespass; Tickets; Words: trespas
Troublemakers, control or expulsion of 19, 23, 81–82, 84, 97, 140, 142, 182
Tutbury 143
Tydd St. Mary, Lincs. 297

Uhtred, earl of Northumbria 76–77, 106n, 277–78

Vacarius 179n, 221
Vegso, Jay 200n
Vengeance, xv, xvii, 3, 6, 9, 39, 55, 64–65, 75, 106, 115; ecclesiastical views on 43–9, 54, 120–27; language of 148; licit 48, 58; need to publicize 11, 66, 80; reserved for God 45–46, 56, 124; royal monopoly of licit 161; sought through God, Christ 65; timing of 5, 20–21, 65n; urge toward xi–xii; at village level 242; within lordship 88, 203
Victims ix–x, 8–9, 51, 147, 157, 167, 172–73, 190, 227, 231
Villeins 97, 138, 141
Viterbo, Italy 254

Walcher, bishop of Durham 131–32, 270–72
Wales 197
Wallace-Hadrill, J. M. 78n
Walter Cantilupe, bishop of Worcester 50, 54
Waltham Abbey 200–201, 301–2
Waltheof I, earl of Northumbria 277
Waltheof II, earl of Northumbria 76, 127–28, 270, 278–79
Warenne, Earl John de 243n, 251–52
Warranty 150
Waste, royal right of 211n
Waugh, Scott 260
Wer 78–79, 83, 88–90, 97n, 140–41, 268

VOLUMES IN THE SERIES

Conjunctions of Religion and Power in the Medieval Past
Edited by Barbara H. Rosenwein

Medieval Cruelty: Changing Perceptions, Late Antiquity to the Early Modern Period
by Daniel Baraz

Unjust Seizure: Conflict, Interest, and Authority in an Early Medieval Society
by Warren Brown

Discerning Spirits: Divine and Demonic Possession in the Middle Ages
by Nancy Caciola

Ermengard of Narbonne and the World of the Troubadours
by Fredric L. Cheyette

Speaking of Slavery: Color, Ethnicity, and Human Bondage in Italy
by Steven A. Epstein

Surviving Poverty in Medieval Paris: Gender, Ideology, and the Daily Lives of the Poor
by Sharon Farmer

Rancor and Reconciliation in Medieval England
by Paul R. Hyams

Order and Exclusion: Cluny and Christendom Face Heresy, Judaism, and Islam (1000–1150)
by Dominique Iogna-Prat

The Bishop's Palace: Architecture and Authority in Medieval Italy
by Maureen C. Miller

The Consumption of Justice: Emotions, Publicity, and Legal Culture in Marseille, 1264–1423
by Daniel Lord Smail

Shifting Landmarks: Property, Proof, and Dispute in Catalonia around the Year 1000
by Jeffrey A. Bowman

CPSIA information can be obtained
at www.ICGtesting.com
Printed in the USA
LVOW01*1619280317
528771LV00008B/104/P